FASCINATING BIBLE FACTS

WEST
SIDE
PUBLISHING

Contributing Writers: Jeanette Dall, Christine Dallman, Dave Gerardi, Jack Greer, Robert V. Huber, J. K. Kelley, Martin H. Manser, Randy Petersen, Betsy Rossen Elliot, Donald Vaughan, Kelly Wittmann

Facts verified by Kathryn Holcomb.

Cover Illustration: Adrian Chesterman

Interior Illustrations: Linda Howard Bittner

Additional Images: Alamy Images, Art Explosion, iStockphoto, Jupiterimages, Photolibrary, PIL Collection, Shutterstock, Thinkstock

Louis Weber, CEO
Publications International, Ltd.
7373 North Cicero Avenue
Lincolnwood, Illinois 60712

ISBN-13: 978-1-4508-1885-8
ISBN-10: 1-4508-1885-4

Manufactured in USA.

8 7 6 5 4 3 2 1

Contents

✤ ✤ ✤ ✤

Searching Through Scripture

⚜ ⚜ ⚜ ⚜

It gives us comfort, guidance, and encouragement, but how much do we *really* know about it? The Bible has been the world's best-selling, most widely read book for centuries—and here's your chance to find out why. *Armchair Reader™: Fascinating Bible Facts* is full of stories, statistics, and studies that will help you understand the content and context of this beloved, ancient book. Read about

- The Brick Testament, a Lego-block retelling of the Old Testament

- Where Jesus Walked, about the world of Jesus, both in his day and now; Great Bible Orators, exploring the lives of history's greatest preachers; and Israel's Neighbors, where you can finally learn exactly who the Hittites, Ammonites, and other "-ites" really were

- Jesus' best comebacks: He was no meek messiah!

- The truth about dragons in the Bible (and is *that* what seraphim look like?)

- Movie apocalypses—film versions of the biblical end of the world

- Greek, Hebrew, and Aramaic word studies that will help make sense of scripture

- Many more stories that will inform and educate

If you've ever wanted a better understanding of the Bible in all its depth and richness, you're holding the right book in your hands. Explore it from Genesis to Revelation in *Armchair Reader™: Fascinating Bible Facts!*

In the Beginning, There Was the Torah (or Pentateuch)

❧ ❧ ❧ ❧

The stories and mysteries of the first five books of the Bible continue to fascinate us centuries later.

Genesis, Exodus, Leviticus, Numbers, and Deuteronomy: Both Jews and Christians believe the first five books of the Bible to be the books of Moses, but they refer to these books by different names. For Jews, they are the *Torah,* which means "teaching" or "doctrine." For Christians, they are the *Pentateuch,* which derives from the Greek words *penta* ("five") and *teuchos* ("book"). For both religions, they are holy and divinely inspired.

From Creation Forward

The Hebrew names of the first five books are *Bereshith, Shemot, Vayyiqra, Bemidbar,* and *Debarim.* The books begin with the creation of humankind in the Garden of Eden and end with Moses dying just as the Jews are about to enter the Promised Land. Arguably the most important story in the Torah is the giving of the Law from God to Moses. Moses then placed this Law before the Israelites and continued to teach them as they departed from Egypt (Deuteronomy 4:44–45). The Torah is the first of three parts of the Tanakh, or Hebrew Bible. In the Torah are 613 *mizvots,* or commandments, to live by. Of these commandments, 365 are negative or restrictive, while 248 are positive or encouraging.

The written text of the Torah is called *Torah Shebichtav,* but the Torah does not end with the written word. The ancient Hebrews also established the tradition of *Torah Shebe'al Peh,* or "Torah that is oral." This was wisdom and practical advice that was handed down from parent to child, generation after generation, which is now contained in the *Talmud* and the *Midrash,* writings that expound on the basic principles laid down in the Torah. According to rabbinical lore, the Torah was given to Moses in the wilderness, rather than in the land of Israel, because God wanted to offer the Law to all people. It was revealed in the 70 languages of the 70 nations that then existed on earth. But only the Hebrews accepted God's Law.

Modern Application

Though God commanded the Israelites to study the Torah, he also made it clear that the Torah was not to be worshipped, for that would be idolatry. Still, Torah study is a very serious matter for Orthodox Jews, and they take Joshua 1:8 to heart: "This book of the law shall not depart out of your mouth; you shall meditate on it day

and night, so that you may be careful to act in accordance with all that is written in it." For Christians, the view of the Pentateuch is not so clear or unified. Different types of Christians believe different things about the first five books of the Bible. Fundamentalists believe that every word of the Bible was written by God through humans, and that there are no metaphors in the Bible, only literal truth. For Christians of a more liberal bent, Christ's teachings in the New Testament render unnecessary many of the instructions of the Old Testament, so though they respect the laws contained therein, they do not feel obligated to follow them to the letter.

It is almost universally recognized by both Jewish and Christian scholars that the Torah/Pentateuch reached its final form long after Moses died, so other writers must have worked on them too. This makes the first five books of the Bible *pseudepigraphical,* or written by many under the name of one. This practice was quite common in ancient times, however, and probably affects all the books of the Bible to one extent or another. It in no way dampens the faith of the devout in either the Jewish or Christian religions; the Torah and the Pentateuch continue to inform their daily lives. And even the nonreligious in Western society have probably been influenced more than they realize by the stories in these first five books.

Safety in Bible Numbers

✤ ✤ ✤ ✤

*Many Bible numbers have special meaning. We've all heard of 666,
the number of the beast, and heard fanciful interpretations that we
probably steer clear of. But what about other numbers?*

Back to Square One

The number one stands for unity, especially of God himself as *One*
(Deuteronomy 6:4): The Bible claims he is the only God.

Almost a Piece of *Pi*

Moving to mathematics for a moment, *pi* (π) is one of the most
famous numbers: 3.14159. . . . In the Bible, the number 3 also goes
on forever, in the sense of the eternal *Trinity*: Father, Son, and
Holy Spirit (Matthew 28:19). At Easter we remember Jesus rising
from the dead on the *third day* after Good Friday (Matthew 16:21;
Luke 24:7). The Old Testament prophecy of Daniel (1:7) talks about
Shadrach, Meshach, and Abednego, who were thrown into the fiery
furnace (Daniel 3). In the New Testament, the *wise men* (Magi)
came to see the baby Jesus (Matthew 2:1–12). Interestingly, the
Bible nowhere says there were three wise men; it records the three
gifts of gold, frankincense, and myrrh that they offered. And then
there's the happy trio of faith, hope, and love (1 Corinthians 13:13).

Enter the Four Horsemen of the Apocalypse

The number four represents completion and creation, e.g. the *four
corners* of the world (Revelation 7:1). Wait a moment—can you hear
the arrival of the *four horses and riders* of the Apocalypse? White,
red, black, and pale green: They represent conquest, bloodshed,
famine, and death that are to ravage the earth (Revelation 6:2–8).

A Six-Shooter?

Six stands for human beings, who according to Genesis, were created by God on the *sixth day* (Genesis 1:27–31). Now we know how
God spent the final part of his working week.

Seven Up!

The number seven symbolizes perfection and fulfillment: The *seventh day* is when God rested from all his work of creation (Genesis 2:2). Seven is seen too in the services on Good Friday that recall the so-called *seven words* of Christ from the cross as recorded in Matthew 27:46; Luke 23:34, 43, 46; John 19:26–27, 28, 30.

Duodecimal Disciples

Twelve stands for the people of God, the 12 tribes of Israel. It is also for the 12 apostles: Simon Peter; Andrew; James and his brother John; Philip; Bartholomew; Thomas; Matthew; James, son of Alphaeus; Thaddaeus; Simon the Cananaean; and Judas Iscariot (Matthew 10:2–4). What a motley crew they were. Fishers, a tax collector, a former terrorist: Would you entrust your whole life's work to any of them?

Forty Winks

Forty represents the development and history of salvation: testing. Jesus fasted in the wilderness for *forty days and forty nights* (Matthew 4:2), and the Bible text plainly records "afterwards he was famished"—which is hardly surprising.

Threescore and Ten

Seventy stands for God's administration of the world: Jesus sent out *70 disciples* to help him in his ministry (Luke 10:1). "Threescore years and ten" as the old King James Version has it, is the normal human span of life (Psalm 90:10). The Bible still seems to have that right today. The Greek translation of the Old Testament is known as the "Septuagint," because it is traditionally thought that it was carried out by *70* scholars in *70* days.

666: At Sixes but Not Sevens

The number 666 is the mark of the beast (Revelation 13:18). Some people have thought the number referred to any of the following: Nero, Caligula, Caesars in general, Cromwell, or Luther. Perhaps the number is best thought of as a series of digits of sixes, which one after another fail to reach the perfect number seven. Failed again and again and again!

Great Bible Orators

The People's Pastor

*Billy Graham ministered to world leaders and the poor alike.
In his eyes, everyone was equal.*

Many evangelists have become internationally renowned through their efforts to spread God's word, but few have achieved the level of international acclaim experienced by Billy Graham. Over the years, his astoundingly popular evangelical crusades filled stadiums—and instilled the Holy Spirit in the hearts of millions.

Born near Charlotte, North Carolina, on November 7, 1918, Graham decided to commit his life to God while still in high school. He briefly attended Bob Jones College in Cleveland, Tennessee, then transferred to the Florida Bible Institute (now known as Trinity College), where he received his Bachelor of Theology degree. In 1939, he was ordained by the Rev. Cecil Underwood, a Southern Baptist.

Graham attended Wheaton College in Wheaton, Illinois, and graduated with a BA in anthropology in 1943. His star rose quickly within the Baptist community, and he became pastor of the United Gospel Tabernacle in Wheaton while still a student.

A Gifted Speaker
Oratory was Graham's greatest gift, and he used it to wonderful effect. He traveled often to preaching engagements while still attending Wheaton College, and in the decades that followed, he became known as one of the greatest Christian leaders of the 20th century. He held evangelistic campaigns, or crusades, throughout the United States, often filling huge stadiums to capacity, then traveled the world to spread the word of God, hosting rallies throughout Africa, Asia, South America, and Europe. Among his most impressive campaigns were the Greater London Crusade in 1954 and the New York Crusade in 1957.

Graham was very cognizant of the image of evangelists as con men who preyed on the poor, and he vowed early on to live a life free of scandal and without a hint of opportunism. He made sure that the finances of his ministry were transparent, and as a result he managed to avoid the travails that afflicted many of his contemporaries. In fact, the Billy Graham Evangelistic Association's annual reports are available online at their website for everyone to read and review.

As a result of his pristine image, Graham was sought out by many of the world's most influential leaders. Over the course of his career, he met and prayed with every president from Harry Truman to Barack Obama. President George W. Bush told Graham that it was a conversation with him that led Bush to become a born-again Christian.

Always eager to save one more soul, Graham reached out to Christians every way he could: through television, several best-selling books, a newspaper advice column, and even motion pictures such as *Two a Penny* (1967), in which he played himself.

Moments of Controversy

Graham's life was not perfect, however, and over the years there were some controversial moments. In the 1950s, he endorsed Senator Joseph McCarthy in what would later become known as McCarthy's communist "witch hunt," and in 2002 Graham was embarrassed by the release of a taped conversation with President Richard Nixon in which Graham said, " . . . a lot of the Jews are great friends of mine, they swarm around me and are friendly to me because they know that I'm friendly with Israel. But they don't know how I really feel about what they are doing to this country." Graham has also been criticized for not doing more to address the nation's social ills, such as civil rights, and for being too close to men of power.

But Graham managed to shrug off most of the criticisms thrown his way, and he continued his ministry until age and frailty finally forced him to retire in 2005. His son, Franklin Graham, also an evangelist, was appointed CEO of the Billy Graham Evangelistic Association in 2000, and he has continued his father's international Christian outreach. In November 2010, the association celebrated 60 years of ministry; Graham started it in 1950.

Billy Graham rose from preaching in small churches and at revival meetings to become a global Christian ambassador. He unerringly viewed God's salvation as the answer to the world's problems—and millions listened. Through Graham's booming voice, a different kind of evangelism was allowed to take root and flourish across the globe.

Biblical Menagerie

⚜ ⚜ ⚜ ⚜

Many types of animals are mentioned throughout the Bible,
both literally and metaphorically.

The Bible is a zoologist's dream. A wide variety of animals are discussed throughout the Old and New Testaments, providing insight into life in ancient times as well as some unique and insightful allegories.

Genesis, as everyone knows, tells us that God created all living things, including fish, birds, and every manner of beast, all of which were named by Adam. Later in Genesis, Noah is instructed by God to build an ark and place within it seven pairs of all clean animals, one pair each of all of the animals that are not clean and seven pairs of all of the birds of the air. The purpose of this massive collection was to preserve all the animals of the earth following the great deluge.

What to Eat, What Not

Later in the Old Testament, specifically in Leviticus and Deuteronomy, the difference between "clean" and "unclean" animals is explained. In a nutshell, mammals that chew their cud and have cloven hooves, such as cattle and sheep, are considered clean and thus okay to eat. Those that do not chew their cud but still have cloven hooves, such as swine, are considered unclean and thus unfit for consumption. Edible seafood is limited to fish that have scales and fins, while unclean birds include scavengers and birds of prey. It is generally believed that such rules were put into place to help guarantee sanitary dining practices.

Certain animals receive special prominence in the Bible. Snakes, for example, are said in Genesis to be "more crafty than any other wild animal that the Lord God had made," and they evoke God's wrath by tempting Eve in the Garden of Eden. As punishment, God condemns the snake to crawl on its belly and eat dust for its entire life.

Lamb of God

Lambs are also mentioned frequently throughout scripture. During Passover, lambs were sacrificed and eaten in commemoration of the Exodus, and in the Gospel of John, Jesus is referred to as "the lamb of God who takes away the sin of the world." The exact meaning of this phrase has caused much debate among biblical scholars. Some believe John saw Jesus as a kind of symbolic sacrificial lamb for the atonement of all sins, while others believe John was recalling the Israelite ritual on the annual Day of Atonement. Still others believe he may have been referring to the horned ram that led a flock, the traditional symbol for the king of Israel.

The dove is another important biblical creature. In Genesis, Noah releases a dove to determine if the floodwaters had receded; on the second try, a dove returns with an olive branch in its beak. In biblical times, doves were a symbol of purity and were often offered up following the birth of a child; Mary made such an offering after the birth of Jesus.

Educating with Animals

Jesus used animal references in his teachings. During his Sermon on the Mount, he observes, "Look at the birds of the air: they neither sow nor reap nor gather into barns, and yet your heavenly Father feeds them. Are you not of more value than they?" Later he says, "Do not give dogs what is holy; and do not throw your pearls before swine, lest they trample them under foot and turn to attack you."

Other animals mentioned in regard to Jesus include fish, which he multiplied (along with bread) to feed the hungry masses, and the donkey, which a pregnant Mary rode into Bethlehem and which Jesus rode during his triumphant return to Jerusalem.

Vivid Animal Descriptions

Interestingly, animals are also used in the Bible to describe the in-describable. Ezekiel, for example, describes the angels around God's throne as having features similar to a lion, a bull, and an eagle. And God himself is compared to a lion, a leopard, a bear, and an eagle.

Animals of all kinds can be found in the pages of the Bible, but it's important to remember one thing—they all belong to God. After all, it was in his wisdom that they were created in the first place.

Kids, Kids, Kids

✤ ✤ ✤ ✤

They are all sizes and shapes, they run and play, complain about doing chores, and eat everything in sight.

Maybe you recognize your own children or grandchildren in those descriptions. It also applies to Bible kids. Kids have basically been the same from the first one, Cain, to the most recent newborn. Of course, many other things have changed. Most of today's kids live longer, healthier lives and can go to school regardless of their status in society. Children were very important in Bible times. Proverbs 17:6 says, "Grandchildren are the crown of the aged." And Jesus said to his disciples, "Let the little children come to me; do not stop them" (Mark 10:14).

Two Stepbrothers—Two Nations

Ishmael and Isaac had the same father, Abraham, but different mothers. Ishmael was the oldest, but Isaac was the child God had promised to Abraham. Sarah, Isaac's mother, didn't want Ishmael to inherit Abraham's property, so he and his mother were sent out into the desert. God helped them survive and promised that Ishmael's descendants would be a great nation (Genesis 21:1–21). Isaac's descendants became the Jewish nation of Israel. Ishmael's descendants became nomads in Arabia (now Yemen, Oman, Saudi Arabia, and Jordan). Muslims trace their lineage to Abraham through Ishmael.

Guardian of the Baby

Baby Moses was floating on the Nile in a basket-boat to avoid being killed by pharaoh's soldiers. But Moses was a helpless infant and needed a trustworthy guardian. This is where his sister, Miriam, plays her part in the life-and-death drama. She patiently hid among the reeds and kept a watchful eye on the basket. When Moses was found by pharaoh's daughter, Miriam boldly asked her if she needed someone to take care of the baby. The caretaker

Miriam got for Moses was their very own mother, so Moses was safe in his own home until he was older (Exodus 2:1–10).

Two Prophets—Four Boys

Elijah and Elisha were Old Testament prophets who performed many miracles. Most of these miracles affected the nation of Israel, but these prophets also cared for children.

When there was a drought in the land and very little food, a widow was desperate. She decided that she would use the last of the oil and flour for a small meal and then she and her son would die. Elijah heard of her plight and said God would take care of them. God did this by never letting the supplies run out (1 Kings 17:7–16). Elisha also helped a poor widow with two sons. She couldn't pay her bills, so her sons were to become slaves. All she had was a little oil. Elisha had her sons borrow all the jars they could find. When the widow poured her oil into the jars, it kept flowing until all the jars were filled. The oil was sold, and the widow was debt-free (2 Kings 4:1–7).

In his travels, Elisha often stayed with a Shunammite woman. One day her only son died, and she sent for Elisha. Elisha prayed to God, and the son was made alive again (2 Kings 4:8–37).

Three Nameless Kids

Some Bible-time children were important in God's plan, but we don't know their names. One young girl had been kidnapped when the Armeneans raided Israel, and she became a servant of the wife of Naaman, an army commander. Naaman had leprosy, an incurable disease. The servant girl told Naaman to go to Elisha for help. Naaman listened to the girl and was cured (2 Kings 5:1–16).

Wherever Jesus went, crowds followed. Once, over 5,000 people gathered to hear him and after a long day were famished. One boy, who had the foresight to bring a lunch, offered it to Jesus. Jesus used this meager lunch of five loaves of bread and two fish to satisfy the hungry horde—and there were even leftovers (John 6:1–15)! In another instance, the young daughter of Jairus was dying, and Jairus begged Jesus to come to his house and touch his daughter. Before Jesus arrived, the daughter died. At the house, Jesus took the girl by the hand and said, "Child, get up!" She instantly came alive and was completely cured (Luke 8:40–56).

What Are the Ten Commandments?

✤ ✤ ✤ ✤

*Scripture records that God gave the Ten Commandments,
also known as the* decalogue *(Greek for "ten words"), directly
to Israel. They are central to Judeo-Christian life, yet many
Christians cannot recite them all.*

The Setting

Both Exodus 20 and Deuteronomy 5 tell the story
(with slight differences). As most believers know,
Moses led the Israelites out of hard labor in Egypt
with God's help. Thereafter, he expected them to
do things his way. As they reached Mount Sinai,
God alerted Moses that something big was com-
ing. God told the Israelite leader to get his people cleaned up, to
stay off the mountain until a trumpet blew, and even then not to
swarm up to the top.

On the third day, God made Mount Sinai behave like Mount
St. Helens, complete with earth tremors and smoke, and crowned
with a monster storm. The ground wasn't the only thing trembling,
because the display of divine power naturally scared the Israelites.
With that, God gave the commandments to Moses and Israel, beginning with the ten and continuing with many specific instructions,
which observant Jews obey to this day as Mosaic Law.

God engraved the commandments on stone tablets for Moses
to show his people so they didn't forget the basics. The Israelites
fumbled early in the game, worshipping a golden calf (Exodus 32).
Not cool! Moses had to talk God out of some serious consequences.

Two Parts

The first four commandments define people's duties toward God;
the final six specify their responsibilities to one another. If Israelites
obeyed his code of moral and righteous conduct, they would please
him; they would live in a nation of law, order, and justice.

Part 1: Responsibilities Toward God

- *You shall have no other gods before me.* God being Israel's savior, Israelites were to worship him alone. No one and nothing took priority over God.
- *You shall not make for yourself an idol.* Israelites were not to manufacture nor worship images of God (golden calves, for example).
- *You shall not make wrongful use of the name of the Lord.* God's name was to be used reverently, never in casual or unholy ways, no matter how hard someone hit his finger with a hammer.
- *Remember the sabbath day, and keep it holy.* One day a week, the Israelites were to rest from their labor in every way, dedicating that seventh (shabbat) day to honoring God.

Part 2: Responsibilities Toward One Another

- *Honor your father and your mother.* Israelites were to respect their parents. As Paul later pointed out, this was the first commandment that included a promise: Obeying it was the foundation for a long, happy life.
- *You shall not murder.* As life was a gift of God, an Israelite wasn't allowed to deprive anyone of it without just cause. On this commandment rested a sense of personal safety in society.
- *You shall not commit adultery.* Married Israelites were to have sex only with their spouses, to prevent jealousy and fracture in the core family unit.
- *You shall not steal.* This enacted the basic right of personal property. Why work hard for things if someone can steal them?
- *You shall not bear false witness against your neighbor.* Israelites were not to lie about their neighbors. God knew that gossip evolved quickly into slander, which creates division in any community.
- *You shall not covet your neighbor's house . . . , wife, slave, ox, donkey, or anything that belongs to your neighbor.* Israelites weren't even allowed to *desire* what wasn't theirs.

Divine Wisdom

As the Israelites made a new beginning in a new land, God wanted them to start right. Even nonbelievers generally share the commandments' values, which says much about their timeless good sense.

Bringing the Plagues of Exodus to Life

✧ ✧ ✧ ✧

Do we need to explain the plagues of Egypt in terms of modern science? No, but for the most part, we can.

Do It or Else!

God told Aaron and Moses to give pharaoh one more chance, in the name of the Lord, to release the Israelites from forced labor. Pharaoh had a bad attitude about this, saying (yes, we're paraphrasing): "Not familiar with this Lord of yours. This is Egypt, and you may have noticed that *I'm* its lord. Now run along, and make your bricks like good forced laborers. In fact, no straw for you, but your brick-making quota remains the same. That'll teach you." God more or less told his people's leaders: "Okay, I'll fix this. Time to bring the pain."

The Bloody Nile

The first lesson involved God turning all the water in Egypt—whether in someone's glass or flowing down the Nile—into blood. Yuck. This killed all the fish (try to imagine the smell of fermenting dead fish in a sunny climate) and made the water undrinkable. While the modern Nile has never turned to actual blood, a couple of known conditions could create this effect. We now know that algae can create red tides in fresh water as well as seawater, causing massive fish kills and reddening the water. Another fair explanation could involve volcanoes in Ethiopia, far up near the headwaters of the Blue Nile, which can fill the river with nasty reddish silt that could kill fish.

Frogs

A week passed, and pharaoh didn't yield. "Tell him I will swamp Egypt with frogs," said God. Pharaoh wouldn't budge, and soon Egypt looked like an Alfred Hitchcock version of *The Muppet Show*.

This time pharaoh showed signs of getting with the program, but after God killed all the frogs—leaving Egypt buried in dead frogs—pharaoh went back on his word. Well, the Old Testament Hebrew word for "frogs" also includes  toads; both are common enough in Egypt. It's possible that the mess in the Nile caused the frogs and toads to jump out on land en masse.

Gnats and Flies

After pharaoh reneged on his commitment, God said: "Okay, have some gnats." The little insects drove everyone crazy. The Exodus account may be describing the dog fly, a very nasty biting insect native to the Nile Delta, or it could simply describe plain old gnats in great clouds; some accounts interpret the word as "lice" (pretty common in the ancient world to begin with).

God then sent flies, which concentrated especially on pharaoh's house and those of his officials. Now pharaoh began to waver, but when God called off the flies, pharaoh flip-flopped again. These flies could also be dog flies—it's hard to specify exactly based upon scripture's rather general description.

Dying Livestock

"Pharaoh doesn't learn, does he?" mused God. "Okay, time for the heavy stuff." Moses warned pharaoh again and got rejected again. Suddenly most camels, horses, cattle, and other livestock in Egypt got sick and died, while the Israelites' livestock kept happily munching grass. The ancient Egyptians knew any number of livestock diseases, including African horse sickness, bluetongue, rinderpest, foot-and-mouth, and anthrax (in descending order of likeliness based on scripture). A combination of outbreaks is quite plausible.

Boils

Pharaoh didn't give in, so God played a little rougher: He sent a plague of boils. This one affected both animals and humans, causing huge disgusting sores that broke and festered. What could this have been? One strong possibility is *glanders,* a disease people can catch from animals. It causes the lymph nodes to swell up and can be fatal even with early modern medical detection; imagine how hard it might have hit the Egyptians.

Thunder and Hail

God next had Moses warn pharaoh to get his people and livestock into shelter, for he was about to send a monster hailstorm. Some did. Those who ignored the warning (plus all the flax and barley crops) perished. Pharaoh again seemed ready to give in, then he reneged again. (By any measure, the guy was a slow learner.) Hail is simple to explain: While rare on the Nile, it isn't unknown there today.

Locusts

God's next plague, the grasshopper (called a locust in its swarming phase), simply ate Egypt alive: crops, trees, anything with leaves. While pharaoh didn't give way yet, this plague is known to anyone who lived through the Dust Bowl days in the American Midwest. When the locusts got thick enough, they could and did eat even the clothes off clotheslines, so no wonder they scoured Egypt, as scripture says.

Darkness

God then socked Egypt with three solid days of darkness. While it didn't bend pharaoh, this also has a very plausible explanation. Egypt is in North Africa, where the *khamsin* (Sahara sandstorm) can last up to three days, burying everything in sand and blotting out the sun. In fact, the *khamsin* has preserved numerous archaeological wonders simply by burying them over the years.

Death of the Firstborn

By now God was absolutely fed up with pharaoh, so he made it personal: He struck down the firstborn of every Egyptian family, from pharaoh's to prisoners' to livestock. The Israelites were untouched. "Okay, enough, get out!" said pharaoh. While there are numerous candidate toxins and diseases that could have caused this, it may not have a corresponding modern explanation.

Whatever the plagues actually were (and giving a scientific explanation doesn't lessen God's power), the Israelites were now free to find a new land where they could worship and live in accordance with the Lord's commands.

Where Jesus Walked

Bethlehem

Perhaps the biblical place best known for its association with Jesus, Bethlehem was ancient by his time.

In Biblical Times
Bethlehem has more Old Testament mentions than New. It was David's city and the burial place of Rachel (Genesis 48). Nonbiblical sources reference it as early as the Amarna letters (c.1400 B.C.). It did not flourish greatly after Christ's time but did not die out. The Samaritans (not the good ones, obviously, but perhaps their cousins the bad Samaritans) sacked Bethlehem in A.D. 529; Islamic troops captured it in A.D. 637.

Jesus' Connection
The story of Jesus begins in Bethlehem. It does not stay there long, however. In Matthew 2, wise men "from the East" (possibly Persian and possibly astrologers) were drawn to the town by a star. When they found the infant, they gave him gifts. Unfortunately for Joseph's family, King Herod was madder than a hornet. He didn't know the baby Jesus by sight, but he figured to kill him by killing every Bethlehem-area child under age two. Joseph took his family to Egypt for safety; how times had changed for Jews, to be trying to enter Egypt rather than escape it! When the vengeful king died in 4 B.C., the family returned but settled in Nazareth.

Bethlehem Today
Modern Bethlehem (Hebrew, *Bait-lechem,* "house of bread"; Arabic, *Bayt lam,* "house of meat") is a predominantly but not overwhelmingly Arab and Muslim city in the West Bank, governed by the Palestinian Authority. It stands six miles almost due south of Jerusalem. Its population is about 30,000, probably far more than in biblical times. The city houses one of the world's oldest continuous Christian populations; the city's law requires its mayor to be a Christian. Pilgrims flock to the Church of the Nativity, built over the site where tradition holds Christ was born. In addition to tourism, Bethlehem survives on sales and exports of hand-crafted items.

Ancient Trash Talk

✤ ✤ ✤ ✤

Think it didn't exist way back when?
Well, it did—in both the Old and New Testaments.

We often bemoan the lack of manners and discretion in our reality TV age, but the truth is, there have always been crude, loudmouthed people who insult others and offer their not-so-welcome opinions on everything under the sun. It wasn't only the "bad guys" of the Bible, however, who resorted to bad-mouthing, mockery, and mud-slinging. Sometimes the "good guys" had to get down to their level in order to prove a point and beat them at their own game.

Unheeded Warnings

One of the reasons we know there was a lot of trash-talking going on in biblical times is because there are so many warnings against it in the Bible. James 4:11 pleads, "Do not speak evil against one another, brothers and sisters." Paul urged the Colossians to "get rid of all such things—anger, wrath, malice, slander, and abusive language from your mouth" (3:8). Matthew 5:21–44 cautions, "You have heard that it was said to those of ancient times, 'You shall not murder'; and 'whoever murders shall be liable to judgment.' But I say to you that if you are angry with a brother or sister, you will be liable to judgment; and if you insult a brother or sister, you will be liable to the council; and if you say, 'You fool', you will be liable to the hell of fire." Then an alternative to slander, insults, and backbiting is offered: "You have heard that it was said, 'You shall love your neighbor and hate your enemy.' But I say to you, Love your enemies and pray for those who persecute you." The ancient Hebrews, however, found this instruction to be easier said than done, as we still do today.

Trash talking in the Bible goes all the way back to Genesis 3, when the serpent bad-mouthed God to Eve, telling her that God was lying about the fruit of the tree in the middle of the Garden of Eden: "But the serpent said to the woman, 'You will not die [if you eat it]; for God knows that when you eat of it your eyes will be opened, and you will be like God, knowing good and evil.'" Eve listened to the serpent, ate some of the fruit, and gave some to her husband, Adam, who proceeded to trash-talk *her* when God confronted him about the incident! "The man said, 'The woman whom you gave to be with me, she gave me fruit from the tree, and I ate.'" So God turned to Eve, who, naturally, blamed it all on the serpent: "The serpent tricked me." This may be the first recorded case of what we now call "passing the buck."

Desperate Tentwives

Later in Genesis, God promises Abraham repeatedly that he will be the father of many children. "Look towards heaven and count the stars, if you are able to count them.... So shall your descendants be." But as the decades go by, Abraham pretty much gives up on God's promise and Sarah can see he's depressed. So she gives him her Egyptian slave-girl, Hagar, and tells him, "You see that the Lord has prevented me from bearing children; go in to my slave-girl; it may be that I shall obtain children by her." Well, what sounded like a great idea in theory predictably escalated into a domestic crisis when Hagar conceived Abraham's first child, Ishmael. Hagar got all high and mighty about it, treating Sarah with contempt. And Sarah wasn't about to put up with it. Not only was she abusive to Hagar, but she chewed Abraham out too, screaming, "May the wrong done to me be on you! I gave my slave-girl to your embrace, and when she saw that she had conceived, she looked on me with contempt. May the Lord judge between you and me!" So Abraham really had his hands full.

A few generations later, Rebekah railed at her husband, Isaac, about their two foreign-born daughters-in-law, who were married to their son Esau: "I am weary of my life because of the Hittite women. If [our other son] Jacob marries one of the Hittite women such as these, one of the women of the land, what good will my life be to me?" Such political incorrectness is rife throughout both the Old and New Testaments. In Ezra 9:1–2, the writer complains, "The people of Israel . . . have not separated themselves from the peoples of the lands with their abominations, from the Canaanites, the Hittites, the Perizzites, the Jebusites, the Ammonites, the Moabites, the Egyptians, and the Amorites. For they have taken some of their daughters as wives for themselves and for their sons. Thus the holy seed has mixed itself with the peoples of the lands." Many ancient Hebrews were what we might now call racist, but their enemies were no better. Ethnic stereotyping and scapegoating were as common then as they are now, and the result was a lot of nasty verbal abuse from all sides.

New Testament, Old Insults

Things didn't really get much better in New Testament times. Tax collectors and prostitutes were the favorite targets of obnoxious loudmouths, and when Jesus decided to hang out with them, he got an earful. The Pharisees reproached him in front of anyone who would listen: "Why does he eat with tax-collectors and sinners?" Many of Jesus' supporters were aghast when he asked the tax collector Matthew to become one of his apostles.

Gossip and slander flew across Israel as Jesus continued to live and travel with what many considered to be shady characters, and he warned that it would only get worse, both for him and his followers. But even so, his message in Matthew 5:11–12 about trash talk was one of hope: "Blessed are you when people revile you and persecute you and utter all kinds of evil against you falsely on my account. Rejoice and be glad, for your reward is great in heaven."

God's Personal Name

Just as the Canaanite high god's personal name was Baal, the Mesopotamian high god's name was Marduk, and the Egyptian high god's name was Ra, so the Israelites' God had a personal name, Yahweh. Its exact meaning is debated; it either means "he creates" or "he is (with his people)."

The Voice

✤ ✤ ✤ ✤

Charlton Heston personifies Moses and the Bible.

No voice is as synonymous with the Bible as Charlton Heston's. His deep, gravelly timber captured the sonorous gravity of the passages like no other.

"Let my people go!"

Heston earned his association with the Bible thanks to two movies: *The Ten Commandments* and *Ben-Hur*. Cecil B. DeMille directed *The Ten Commandments* in 1923 as a silent movie. He wanted to remake it in color with sound and got total control from the studio. DeMille noticed the uncanny resemblance between Michelangelo's statue of Moses at the Church of St. Peter and Heston, right down to the broken nose from Heston's football days. At the time, Heston had not yet established himself, but DeMille surrounded him with stars, including Yul Brynner, Anne Baxter, and Edward G. Robinson. They shot in Egypt, and Heston climbed Gebel Musa (Mount Sinai for all intents and purposes) barefoot. The experience on Sinai and the research into Moses changed him, Heston said. Heston's newborn even played Moses as an infant. When the picture opened in 1956, DeMille applauded Heston's performance. Heston was less enthusiastic, saying the role was beyond his capacities.

Only a few years later, Heston starred in another biblical remake: William Wyler's *Ben-Hur* (1959). Based on the fictional novel by Lew Wallace, *Ben-Hur* is about a Jewish prince sold into slavery whose life dovetails with Jesus Christ's at crucial parts of the New Testament. The shoot was grueling, and Heston did most of the charioteering in the epic race himself. He won an Oscar and the film reaped ten more.

"It's Moses!"

Wherever he went, Heston was often greeted with, "It's Moses!" Heston wore this role well. After all, chapter one of his autobiography starts, "In the beginning..."

Video Games Based on the Bible

❧ ❧ ❧ ❧

Though the history of Christianity isn't normally associated with
"fun," religious leaders are nothing if not business savvy. With
the explosion in video-game popularity over the past two decades,
Christian publishers and video-game producers have sought to get in
on the act, sometimes with comic results. Here are some of the best,
worst, and most controversial video games based on the Bible.

1. Super 3D Noah's Ark
Wolfenstein 3D, one of the most popular video games of all time,
featured the player roaming the passageways of a castle, shooting
Nazis. Wisdom Tree, the makers of *Super 3D Noah's Ark*, somehow
believed that taking *Wolfenstein* and turning it into a Nintendo game
about throwing fruit at animals would be a big hit. It wasn't. Not
only that, but *Noah's Ark* was an illegal, unlicensed game, requiring players to go through a convoluted process for the game to even
function on a Nintendo system.

2. The Bible Game
Doesn't a video game that's supposed to be a Bible-trivia game show
featuring a cheesy rock soundtrack sound like fun? It doesn't to us
either. Though *The Bible Game* was designed for small children, the
trivia questions were obscure enough to stump seminary students.
In addition to the game-show component, it also featured random,
unconnected "mini games," including running around a maze
whacking demons with a Bible. It is perhaps not surprising that the
game was poorly rated by gamers across the board.

3. Catechumen
In terms of sales, *Catechumen* was the first popular Christian video
game, with more than 80,000 games sold in its first five years of release. The game features a player wandering around ancient Rome
killing pagan soldiers. Though it wasn't ranked very highly for its

game play, *Catechumen* was the first game to catch on to the idea that gamers like "first-person shooter," and it introduced the idea of spiritual warfare to Christian video gaming.

4. Left Behind: Eternal Forces

The most controversial and popular Christian book series in history is the inspiration for the most controversial and popular Christian video game. *Left Behind: Eternal Forces* allows the player to roam the streets of New York City, battling the forces of the Antichrist in the wake of the Rapture.

Left Behind: Eternal Forces was the first major-league video game in history, a multiplayer role-playing game in the vein of *Modern Warfare* and other massive video-game hits. The game immediately drew controversy, inciting cries of racism and bigotry that caused even Christian groups to protest its release. The game

> Estimated total sales of Christian-based video games, 2008:
> **$400 million**
>
> Anticipated sales of Christian-based video games, 2014:
> **$648 million**

created further controversy when it was revealed that players were allowed to play the role of "secularists" attempting to lead good Christians astray. Still, it is the most popular Christian video game to date, largely due to an AOL-like campaign to bombard the nation's mailboxes with free copies.

Hebrew Shorthand

Rabbis interpreted some words in the Hebrew Bible as actually standing for entire phrases. That is, they argued that each letter of certain words represented a different word of a phrase. The first word of the Bible, *Br'shyt* ("in the beginning") was said to represent several different phrases, one of which was "in the beginning God saw that Israel would accept the Torah."

Five Words from the Hebrew Scriptures You Should Know

⚜ ⚜ ⚜ ⚜

Some of these you know already, but what do they really mean?

Hallelujah

It's originally a Hebrew phrase, from the root word *halal,* meaning "praise" or "boast." The short form of God's name, Jah, is added, so the precise translation is "Let us praise the Lord."

In the Hebrew scriptures, it only appears (23 times) in Psalms 104–150, usually at the beginning or end of a psalm. This makes scholars think it was already a ritual phrase, calling people to worship. Its only New Testament use is in Revelation 19:1–6 (written as *Alleluia*), where God's ultimate victory over evil is celebrated.

Shalom

Commonly translated "peace," *shalom* has a much broader meaning. It is not only the lack of discord between people, but solid relationships, peace of mind, and general well-being. In biblical times, a common "How are you?" greeting was literally, "Is there *shalom* with you?" (see 2 Samuel 20:9).

Though the early origins of the place name are unclear, Jerusalem (in Hebrew *Yerushalayim*) was understood literally as the "seeing of *shalom,*" and thus it is known as the City of Peace.

Amen

This comes from a root word for certainty, firmness, assurance. You could translate it as "yes" or "so be it" or "that's right" or (in a modern parlance) "solid." We see it a few times in the Hebrew scriptures as common agreement, sort of an "Aye, aye, sir" (1 Kings 1:36). But very early in Jewish history, it was used in religious settings to affirm the truth of the proceedings.

Jesus used the word as a preface, rather than a response. Before important statements, he often said, *"Amen, Amen,* I tell you ... "

(usually translated "Very truly"—see John 3:3). In 2 Corinthians 1:20, the apostle Paul notes that Jesus puts the "amen" on God's promises, and the book of Revelation actually calls Jesus "the Amen, the faithful and true witness" (3:14).

Messiah

The Israelites had a ceremony of dedication in which they poured oil on the head of a king, a priest, or a prophet. This anointing symbolized God's choosing and empowering. The word Messiah (*mashiyah*) means "anointed one."

In Israel, the king had special honor as "the Lord's anointed" (1 Samuel 26:9). Even the Persian king Cyrus is called "the anointed one" for his God-chosen role in releasing the Jews from captivity (Isaiah 45:1).

Daniel had a vision of an "anointed prince" who would show up in the future and be "cut off" (Daniel 9:25–26). And Isaiah prophesied about an anointed person who would preach, heal broken hearts, and free captives (Isaiah 61:1). Jesus read that Isaiah text to launch his public ministry (Luke 4:16–21).

By that time, several groups were looking for a *messiah*—an anointed king, priest, or prophet—who would restore the nation to faith, righteousness, and/or independence. Though he was careful about claiming the title, others called Jesus the Messiah (John 1:41; 4:29). The Greek name *Christ* (*Christos*) means "anointed one."

Torah

It's usually translated as "law," but the word literally means "teaching." It's used in the Hebrew scriptures and tradition for all that has been taught by God.

First it referred to the specific commandments given at Mount Sinai. It came to include all the instructions for Israel's worship rituals. When the long-forgotten "book of the law" was found during Temple renovation (2 Kings 22:8), it might have been just the book of Deuteronomy. Over time, *Torah* became the term for the first five books of the scriptures, the books of Moses (as opposed to the "Prophets" and the "Writings"), but some would use it for all the Hebrew scriptures, including the Talmudic commentary. And, as God's "teaching," *Torah* sometimes refers to all of Jewish tradition.

Jonah, the Reluctant Prophet

✤ ✤ ✤ ✤

Most people know that Jonah was swallowed by a "whale" because he refused God's commission to preach to the people of Nineveh. Few realize why he refused. And fewer still realize how angry he became when he finally did preach to the Ninevites and they responded. The story of Jonah's anger and God's response is found in the last quarter of the book of Jonah, which many people don't bother reading—and in fact, there are no whales.

Although Jonah was an actual prophet, the book that bears his name is not a record of his prophecies, as are the other prophetic books, but a cautionary tale. It tells us that God is concerned with all the people of the world and not just the Israelites. It also tells us to do what God wants when he wants it done. Jonah tried to "worm" out of his commitment to God, and he was almost undone by an actual worm before it was all over.

The historical Jonah was a prophet in the court of Israel's King Jeroboam II, who reigned from 786 to 746 B.C. According to 2 Kings 14:23, Jonah correctly predicted that Jeroboam would restore some of the lands lost to Israel since the time of Solomon.

In Jonah's day, the Assyrians were the archenemies of the Israelites and several decades later would invade them and wipe out 10 of the 12 tribes of Israel. The capital of Assyria was Nineveh, a resplendent city on the Tigris River. It was the last place any Israelite would want to go, and Jonah was no exception.

Jonah's Unwelcome Mission

The book of Jonah starts out abruptly. God calls Jonah and tells him to go to Nineveh and cry out against the city for its wickedness. It's as simple as that, but Jonah reacts strangely. He sets out in the opposite direction of Nineveh in a pathetic attempt to flee "from the presence of the Lord" (Jonah 1:3). At Joppa, Jonah finds a ship headed for Tarshish, a far-distant city on the Mediterranean. Jonah promptly pays his fare and boards the ship, but soon after leaving port, the ship is caught in a horrific storm, which God has brought to stop Jonah's escape.

The sailors panic and try to discover the reason for the storm. Oddly enough, Jonah is sleeping through it all, but they wake him and quickly discover that his God has sent the storm because of him. Jonah tells the sailors to toss him overboard. They hesitate, not wanting to be "guilty of innocent blood" (Jonah 1:14). Eventually they do throw Jonah into the sea, and the storm stops immediately, converting the sailors to belief in Yahweh.

Big Fish Story

Jonah is then swallowed by a whale—actually the Bible says "the Lord provided a large fish to swallow up Jonah" (Jonah 1:17). The reluctant prophet remains inside the whale/fish for three days, singing a psalm. Surprisingly, the psalm isn't one of petition (get me out of this fish!) or atonement (I'm sorry I messed up!), but one of thanksgiving (thanks for sending the fish?). "Then the Lord spoke to the fish, and it spewed Jonah out upon the dry land" (Jonah 2:10). The land, of course, is not Nineveh, but God calls Jonah again and recommissions him to travel to Nineveh and deliver his message.

Begrudgingly, Jonah drags himself across the many miles to Nineveh and walks through the city, proclaiming: "Forty days more, and Nineveh shall be overthrown" (Jonah 3:4). This is the only prophetic message in the entire book. The city of Nineveh is said to be so large that it takes Jonah three days to walk across it, delivering God's message.

Nineveh's Surprising Response

Jonah is not ready for what happens next. The people of Nineveh, whom he fears and detests, take his prophecy seriously. They believe

God, even though he is to them a foreign deity, not one they themselves worship or even know. Afraid that Jonah's prophecy may come true, they proclaim a fast and everyone puts on sackcloth—signaling repentance. When word reaches the king, he too believes, covers himself with sackcloth, and sits in ashes. The king then proclaims a decree mandating that all people—and all animals too—cover up with sackcloth, cry out to God, and stop their evil ways. "Who knows," says the king, "God may relent and change his mind." And that is exactly what happens. Moved by the people's repentance, God decides to spare their city.

Jonah's Hissy Fit

When God revokes his threat against the repentant Ninevites, Jonah is fit to be tied and even wishes to die. First he vents his anger against the Lord, claiming that he'd been afraid this would happen all along and that is why he'd tried to run off to Tarshish. Why exactly is Jonah so angry? Because God is merciful! He complains: "I knew that you are a gracious God and merciful, slow to anger, and abounding in steadfast love, and ready to relent from punishing" (Jonah 4:2). Jonah is angry that his enemies, the Ninevites, will be spared—probably to fall into sin again and return to invade Israel. He is also angry because he will be judged a false prophet when his prediction of doom does not come true. In a total funk, he begs God to let him die, then he stalks off in a huff and sits down outside the city waiting to see what will happen.

Shady Bush and a Worm

God, still loving despite Jonah's bad temper, causes a bush to magically spring up and shade Jonah from the blistering sun. Jonah calms down a bit, grateful for the bush. That night, however, God appoints a worm to destroy the bush. The next day, Jonah is devastated by the heat and again wishes to die. When God asks Jonah if it is right for him to be angry about the bush, Jonah answers, "Yes, angry enough to die" (Jonah 4:9). In response, God asks Jonah why he cares so much about a bush he had no part in creating yet resents God's caring for the 120,000 people of Nineveh who need his care.

The verdict is in. God is compassionate and loving to all his creatures.

Poetic License

Having trouble reading the book of Psalms?
Perhaps it's time to practice your Hebrew!

The psalms of the Old Testament can sometimes be a bit confusing to contemporary readers because many of them are in the form of ancient Hebrew poetry. However, they become a bit more clear if you understand the conventions and rich traditions of this unique literary form.

Hebrew 101
Hebrew contains only 22 letters—all of them consonants. The language is read from right to left. If you're Jewish, you know this. If not—surprise!

Hebrew poems often took the form of an acrostic, in which the first letter of each line forms a word or phrase. (Some also form the alphabet.) Acrostic psalms include 9, 10, 25, 34, 37, 111, 112, 119, and 145.

The structure of an ancient Hebrew poem involves a hierarchy of six levels: They are the stress unit, which is the most basic measurement of counting; verset; line; strophe; stanza; and section. In most cases, two or three stress units make up a verset; two or three versets make up a poetic line; two or three lines equal a strophe; two or three strophes make up a stanza; two or three stanzas create a section; and two or three sections make up a poem.

A Passion for Parallelism
Perhaps the most significant characteristic of ancient Hebrew poetry is something called parallelism. One example is the repetition of words, such as the first and last verses of Psalm 8:1, 9: "O Lord, our Sovereign, how majestic is your name in all the earth!" The repetition of the same thought is another example of parallelism (see Psalm 51:2).

Then there's the completion of an idea: "but their delight is in the law of the Lord, and on his law they meditate day and night" (Psalm 1:2).

Understanding the characteristics of ancient Hebrew poetry can bring fresh meaning to the book of Psalms. But don't feel bad if you don't quite get it—their true inspiration will still find its way into your heart.

Biblical Dragons (or Sea Serpents)

✧ ✧ ✧ ✧

Who says that there were never any dragons? The Bible talks about them, so they must have existed. In fact, the Bible gives two different names to dragons, or sea serpents: Leviathan, which means "twisting one," and Rahab, which means "boisterous one." There's also that dragon in the book of Revelation.

When God created the universe, he did not start from nothing but brought order out of a watery chaos (Genesis 1:1–2). According to myths from Babylon and the Canaanite city of Ugarit, before creating the universe we know today, it was necessary to destroy a seven-headed dragon that represented chaos. Although there is no mention of this dragon in Genesis, Psalm 74, in addressing Yahweh, reminds him that at the Creation, "You divided the sea by your might; you broke the heads of the dragons in the waters. You crushed the heads of Leviathan" (Psalm 74:13–14). The dragon, or sea serpent, Leviathan (also called Rahab) is a monster from the past, present, and yet to come.

Primeval Dragon of Chaos

The book of Job has the most to say about the primeval dragon of chaos. In responding to Job, God appears in a whirlwind and reminds him that he is insignificant in comparison with himself, the Almighty. Job was certainly not present at the Creation, when Yahweh formed all that is. It is God, not Job, who is all-powerful, for "by his power he stilled the Sea; by his understanding he struck down Rahab" (Job 26:12).

God gives some physical details about this beast, telling Job that it has a double coat of mail and its back is made of a row of shields and "there is terror all around its teeth" (Job 41:14). Most dragonlike of all, "From its mouth go flaming torches; sparks of fire leap out. Out of its nostrils comes smoke, as from a boiling pot and burning rushes. Its breath kindles coals, and a flame comes out of its mouth" (Job 41:19–21). And no humanmade weapon can harm it. Finally, "It makes the deep [sea] boil like a pot" (Job 41:31).

God asks Job if he thinks he can capture such a monster: "Can you draw out Leviathan with a fishhook, or press down its tongue with a cord?" (Job 41:1). God further derides Job by asking: "Will you play with it as with a bird, or will you put it on a leash for your girls?" (Job 41:5). He is probably referring to Psalm 104, in which God seems to regard Leviathan as a kind of personal plaything.

Dragons of Biblical Times
While Leviathan/Rahab does not appear in the historical accounts of the Israelites, the beast is sometimes summoned as a metaphor for Israel's enemies. Rahab is used as a name for Egypt in Isaiah 30:7, and the pharaoh is called a great dragon in Ezekiel 29:3–5 and 32:2–8. Jeremiah and Habakkuk also refer to the Babylonians as dragons and monsters. In the additions to the book of Daniel (part of the Protestant apocrypha but included in the Catholic Bible as chapter 14 of Daniel), the king of Babylon tells the prophet Daniel that a great dragon in the land (a giant reptile?) is an immortal god. With the king's permission, however, Daniel feeds the beast a mixture of pitch, fat, and hair boiled together. After consuming the mixture, the dragon bursts open, showing that it was no god after all.

Dragons Yet to Come
As it was in the beginning, so will it be at the end of time, for the battle against Leviathan will be fought again: "On that day the Lord with his cruel and great and strong sword will punish Leviathan the fleeing serpent, Leviathan the twisting serpent, and he will kill the dragon that is in the sea" (Isaiah 27:1).

In chapter 12 of Revelation, the archangel Michael slays the red dragon with seven heads, which is equated with Satan. Finally, in Revelation 13:1–10, there is an echo of this same monster in the seven-headed beast from the sea, which represents Rome.

Dragons are (almost) forever.

Snakes Alive!

✤ ✤ ✤ ✤

From Genesis to Revelation, they slither
throughout the pages of Scripture.

Whether you think they're creepy, alluring, frightening, or fascinating, you'll find snakes showing up from time to time in the Bible. Following are some of their notable "special appearances."

So, What Kinds of Snakes Are We Talking About?

Translating the various Old Testament words that refer to specific types of snakes is tricky work. Only one of these eight Hebrew words can be translated with some certainty. While particular snakes are not so easily identifiable, the general word for snake in Hebrew that corresponds to the English word for "serpent" or "snake" is easily translated. That being said, there are several kinds of venomous snakes—and lots of them—found in the lands where the Bible events occurred, including vipers, adders, and cobras.

An Infamous "Garden Snake"

In the opening verse of Genesis 3, we read that the serpent was "more crafty than any other wild animal that the Lord God had made." This sneaky snake is portrayed in Genesis 3 as being the instigator of the temptation that led to our "first parents'" first sin in the Garden of Eden.

It's interesting to note that nowhere in the Genesis account is the serpent identified as being the devil in disguise. Apparently the Satan-serpent connection was understood by the ancients. It was not explicitly noted in the scriptures until the apostles Paul and John wrote of it—directly and by allusion (see Romans 16:20; 2 Corinthians 11:3; Revelation 12:9).

Some have inferred from the curse God declared for the serpent that it may have originally moved about upright, but there is not sufficient evidence for this theory. Still others have wondered, because of Eve's dialogue with the serpent, if there may have been verbal communication between humans and animals prior to the Fall.

Transformer Snakes

Snakes show up again in the Exodus story, but this time as a sign of divine power, not a vehicle for Satan's deceit. In the desert, where Moses encountered God in the burning bush, God gave Moses a couple of miraculous signs to convince the elders of the Hebrew people that Moses really was sent by God to lead the people to freedom. One of these signs included Moses' staff turning into a snake when he threw it down on the ground. Then when he picked it up by the tail (gasp!), it turned back into a staff (whew!).

Later, however, when Moses and his brother, Aaron, stood before pharaoh, it was Aaron's staff (not Moses') that was used in the staff-turned-snake miracle. It's a familiar story, but an often overlooked aspect of it is that pharaoh's magicians could duplicate the stick-to-snake transformation. Aaron's staff-snake ended the showdown, however, by swallowing the other snakes. Guess pharaoh's magicians had to whittle some new magic wands.

Asp Attack!

Translators aren't really certain about the type of "fiery serpent" that God unleashed on the people who were griping, accusing God and Moses of leading them into the wilderness only to die. But the adjective *fiery* may have described the type of pain the venom inflicted, or merely that these serpents were deadly.

This wasn't some capricious act of judgment on God's part, however. Despite his provisions, protection, and a recent victory he'd given over an aggressive foe, the people were quick (as we often are) to turn ugly at the first sign of difficulty. Rather than calling on God for what they needed, they made it clear to him that they were fed up (literally) with the manna they'd been dining on and wanted no more of God's or Moses' leadership. That's when their complaints about being led into the wilderness to die began to be realized. Enter fiery serpents.

The people quickly realized their mistake, confessed their sin to Moses, and asked him to intercede. Moses prayed. God's antivenom was unconventional to say the least: a bronze serpent on a pole, held up for people to look on and get relief from their snakebites.

Figuratively, many Bible theologians see a type, or representation, of Christ in the bronze serpent that was lifted up for people to look upon and be saved. Jesus—who became redeemer of the world by carrying the judgment of our own sins upon himself as he hung on a cross—has taken away the sting of death, promising eternal life to those who look to him for salvation from sin.

A postscript to this story: Later in Israel's history, this bronze serpent became an object of idolatrous worship, so King Hezekiah targeted it for destruction as he sought to turn the people's hearts back to their God.

Snakebite-Proof Apostle

Paul had been sailing to Rome as a prisoner. The vessel he was traveling in broke apart in a storm, and the crew and passengers—276 in all—had swum to the shores of the island of Malta, where they were welcomed by the natives. They built a fire, and while Paul stoked it with some sticks he'd gathered, a deadly snake, driven out by the heat of the fire, bit his hand and hung there by its fangs. Shaking it off into the fire, Paul went about his business. Surmising this was divine judgment, the natives waited for the apostle to drop dead. Much to their amazement, he never did, and they quickly changed their opinion.

As Jesus commissioned his disciples to go out and preach the gospel, he said this: "And these signs will accompany those who believe: by using my name they will cast out demons; they will speak in new tongues; *they will pick up snakes in their hands,* and if they drink any deadly thing, it will not hurt them; they will lay their hands on the sick, and they will recover" (Mark 16:17–18, emphasis added).

In some times and places, there have been church groups advocating and practicing poisonous snake handling to test or demonstrate the authenticity of their faith. They base their actions on Mark 16. However, Jesus' message has been understood by most Christian groups to mean that there would be some unusual evidence that would accompany (and so authenticate) the apostles' message (as we see in Paul's case on Malta). Most Christians don't think the passage advocates putting oneself in harm's way as a matter of habit or ritual.

The "Old Serpent's" Destiny

Revelation 12:9 quite clearly identifies the devil—as he is revealed and understood in scripture—with that deceiving serpent in Eden: "The great dragon was thrown down, that ancient serpent, who is called the Devil and Satan, the deceiver of the whole world—he was thrown down to the earth, and his angels were thrown down with him."

And while he has been at large in the world up to this day, working his deceptions, a final end has been decreed for him: "And the devil who had deceived them was thrown into the lake of fire and sulfur, where the beast and the false prophet were, and they will be tormented day and night forever and ever" (Revelation 20:10).

Sounds like he'll meet a fate similar to the Apostle Paul's viper... just a more permanent one. How's that for an ending to the snakiest of all snakes?

Maccabees

The Maccabees founded the Jewish Hasmonean kingdom of Israel, which maintained a free Jewish state from 142-37 B.C. In 167, the Jews were thoroughly fed up with their Seleucid (Greek) overlords, who had tried to ban Jewish worship. Seleucids evidently didn't read the Old Testament, or they'd have known how pointless that was.

The rebellion began when Mattathias, a rabbi, killed a Seleucid officer and a Jew who were offering pagan sacrifices in obedience to Seleucid decrees. The resulting guerrilla war, first led by Judas Maccabeus ("Judah the Hammer"), gave the Seleucids fits. It's no accident that the modern Israeli Defense Forces find great inspiration in their Maccabean ancestors, who proved tough, resourceful, and utterly dedicated to winning or dying. The Seleucids eventually decided to leave the troublesome Maccabees to their own devices, enabling an independent Jewish state to rule Israel until the Romans absorbed all Judea.

Brick House (of the Lord)

⚜ ⚜ ⚜ ⚜

The Brick Testament presents hundreds of Bible stories recreated entirely out of Legos!

The Bible has been presented in many formats, but one of the most unique has to be The Brick Testament, which features more than 4,530 scenes retelling more than 420 stories from scripture.

Labor of Love

A labor of love by the Rev. Brendan Powell Smith (who is not an ordained minister of any official church), the project started in 2001 as a website (www.thebricktestament.com) and more recently has been published as a series of picture books. Smith explains on the project's website: " ... the goal of The Brick Testament is to give people an increased knowledge of the contents of the Bible in a way that is fun and compelling while remaining true to the text of the scriptures."

The Brick Testament starts with Genesis and works its way through Revelation. An eclectic array of important stories, including the life and teachings of Jesus, are told along the way. Each tale is revealed through a variety of photographic images and is given a special rating in regard to sex, nudity, violence, and cursing.

Nothing but Legos

Smith has strived to stay true to the basic concept of the project by creating as many aspects of the scenes as possible out of Lego bricks. In a few instances, some pieces have had to be modified, he says on the project's website, but the vast majority of re-creations use unaltered Lego parts from sets released from the 1960s to the present.

The Brick Testament has become so popular that Smith has made available a selection of special items for fans. Among them are a 36-inch poster of the Last Supper made entirely out of Legos, along with custom sets of the Holy Trinity, Ark of the Covenant, Angel vs. Devil, and Moses and the Ten Commandments.

The Naked Truth

❦ ❦ ❦ ❦

*Whether presented in metaphor or in stark reality,
the Bible doesn't shy away from the topic of nakedness. The lack
of prudish skirting around potentially embarrassing episodes and
truths in the scriptures might surprise some, might make a few
uncomfortable, and might offend still others, but that's just the way
it is when you're dealing with naked truth. (Note: Instances
of nakedness referred to may be entire or partial.)*

- **Innocence Lost (Genesis 2:25–3:11, 21):** Created in innocence
  and freedom, Adam and Eve enjoyed a shame-free state of being in
  the buff until they sampled fruit from the only off-limits tree in the
  Garden of Eden. Once the knowledge of good and evil was attained
  through their moral freelancing, their nakedness became evident to
  them, and they hid. In an attempt to cover up, they tailored makeshift
  fig-leaf garments. After confessing their sin to God, he outfitted them
  with animal-skin duds.

- **Arrive Naked, Leave Naked (Job 1:13–22):** An icon of suffering,
  Job had it all and then lost it all tragically—all his children, his wealth,
  and his health. Only his own life and his wife were spared in the
  onslaught of calamity. Amazingly, Job's first response to his epic trials
  was one of worship: "Naked I came from my mother's womb, and
  naked shall I return there; the Lord gave, and the Lord has taken away;
  blessed be the name of the Lord."

- **A Biblical "Peeping Tom" (Genesis 9:20–27):** Noah, his wife, and
  three sons—Shem, Ham, and Japheth—along with their wives emerged
  from the ark after the Great Flood, and they began their little chore
  of reestablishing civilization. At some point in the process, Noah had
  planted a vineyard and was enjoying the fruits of his "label." One day,
  he imbibed to the point of getting drunk and then fell asleep naked in
  his tent. Ham happened to peek in and see his dad lying there nude.
  Rather than keeping what he'd seen to himself or covering up his dad,

Don't Say That Name!

The personal name of God (written as Y-H-W-H) was so holy to the Jews that they eventually stopped pronouncing it because they felt unworthy. When they encountered this name in the Bible while reading aloud, they substituted one of God's titles, *adonay* or *adonai* ("the Lord"). In most English Bibles today, God's personal name is written as "the LORD."

he exposed Noah to further shame by broadcasting his discovery to his brothers. Fortunately, Shem and Japheth had more respect for their father and walked into his tent backwards, eyes averted, with a covering. When Noah awoke and realized what had happened, Ham found himself on the receiving end of a curse from his father, while Shem and Japheth were blessed for their efforts.

- **Custom Undies (Exodus 20:26, 28:40–43):** Priests who served at the altar of God had to wear special underwear. Why? Was there something magical or super-powerful about these hip-to-thigh length briefs? Nope. They were simply for the practical and moral purpose of covering their nakedness as they ministered before God.

- **Naked No-Nos (Leviticus 18:6–20):** To "uncover the nakedness" of someone is a biblical euphemism for having sexual relations with them. The moral law, given to Moses by God for the Hebrew people, had explicit rules about who was sexually "out of bounds." Society retains many of these same standards today.

- **A Naked King (1 Samuel 19:18–24):** In a fit of jealous rage, Israel's first king, Saul, was chasing David, who would later become king. When Saul approached the place where David was staying with the prophet Samuel, Saul's intention was to kill David. Instead, God prevented Saul from carrying out his plans by sending him into a prophetic "frenzy" in the presence of Samuel. In his overwhelmed state, Saul stripped off his clothes and lay naked all day and night, unable to lay a hand on David.

- **A Naked Prophet (Isaiah 20:1–6):** As an object lesson foreshadowing the fate of Egypt and Ethiopia at the hands of Assyria, God ordered his prophet Isaiah to go naked and barefoot for three years.

- **A Naked Escape (Mark 14:51–52):** The Gospel of Mark is the only one of the four gospels to mention the episode of a young man who escaped naked from the Garden of Gethsemane at Jesus' arrest. The details seem too autobiographical for the reference to not be the book's author—Mark himself.

- **A Naked Disciple (John 21:4–8):** Simon Peter was fishing with the other disciples when Jesus appeared to them after his resurrection. Upon realizing it was Jesus who was talking to him from the shoreline, Peter quickly dressed—he'd been fishing in stripped-down mode—before jumping into the water to make his way to see the Lord.

- **Run (Naked) for Your Lives! (Acts 19:11–20):** Seven young men, attempting to wield power to exorcise demons, used the names of Jesus and Paul in their incantations over a demonized man. The demon overpowered all seven of them, telling them that while it knew about Jesus and Paul, it knew nothing of them. The book of Acts reports that all seven of the wannabe exorcists ran from the house naked and bleeding.

> # Who Is El Shaddai?
>
> One of God's titles was El Shaddai, which is usually translated as "God Almighty." God told Moses that he had appeared to Abraham, Isaac, and Jacob as El Shaddai, but that he did not reveal to them the full implications of his personal name, Yahweh (Exodus 6:3).

- **Naked Before God? (Hebrews 4:12–13):** "Indeed, the word of God is living and active, sharper than any two-edged sword, piercing until it divides soul from spirit, joints from marrow; it is able to judge the thoughts and intentions of the heart. And before him no creature is hidden, but all are naked and laid bare to the eyes of the one to whom we must render an account."

New Look at an Old Book

✤ ✤ ✤ ✤

Underground cartoonist Robert Crumb generated more than a little controversy with his adaptation of the book of Genesis.

Robert Crumb is arguably the most influential member of the Underground Cartoonist movement of the 1960s and '70s. Many of his creations, including libidinous Fritz the Cat, have become cultural icons, and Crumb's original artwork typically sells for hundreds and even thousands of dollars. Not bad for a Philly boy who got his start illustrating cards for American Greetings.

Crumb is no stranger to controversy—and that trend has continued with the publication of the artist's most recent work, an illustrated adaptation of the book of Genesis.

Definitive Version

Five years in the making, *Book of Genesis Illustrated by R. Crumb* (W. W. Norton & Company, Inc., 2009) is exactly as its title suggests: an adaptation containing almost every word of the first 50 chapters of the Bible. It's a remarkable endeavor and, in the view of many critics, one of Crumb's most thought-provoking works.

Not everyone praised the book, which features quite a bit of sex and violence. One critic condemned the project for "turning the Bible into titillation." Others, however, acknowledged Crumb for strictly adhering to the biblical text. "It may surprise people but the Bible does contain nudity, sex and violence," commented a representative of the Bible Society. "That's because it contains real stories about real people. If by reading the book people are encouraged to re-engage with the Bible, then that can only be a good thing."

Crumb's Beliefs

What about Robert Crumb? The artist admits to being an agnostic, and he doesn't view the Bible as the literal word of God. "The idea that people for a couple thousand years have taken this so seriously seems completely insane and crazy, totally nuts," he said during a press conference. "But the human race is crazy if nothing else."

Who's a Bible Hero?

❖ ❖ ❖ ❖

Who comes to your mind when you think of a Bible hero?

Maybe it's Noah the ark-builder or David the giant-killer. The list could also include the rich and wise King Solomon or Moses the leader of millions. These people and other warriors, leaders, and kings can be called the main characters in Bible heroics. However, there are other people that were also heroes in their own way. These were the supporting actors, standing in the wings, ready to give their help and support when it was needed. Some of them were only on the scene for a short time and others are virtually unknown. But all of them were heroes, lending richness to the people, places, and events recorded in the Bible.

Deborah—Original Multitasker
Deborah (whose name means "honeybee") bucked the trend in ancient Israel's definition of the woman's role. She was a wife, a songwriter, a prophetess, and a judge. Deborah was the only female of the 12 judges who guided Israel, and it was a position that she held for 40 years. In a male-dominated society, her legal advice in disputes and in matters concerning security and warfare were sought after and followed. As a prophetess, Deborah received orders from God and passed them on to Barak, the commander of Israel's army. When Deborah told Barak to attack the much larger army of General Sisera, Barak responded like a petulant child. "I won't go unless you go with me!" he declared. So Deborah packed up and went along. With God's help, she knew just the right time to shout, "Attack!" Barak listened to her and won an amazing victory—though because of his hissy fit, Deborah got all the credit. After the complete defeat of the enemy, Deborah wrote a song of praise and victory describing God's deliverance (Judges 4—5), which Barak sang.

Jehoiada—Protector of the Future King
Ahaziah, king of Judah, had been killed, and the empty throne was left by default to Athaliah, Ahaziah's wicked mother. To assure

that no one would rise up and oppose her, Athaliah embarked on a bloody massacre. She slaughtered all remaining members of the royal family that she could find—many of them her own flesh and blood. But Athaliah's plans were foiled by the high priest, Jehoiada. He and his wife took Ahaziah's infant son, Joash, and stole him away from the king's children that were about to be killed. Jehoiada hid Joash in the temple for six years. When Joash was seven years old, Jehoiada engineered a plan with army officers and other leaders to crown Joash king. The coup was successful, Athaliah was assassinated, and Joash was king of Judah. For as long as he lived, Jehoiada counseled Joash and helped him to be a wise and godly king (2 Chronicles 22:10–24:16).

Nicodemus—Visitor in the Night

Nicodemus had a lot going for him—he was a rich man, a teacher, a Pharisee, and a member of the Jewish ruling council. But at first glance, he certainly doesn't seem to be in line for a "hero" award. Nicodemus wanted to have a serious conversation with Jesus but not out in the open where others could see him. Instead, Nicodemus

waited for night and then quietly hurried along the streets of Jerusalem under the cover of darkness to meet secretly with Jesus. Nicodemus became bold and heroic at the end of Jesus' life. He objected when the council condemned Jesus without a hearing. He also spent a great deal of money for spices to prepare Jesus' body for burial. In the end, Nicodemus finally understood Jesus' teachings and changed from a timid, secret disciple to one who made his beliefs manifest (John 3:1–21; 19:39–42).

Susanna and Joanna—First "Groupies"

Doing laundry, sewing, and cooking were probably not part of the job description for Jesus' disciples. Regardless of that, they did need to eat and their clothes certainly got dirty walking around on the dusty roads. And eventually even the best-made clothes wear out. This is where some women acted as "quiet heroes," taking care of the physical needs of Jesus and his followers. Two of these women were Susanna and Joanna, both of whom had received Jesus' healing for various physical or mental conditions. Joanna's husband was Herod's steward, overseeing financial and property matters for Herod and seeing to the education of the children in the royal household. This put Joanna in the upper class of society. These women were helping to support Jesus and his disciples out of their own means. This would have been viewed as scandalous behavior in those days. But they were responding to Jesus' message in a positive, loving way (Luke 8:1–3).

Joseph—Final Act of Love

Joseph of Arimathea, like Nicodemus, was a member of the Jewish ruling council—the Sanhedrin. He was also a rich man with a highly honored reputation. Joseph had not consented to the crucifixion of Jesus. He had been a secret disciple of Jesus, but after Christ's death, Joseph got rid of all secrecy. He boldly went to Pilate and asked for the body of Jesus. Joseph risked excommunication for such actions, but he wanted Jesus to have the best resting place available. So Joseph gave Jesus a tomb that he had prepared for himself, a vault chiseled out of rock in a quiet garden. It was a rich tomb in which no one had ever been buried, the very best that Joseph could give to Jesus (Mark 15:43; Luke 23:50–51; John 19:38–42).

Tabitha—Faith in Action

During the days of the early church, Tabitha (who is also known as Dorcas) lived in the city of Joppa. People knew that she was a follower of Jesus not only by what she said but also by what she did. Tabitha helped anyone in need, especially widows. She worked hard and gave the widows and others many handmade items. Tabitha was a quiet hero who lived a life of service. The people she ministered to came to know Jesus through her (Acts 9:36–43).

The Fabrics of Their Lives

✤ ✤ ✤ ✤

East of Eden, the ancient Israelites learned to cover themselves.

In Genesis 3, God banishes Adam and Eve from the Garden of Eden and, as they are now aware of their nakedness, provides them with animal skins to wear. Adam and Eve's descendants, however, would not be content with skins. Instead, they would discover cloth fabrics that were far more comfortable to wear in the often hot climate in which they lived and worked. Shelter, too, was affected by the production of woven fabrics, whether that meant living in a tent or simply using a blanket to sleep at night. Linen, wool, goat's hair, camel's hair, silk, and cotton were all used to various degrees at different periods in biblical history, though their use depended largely on an individual's wealth and social standing. But rich or poor, fabric was an absolute necessity for every man, woman, and child.

Seen and Herd

The importance of the shepherd in biblical times cannot be overstated. Goats and sheep were in constant peril from wild predators, and the people who protected these flocks of ancient Israel were the shepherds. Though shepherds were almost always humble men at the bottom of the social ladder, the profession was considered so vital to Jewish society that both the Old and New Testament are rife with shepherd imagery. God calls King David a shepherd in Ezekiel 34:23. In Luke 2:8–20, David is referenced when angels appear to shepherds tending their flocks at night and announce to them the birth of Jesus. These shepherds are honored to be some of the first to visit the Christ child. Later, in John 10:11, the adult Jesus tells his followers, "I am the good shepherd. The good shepherd lays down his life for the sheep."

Of course, goats and sheep were also used for their meat and for sacrifices, but the value of their hair and wool was immense. Along with woven camel hair, woven goat's hair and sheep's wool were the most common fabrics in ancient Israel. Garments made from the

hair of these animals are often called "sackcloth" in the Bible. In both the Old and New Testament, sackcloth is the clothing of the poor, the powerless, and the mourning. When God threatens to destroy the city of Nineveh in Jonah 3, its king and all residents don sackcloth to show repentance for their sins, so God withdraws his threat. In Matthew 3:4–5, John the Baptist wears a hair shirt to show his humility and devoutness as he prepares the way for Jesus: "Now John wore clothing of camel's hair with a leather belt around his waist, and his food was locusts and wild honey. Then the people of Jerusalem and all Judea were going out to him."

Fields of . . . What?

We know that the ancient Israelites made clothing out of some kind of plant, for the Hebrew word *pishtah* meant a type of fabric made from plants. But what kinds of plants? Flax and cotton are the two most likely. Jews almost certainly grew and harvested flax themselves, but historians differ on whether they grew their own cotton or imported it from other countries. In New Testament times, large amounts of both cotton and silk were sold in the Jerusalem marketplace, but both were considered luxury items. For the average person, they were just too expensive.

This is why flax, which was used to make linen, was so important in ancient Israel. It was an easily cultivated crop that had been grown in the region since the early Bronze Age, and according to recent archaeological discoveries, humans may have begun dyeing its fiber as long ago as 30,000 years. When flax was ready to be harvested, the plants were pulled up at the roots rather than cut. This maximized the length of the fiber. The plants were then put in the ground for two weeks in a process called retting, in which enzymes separate the fiber from the straw. Once the straw had been fully retted, it was ready to be threshed.

Fruit of the Loom

After hair and wool was shorn from animals or *pishtah* harvested by the men of ancient Israel, the women took over and wove them into fabric. The spinning wheel had not yet been invented in biblical times, so the women used distaff spinning to make cloth. A distaff was a stick to which the wool or flax was attached, while a cylindrical object called a spindle was turned by hand in order to twist the fibers into thread. This women's work was exalted in Exodus 35:25–26: "All the skilful women spun with their hands, and brought what they had spun in blue and purple and crimson yarns and fine linen; all the women whose hearts moved them to use their skill spun the goats' hair." In Proverbs 31, which describes the ideal wife, spinning and the manufacture of clothing are given prominent mention: "She puts her hands to the distaff, and her hands hold the spindle.... She makes herself coverings; her clothing is fine linen and purple."

Once the thread was spun, the women would use a flat, narrow piece of wood called a shuttle to weave cross threads between lengthwise threads. Sometimes the fabrics they created on these primitive looms were coarse and utilitarian, but others were more like works of art. During the time of slavery in Egypt, Israelite women learned new and more complex methods of creating garments and wall hangings. In Exodus 35:35, Moses tells them that their talent in this area is a gift from God: "He has filled them with skill to do every kind of work done by an artisan or by a designer or by an embroiderer in blue, purple, and crimson yarns, and in fine linen, or by a weaver." In thanks, the women of ancient Israel took the jobs of spinning, weaving, dyeing, and embroidery very seriously, and they worked as hard as the men to create practical beauty in times of darkness and despair.

"I Am Who I Am"

When Moses asked God what his name was, God responded with this cryptic phrase: "I am who I am" (Exodus 3:14). These words in Hebrew are related to God's personal name, Yahweh. God may have been revealing something profound about himself, or he may have been reminding Moses of his earlier promise that "I will be with you" (verse 12).

Fast Facts

- The New Testament was originally written in Greek. Nearly 5,650 hand-written copies survive in the original language and around 10,000 copies in Latin. When you throw in other languages, a total of approximately 25,000 ancient copies of the New Testament are still in existence.

- After the New Testament, the second most common ancient text in existence is Homer's Iliad, with 643 known copies.

- Until the 18th century, the vast majority of devout Christians believed that the earth was created 4,000 years before the birth of Christ and that every event reported in the Bible actually happened in real time as we know it. It was the science of geology and James Hutton's groundbreaking 1788 book Theory of the Earth that made people start to think they might be wrong about the age of the earth.

- You can thank Cardinal Hugo de S. Caro  for the concept of biblical chapters, which he introduced in A.D. 1238. Verse notations were added over 300 years later by Robertus Stephanus, following the invention of the Gutenberg printing press.

- The University of Göttingen in Germany houses a Bible written on 2,470 palm leaves.

- The number of new Bibles that are sold, given away, or distributed in the United States through other means totals around 168,000 per day, according to Wycliffe International, the Society of Gideons, the International Bible Society, and other sources. So if you don't own one, you have no one but yourself to blame.

- The Bible can be read aloud in its entirety in approximately 70 hours—unless you're a really slow reader, in which case it will take much longer. This time does not include bathroom breaks or interruptions from audience members for you to "speak up, we can't hear you in the back!"

- There are a combined total of 66 books in the Old and New Testaments of the Bible.

- Since its creation, the Bible has been translated into more than 1,200 languages—including Klingon.

Early Reading

❖ ❖ ❖ ❖

The Dead Sea Scrolls provide a remarkable glimpse
into the creation and history of the Old Testament.

In 1946, a couple of Bedouin shepherds looking for a stray goat stumbled upon some ancient desert caves near the shore of the Dead Sea in Israel. They returned with what would turn out to be one of the world's most important archaeological finds—the oldest biblical and extra-biblical documents ever uncovered.

In the following years, nearly 900 manuscripts were recovered from 11 caves in the ancient settlement of Qumran, about 13 miles east of Jerusalem. Known as the Dead Sea Scrolls, the documents, many of which are fragments, have provided astounding insight into ancient Hebrew life and the contents of the Bible.

Biblical Cornucopia

The scrolls are believed to date from the 3rd century B.C. to A.D. 68 and are written in Hebrew, Aramaic, and Greek. They have been divided into two categories: biblical and nonbiblical. The documents in the biblical category include fragments from every book of the Old Testament except for the book of Esther. Included among them are 19 copies of the book of Isaiah, 25 copies of Deuteronomy, and 30 copies of the book of Psalms. The documents also contained some surprises, including prophecies by Ezekiel, Jeremiah, and Daniel not found in the Bible, as well as previously unseen psalms attributed to King David and Joshua.

Of equal interest are the documents that do not pertain to the Bible. Many deal with common life and Jewish law, and they include rule books for the community, war conduct, hymnic compositions, and writings of wisdom. Perhaps most intriguing, however, was what has come to be known as the Copper Scroll, found in cave 3. It features a list of 64 underground hiding places throughout Israel said to contain gold, silver, aromatics, and manuscripts. Some scholars believe that these deposits, if they still exist, may be treasures from the temple of Jerusalem that were hidden for safekeeping.

Authors Unknown

Following the discovery of the scrolls, archaeologists were understandably eager to learn who created them and hid them in the protective caves. Archaeologists excavated the Qumran ruin, a series of structures located on a terrace between the Dead Sea and the caves where the scrolls were found, but they learned little. The excavation did shed some light on life in ancient times but provided little additional information regarding the amazingly preserved manuscripts.

The biggest question, of course, was why the keepers of the scrolls, believed by some to be a Jewish sect known as the Essenes, felt it necessary to hide the documents. Some scholars believe the scrolls were hidden away during the First Jewish Revolt between A.D. 66–70 to protect them from advancing Roman forces sent to hunt down rebel Jews. There is some debate about this, however, and the controversy continues.

Time has taken a toll on the documents, which today are extremely fragile, but so did their discovery. Muhammed edh-Dhib, the Bedouin who found the first scrolls, hung them from a tent pole while he tried to decide what to do with them, taking them down occasionally to show people. The documents passed through many hands before finally being placed under the protection of the Israel Antiquities Authority. In March 1948, the Arab-Israeli War prompted officials to temporarily relocate the invaluable scrolls to Beirut, Lebanon; they were returned when the conflict ended.

Solving the Puzzle

Researchers have been poring over the Dead Sea Scrolls for more than 50 years, attempting to learn as much as they can about their contents, their significance in regard to Judaic and Christian history, and the people who created and later hid them. Detailed photographs of a large percentage of the intact scrolls and fragments have been made to give scholars around the world greater access.

The importance of the Dead Sea Scrolls cannot be overstated. Until their discovery, the oldest Hebrew manuscripts of the Bible dated back only to 9th century A.D. The scrolls pushed that date back another thousand years, while simultaneously providing scholars with astounding new insight into one of the most influential texts in human history.

All Work and No Play?

⚛ ⚛ ⚛ ⚛

The work week has been long and you are really beat.
Or you have run up against a frustrating problem and just can't
seem to unravel the mess. Or the kids have been sick and you've been
cooped up in the house for days. Do these scenarios sound familiar?
How do you unwind and recuperate mind and body?

Some of us engage in physical activities or sports to unwind. Others
enjoy music or dramatic presentations. Then there's always "vegging
out" in front of the TV or perhaps taking a short vacation. Bible-time
people also experienced hard work, frustrating problems, and cranky
kids. And just like us they needed something to break up the mo-
notony of everyday life. They didn't have high-tech amusements or
activities, but they did have fun and enjoy themselves.

Music and Dance
The first biblical record of music is found in Genesis 4:21, "[Jabal's]
brother's name was Jubal: he was the ancestor of all those who play
the lyre and pipe." Music was used from a very early date, as in
Genesis 31:27, as an accompaniment to song and dance. Singing and
the playing of musical instruments were integral parts of the worship
service. The book of Psalms is the songbook of the Bible, and many
of the psalms indicate which musical instruments were to be used as
an accompaniment to the singing. The sacred song and dance always
went together; words, motion, and music together helped to express
joy and celebration or sorrow. David was filled with joy when he
brought the Ark of the Covenant to Jerusalem and "danced before
the Lord with all his might" (2 Samuel 6:14). Moses sang a song of
victory after crossing the Red Sea, and Miriam and all the women
sang and danced to celebrate their delivery from the Egyptians
(Exodus 15:1–21).

Children's Games
The Bible doesn't list specific games that children played, but in
Zechariah 8:5 it mentions, "boys and girls playing in [Jerusalem's]

streets." And in Matthew 11:16–17, Jesus speaks of children singing songs to each other. Most of their games were probably played outdoors, such as running races, participating in feats of strength and agility, and using slingshots. Bible-time children played ball games with a ball probably made of solid leather. Girls played knucklebones, which is like jacks. Archaeologists have found marked-off squares that could have been used for hopscotch. Rattles, whistles, game boards, tiny clay pots, marbles, and furniture have also been found in some digs.

Biblical Sports
In 1 Corinthians 9:24–27, Paul speaks of physical training and running races. The people of the Bible were very much like us, and they enjoyed the competition and fellowship of participating in contests that challenged them physically and mentally. Some biblical archaeological studies refer to ancient sports and recreation. These included primitive versions of soccer, cricket, field hockey, and a baseball-like game called round ball.

Brain Games
Riddles and quizzes were a favorite form of entertainment, often used at parties or other gatherings. Someone would present a riddle and others would try to figure out the answer. An example of this is found in the story of Samson in Judges 14:10–18. Unfortunately, the guests couldn't solve the riddle and needed to turn to trickery to get the answer—with disastrous results. (See the story on page 96.) We can only hope that most riddle challenges ended in fun and peace!

Juggling
An ancient section of the Talmud, the Mishna, speaks of juggling as part of the celebration of the festival of Sukkot. "Pious and prominent men used to dance with burning torches in their hands before the thousands of celebrants; they sang before them songs and praises to God. The Levites played on harps and lyres, and with cymbals, trumpets, and numerous musical instruments." Other Jewish scholars expand on this, saying that the torches were thrown into the air and then caught. They used anywhere from four to eight torches—constantly juggling them up and down, up and down.

The Bible Says Don't!

✥ ✥ ✥ ✥

The Bible is chock full of important rules—
but not all of them make sense in the 21st century.

No matter how hard you try to adhere to the teachings of the Bible, chances are you're still going to break a few rules. A lot of stuff in the Bible—especially the Old Testament—doesn't apply today. In fact, if you're doing any of the following, you're not a strict adherent of the Bible:

• Have a rounded haircut. According to Leviticus 19:27, one should not "round off the hair on your temples or mar the edges of your beard." Bad news for the '60s-era Beatles and their bowl-cut–wearing fans.

Problems with Pigs

• Football: Even touching pig skin is a no-no, warns Leviticus 11:8, because swine are unclean animals. So take that, NFL!
• Fortune tellers: Leviticus 19:31 tells us not to turn to mediums or spiritualists, lest we face exile.
• Gossip: Proverbs 11:13 says it best: "A gossip goes about telling secrets, but one who is trustworthy keeps a confidence."
• Tattoos: According to Leviticus 19:28, "You shall not make any gashes in your flesh for the dead or tattoo any marks upon you." So don't even think about getting that cute kitten tattoo.

Better to Stay Together

• Divorce: Notes Mark 10:11–12, "Whoever divorces his wife and marries another commits adultery against her; and if she divorces her husband and marries another, she commits adultery."
• Clothes made from blends: The authors of the Bible really dislike mixed things. Leviticus 19:19 states: "You shall not let your animals breed with a different kind; you shall not sow your field with two kinds of seed; nor shall you put on a garment made of two different materials." That cotton/polyester sweater you love? Ditch it or face the wrath of God.

Where Jesus Walked

Nazareth

Christ was, of course, a Nazarene.
So what was, and is, the town of Nazareth?

In Biblical Times
Nazareth's site would seem a very attractive place to live, to go by its history of occupation. The earliest archaeological finds in the immediate area have been dated to the late Stone Age. By Christ's time, Nazareth was a small farming town; it could even be considered, in our lingo, somewhat podunk. In John 1, Nathanael responded to Philip's word of Jesus by asking, "Can anything good come out of Nazareth?" Luke describes it as the site of the Annunciation. It had a significant Jewish population until about A.D. 630, when the Eastern Roman Empire ran them out. Soon thereafter, Islamic forces captured the town.

Jesus' Connection
After King Herod died, Joseph brought his family to Palestine from Egypt. After a vision from an angel, Joseph settled in Nazareth, Galilee. Young Jesus grew to maturity there, and then he went out to minister. When he returned to Nazareth, he didn't get much respect. In Luke, he attended Shabbat at synagogue in Nazareth and tried to preach but was rejected and almost thrown off a cliff. Mark also refers to this episode. Christ took it philosophically, authoring the famous sentence: "Prophets are not without honor, except in their home town, and among their own kin, and in their own house." Scripture does not record Jesus returning to Nazareth.

Nazareth Today
Modern Nazareth (the Hebrew name is *Natzrat* or *Natzeret;* in Arabic it's *An-Nasira*), the "Arab capital of Israel," is some 16 miles west southwest of the Sea of Galilee. Over 60,000 people live in Nazareth proper, predominantly Arabs, who are roughly two-thirds Muslim and one-third Christian. It is part of a greater metro area with nearly 200,000 people. The chief modern attraction is the Church of the Annunciation, built over the spot where tradition says Gabriel appeared to Mary.

Moviepocalypse

❧ ❧ ❧ ❧

There is a cottage industry of films based on Revelation that could fill a book in their own right. The ones listed below will give you a good start for your popcorn Armageddon.

- **The Omen (1976):** The Antichrist walks the earth in *The Omen* as a little boy named Damien. Gregory Peck learns his biological son was stillborn and switched at birth with the Antichrist. Dark forces surround and protect Damien, leaving a trail of bodies in his wake. In terms of biblical passages, the movie focuses solely on references to the beast in the books of Daniel and Revelation (as *Rosemary's Baby* did).

- **Constantine (2005):** It's hard to take Keanu Reeves seriously in anything, but he's very watchable as a former attempted suicide who fights demons to earn his right to get into heaven. The plot has some force using the Spear of Destiny to unleash Satan's son on the world. Based on the comic *Hellblazer,* there's a lot of Revelation material mixed in with medieval legends and Dante's *Inferno* to create a cool, if jumbled, mythology. The conversation between Reeves and an angel about humanity's squandering of God's gift elevates the film above a genre picture.

- **The Seventh Sign (1988):** The well of souls is empty, and Jesus has returned to end the world. Only Demi Moore can prevent him from opening the seventh seal. The story of Longinus (the Roman soldier who stabbed Christ on the cross with his spear) is inexplicably tied into the apocalypse, by way of the priest who investigates all the strange happenings as a result of the opening of the first six seals. There's no law against it, but Longinus was not in Revelation (nor in the Gospels, at least not by name).

- **The Prophecy (1995):** What's so interesting about *The Prophecy* (other than Christopher Walken as the angel Gabriel) is that the main character (Elias Koteas) finds a Bible on the body of a dead angel/

demon with a 23rd chapter of Revelation (the Bible has 22). The 23rd chapter talks of a second war in heaven started by Gabriel. The movie doesn't take much from the Bible at all, but its expanded mythology is interesting and shares some elements with *Constantine.*

- **Legion (2010):** This recent film is notable because it diverges completely from the biblical apocalypse. God has given up on humanity and has sent down the angels to kill us all. The film suffers from pacing issues, but the message of sacrifice and redemption (plus angel vs. angel combat) is worth a viewing.

> ## Interbiblical Quotes
>
> The New Testament quotes the Old Testament hundreds of times, but only once does a New Testament author mention another New Testament writer by name. Peter cites Paul in support of his own views on God's patience (2 Peter 3:15).

- **Left Behind: The Movie (2000):** Based on the series of best-selling books, *Left Behind* is about a group of people who are literally left behind after the rapture. One of those people is played by Kirk Cameron from *Growing Pains.* Two sequels followed (the third stars Louis Gossett Jr. as the president of the United States). The Antichrist is revealed, and the group must elude his minions to spread the word of God. Fair warning: You will be preached at by bad dialogue.

    The books were coauthored by an evangelical minister and fictional license was taken with the events, so how close the series adheres to the Bible depends on one's interpretation. (Roman Catholics, for example, believe Jesus' thousand-year reign is spiritual and not physical.)

- **The Rapture (1991):** This movie is a very literal depiction of the apocalypse without resorting to preachy-ness. It's got the four horsemen, eerie trumpets, people disappearing to heaven, you name it. It also has one of the thornier ethical quandaries put to film. Sharon (Mimi Rogers) has abandoned her immoral life to embrace God. She is put through a Joblike trial and she passes, but in the end (literally the end; it's the apocalypse after all) she must decide if *she* can forgive God for *his* actions.

Where Did All the Priests Go?

❧ ❧ ❧ ❧

*When Israel split into two kingdoms after the death of Solomon, the
king of the newly formed northern kingdom created his own priests,
angering the priests established by the Law of Moses. The Bible says
almost nothing more about any priests in the North after that time.
Why? Perhaps the biblical authors deliberately kept them out.*

When Solomon's son Rehoboam became king of Israel, he threatened to deal ruthlessly with the people in the northern reaches of
his realm. In response, the people of the North rejected him as ruler
and formed their own northern kingdom, which retained the name
Israel. (The smaller southern part of the original kingdom, which
included Jerusalem, came to be called Judah.) Soon after the split,
Jeroboam, the first king of the northern kingdom of Israel, built
shrines featuring images of calves, scandalizing orthodox believers
because idols violated the Law of Moses. To make matters worse,
Jeroboam dismissed the established priests, who came from the
tribe of Levi (as required by Mosaic Law), and indiscriminately
appointed priests from among the people. In fact, it got so bad that
"any who wanted to be priests he consecrated" (1 Kings 13:33).

Getting Even

It is believed that descendants of the ousted priests later joined
together in Jerusalem and compiled and edited the books of Kings.
Significantly, after reporting the ouster of the legitimate priests and
the creation of the new ones, the books of Kings make only two references to northern priests—and neither is upbeat. One says that all
of King Ahab's priests were killed (2 Kings 10:11). The other mention relates that when the Assyrians conquered the northern kingdom (in 721 B.C.), they exiled all the priests from the land, though
they later sent back one priest to teach the people (2 Kings 17:27).

It seems as though the authors of 2 Kings were showing contempt by ignoring the wrongfully appointed priests of the North.
They ousted these men from the Bible just as their ancestors had
been ousted from the priesthood in the North.

Shabbat

Shabbat finishes the Jewish week with a day of obligatory rest.

Biblical Basis

Exodus 20:8–11: "Remember the sabbath day, and keep it holy. Six days you shall labor and do all your work. But the seventh day is a sabbath to the Lord your God; you shall not do any work—you, your son or your daughter, your male or female slave, your livestock, or the alien resident in your towns. For in six days the Lord made heaven and earth, the sea, and all that is in them, but rested the seventh day; therefore the Lord blessed the sabbath day and consecrated it." It doesn't get much clearer. It is also why the Jewish week ends at sundown on Saturday, and why Sunday in Hebrew is *Yom Rishon*—"the first day."

Biblical Practice

The Israelites interpreted "remember" and "observe" very seriously, like their modern descendants. To remember meant remembering not only Creation, but also their deliverance from Egyptian bondage. To observe meant to celebrate, gather, pray, and above all, refrain from work—either creative work or work that controlled one's environment. That included travel, using a tool for work, and so on. Over the millennia, rabbis have spent endless hours debating and defining what is allowed on Shabbat.

Modern Practice

Shabbat (pronounced "shah-BOTT") begins Friday night at sundown. As a commandment, Shabbat observance is obligatory for observant Jews. No less than 18 minutes prior to official sundown, the woman of the house lights two candles: one for remembrance, one for observance. After synagogue, the family goes home for a meal. (Since one can't cook on Shabbat, the slow cooker is a blessing.) The man of the house recites a prayer over wine; before dinner, everyone eats braided bread called *chal-lah*. The mood is festive, for Jewish tradition likens Shabbat to a bride, welcomed with honor and joy. Food, prayers, and blessings continue until Shabbat ends at sundown Saturday night.

Going Out and Coming In

Jews honor God's command at their doors.

In Steven Spielberg's 1993, Oscar-winning film *Schindler's List,* Nazis move into the Polish city of Krakow and all Jews are required by law to move into a ghetto. A wealthy, middle-aged Jewish couple is forced at gunpoint to pack up in minutes and leave their comfortable home, which will be given to Oskar Schindler. When they go, the man turns around at the door and pries a small, silver case from the doorframe, kissing it before putting it into his pocket. This case is a *mezuzah,* and like many Jews, its owner thought it invaluable.

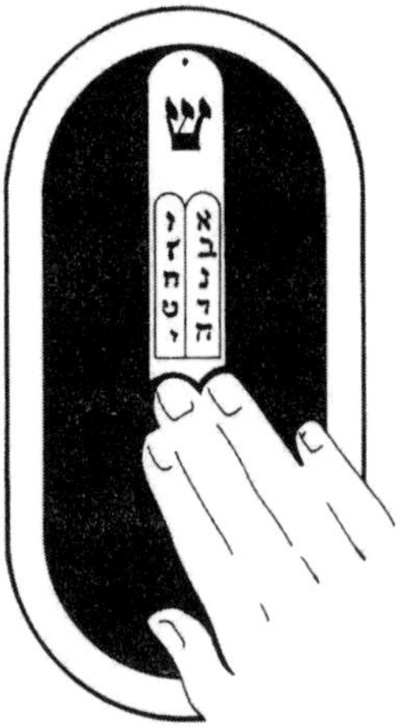

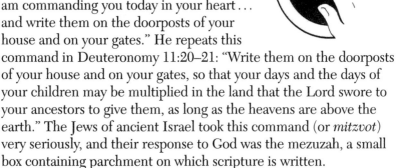

Command Taken Literally

In that box, on a piece of paper, is Deuteronomy 6:4: "Hear, O Israel: The Lord is our God, the Lord alone." In Deuteronomy 6:6–9, God told the Jews, "Keep these words that I am commanding you today in your heart . . . and write them on the doorposts of your house and on your gates." He repeats this command in Deuteronomy 11:20–21: "Write them on the doorposts of your house and on your gates, so that your days and the days of your children may be multiplied in the land that the Lord swore to your ancestors to give them, as long as the heavens are above the earth." The Jews of ancient Israel took this command (or *mitzvot*) very seriously, and their response to God was the mezuzah, a small box containing parchment on which scripture is written.

But why doorposts? What was the significance? Well, back in Exodus 12:21–23, God had protected the enslaved Jews of Egypt using their doorposts. In one of the ten plagues designed to convince pharaoh to release his people, God decided to kill every firstborn male in Egypt. But he didn't want to kill any Jewish people. So,

"Moses called all the elders of Israel and said to them, 'Go, select lambs for your families, and slaughter the passover lamb. Take a bunch of hyssop, dip it in the blood that is in the basin, and touch the lintel and the two doorposts with the blood in the basin. None of you shall go outside the door of your house until morning. For the Lord will pass through to strike down the Egyptians; when he sees the blood on the lintel and on the two doorposts, the Lord will pass over that door and will not allow the destroyer to enter your houses to strike you down.'"

Living the Law Today

Just as their ancestors took God's commandment seriously, so do many modern-day Jews. Most Jews feel that one mezuzah per home, at the main entrance, is sufficient, but more devout Jews affix a mezuzah to every door in their home aside from bathrooms and closets. A mezuzah is placed on the right side of the door, at approximately shoulder level. Jews who live outside of Israel have 30 days to get their mezuzah up, but those living in the Holy Land must affix their mezuzah immediately. How one decides to attach a mezuzah is not a big deal: nails, screws, glue, tape—as long as it's up there. Some *mezuzot* (the plural for mezuzah) are wrapped in plastic to protect them from inclement weather. Rabbis for centuries have argued about whether the mezuzah should be hung vertically or horizontally, so most Jews slant their mezuzot toward the home, just to cover all their bases. A blessing is recited as the mezuzah is affixed: "Blessed are you, Lord our God, King of the Universe, who sanctified us with his mitzvot, and commanded us to affix a mezuzah."

The making of a mezuzah is a very sacred and serious responsibility, and the scribes who produce them study their craft for many years. Strict procedures are followed as they write the scripture onto the parchment. Then the parchment is rolled tightly and placed carefully in the case so that the word *shaddai* ("Almighty") can be seen through a small hole near the top of the mezuzah.

When their work is done, they can rest in peace, knowing that Jews all over the world are touching their fingers to their lips and then placing them on their creations, reciting Psalm 121:8: "The Lord will keep your going out and your coming in from this time on and for evermore."

Jacob the Trickster

❧ ❧ ❧ ❧

Jacob was the patriarch from whom the 12 tribes of Israel were descended, but he was no plaster saint. Rather, he was a conniving rascal who twice cheated his brother, Esau, out of what was rightfully his and then went on to outwit another rascal, his father-in-law, Laban. But smart as Jacob was, he foolishly flaunted his favoritism—twice with almost fatal consequences.

Jacob, the son of the patriarch Isaac and Rebekah, his wife, was a marvelously colorful figure who delighted in trickery. Before he is born, his mother senses a great struggle in her womb and exclaims, "If it is to be this way, why do I live?" (Genesis 25:22). But she does live and gives birth to twins who fight to come out first. "The first came out red, all his body like a hairy mantle; so they named him Esau" (Genesis 25:25). *Esau* means "red." Jacob comes out next, "gripping" Esau's heel. He missed being the first-born—and his father's chief heir—by minutes! Even as a newborn infant, this seems to infuriate him.

When the twins grow up, Esau, a super-macho hunter, is his father's favorite. Jacob, a shepherd, is a mama's boy. Favoritism will run rampant in this family and almost bring it down.

Conniving to Get Esau's Birthright and Blessing

One day when Esau comes in from hunting, exhausted and famished, he sees Jacob cooking red lentil stew and begs: "Let me eat some of that red stuff, for I am famished!" (Genesis 25:30). Jacob demands his birthright in return. Esau is a naive hunter who is used to living day to day and eating whatever game he snares. He grumbles, "I am about to die; of what use is a birthright to me?" (Genesis 25:32). So he swears to hand his birthright over to Jacob. In exchange for the right to inherit twice as much as his brother, Esau gets a bowl of stew along with some bread. And Esau "ate and drank, and rose and went his way" (Genesis 25:34). It was as simple as that.

When Isaac grows old and blind and believes he is about to die (though he's not), he decides to give Esau his final blessing. This highly regarded blessing was thought to release a power that determined the character and destiny of its recipient. Isaac tells Esau to hunt some game, cook it, and bring it to him, at which time he will confer the blessing. While Esau is off hunting, Rebekah, who has overheard the plan, shows that she too can be a trickster. She quickly prepares meat for Isaac and dresses Jacob in Esau's clothes, then covers Jacob's exposed skin with animal skins to mimic Esau's hairiness. Jacob then brings the food to his father, who, unable to see, asks who is there. Jacob lies, insisting that he is Esau. Isaac has him approach and feels him. He says, "The voice is Jacob's voice, but the hands are the hands of Esau" (Genesis 27:22). And so Isaac blesses the disguised Jacob. When Esau discovers that Jacob has tricked him out of the blessing, he flies into a rage and threatens to kill his brother. Mama helps again, conniving to have Isaac send Jacob to stay with her brother, Laban, in distant Haran.

On the way to Haran, Jacob has a dream in which angels ascend and descend a ladder that is stretched between heaven and earth. God also appears in the dream and renews the promise he'd made to Jacob's grandfather, Abraham, to give his people the land of Canaan and to make his descendants as plentiful as the dust of the earth.

The Trickster Tricked

Laban has two daughters: beautiful Rachel and not-so-beautiful Leah. Jacob falls hopelessly in love with Rachel at first sight and offers to work for Laban for seven years for the privilege of marrying her. Laban agrees.

At the end of the seven years, a weeklong wedding takes place, but on the day the actual knot is tied, Laban, another trickster, hides Rachel away and tells Leah to put on Rachel's wedding clothes, which include a heavy veil. Leah marries Jacob in her sister's place. The next morning, when Jacob discovers that he has married Leah, he is probably as angry as Esau had been when he discovered that Jacob had cheated him out of his blessing. Jacob goes straight to his uncle to vent his rage. The wily Laban tells Jacob that it is the custom in his country for the oldest daughter to marry first, but he promises to give him Rachel as a second wife right away if he will contract with him to work another seven years. Totally besotted with Rachel, Jacob begrudgingly agrees. The trickster has been tricked.

Tricking the Trickster's Trickster

In the following years, Jacob's beloved Rachel bears him no children but Leah has six sons and a daughter. Jacob also has four sons by his wives' maids before Rachel finally bears a son, whose name is Joseph. Learning nothing from the trouble that family favoritism has already played in his life, Jacob immediately begins showing a great preference for Joseph, his favorite wife's only son.

Once his years of contracted service are completed, Jacob connives to get back at Laban. He convinces Laban to pay him for future work by letting him have the black lambs and speckled or streaked goats that are born under his care. Laban agrees. Jacob then waters Laban's strongest animals within sight of streaked stakes, which apparently result in the animals' bearing black, streaked, and speckled offspring. Because, according to the agreement with Laban, all these animals belong to Jacob, Jacob grows rich and Laban poor. As Laban grows angrier and angrier at having been duped and virtually robbed, Jacob takes the precaution of returning to Canaan along with his wives and their maids, 11 sons, daughter, and livestock.

Wrestling for a New Name

The night before Jacob is to meet his brother, Esau, on the road home, he wrestles with a mysterious stranger, who at dawn blesses

Jacob and gives him a new name: Israel ("the one who strives with God"). The next day, Jacob, worried that Esau may still want to kill him, positions Rachel and Joseph out of harm's way at the back of his camel train. "But Esau ran to meet him, and embraced him, and fell on his neck and kissed him, and they wept" (Genesis 33:4).

Jacob settles down near Shechem, but Rachel soon dies giving birth to Jacob's twelfth son, Benjamin. The descendants of Jacob's (now Israel's) sons are the 12 tribes of Israel. Isaac also dies, and Jacob and Esau bury him.

Favorite Sons

With Rachel dead, Jacob thoughtlessly increases his show of favoritism to her son Joseph, arousing the jealousy of his older sons. Jacob even gives Joseph a special coat and allows him to lord it over his brothers. Then, one day, the jealous brothers sell Joseph to slave traders, bring to Jacob Joseph's coat soaked in blood, and let their father believe that Joseph was killed by a wild animal.

Jacob barely survives his grief, but when he does he transfers all his affections to Rachel's other son, Benjamin. (He is Joseph's younger brother.) When a famine strikes and Jacob must send his sons to Egypt to buy grain, he insists upon keeping Benjamin with him. When the sons return home and tell Jacob that Joseph is not dead but living in Egypt in a position of great power, Jacob travels to Egypt for a joyful reunion with Joseph. He and his family settle there with Joseph's help.

Jacob's Last Double-Cross

Even on his deathbed, Jacob can't help pulling a fast one. Still playing favorites when asked to bless Joseph's two sons, Jacob mischievously gives the younger son the blessing due the older one. Here's how: At this point Jacob is blind and Joseph has to place his hands on the children for him—the child blessed by the right hand gets the greater blessing. After Joseph places his father's hands where they should go, Jacob craftily crosses his arms and gives the greater blessing to the younger boy. By crossing his arms, he double-crosses Joseph. So we have a kind of flashback to the time when he stole his own blind father's blessing. Jacob remains a trickster to the very end.

Quiz

Daniel I

This prophet-advisor-hero was far more than lion chow.

1. Of these four stories from the book of Daniel, which comes first?
   - a. Daniel spends the night in the lions' den
   - b. Daniel and other Jewish captives suggest a different menu
   - c. Daniel interprets the writing on the wall
   - d. Daniel's three friends are thrown into a blazing furnace

2. Why was Daniel condemned to the lions' den?
   - a. He spoke out against the immoral policies of the king
   - b. He tried to flee back to his homeland, Judea
   - c. He prayed openly to someone other than the king
   - d. He refused to bow down to the idol the king had put up

3. How did King Darius respond after Daniel survived the den of lions?
   - a. He was relieved, he praised God, and he punished Daniel's enemies
   - b. He was furious, he vowed revenge, and he was attacked by the lions
   - c. He was puzzled, he summoned his advisors, and he ordered the lions killed
   - d. He went mad, he tore off his robes, and he ate grass like a cow

4. What are Mene, Mene, Tekel, and Parsin?
   - a. The Persian names of Daniel and his three friends
   - b. The ancient names of the gems used in Nebuchadnezzar's statue
   - c. The words of the "writing on the wall"
   - d. Daniel's nicknames for the lions

Answers: 1. b (Daniel 1); 2. c (Daniel 6:12); 3. a (Daniel 6:19–27); 4. c (Daniel 5:25)

From Baseball to Bible Thumper

Billy Sunday was a good baseball player—
and an exceptional evangelist who preached to millions.

Preachers often come from unusual backgrounds, but it's safe to say that Billy Sunday is the only one to play professional baseball before taking up the Lord's calling.

Born on November 19, 1862, near Ames, Iowa, Sunday's early life was less than ideal. His father died weeks after he was born, and his step-father died prematurely as well. As a result, his impoverished mother had no choice but to send Sunday and his older brother to the Soldiers' Orphans Home in Glenwood, Iowa, when Sunday was around 10 years old. There, Sunday received a good education and developed the prowess that would serve him well as a professional athlete.

From Player to Preacher
Sunday experienced a religious conversion in 1886, and he began speaking at churches and YMCAs throughout the Chicago area. In 1891, he turned down a $3,000 baseball contract to accept an $83-per-month position with the Chicago YMCA, where he honed his preaching skills. Two years later, Sunday became the full-time assistant to renowned evangelist J. Wilbur Chapman, who gave Sunday a crash course in public speaking.

Sunday eventually struck out on his own. A savvy promoter, he used his reputation as a baseball player to help publicize his revival meetings, which drew huge crowds.

Impressive Numbers
It is believed that Sunday preached to more than one million people over the course of his career—all without the aid of a microphone. He made a small fortune as a result, but he donated large amounts to various chari-ties. Billy Sunday died in 1935, following a mild heart attack.

A Biblical Life!

✤ ✤ ✤ ✤

Is it possible to live by all the rules set forth in the Bible?
One man decided to find out.

It's one thing to read the Bible, it's something else entirely to live it. But that's just what journalist A. J. Jacobs did—for a year. Then he wrote a book about it, called *The Year of Living Biblically*.

Jacobs, a frequent contributor to *Esquire* magazine, wrote down every rule, guideline, and suggestion he could find in the Bible. It was a long list: more than 700 rules that ran 72 pages. Many of the rules were wise, he writes on his website, but others were simply baffling. Regardless, he decided to follow all of them as best he could, which wasn't always easy in this modern age.

Rules to Live By

Interestingly, Jacobs found many of the rules life-enhancing. "Keep the sabbath," for example, resulted in "the beauty of an enforced pause in the week. No cell phones, no messages, no thinking about deadlines. It was a bizarre and glorious feeling," he observed.

Jacobs also benefited from the rule to "let your garments be always white" (Ecclesiastes 9:8). "You can't be in a bad mood when you're dressed like you're about to play the semi-finals at Wimbledon," he writes. The directive to give thanks was another rule that he saw benefits from: "I gave thanks for everything—for the subway coming on time, for the comfortableness of my couch, etc.... Never have I been so aware of the thousands of little things that go right in our lives."

Other rules, however, were more difficult to follow. Among them: Do not trim the corners of your beard (Leviticus 19:27). "My rabbinical beard became wildly uncomfortable," Jacobs notes on his website, "plus I was subjected to every beard joke in the history of facial hair, with about 412 ZZ Top references."

Put to death people who commit adultery. Jacobs didn't kill anyone, but he did "stone" one adulterer—a grumpy 70-something man he met in the park—by tossing pebbles at him.

How Samuel Became the Last Judge

✤ ✤ ✤ ✤

*The child Samuel was literally an answer to his
mother's prayers, and in gratitude, his mother, Hannah,
dedicated her son to God. The boy grew up to become a prominent
priest, prophet, and judge (ruler) of Israel. He also appointed
the first two kings of Israel, ending the period of the judges
that had lasted about two centuries.*

After the Israelites settled in Canaan—the land that God had promised them—they divided it into 12 tribal territories, each with its
own judge. A judge was a combination interpreter of legal matters,
a ruler, and often a military leader. The Israelites boasted that they
had no king but God and the laws they followed were the laws God
had given them through Moses. However, by the 11th century B.C.
(the 1080s or thereabouts), the people of Israel had fallen into moral
chaos and seemed incapable of extricating themselves from turmoil.
They were also politically weak, economically disadvantaged, and
subject to invasion by their neighbors, the Philistines. Israel badly
needed a strong moral leader, and the only person who fit the bill
was the elderly priest Eli, who was currently serving as judge but
declining physically and mentally.

The Birth of Samuel

The first book of Samuel begins at this point in time and tells the
story of Hannah, a woman who is advancing in years but still childless. Hannah goes to the shrine at Shiloh and weeps and prays,
vowing that if she has a son, she will dedicate his life to serving God.
Hannah's prayer is answered. She gives birth to a son, Samuel, and
as soon as the boy is old enough, Hannah brings him to Shiloh to
begin his life of service to God under the tutelage of Eli, the priest
and judge.

At Shiloh, the boy grows and matures, moving closer and closer
to Yahweh, while Eli's sons, who are expected to succeed him, turn
out to be sexually promiscuous cheats. In other words, like much

else in Israel, the priestly order is deteriorating. When Eli tries to discipline his sons, they ignore him.

The Call of Samuel

Late one night, the young Samuel is awakened by someone calling his name. He runs to Eli, and replies, "Here I am, for you called me" (1 Samuel 3:5). But Eli hasn't called Samuel, so he tells the boy to go back to sleep. After the same thing happens a second and then a third time, Eli realizes that God might be calling to Samuel. He tells the boy if he hears the voice again to respond: "Speak, Lord, for your servant is listening" (1 Samuel 3:9).

Again, someone calls Samuel. Although terrified, the boy follows Eli's instructions and pipes out in a shaky voice: "Speak, Lord, for your servant is listening." What follows is shocking, for God tells the boy that Eli's sons aren't righteous like their father but dishonest, and God would no longer allow Eli's sons to be priests.

Samuel lies awake until morning, afraid to tell Eli what God had told him, but the old man insists on knowing everything. The young Samuel has to explain that Yahweh will punish his aged mentor and his heirs "because his sons were blaspheming God, and he did not restrain them" (3:13). When Eli hears the crushing news, he accepts God's will. Samuel has gone from being totally dependent on Eli to having Eli totally dependent on him for hearing Yahweh's word. "As Samuel grew, the Lord was with him and let none of his words fall to the ground. And all Israel . . . knew that Samuel was a trustworthy prophet of the Lord" (1 Samuel 3:19–20).

When Eli is 98 years old, his sons are killed in battle. Upon hearing the news, Eli falls over backward, breaks his neck, and dies. He had judged Israel 40 years. Soon after, Samuel calls together the people of Israel and exhorts them to abandon idolatry and worship only Yahweh. He officially takes over as judge, traveling the land, governing the people, and settling disputes.

Samuel, Maker of Kings

When Samuel grows old, he makes his sons judges in his place but discovers that they are just as corrupt as Eli's sons had been. Who is going to take Samuel's place as leader? The people come to Samuel and demand of him: "You are old and your sons do not follow in your ways; appoint for us, then, a king to govern us, like other nations" (1 Samuel 8:5). Obviously the Israelites have forgotten that Yahweh is their king, ruler, and protector and they have no need for a human king. Samuel is horrified by this request for a king, but Yahweh tells him to give the people what they want—but to first warn them of what they may be getting themselves into.

Samuel accordingly makes a speech warning the people that a king might take their sons, their servants, and their crops for his own use, tax them heavily to build up his own wealth, and turn them into virtual slaves—abuses that later materialized under King Solomon. The people still want a king, so Samuel anoints Saul. Most of the people accept Saul, but a few "worthless fellows" ask: "How can

this man save us?" (1 Samuel 10:27). They were referring to the tradition that only God could serve as king of the Israelites, for only God, and no mere human, could bring salvation. About a month later Saul succeeds in repelling an enemy attack, and all the people accept him as the first king of Israel. Saul reigns as king for many years, but he eventually offends God, who tells Samuel to anoint David as Israel's next king—and its greatest.

Living in Retirement

Soon after Saul became king, Samuel called the people together, exhorted them to always follow God's will, and retired as judge, though he continued to serve as priest and prophet. As prophet, Samuel advised the king, a role that prophets would retain far into the future. Samuel was the last of the judges of Israel, which would be ruled by kings for centuries. When Samuel died, all Israel mourned him. Though the last of Israel's judges, he was the first prophet to advise the nation's kings.

10 Things

Dumb Things People Said in the Bible

Ever utter something and then regret it? Join the club.

1. Adam: *"The woman whom you gave to be with me, she gave me fruit from the tree, and I ate" (Genesis 3:12).*

The forbidden fruit had just been eaten, and God wanted answers. By blaming everything on his wife, the first man launched the opening volley in the battle of the sexes.

2. Aaron: *"You know the people, that they are bent on evil. They said to me, 'Make us gods, who shall go before us; . . . so they gave [gold] to me, and I threw it into the fire, and out came this calf!"* (Exodus 32:22–24).*

Moses was understandably upset when he came down from the mountain to see the people dancing around an idol of a golden calf. Brother Aaron managed to explain the situation without taking any responsibility.

3. Haman: *"Whom would the king wish to honor more than me?"* (Esther 6:6).*

The king asks Haman how to reward a loyal servant. Assuming that he himself is the honoree, Haman recommends extravagant treatment—royal robes, a noble steed, a crown, and a proclamation from the king himself. Then Haman finds out the honors are going to his archrival, Mordecai.

4. Fools: *"There is no God" (Psalm 14:1).*

The psalmist takes a shot at the atheistic opposition. The Lord looks down from heaven, the next verse says, for anyone who is wise enough to seek him. But to start out with the assumption that God doesn't exist is just plain foolish.

5. The timid servant: *"Master, I knew that you were a harsh man . . . so I was afraid, and I went and hid your talent in the ground. Here you have what is yours"* (Matthew 25:24–25).

In Jesus' parable of the talents, three servants are given amounts of money to invest and double. The third servant is afraid he'll lose the money, so he buries it. The master is far from pleased with him.

6. The disciples: *"Teacher, do you not care that we are perishing?"* (Mark 4:38).

You might excuse these guys, since they were sailing through a massive storm on the Sea of Galilee and Jesus was fast asleep. Still, the idea that Jesus did not care about them is ridiculous.

7. James and John: *"Lord, do you want us to command fire to come down from heaven and consume them?"* (Luke 9:54).

A Samaritan village refused to welcome Jesus and his disciples, and these two were miffed. But what part of "Love your enemies" did they not understand?

8. Peter: *"You will never wash my feet"* (John 13:8).

Peter could have his own list of dumb things he said, since he was always putting his foot in his mouth. All the more reason to have his feet washed. Jesus was teaching a powerful lesson by kneeling to wash his disciples' feet, even though he was their master. Peter saw the irony in that, but he didn't learn the lesson. Proudly, he initially refused to let Jesus serve him.

9. Sapphira: *"Yes, that was the price"* (Acts 5:8).

People were selling land and giving proceeds to the church, so this couple wanted to do the same—except they held back some of the money. Sapphira's husband had brought the donation to Peter a few hours earlier, lying about the price of the land. He was struck dead for lying to the Holy Spirit. Later checking up on the situation, the wife lied too—and got the same result.

10. Simon Magus: *"Give me also this power so that anyone on whom I lay my hands may receive the Holy Spirit"* (Acts 8:19).

This magician was dazzled by the apostles' power, and he wanted to buy it. Peter gave him a thorough scolding: "May your silver perish with you."

What Enoch Did After Leaving Earth

✤ ✤ ✤ ✤

*According to the Bible, Enoch did not die but was simply taken
up to heaven by God. This spurred questions about what Enoch
did later. One answer is that he wrote books about what he saw and
learned in heaven. We can still read them today.*

Little is known about Enoch. After reporting his birth, Genesis
devotes only a few verses to him. They report that Enoch was the
oldest son in the sixth generation. That's the sixth generation ever, as
Enoch was descended from Adam's third son, Seth. In other words,
Enoch was the great-great-great-great-grandson of Adam and Eve.
(There was another Enoch, but he was the son of Cain and an entirely different person.)

Walking with God into Heaven

In primordial times (just after the Creation), people lived long
lives. Enoch's father, Jared, lived 962 years and Enoch's first son,
Methuselah, lived to be 969, making him the oldest person in the
Bible—or maybe not, because Enoch probably never died. Aside
from genealogical information, all the Bible reports about Enoch is
that he had a close relationship with God—"Enoch walked with God
after the birth of Methuselah three hundred years" (Genesis 5:22).
But the clincher is that, after living 365 years, Enoch "was no more,
because God took him" (Genesis 5:24). Apparently Enoch didn't die
but was taken into heaven to be with God. The New Testament's
Letter to the Hebrews explains that because Enoch had pleased
God so much, "he did not experience death" (Hebrews 11:5). The
only other person to avoid death was the prophet Elijah, who was
taken up to heaven in a fiery chariot.

Enoch's mysterious end led to lots of speculation about what
happened to him after God took him. Ancient Jewish traditions
hold that even before his final exit, Enoch had spent "hidden years"

with the angels, who taught him things unknown to others. These traditions continued to grow, and then, sometime between the 2nd century B.C. and the early Christian era, three books appeared that claimed to record Enoch's special wisdom—and his warnings about the end times. These books of Enoch never made it into the Bible, but they became very influential. They even inspired two great epic poems: Dante's *Divine Comedy* and Milton's *Paradise Lost*.

1 Enoch

The First Book of Enoch, or 1 Enoch, falls into five parts in imitation of the Pentateuch—the first five books of the Bible, which are considered the Jewish Law, or Torah.

The first part, the Book of the Watchers, tells of the fall of the angels, a tale not in the Bible, though it is firmly rooted in Christian lore as the origin of Satan. It also relates how angels took Enoch on two tours of the universe, showing him the cornerstone of the earth, the forbidden tree in the Garden of Eden, and the mountain that holds the spirits of the dead awaiting the Day of Judgment.

Part 2, the Book of Parables, tells of Enoch's journey through the cosmos to the heavenly throne, where God appoints an end-time judge who will reverse the fortunes of the oppressed and condemn their oppressors. Oddly enough, the judge—who is variously called the righteous one, chosen one, messiah, and son of man—turns out to be Enoch.

In the Astronomical Book, part 3, the angel Uriel explains to Enoch the structure of the universe and the movement of the stars and winds, all of which God controls.

In the Book of Dreams, part 4, Enoch experiences two visions. The first tells of the coming Flood. The second (the Animal Apocalypse) presents biblical history with animals in place of people! The patriarchs are bulls, the gentiles are wild beasts, and Israel is a flock of sheep. The history ends with the story of the Maccabean Revolt in the 2nd century B.C., the probable time of the book's composition.

The Epistle of Enoch, part 5, includes a story about the birth of Noah, suggesting that just as God brought salvation after the Flood through Noah, so too will salvation follow the end of the world. A section called the Apocalypse of Weeks divides history into uneven units of time, called weeks. Enoch warns his people to repent, for they are already in the seventh week and the last judgment will begin in the eighth.

2 Enoch

In the Second Book of Enoch, probably written in the first century, two angels lead Enoch through seven so-called heavens—though some are more like hell. In the first heaven, Enoch sees angels tending the stars and the sources of the weather. In the second, he finds people who have turned away from God weeping. In the third, he sees the Garden of Eden, which is meant for the righteous, and a place of punishment for sinners. The fourth heaven contains the paths for the sun and moon. The fifth holds the fallen angels prisoner. In the sixth heaven, all the orders of angels, archangels, cherubim, and the like sing to the glory of God, and some keep records of the deeds and misdeeds of every human.

In the seventh heaven, Enoch meets God, who gives him an account of history from the Creation to the final judgment. Enoch returns to earth to impart his discoveries to his descendants, exhorting them to observe God's laws. He then returns to heaven for good.

3 Enoch

The final work associated with Enoch is a collection of writings in which Ishmael Ben Elisha, a renowned rabbi of the 2nd century A.D., ascends to the seventh heaven and is greeted by the archangel Metatron, who turns out to be none other than Enoch—transformed into an angel. Ishmael takes a tour of heaven, discovering its mysteries. However, these mysteries seem to reflect those explored by the Kabala, a Jewish mystical movement, in the 5th to the 6th centuries—the most likely time of the book's composition.

If Enoch wrote these books, he took 2,000 years to do so. But, in fact, he probably didn't write a word. Scholars agree that the books of Enoch belong to a category known as pseudepigraphia—books written under the pseudonym of an important person of the past (a common practice). That means we still have no idea what Enoch did after leaving earth.

How Many Times Did Goliath Die?

❖ ❖ ❖ ❖

The boy David kills the giant Goliath with his slingshot,
but years later somebody else supposedly kills Goliath.
This presents a puzzle, but one with possible solutions.

The boy David stays home to tend sheep while his brothers go to
fight in the war between Israel and the neighboring Philistines.
One day, according to 1 Samuel 17, David's father sends him to the
battlefield with lunch for his brothers (plus extra cheese to butter up
their commander). When David arrives, he hears that the nine-foot-
tall Goliath has challenged any single Israelite to fight him to decide
the war's outcome. No one dares take the challenge—except David.
After failing to dissuade the boy, King Saul lends him his armor.
David can't move in the heavy equipment, so he discards it and
strides out defenseless to meet the giant. While Goliath is busy
mocking the lad, David loads the sling he had often used to kill
wolves that stalked his sheep. Then he deftly sends a stone sailing
into Goliath's forehead, killing him instantly.

Goliath is stone cold dead, but 2 Samuel 21:19 reports that years
later the same giant dies in a different battle. This time his killer is
Elhanan, one of King David's warriors.

Possible Solutions to the Puzzle

The story of David the giant killer may be a folktale that was applied
to David because of his fame. It was not unusual to circulate stories
of a hero's childhood to hint at his future accomplishments, and the
tale of the slingshot doesn't fit its spot in 1 Samuel. After the killing,
Saul asks who the young man is, showing he had no previous knowledge of David, who (according to 1 Samuel 16:21–23) had been
playing the lyre for him.

It is also possible that the name of the giant killed by David was
unknown and the name of Elhanan's victim (from this later war of
David's) was later used for him. Finally, the second killing may have
been erroneously reported, for 1 Chronicles 20:5 holds that Elhanan
killed not Goliath, but his brother Lahmi.

Bible Bookstore Statistics

✧ ✧ ✧ ✧

As the most important book in the history of Western civilization,
it is perhaps not surprising that, in terms of bookstore numbers,
the Bible simply dwarfs the competition. Here are a few biblical
bookstore stats that put today's best sellers in perspective.

All-time Best Seller

While it's difficult to calculate how many Bibles have been sold over
the course of history—after all, a great percentage of Bibles in print
were distributed free of charge—historians agree the Bible is by far
the best-selling book of all-time, selling more copies than the rest of
the top ten all-time best sellers put together. Here's a list:

The Bible: 2.5–6 billion
Quotations from Chairman Mao Zedong: 800–900 million
The Qu'ran: 800 million
Xinhua Zidian (Chinese dictionary): 400 million
Chairman Mao's Poems: 400 million
Selected Articles of Mao Zedong: 252 million
A Tale of Two Cities, Charles Dickens: 200 million

Fantasy Best Sellers

While some critics dismiss the Good Book as fiction best suited for
fantasy buffs, it is another fantasy series that is giving the Bible a run
for its crown: the *Harry Potter* series, written by J. K. Rowling.
Number of Bibles sold, 1997–2007: 250 million
Number of *Harry Potter* books sold, 1997–2007: 325 million

Thou Shalt Not Steal

Bukowski? Sure. Ginsberg? Makes sense. Kerouac too sounds about
right. But the Bible? *The Bible?* Though God is pretty clear that
theft is condemned, not everybody seems to have gotten the message. According to bookstore statistics, the Bible is by far the most
shoplifted book in the United States.

Where Jesus Walked

Bethany

It's not just a popular name for girls.
Both towns of Bethany occupy special places in scripture.

In Biblical Times

The New Testament mentions events in both Bethanys, but it doesn't describe either town much. We don't even know the location of the Bethany on the Jordan's East Bank (where John was baptizing folks); the King James Version calls it Bethabara, for unclear reasons. Let's call it Bethany A. We know rather more about what we'll call Bethany B, the location of the Ascension along the Mount of Olives and just east of Jerusalem. It seems to have housed a major hospital, making it an excellent place for the Messiah to perform miracles.

Jesus' Connections

At Bethany A, priests and Levites asked John who he was. Was he Elijah? No. Okay, then who are you? John replied that after him would come someone whose sandals he was unworthy to untie. The next day, John pointed out Jesus as the Lamb of God.

Bethany B had a busier scriptural history. Jesus began his Palm Sunday trip here, cursing a fig tree because it wasn't fig season. Leaving Bethany for Jerusalem, he turned over vendors' tables in the temple. Later, Jesus was near Bethany when Mary and Martha told him of Lazarus's death, so he hiked into town and raised Lazarus from the dead. Another time, at a dinner in Jesus' honor at Bethany, a woman anointed him with expensive perfume. Judas complained that the money could have gone to the poor, but John snipes that Judas's favorite charity was Judas himself. And, in one of his most storied acts, Jesus ascended into heaven at Bethany.

Bethany Today

Bethany A could be anywhere on the East Bank of the Jordan River. Bethany B is traditionally associated with *Al-Izzariya* ("Place of Lazarus"), a city of about 17,000 just east of Jerusalem; its name in Hebrew is *Beitanya*. It is almost exclusively Arab and Muslim today. Is it ancient Bethany? There's no proof, but it's in the right area.

Moses Kills a Man

⚜ ⚜ ⚜ ⚜

*Moses always sought to save his people from Egyptian repression,
but his first attempt to do so ended in his committing murder.
We don't usually think of Moses as a killer, but he was. Later,
as God's agent, Moses redeemed his first clumsy and criminal
attempt by truly freeing his people from bondage.*

At the time of Moses' birth, the descendants of Jacob (aka Israel)
were living in Egypt and multiplying at an alarming rate—or so
the native Egyptians thought. The Israelites had come to Egypt to
escape a famine in their own land and had settled there with the
help of Jacob's son Joseph, who held a high political post in Egypt.
Nearly 400 years later, most of the Israelites were slaves and their
growing numbers were perceived as a threat to the native population. Consequently, the pharaoh decreed that all male infants born
to the Israelites must be put to death. The infant Moses was saved
only through the ingenuity of his mother. She set him afloat in a
basket on the Nile, where a daughter of the pharaoh rescued him
and eventually raised him in comfort. Moses turned killer soon after
he reached manhood and probably while he was still living in the
luxurious royal court. The story is told succinctly in five brief verses:
Exodus 2:11–15.

Moses Looks Before He Leaps

One day Moses takes a walk to survey a work site in the desert.
There he sees an Egyptian man beating an Israelite, one of Moses'
kinsmen. Moses is furious, but he does not strike out immediately in
blind rage. We are told that first he deliberately looks this way and
that and sees no one. It is only then that Moses acts. Believing that
there are no witnesses, he lunges at the offending Egyptian and kills
him, then buries the body in the sand.

Moses has committed murder. Even though the Egyptian had
been beating his kinsman, Moses had no right to kill him. In fact,
the Egyptian was very likely an overseer of the workforce who was

within his right to beat an Israelite slave who refused to comply with his commands. We don't know what the Israelite had done to deserve a beating, but neither did Moses. He had leapt into action without ascertaining the facts. He had repaid a beating with death—a harsh punishment for a far lesser crime—if any crime had been committed at all. Such a killing would be roundly condemned in the laws Moses was later to receive on Mount Sinai.

Moses Runs for His Life

The next day, Moses returns to the work site and sees two Israelites fighting. He asks the man who had started the fight why he was striking a fellow Israelite. The offender snaps back at Moses: "Who made you a ruler and judge over us? Do you mean to kill me as you killed the Egyptian?" (Exodus 2:14). Apparently the man Moses had helped the day before has blabbed.

Moses realizes he is in trouble, and sure enough he is. The pharaoh gets wind of the murder and calls for Moses' execution. But by that time Moses has taken to his heels and made a run for it.

Moses settles in the Sinai and marries a local woman. One day the Lord appears to him in a burning bush and commissions him to return to Egypt and free his people. This time, however, Moses is not to play the vigilante, meting out rough justice. He is to play out his mission with God's help and he will succeed.

The quarrelsome Israelite in Egypt had asked who had made Moses their ruler and judge. Moses had not been able to answer. On his return to Egypt, however, he will have a ready answer, supplied by God himself, who instructs Moses to say "I Am [Yahweh] has sent me to you. . . . the Lord, the God of your ancestors, the God of Abraham, the God of Isaac, and the God of Jacob has sent me to you" (Exodus 3:14–15). What Moses could not do himself he would do with God's help.

The Psalms of Music

Some psalms were meant to be read.
Others were meant to be sung—with gusto!

Psalms are a popular part of spoken church services, but back in the day it wasn't uncommon for them to be sung. You've probably noticed that many psalms include the word "mizmor," which is Hebrew for "a poem sung to the accompaniment of a stringed instrument." The Greek equivalent is "psalmos," from which the English word "psalms" derives.

Which Psalms to Sing?
Which psalms were meant to be sung? The word "selah" is a tip-off. It's found 71 times in Psalms and three times in Habakkuk, and it commands people to literally sing their praises as part of a musical interlude.

A wide variety of musical instruments were used in biblical times to accompany psalms meant to be sung. The kinnor, a small harp also known as a lyre, was one of the most commonly used string instruments. Also a part of these ancient jam sessions were horns, including the ram's horn, or shofar (which is still used in synagogues today), and percussive instruments ranging from primitive tambourines to cymbals to jingling bells. It wasn't exactly Lollapalooza, but they got the people a singin'.

Inspiration for Classical Composers
Many psalms have been set to music by some of the world's greatest classical composers, including Handel, Berlioz, Mendelssohn, and even Johann Sebastian Bach, whose composition "Psalm 51" is a popular favorite. Several traditional hymns have also been inspired by psalms, such as "A Mighty Fortress" by Martin Luther, "The Lord Is My Shepherd" by Handel, and Henry Lyte's "Praise My Soul, the King of Heaven."

Contemporary artists similarly inspired include Darlene Zschech ("Shout to the Lord"), Ralph Carmichael ("The New 23rd"), Rebecca St. James ("Psalm 139"), and even Leonard Bernstein ("Chichester Psalms").

So the next time you're in church and psalms are part of the program, don't hold back. God wants you to sing with everything you've got.

Quiz

Daniel II

*More questions about the prophet-advisor-hero
who was far more than lion chow.*

1. King Belshazzar threw a rockin' party, but he went over the top when he brought these out.
   a. horn, pipe, lyre, trigon, harp, drum
   b. carnivorous crocodiles imported from India
   c. Assyrian slaves serving as waiters
   d. sacred vessels captured from the temple in Jerusalem

2. Daniel interpreted a dream for King Nebuchadnezzar in which there was a statue with head of gold, chest and arms of silver, midsection and thighs of bronze, and legs of iron. What were its feet made of?
   a. a mixture of all the other metals
   b. stone
   c. iron and clay
   d. flesh

3. After throwing Daniel's three friends into the blazing furnace, the king was amazed at what he saw there. What did he see?
   a. a dove flying out of the flames
   b. his own image burning up
   c. flames slowly dying down to nothing
   d. four men, not three, walking unhurt in the flames

4. As captives being groomed for government service, Daniel and his three Jewish friends had a problem with the food they were being served. What was the problem?
   a. diet was too rich; they preferred veggies and water
   b. diet was non-kosher; they would not eat unclean food
   c. diet was too meager; they needed more food

Answers: 1. d (Daniel 5:2); 2. c (Daniel 2:32–33); 3. d (Daniel 3:24–25); 4. b (Daniel 1:8, 12)

Life at the Top

❧ ❧ ❧ ❧

Though most Jews in biblical times were poor,
a lucky few were very wealthy.

Throughout the Bible, the Hebrew people were oppressed by one
people after another—most notably by the Egyptians and Romans.
For that reason, most Jews were impoverished, kept "in their place"
by slavery, indentured servitude, high taxes, and prejudice. But a
small minority of Jews flourished financially in these harsh environ-
ments, and not all of them were traitors to their people.

Times of Freedom

Of course, the Jews were not oppressed at all times. Before the exile
to Babylon, they were ruled by such mighty Hebrew leaders as King
Saul and King David. Both Saul and David were wealthy, but by the
time David's son Solomon rose to the throne, money was flowing like
water. We cannot be sure exactly how Solomon made his money, but
we know that he took in about 25 tons of gold a year. From biblical
accounts he appears to have been quite the international wheeler
and dealer, though there is no trace of him in any historical sources
but the Bible. Solomon was known for his wisdom, but he just didn't
know when to say "when" in matters of money or women. He began
to be influenced by the materialistic ways of the foreigners with
whom he traded, and he amassed a harem of 700 wives and 300 concubines. Extremely displeased, God tore the kingdom of Israel from
Solomon and divided the nation—though he did allow Solomon's
descendants to inherit a portion of the land.

Solomon is probably the most famous rich Israelite in the Bible,
and the wealthiest of the wealthy, but he was not alone in fortune.
Hebrew kings of the Old Testament surrounded themselves with
sophisticated courtiers and well-connected high priests. These men
usually lived in luxury; their homes were built not of mud or common concrete, but of marble and often featured extravagant gold
trim, lush courtyard gardens, and tiled bathing pools. One feature

they usually did not have, though, was many windows. Crime was a big problem for the wealthy in the Bible, because there were so many poor people and so few efficient police forces. Homes of the rich were built like fortresses by necessity.

Taste of Their World

The high crime rate, however, did not dissuade the rich from offering hospitality to fellow members of the upper class. Once inside such homes, guests would enjoy the sight of elaborately carved wooden furniture, beautifully embroidered silk pillows and cushions, and skillfully woven wall hangings and carpets. Wealthy Hebrew men liked to give banquets at which they could show off their stylishly dressed wives and/or concubines. At their feasts, they spoiled guests with bottomless glasses of the finest wine, delicious slow-roasted meats, and pastry and fruits. Their every whim was catered to by slaves and servants, and hired musicians serenaded the partiers with wind and stringed instruments, drums, and cymbals. This life of affluence and leisure was easy to get used to, and the men who lived it were constantly tempted to cut moral corners in order to keep it.

The ethical quandaries only increased in later years, first when the Jews were exiled in Egypt, and then when Israel was occupied by the Romans. In both cases, it was far easier to "go along to get along," and those who questioned or confronted these oppressive regimes had absolutely zero chance of ever escaping poverty. Still, some Jews made comfortable livings without exploiting their own people, and they looked to the Law as their guide in doing so. Though the Old Testament makes it clear that there is nothing wrong with being wealthy, it also cautions against greed and injustice. Proverbs 13:11 warns, "Wealth hastily gotten will dwindle, but those who gather little by little will increase it." Jeremiah 22:13 condemns he who would exploit his fellow man: "Woe to him who builds his house by unrighteousness . . . who makes his neighbors work for nothing, and does not give them their wages."

Old Problem, New Ideas

Some things never change, and wealthy Israelites often felt the same way the rich feel today: "More money, more problems." The higher their income, the more taxes they would have to pay, and taxes always seemed to increase, never decrease. By the time of Christ, a rich Hebrew would be saddled with taxes to three institutions: the Roman government, the Herodian provincial government, and his temple. Then, of course, there were other taxes on trading, traveling, and products. So much time and energy was taken up on financial planning and taxes that many rich people questioned whether it was all worth it. Still, few were willing to give up their luxuries. And until Jesus Christ came along, no one told them they had to.

Jesus was tough on the rich, perhaps most famously in Matthew 19:16–24, when a wealthy young man tells Jesus he's been keeping the commandments scrupulously, yet still feels he's lacking something. "Jesus said to him, 'If you wish to be perfect, go, sell your possessions, and give the money to the poor, and you will have treasure in heaven; then come, follow me.'" This went over like a lead balloon, and the seeker walked away in frustration. Christ turned to his apostles and said, "Again I tell you, it is easier for a camel to go through the eye of a needle than for someone who is rich to enter the kingdom of God." After his death, Jesus' disciples continued to warn those in Israel about the dangers of greed. Timothy told his Christian brethren, "But those who want to be rich fall into temptation and are trapped by many senseless and harmful desires that plunge people into ruin and destruction" (1 Timothy 6:9). James too warned that the rich would have a day of reckoning: "Come now, you rich people, weep and wail for the miseries that are coming to you" (James 5:1–4).

Old Testament or New, the rich usually found that they got more than they bargained for.

Hallelu-Yah!

The word *hallelujah* is Hebrew for "praise the Lord." It contains a shortened form of God's name: Yah (for Yahweh). Many biblical characters' names end similarly: Hezekiah is *chizqi-yah* "Yahweh is my strength," and Isaiah is *yesha-yahu* "Yahweh saves."

Fast Facts

- *The Bible contains words from a wide variety of languages. In fact, in the King James Version, there are more than 8,670 different words in Hebrew, 5,624 different words in Greek, and a whopping 12,143 different words in English.*

- *As bizarre as it may sound, several verses in the King James Version of the Bible contain all letters of the alphabet but one. Ezra 7:21, for example, contains every letter except for "J." In addition, Joshua 7:24, 1 Kings 1:9, 1 Chronicles 12:40, 2 Chronicles 36:10, Ezekiel 28:13, Daniel 4:37, and Haggai 1:1 contain every letter except for "Q." 2 Kings 16:15 and 1 Chronicles 4:10 contain every letter except "X," and Galatians 1:14 contains every letter except "K." What does this mean? Nothing, except that the person who uncovered this interesting fact had way too much time on his hands.*

- *Some important numbers with which to amaze your friends: the Bible contains 1,189 chapters, 31,071 verses, 783,137 words, and a grand total of 3,116,480 letters. If you don't believe us, count them yourself! (Totals may vary depending on which version of the Bible you're using.)*

- *Believe it or not, the Bible contains:*
    - *1,260 promises*
    - *6,468 commands*
    - *More than 8,000 predictions*
    - *3,294 questions*

- *The long and short of it:*
    - *The longest name in the Bible is Mahershalalhashbaz (Isaiah 8:1).*
    - *The longest verse in the Bible is Esther 8:9. (The number of words it contains varies according to which Bible version you're reading, but it's a loooong sentence.)*
    - *The shortest verse is John 11:35 ("Jesus wept").*
    - *The longest book is Psalms, with an impressive 150 chapters.*
    - *The shortest book, by number of words, is 3 John.*
    - *The longest chapter is Psalm 119 (a dizzying 176 verses).*

- *Unsurprisingly, God plays a prominent role in the Bible. In fact, he's mentioned by name a total of 3,358 times. The word "Lord" appears 7,736 times.*

The Strength of Samson

❧ ❧ ❧ ❧

With great power comes great responsibility.

Before there was Schwarzenegger, Stallone, or Seagal, there was Samson. A latter-day action hero, Samson was as flawed as he was powerful.

From Hair, Strength

Samson was born to a previously barren woman, and his birth was therefore seen as the result of divine power. As such, Samson's parents undertook for him one of the vows of divinity: His hair must never be cut from birth until death.

The Philistines and Israelites were great enemies, so it is somewhat surprising that Samson chose a Philistine to be his wife. At the wedding, he offered a riddle to 30 of the guests. If they guessed correctly, each man would get a new set of clothes; if not, they each had to give Samson one. Some time earlier, Samson had killed a lion. Bees settled in the dead lion's body, and Samson took the bees' honey home to his parents. His riddle was, "Out of the eater came something to eat. Out of the strong came something sweet." Samson's wife's friends pleaded with her to get the answer, as they didn't want to pay Samson 30 garments. She begged and begged until Samson revealed the answer to her. So angry was Samson when he learned she betrayed him that he killed 30 men and gave their garments to the wedding guests. He left, and the bride's father gave the woman to the best man. When Samson found out, he put torches in the tails of foxes and sent them into the fields, burning the Philistines' crops.

The Philistines wanted revenge and chased the fugitive into Judah. The Judahites convinced Samson to let them hand him over to the Philistines. But just when things looked bad for ol' Samson, he broke free from his ropes and killed the assembled Philistines with the jawbone of an ass. God even opened up the ground to quench Samson's thirst with fresh water. (Things move quickly in the stories about Samson. It's a bit like a Michael Bay movie.)

Samson and Delilah

The Philistines were ticked off because Samson had to this point proven invincible. They paid his new love, Delilah, to find the secret of Samson's strength. She asked him, but he lied. First he told her seven fresh bowstrings could hold him. It didn't work. Then he said unused ropes would do. They didn't. Finally, he revealed that if he broke the vow of uncut hair, he would be weakened. Delilah lulled him to sleep, cut his hair, and the Philistines captured him and gouged out his eyes.

At a feast, the Philistines brought out their trophy prisoner, but Samson's hair had grown again. He stood between the pillars of their pagan temple, prayed to God, pushed the pillars, and brought the entire building down on himself and his enemies.

Power and Betrayal

Samson led a life of excitement and adventure. He's a precursor to the modern-day action hero: He gets all the women; he kills all the bad guys; he dies a hero's death by sacrificing himself to kill even more bad guys.

But Samson's strength came from his hair and the vow he took (through his mother) for God. In a very real sense, the power didn't come from the *hair*; it came from *God*. Samson didn't use his power for good, however; he used it to kill. He did kill the enemies of the Israelites, but he did it mostly in anger and for revenge. His power was a wanton power. It was more driven by lust and passion than a desire to do good.

Throughout his life, Samson's tales of strength are preceded by him chasing a woman. His affair with Delilah was no different. In the end, Samson's naked lust was his own undoing. Although Delilah betrayed Samson, Samson betrayed his vow to God. He revealed the secret of his hair, and God sapped him of his strength. It was only later, when his hair grew back, that Samson prayed to God. Only then did his strength return, enabling him to destroy a whole temple in a terrific crash. Just like in a Michael Bay movie.

A Taste of Proverbs

❧ ❧ ❧ ❧

*Attributed to Solomon, Proverbs offers so much in the way
of life guidance. Here are some of the choicest morsels.*

Anger/Quarreling
- *Do not quarrel with anyone without cause, when no harm has
been done to you (3:30).*
- *A soft answer turns away wrath, but a harsh word stirs up
anger (15:1).*
- *Like a city breached, without walls, is one who lacks self-
control (25:28).*
- *Like somebody who takes a passing dog by the ears is one who
meddles in the quarrel of another (26:17).*

Fools/Foolishness
- *The fear of the Lord is the beginning of knowledge; fools despise
wisdom and instruction (1:7).*
- *In vain is the net baited while the bird is looking on (1:17).*
- *The lips of the righteous feed many, but fools die for lack of
sense (10:21).*
- *A rebuke strikes deeper into a discerning person than a hundred
blows into a fool (17:10).*
- *Even fools who keep silent are considered wise; when they close
their lips, they are deemed intelligent (17:28).*
- *Do not answer fools according to their folly, or you will be a fool
yourself (26:4).*
- *The legs of a disabled person hang limp; so does a proverb in the
mouth of a fool (26:7).*

Love/Friendship
- *Better is a dinner of vegetables where love is than a fatted ox and
hatred with it (15:17).*

- *Some friends play at friendship but a true friend sticks closer than one's nearest kin* (18:24).

Wealth/Money
- *Wealth hastily gotten will dwindle, but those who gather little by little will increase it* (13:11).
- *Better is a little with righteousness than large income with injustice* (16:8).
- *The rich rule over the poor, and the borrower is the slave of the lender* (22:7).
- *Whoever is kind to the poor lends to the Lord, and will be repaid in full* (19:17).

Wicked/Wise
- *There are six things that the Lord hates, seven that are an abomination to him: haughty eyes, a lying tongue, and hands that shed innocent blood, a heart that devises wicked plans, feet that hurry to run to evil, a lying witness who testifies falsely, and one who sows discord in a family* (6:16–19).
- *A scoffer who is rebuked will only hate you; the wise, when rebuked, will love you* (9:8).
- *The wicked flee when no one pursues, but the righteous are as bold as a lion* (28:1).

Wine/Drink
- *Wine is a mocker, strong drink a brawler, and whoever is led astray by it is not wise* (20:1).
- *Do not look at wine when it is red, when it sparkles in the cup and goes down smoothly. At the last it bites like a serpent, and stings like an adder. Your eyes will see strange things, and your mind utter perverse things* (23:31–33).

Women/Mothers
- *Like a gold ring in a pig's snout is a beautiful woman without good sense* (11:22).
- *The rod and reproof give wisdom, but a mother is disgraced by a neglected child* (29:15).

Israel's Neighbors

AMMONITES

Readers will note the name "Amman" as the capital of the modern Hashemite kingdom of Jordan. Perhaps fittingly, it refers to one of the nations that the Israelites often fought against: Ammon.

Who Were They?
The Ammonites were ethnically close to the Israelites, even if they weren't politically close. The Ammonite kingdom was an ancient Semitic nation immediately east of the Israelites, north of Moab and east of the River Jordan, roughly the same size as Israelite territory. It was an independent nation from roughly the 13th century B.C. to the 8th century, during which it had frequent conflicts with the Israelites. The Ammonites lived in a fairly poor country and paid tribute to the Assyrians—pretty smart on their part, because the Assyrians got crabby if one didn't pony up. They worshipped a god called Molech/Milcom (probably two names for the same god). Their language was most likely Hebrew sprinkled with Aramaic.

Where Are They Now?
Their former territory lies within modern Jordanian lands. The Ammonites maintained some independent cultural identity after they lost their political independence, but Arab culture ultimately absorbed them after the rise of Islam (7th century A.D.). There is a certain irony in the fact that the only surviving cultural aspect of the Ammonites today rests within the modern nation of their ancient Hebrew adversaries: the State of Israel.

Biblical Mentions
According to the Old Testament, the Ammonites were descendants of Lot's involuntary incest with his younger daughter. The Bible doesn't speak too highly of them. Prone to great cruelty, they played regional politics to their perceived advantage, siding with the Babylonians against Israel. King Saul defeated the Ammonites after sending the tribes pieces of dead ox, as a blatant hint to unify under his banner or face ugly repercussions. King David also conquered Ammon, though it regained independence from King Solomon. It was a big no-no for Israelites to worship Ammonite gods.

Quiz

Kings and Queens I

What do you know about the royals of old?

1. Melchizedek was a mysterious king who showed up in the book of Genesis and is mentioned again in the New Testament book of Hebrews. What biblical patriarch paid homage to this king?
   - a. Adam
   - b. Abraham
   - c. Jacob
   - d. Moses

2. Esther was a nice Jewish girl who became queen of Persia. How did she get that job?
   - a. she showed kindness to the king when he stopped at a well
   - b. she was recommended by the elders of her people
   - c. the Lord told the king about her in a dream
   - d. she won a beauty contest

3. King Herod gave an address to a crowd that was seeking his favor, so they shouted his praises: "The voice of a god, and not of a mortal!" What did Herod do next?
   - a. he began to babble nonsense
   - b. he had them killed
   - c. he dropped dead
   - d. he rose into the sky and was seen no more

4. King Ahab was dominated by a foreign queen who tried to spread false worship in Israel. What was her name?
   - a. Jezebel
   - b. Sapphira
   - c. Hulda
   - d. Elizabeth

Answers: 1. b (Genesis 14:18–20, Hebrews 7:1–4); 2. d (Esther 2); 3. c (Acts 12:20–23); 4. a (1 Kings 16:31; 21:25)

Remembering Ruth and Esther

❧ ❧ ❧ ❧

A number of women played key roles in biblical history, but only Ruth and Esther got "book deals."

Messianic Line Would Be "Ruth-less" Without Her

Ruth's Ancestry: Ew!: Ruth was a gentile woman, a Moabite to be exact. The Moabites were descendents of Abraham's nephew Lot. Lot escaped the destruction of the cities of Sodom and Gomorrah by fleeing to a tiny town called Zoar and then to the mountains, living in caves with his two daughters. Afraid there was no hope for carrying on their family line because of their isolation, Lot's daughters impregnated themselves by their dad after getting him drunk on a couple of occasions. The eldest daughter named her son Moab, which may literally mean "from father." And while that reality may mess with our moral sensibilities, it is nonetheless where the Moabite people came from.

Ruth's Progeny: Wow!: The most notable thing about Ruth, historically speaking, is that her name appears in the genealogy of Christ, as recorded in Matthew 1. Some might be surprised at the presence of gentile blood in the lineage of Jesus, but even more surprising, perhaps, is that Rahab is listed too. Rahab was Ruth's second mother-in-law, a gentile woman who had been assimilated into the Israelite community after her career ended as a prostitute in the city of Jericho. Because she had helped the Israelite spies hide from Jericho's authorities, Rahab was rewarded by being spared when God caused the city walls to collapse. She married a man named Salmon and gave birth to Boaz, who became Ruth's second husband. This distinction of being included in Christ's ancestry—an honor accorded to both Ruth and Rahab—seems to clearly underscore God's divine intention to extend his grace and mercy to Jew and gentile alike.

Ruth's Fairy-tale Ending: Ah!: Ruth's own story is one of loyalty and love; romantic and heartwarming, it comes complete with tragic beginning and happy ending. The most famous passage in the book is still used in some wedding ceremonies today: "Where you go, I will go; where you lodge, I will lodge; your people shall be my people, and your God my God" (1:16). This is not, however, Ruth's wedding vow to her second husband, Boaz, but her pledge of loyalty to stay with her first mother-in-law, Naomi, whose widowhood forced her to return home to Israel from the land of Moab.

Though Ruth had also been widowed when her own husband (Naomi's son) died, Ruth chose to cling to Naomi rather than remain with her own people. Her gift of devotion and love to Naomi went far beyond anything Naomi could have expected or even hoped. Ultimately, Ruth's marriage to Boaz is the fairy-tale ending of the story. Boaz nobly "redeems" Ruth and Naomi from poverty and reestablishes Naomi's family heritage (as well as her joy) through Obed, the first son born to Boaz and Ruth. The rest is history, and the four-chapter book bearing Ruth's name can be read in one sitting.

The Queen Who Saved Her People

Purim: Check Your Calendar: Ever heard of the Jewish festival of Purim? If it's indicated on your wall calendar, you'll find it in either February or March. Did you know that this festival is all about what a young Jewish woman named Esther did to save her people from genocide while they were living in Persia as exiles? The events described in the book of Esther take place between 483 and 473 B.C., somewhere in the neighborhood of 600 years after Ruth's lifetime.

From Ruth to Esther: A lot of water had passed under the bridge in that time. Ruth's great-grandson, David, had ruled as Israel's second king, followed by his famous son Solomon. Under Solomon's son, the kingdom began to unravel, splitting in two.

After a series of corrupt kings in the northern kingdom of Israel, the people were carried into exile by Assyria. A number of years later, the southern kingdom of Judah, also weakened by corruption, was overthrown when King Nebuchadnezzar's army conquered

Jerusalem. Off into exile went Judah. While living in Babylon, the people of Judah saw a changing of the guard as the Medo-Persian Empire conquered the Babylonians. After this happened, the Jewish people got a permission slip from King Cyrus, just as the prophet Isaiah had foretold, to return to Jerusalem and rebuild the temple. Jews who chose to return to their homeland did so in three separate waves. It was between the return of the first and last groups that the events of the book of Esther took place.

From Jewish Orphan to Queen of Persia: Since her parents had died, Hadassah—aka Esther—lived under the protection and provision of her cousin Mordecai in the Persian capital city of Susa. Meanwhile, the Persian King Ahasuerus—aka King Xerxes—after being badly "dissed" by his queen, held a beauty contest to select Queen Vashti's successor. From among the many contestants, Xerxes fell for Esther, appointing her his new queen.

An Evil Plot: There's so much intrigue and providential intervention in this book that one really must read it to enjoy the account fully. However, the main storyline has to do with a villain named Haman—the king's preeminent noble—who works to orchestrate a complete annihilation of the Jews in Persia. Why? Because of a grudge Haman has against Esther's cousin, Mordecai, who refuses to bow his knee to Haman.

Apparently not realizing that Esther herself is a Jew, Xerxes signs a decree, drafted by Haman, that sets a date for the Jews' destruction. Haman deceitfully promotes the decree to the king as being in the empire's best interest because, Haman says, the Jews are undermining the kingdom's unity.

Esther's Shining Moment: When the decree is read throughout the kingdom, Mordecai turns to Esther for help. He urges her to go to the king to appeal the edict. But Esther is reluctant, explaining that no one is permitted to enter the king's presence unless summoned. It's a huge risk for her to approach him, for unless Xerxes extends his golden scepter in welcome, she will be executed.

Mordecai responds, "Do not think that in the king's palace you will escape any more than all the other Jews. For if you keep silence at such a time as this, relief and deliverance will rise for the Jews from another quarter, but you and your father's family will perish.

Who knows? Perhaps you have come to royal dignity for just such a time as this."

And at this pivotal point, Queen Esther's response to Mordecai is stirring: "Go, gather all the Jews to be found in Susa, and hold a fast on my behalf, and neither eat nor drink for three days, night or day. I and my maids will also fast as you do. After that I will go to the king, though it is against the law; and if I perish, I perish."

Purim: The Rest of the Story: The events that transpire after Esther's brave decision are recorded in chapters five through nine of the book bearing her name. Interestingly, God is never mentioned throughout the entire story—a fact that has caused some to question the book's qualification to be included in the biblical lineup. However, Mordecai's faith in God is clearly demonstrated, and God's intervention on behalf of his people is undeniable. And Purim? It is the celebration—initiated during Esther's time and still observed by devout Jews today—of how God delivered his people from Haman's wicked plot by means of Esther's courageous heart.

Essenes

One might characterize the Essenes as Jewish monks whose Palestine heyday lasted a couple of centuries, from roughly 150 B.C. to A.D. 50. They numbered perhaps a few thousand and devoted themselves to an austere lifestyle to avoid the taint of the surrounding world and achieve greater holiness. Most lived in Essene communes, owning property jointly and not pursuing wealth. Fasting, prayer, and celibacy were central to Essene life. They strove for cleanliness and an even disposition.

Our knowledge of Essene ways comes from other ancient sources. It is possible that John the Baptist was an Essene, though we lack solid confirmation of this. Modern awareness of the Essenes owes much to the discovery of Hebrew Bible manuscripts in the form of the Dead Sea Scrolls (1946), believed by many scholars to be Essene writings.

A Man of Accomplishment

Dwight Moody went from selling shoes to saving souls.

Dwight Moody was one of the most popular evangelists of the 19th century; he founded the Moody Bible Institute and Moody Publishers.

Born in Northfield, Massachusetts, on February 5, 1837, Moody's initial goal was to make $100,000—a goodly sum in those days. He worked first in his uncle's shoe store in Boston, then he became a successful salesman in Chicago. After converting to Christianity in 1855, however, Moody decided on a different path—he became a preacher. He first ministered to the poor in Chicago, becoming involved with the U.S. Christian Commission of the YMCA, ministering to Union soldiers during the Civil War.

Rewarding Partnership

Moody started the Illinois Street Church in Chicago, and in June 1871, he partnered with gospel singer Ira D. Sankey. That relationship made Moody a household name. He traveled the nation and world spreading God's word to crowds that often numbered in the thousands.

As a preacher, Moody strived to appeal to the common man. His style was simple, lively, and to the point. He promoted a theology in which the word of the Bible was literal and absolute.

Final Days

Moody visited the Holy Land in 1892, and he returned to England that fall with a heart condition that forced him to slow his schedule. He began eschewing large revivals in favor of sermons before smaller congregations, and it was while holding such a service in Kansas City, Missouri, on November 16, 1899, that he experienced some kind of physical breakdown. He managed to make it home but died shortly after.

Dwight Moody is considered by many to be one of the greatest evangelists who ever lived. No matter where he preached, his message was always the same—salvation is readily available within the word of God.

Biblical Nicknames: They Had 'Em Too!

✤ ✤ ✤ ✤

The things we do, the way we do things, what we look like, events we experience . . . these biographical details have the potential of earning "pet" names among our peers or family members. It's interesting to see in the Bible how often nicknames (or other names) are employed, sometimes for the same reasons we get tagged with them today.

See if you can match up the given name of each biblical character with his or her nickname.

1. Azariah	a. Abednego
2. Daniel	b. Barnabas or Son of
3. Disciples of Christ	Encouragement
4. Esau	c. Belteshazzar
5. Gideon	d. Christians
6. Hananiah	e. Dorcas
7. Jacob	f. Edom
8. James and John	g. Iscariot
9. Jedidiah	h. Israel
10. John (born to Zechariah	i. Jerubbaal
and Elizabeth)	j. Meshach
11. Joseph of Cyprus	k. Peter
12. Judas	l. Shadrach
13. Mishael	m. Solomon
14. Simon (disciple of Jesus)	n. Sons of Thunder
15. Tabitha	o. The Baptist
16. Thomas	p. The Twin

Cities of Refuge

❧ ❧ ❧ ❧

*Family vendetta was the law of the Israelites in the early days,
but then Mosaic Law set up six cities of refuge, where a person
accused of murder could find protection and get a fair hearing.*

As in most primitive societies, the Israelites who lived before the
time of Moses had no laws to regulate punishment for criminal acts.
If a person was a victim of a crime, he or a near relative took it upon
himself to exact retribution. Because that retribution was often more
excessive than the original crime, the precept of "eye for eye, tooth
for tooth" (Exodus 21:23–25) was brought into play. Although this
concept sounds brutal, it was actu-
ally moderating. The punishment
should fit the crime, not go beyond
it. If someone steals your chicken,
you should not take three of his
cows in retaliation. If someone
blinds you, you are not justified in
taking his life.

Blood Vengeance

When one person deliberately
took another's life, the stakes were
higher. The victim's nearest male
relatives were expected to act as
"redeemers" and seek revenge. Under the old law, "anyone who kills a
human being shall be put to death"
(Leviticus 24:17). Even if the killing was an accident, it was considered the duty of the victim's relatives to find the killer and take his
life. There was nowhere an innocent person could reside without
fear of blood revenge. All he could attempt to do was to claim sanctuary by holding on to an altar. But how long could a person remain
in such a position?

> ## Biblical Onomatopoeia?
>
> Onomatopoeia refers to
> words that sound like what
> they describe, such as
> "buzz" or "boom." An inter-
> esting Hebrew example
> refers to the "galloping, gal-
> loping" sounds of Canaanite
> warhorses in an Israelite
> victory song: "daharote,
> daharote" (Judges 5:22).

Something needed to be done to prevent the shedding of innocent blood, as such acts generally led to more and more violence. One man might kill another whom he mistakenly believed murdered his father, then a brother of the innocent man would seek revenge for his brother's wrongful death, resulting in still another act to be revenged. In the end, one accidental death could result in the annihilation of an entire family. This clearly had to be stopped.

Hope for the Innocent

In response to the excesses of blood vengeance, the Law of Moses established six so-called cities of refuge, where a person responsible for someone else's death could find asylum. A person who killed another intentionally was still executed, but if he unintentionally caused another's death, he could flee to one of six cities: Golan, Ramoth-Gilead, or Bezer on the east side of the Jordan River, or Kedesh, Shechem, or Hebron on the west side of the river.

There were still loopholes. If the avengers caught the suspect while he was traveling to a city of refuge, they could legitimately kill him without a trial. Consequently, according to Jewish rabbis of the first few centuries A.D., the Sanhedrin, the official Jewish governing council, had the job of keeping the roads to the cities of refuge in good repair, allowing the suspect a fair chance of reaching sanctuary. The rabbis wrote that the roads were wide and smooth and without hills, that bridges spanned all the rivers, and that guideposts displaying the word "Refuge" were placed at every turn. Furthermore, the rabbis claimed, two students of the law accompanied every fleeing man to attempt to pacify the avenger should he overtake them.

Partial Vindication

In the cities of refuge, the accused person was given a trial before the community at the city gate (the traditional place for judgments). If the city leaders found a person guilty of murder, they sent him to the victim's family for execution. But if they decided that the killing was an accident—or otherwise unintended—they let the accused live in their city, protected from blood vengeance, until the death of the high priest. Even though the accused was not put to death, he was still forced to live in exile. The death of the high priest was apparently seen as a kind of expiation for the killing.

10 Things

Important Meals in the Bible

As in modern times, major transactions in scripture often took place over food.

1. Abraham and Sarah Entertain Guests (Genesis 18:1–15) Veal and new-baked bread were on the menu when this aged couple ate with three visitors. (The text hints that God himself was one of these guests.) Sarah overheard the dinner conversation, which included a promise that she would bear a child, and she did what any 90-year-old would do—she laughed. Thus the child was named Isaac, which means "laughter."

2. The Passover (Exodus 12) This became the most sacred meal in the Jewish calendar, but it started as a quick getaway. The Lord was unleashing his final plague on Egypt, and the Israelite slaves would soon be freed. No time for bread dough to rise. The meal—lamb roasted in bitter herbs, unleavened bread—was eaten in traveling attire. And if they painted the lamb's blood on their doorframes, the angel of death would "pass over" them.

3. The Lord Prepares a Table (Psalms 23:5) The best-known psalm includes the image of a feast prepared by the Lord himself for his followers. There is "anointing" of the head with oil, a common way of freshening up (but also a sign of God's choosing). And there is an ample supply of wine ("my cup overflows"). This is all done "in the presence of my enemies," and the psalmist revels in this show of support.

4. Esther Prepares Dinner for the King (Esther 7) Though she was the queen, Esther had little power in the court of King Xerxes. When she became aware of a plot against her people, the Jews, by Haman, the leading nobleman in the country, she had to find a roundabout way to tell the king. So she threw a banquet, at which she invited the king to *another* banquet the next day. Then she unveiled the plot and pointed out the plotter.

5. The Last Supper (Matthew 26:17ff.) This was a Passover meal Jesus shared with his disciples on the night he was arrested. From scripture and tradition, the Passover had developed a distinct menu and liturgy, and we see hints of that in the Gospels' account of the Last Supper. Along with Judas, Jesus dips his (unleavened) bread in the dip (which represented the mortar the Israelites used as slaves).

6. Jesus Feeds 5,000 (John 6:1–14) A huge crowd came, and it was getting to be dinnertime. How would they all be fed? While Jesus' disciples were puzzling over the options, one of them found a boy with a bag lunch—or the ancient equivalent. Jesus took the five small barley loaves and two small fishes, and he fed everyone, with 12 baskets left over. This made Jesus even more popular, especially among the hungry.

7. Jesus Cooks Breakfast by the Sea (John 21:4–14) It was after the Resurrection, and though they'd seen the risen Lord, it seems as if the disciples hadn't had much contact with him. Some were fishing on the Sea of Galilee. On the shore, they saw Jesus cooking a breakfast of fish and bread. They weren't sure it was him, but when he miraculously helped them get a record catch, they had a pretty good idea.

8. The Banquet with Barnabas and Peter (Galatians 2:11–14) At first the Christian church was all Jewish, and Jewish tradition held that it was sinful to eat with a gentile. As the church expanded, this made some church dinners difficult. The apostle Paul, who strongly argued for unity, gave a thorough scolding to Peter and his own partner Barnabas when they buckled to pressure from church segregationists and stopped eating with gentiles.

9. Jesus with the Believer (Revelation 3:20) Revelation isn't all about strange beasts and conflicts. The first few chapters contain messages to specific churches from Jesus. To one church he says: "Listen! I am standing at the door, knocking; if you hear my voice and open the door, I will come in to you and eat with you, and you with me."

10. The Marriage Supper of the Lamb (Revelation 19:9) In the rich imagery of Revelation, Jesus is portrayed as the sacrificial Lamb, but at the end of the story, he's very much alive—and he's getting married. The church is described as his bride, and the world ends with a party to end all parties—a reception, if you will. "Blessed are those who are invited to the marriage supper of the Lamb."

Major Gilbert Wins by the Book— the Good Book!

✤ ✤ ✤ ✤

While the Bible wasn't one of the texts for Major Vivian Gilbert's British officer training, scripture helped his brigade to a victory over the same ground where Saul's Israelites once battled the Philistines.

Palestine, 1918

World War I in the Holy Land mainly pitted the British, Australians, and New Zealanders against Turkish soldiers from the Ottoman Empire. As any veteran knows, in wartime many lives and even battles are lost simply because someone didn't know the land, the enemy's location, or their strength. Major Gilbert was serving with the 180th British Brigade outside the town of Michmash in February 1918, about ten miles north of Jerusalem.

The Turks held Michmash in strength. For the British to advance, they would have to capture it; if they bypassed it, a strong Turkish force would be at their rear. The brigade commander, General C. F. Watson, decided upon a frontal assault across the intervening *wadi* (a steep, dry canyon created by many flash floods, very common in Palestine) with machine guns and artillery support. Like the British, the Turks were brave fighters, also armed with artillery and automatic weapons. It could be a bloody battle, especially if the attackers got pinned down climbing the steep far side of the wadi.

Divinely Inspired Idea

Michmash sounded familiar to Major Gilbert, who stayed up late reading his Bible. Just when he was about to give up, he found the key passage in 1 Samuel 13–14. The Bible described how Saul's son Jonathan had snuck up on the Philistines near Michmash with just his armor-bearer. The two Israelite warriors knew the land: They crept up to two sharp rocks called Bozez and Seneh, which flanked about an acre of land that was easier to cross than the wadi. They attacked alone, catching the Philistines sleeping on the other side. So surprised were the Philistines that they fled before Jonathan and his armor-bearer's assault, and Saul followed up with 600 Israelites to seize Michmash. Scripture recorded a decisive victory for Saul and Jonathan and an embarrassing loss for the Philistines.

Inspired, Major Gilbert woke up General Watson to share his findings. Watson read 1 Samuel with Gilbert, and he decided to send some patrols to scout the area under cover of darkness. Guided by the scriptural description, the scouting patrols soon returned with their report: They had found the Michmash Pass, just as described in 1 Samuel, two sharp upthrust rocks bracketing an acre or there-abouts where it was easy to cross the wadi. Best of all, this pass was lightly guarded by the Turks, who evidently hadn't stayed up late reading 1 Samuel.

Using Jonathan's Tactics

General Watson altered his plan of attack. He ordered a company of infantry to prepare for immediate action. The company commander was to lead his force to Michmash Pass by stealth, making silent kills where possible, and secure the pass. If Jonathan's ancient plan worked, at dawn the 180th Brigade would be able to rush Michmash before the Turks could hurry to defend the pass in numbers.

The company commander led his troops well. Moving silently along Jonathan's biblical route, they captured or killed the few Turk-ish sentries they met. It was a long night's work, but as dawn approached, they seized Michmash Pass and sent word back to General Watson. Anticipating success, the British general had the rest of his force ready to make a move.

Victory

As the sun rose over the Holy Land, the 180th Brigade swooped down on Michmash to encircle and assault the town. Thanks to Major Vivian Gilbert—and to scripture—the Turkish defenders were now in an even worse pickle than Jonathan and Saul had placed the Philistines in biblical times. The result was a general panic. Turkish morale broke, and their entire force tried to flee. Few escaped the carnage and subsequent capture, and the British had Michmash with scant loss of life on their side.

Fast Facts

- *The Bible was written by 40 different authors. Some experts think it may have been more.*

- *The Old Testament contains 39 books, 929 chapters, 23,114 verses, 602,585 words, and 2,278,100 letters.*

- *The New Testament contains 27 books, 260 chapters, 7,957 verses, 180,552 words, and 838,380 letters.*

- *The word "Bible" comes from the Greek word "bibla," which means books. Grammatical purists may frown, but it's accurate because while the Bible is generally considered a single volume, it's actually comprised of many individual books.*

- *A good book can take a long time to write. In the case of the Good Book, it was nearly 1,600 years. The very first scripture was penned around 1500 B.C., and the final i's dotted and t's crossed on the New Testament around A.D. 100.*

- *King Solomon must have been one tired dude. According to the Bible, he had 700 wives and more than 300 concubines. The biggest question: How did he remember all his wedding anniversaries?*

- *The fight between David and Goliath (1 Samuel 17) is one of the Old Testament's most well-known tales. But exactly how tall was Goliath? According to the Bible, the big guy stood "six cubits and a span," which is over nine feet. (Nine-feet-two-inches plus in sandals.)*

- *If one views the Bible literally, then people lived very long lives back in ancient times. Methuselah, for example, lived to be 969 years old, kicking the bucket the same year as the Great Flood. Methuselah's father, Enoch, never died at all; he ascended to heaven while still alive.*

- *Small armies conquering overwhelming numbers are commonplace in the Bible, but Gideon really knew how to kick butt. He fought off 135,000 Midianite invaders with just 300 soldiers and 300 trumpets.*

- *Samson is considered the strongest man in the Bible. The wisest? That trophy goes to King Solomon.*

God Sues Israel

❖ ❖ ❖ ❖

In Micah 6, the prophet sets forth God's complaints
about Israel in terms very much like a lawsuit.

Officers of the Court

With God as counsel for the plaintiff (representing himself), heaven
and earth on the bench, and the prophets witnessing the proceedings, it sounds like a lawsuit God can't lose. The way Micah presents
his prophecy brings to mind a court in heaven (presumably far more
supreme than any earthly Supreme Court), with Israel on the docket
for a number of civil torts.

Counsel, You May Proceed

First God asks: What wrong has he done to Israel? He bailed his
people out of a lousy life in Egypt; sent them classy leaders such as
Moses, Aaron, and Miriam; stuck up for them when Balak of Moab
tried to hire a first-class professional curser to curse them; and generally shielded them from various threats on the way to Israel. The
implication: God has kept his covenant but Israel hasn't. He asked
only that Israel be just, kind, and walk humbly with him—requests
he considered quite reasonable.

Judgment for the Plaintiff (What a Surprise)

God finds many faults with Israel in Micah 6–7: dishonest weights in
commerce, cruelty by the wealthy, obeying ungodly laws, and patho-
logical lying. The verdict specifies that Israel will go hungry, save
up supplies that will be lost, work hard at farming but produce no
harvests, suffer scorn and hissing, and generally pay a painful price
for its sins. All is not lost, however. At the end of this section, Micah
reminds the Israelites of God's merciful nature. He will cast away
their sins into the sea by way of pardon and clemency, taking delight
in mercy, and the Israelites will once again show proper faithfulness
to Abraham and Jacob. In other words, they will return to the old
and true ways.

A Harvest of Hope and Health

✤ ✤ ✤ ✤

Olives were not just a crop, they were a symbol.

After enduring 40 days of the flood in his ark, Noah noticed that the waters were finally starting to recede. He sent out a raven and a dove, both of which were gone for a long time because they could not find a dry place to land. But after being sent out a second time, "the dove came back to him in the evening, and there in its beak was a freshly plucked olive leaf; so Noah knew that the waters had subsided from the earth" (Genesis 8:11). It is fitting that an olive leaf would be a symbol of new and renewed life for Noah and his family, because olive trees and their fruit would help to sustain his people for thousands of years to come.

Hardy Little Tree

Averaging 26 to 49 feet in height, an olive tree is short and squat—about the size of an apple tree. Native to the Mediterranean, Africa, and Asia, this evergreen has silvery green, oblong leaves; a twisted, gnarled trunk; and beautiful clusters of white flowers. The fruit of the olive tree is a small *drupe*. A drupe is a fruit in which a hard inner shell, or pit, is surrounded by outer flesh. Drupes are sometimes also called "stone fruits." Though olive trees do not bear fruit until they are 15 years old, they live for hundreds of years; in fact, an olive tree in Algarve, Portugal, has been radiocarbon dated at 2,000 years old. This means that it is possible that there are olive trees in Israel that have been alive since the time of Christ!

The Israelites were not the only ancient people who valued the olive tree and its fruit. The Greeks in particular loved olives, and Homer included them in both the *Odyssey* and the *Iliad.* In Greek mythology, Athena won the favor of Attica by creating and giving him the olive. For this reason, Athenians insisted the olive tree originated in Athens and stamped an image of the olive on their coins. The Romans were also very fond of olives and integrated them into their diet (olives would eventually become a staple of

Italian cooking). In Persia and across Arabia, olives were considered so healthy they were almost thought to be a miracle food. They are mentioned seven times in the Quran, and Muhammad is said to have called the olive tree "a blessed tree."

So Many Uses

In ancient Israel, olive trees were grown inland because farmers believed coastal areas were not compatible to their growing, but this was later found to be untrue. In fact, olive trees seem to love poor soil. In rich soil, they are more likely to become diseased. Green olives were harvested from September to October in a process that involved shaking them off the trees and onto blankets to be sorted. Some olives were then pickled or packed in salt, but most were pressed for their oil. They were sometimes pressed by stomping feet, as grapes were, but a more effective way was to use a large millstone. As the millstone crushed the olives, the oil ran into large vats. The oil was then poured into jars for storage.

Olive oil was consumed in all kinds of food, such as pottage (stew), bread, and salad. Its use went beyond the culinary, however. Olive oil was extremely important as a source of light. Every home in ancient Israel was lit with oil lamps, some quite primitive and some quite elaborate. The poor used clay lamp stands, while the rich owned impressive metal candelabras. Olive oil was also used in grooming, both as a moisturizer for skin and a leave-in conditioner for hair. While the thought of oily hair may gross us out today, in biblical times it was considered quite attractive.

When a host welcomed a guest into his home, he would almost always anoint his head with oil as a sign of respect. Indeed, one of the most famous stories in the New Testament is of Jesus being anointed by an unnamed woman in Mark 14:3–9: "She has done what she could; she has anointed my body beforehand for its burial."

Where Jesus Walked

Cana

It saw Jesus' first recorded miracle; yet, for that monumental scriptural significance, we aren't even sure where it is.

In Biblical Times
It's unclear what Cana was like in Jesus' day. We can infer that it was big enough, at least, to have a major wedding. You don't need over a hundred gallons of wine for a small wedding festival unless the god being worshipped is Dionysos (the Greek god of wine). But these were biblical Jews, not Greek pagans, and one can assume the wedding party-goers were not serious alcoholics; hard to imagine Jesus as an enabler for lushes. The simple fact that we can't find the town's ruins, along with its mere three biblical mentions, suggest that it wasn't enormous. It seems reasonable to consider Cana a smallish Galilean town, not noteworthy except for Christ's miracle and being the hometown of Christ's follower Nathanael.

Jesus' Connection
Jesus, his mother Mary, and the disciples were all invited to a wedding in Cana of Galilee early in his ministry. The party ran out of wine. At first Jesus told Mary that bad wedding planning wasn't his problem. Either she was persuasive or he perhaps took pity on the wedding party; maybe both. In any case, he told someone to have six 20–30-gallon water jars filled up, then he changed the water into wine. The steward, upon tasting the wine, complimented the groom on saving the best wine for last.

Cana Today
Several Galilee sites claim the honor of being the traditional location of Cana. They can't all be right, obviously, and it's possible none are. It might have been near Capernaum, a location known to us, since that's where Jesus went shortly after the wedding miracle. Arab tradition dating back to the 8th century A.D. places Cana at Kafr Kanna, a modern Arab town of 17,000 that is four miles northwest of Nazareth. That might make Kafr Kanna the most reasonable guess—but it's still only a guess.

Quiz

Kings and Queens II

What do you know about the royals of old?

1. King Hezekiah got some bad news and asked God to rescind it. What happened?
   - a. he heard that the Persians were going to conquer the land, but their attack was thwarted
   - b. he watched the Babylonians steal the Ark of the Covenant, but it was returned
   - c. he learned that he was about to die, but God gave him 15 more years to live
   - d. he was told that the scrolls of the law were burned in a temple fire, but they weren't even singed

2. You might know that King David committed adultery with Bathsheba, but what famous son did she later give birth to?
   - a. Saul
   - b. Solomon
   - c. Absalom
   - d. Trick question: She wasn't allowed to bear children

3. In the book of Isaiah, King Cyrus of Persia is called "the Lord's anointed." What did he do to earn that description?
   - a. he allowed the Jews to return to their homeland
   - b. he defeated the enemies of Israel
   - c. he prophesied before all the people of Nineveh
   - d. he married Esther

4. As a prisoner, the apostle Paul spoke before the Jewish king Agrippa and his sister/queen Bernice, telling them all about his faith. To what ruling dynasty did Agrippa and Bernice belong?
   - a. Caesars
   - b. Maccabees
   - c. Essenes
   - d. Herods

Answers: 1. c (2 Kings 20:1-6); 2. b (2 Samuel 12:24); 3. a (Ezra 1:1-3; Isaiah 45:1); 4. d (Acts 26)

119

Ezekiel's Wheel: What in the World? Vision? UFO?

This scriptural passage is responsible for some of the most interesting speculation in the Bible's history. What was Ezekiel seeing?

Scriptural Description

Going to the source (Ezekiel 1), first the prophet describes some extremely strange living creatures in a fiery cloud: humanoids with four faces (human, eagle, ox, lion), four wings, bronze bodies, surrounding something like fiery coals. Then (verses 15–21):

As I looked at the living creatures, I saw a wheel on the earth beside the living creatures, one for each of the four of them. As for the appearance of the wheels and their construction: their appearance was like the gleaming of beryl; and the four had the same form, their construction being something like a wheel within a wheel. When they moved, they moved in any of the four directions without veering as they moved. Their rims were tall and awesome, for the rims of all four were full of eyes all around. When the living creatures moved, the wheels moved beside them; and when the living creatures rose from the earth, the wheels rose. Wherever the spirit would go, they went, and the wheels rose along with them; for the spirit of the living creatures was in the wheels. When they moved, the others moved; when they stopped, the others stopped; and when they rose from the earth, the wheels rose along with them; for the spirit of the living creatures was in the wheels.

Any lesser person than an Old Testament prophet of God might take a few aspirin and swear off "drink" for life.

Otherworldly Interpretations

Plenty of artists have tried to depict Ezekiel's wheel. Most efforts look like gyroscopes: two shining circles intersecting. Picture a globe with a steel-blue ring around the equator. Imagine another metallic ring at a right angle to the first, passing through the North and South

Poles. Subtract the globe. Could this be an ancient spaceship? All we have going for us is our science-fiction ideas of alien spacecraft. Some very educated minds suggest that Ezekiel is indeed describing a credible alien spaceship. We can't prove either way.

One book that fueled much of the speculation was *Chariots of the Gods* (1968, Erich von Däniken). Von Däniken's thesis—that many ancient writings about gods, including the Bible, refer to contact with aliens—is unacceptable to most believers. Therefore, his thesis hasn't gained lasting traction with Jews and Christians. Nevertheless, some suspect that, with regard to Ezekiel 1, von Däniken had a grain of the truth.

Non-science-fiction Views

Since we can only speculate, let's do so:

The simplest explanation might be an angelic vision of the Lord's might. Ezekiel seems to have thought so (see Ezekiel 10) when he reflected on the matter. Perhaps the four forms represent archangels. They could also represent the four Gospels, identifying Matthew with the lion, Mark with the ox, Luke with the man, and John with the eagle.

Considering that Ezekiel's vision came from God, one might consider the "rims . . . full of eyes all around" to mean that God sees everything in all directions. One supposes that Ezekiel, as a believer, wouldn't normally need a reminder of this—but perhaps the Lord felt he did, or he wanted to dramatize it. That veers into trying to guess God's motives, which is problematic for the human mind.

One mainstream Jewish view, according to rabbinic wisdom and analysis, is that Ezekiel saw a heavenly chariot/throne bearing *Hashem* (God). It represented a vision of the Lord, a symbol of his ultimate generosity in showing his glory to his people. Given the location—near Babylon (modern Iraq)—it could foretell the equipment the region's main product (oil) would fuel someday.

We don't know. We can, however, compare the theories of the learned and determine for ourselves with the minds God gave us.

Punishment, Biblical Style

✤ ✤ ✤ ✤

*Scripture provides numerous examples of punishments
that we might find a bit steep today.*

- **Exile:** The first instance, of course, involved the first people. In Genesis 3, Adam and Eve get the heave-ho from the Garden of Eden for eating (presumably fruit) from a tree after God said not to. Ezra 7 also describes the penalty of exile, though it's handed down by a far lesser authority: King Artaxerxes of Persia.

- **Chucked in a Cistern:** In Jeremiah 38, Jeremiah was thrown into a cistern (well) with no water, just mud.

- **Pulling Out Hair:** Nehemiah (Nehemiah 13) was irritated with the Jews (especially Jewish women) for marrying people from Moab, Ashdod, and Ammon. He was so irritated, according to the Bible, that he started beating up the offenders and yanking their hair out. Ow.

- **Scourging:** Deuteronomy 25 proposes a severe penalty for losing a lawsuit. If the judges decided that the loser was badly in the wrong, in addition to whatever other penalties were imposed, the loser would take a whipping. At least they established an upper limit of 40 lashes. That might cut down on silly lawsuits today.

- **Cutting off Thumbs and Toes:** Adoni-bezek was a Canaanite king who lost a battle to the armies of Judah and Simeon. Since Adoni-bezek had cut off the thumbs and big toes of 70 kings (so they couldn't fight), the same was done to him (Judges 1). From his comments on the topic, Adoni-bezek seems to have expected something like this eventually. As ye sow...

- **Slicing off Noses and Ears:** In Ezekiel 23, the prophet rails against the corruption of Samaria and Jerusalem by comparing them to loose women. He says that they will have their noses and ears severed, a punishment also known among the Assyrians (the acknowledged, feared, and despised masters of mutilation in the ancient Near East).

- **Death by Being Cut/Torn in Pieces:** A passage in Hebrews 11 describes a terrible punishment: being cut in two. That must have been fairly slow and very unpleasant, to say the least. In Daniel 2, King Nebuchadnezzar, who leaned toward grotesque penalties, threatens to tear his dream-interpreters into pieces if they can't reveal both his dreams and their meanings. (Perhaps people listening to modern economic forecasts on TV news today feel the king's frustration.)

- **Death by Burning:** In Genesis 38, Judah was ready to burn Tamar for sleeping around and getting pregnant, but he changed his mind when he learned he was the father. Leviticus 20 makes it quite clear that a man mustn't sleep with a woman and her daughter at the same time, lest the whole threesome be burned. In Daniel 3, the burning punishment backfired against King Nebuchadnezzar of Babylon, who threw Shadrach, Meshach, and Abednego into a furnace for refusing to worship an idol. They didn't burn, and witnesses reported a fourth figure among them. Wonder who that might have been?

- **Death by Being Fed to Animals:** The most famous example of this came in Daniel 6, where King Darius threw Daniel into the lions' den. God shut the lions' mouths, and Daniel suffered no harm. Darius, highly impressed, decided instead to throw Daniel's accusers (including their whole families) into the lions' den. This time God didn't shut the animals' mouths.

- **Death by Stoning:** Leviticus 24, Deuteronomy 13, and Acts 7 all mention this relatively common ancient death penalty. In Leviticus, God specified stoning to punish blasphemy; in Deuteronomy, for inciting God's people toward worship of other gods. Acts mentions that Stephen was stoned for preaching the Gospel to an angry mob.

- **Death by Being Thrown off a Cliff:** This punishment is from 2 Chronicles 25, in which Judah's army kills 10,000 men of Seir in the Valley of Salt. That left 10,000 captives remaining. Judah's people threw all of them off a steep height so that they broke into pieces.

Passover

Pesach is so important that even many secular Jews celebrate it.

Biblical Basis
In Exodus, we learn the story of God's final punch to pharaoh's gut regarding the Israelites' liberty: the death of every firstborn male in Egypt. God told his people to smear lamb blood on their doorposts, so his spirit would "pass over" them as it ran around doing the killing. After this tenth and final plague, pharaoh was glad to see the Israelites gone; for their part, they took off so quickly they didn't even wait for their bread to rise. No point giving pharaoh a chance to change his mind, after all, as he had already proven a slow learner and a breaker of his oaths.

Biblical Practice
Scripture records the annual remembrance as a direct command from the Lord, with numerous and specific requirements. He commanded them to begin by setting aside an unblemished sheep or goat for sacrifice. His people were to refrain from eating leavened bread for a week; not only that, they could not even leave any yeast or leavened bread scraps lying around. On the first and seventh days, they were not to work at their usual jobs and must instead gather for worship. They were to give burnt offerings to the Lord each day and could not eat any of the offerings.

Modern Practice
Passover begins on the 15th of Nisan by the Jewish calendar—usually March or April. Even moderately devout Jews will abstain from leavened bread for the full week, and many will scour their homes to be rid of anything contaminated with *chametz* (leaven). *Matzoh*, unleavened bread, becomes the staple during this time. The week begins with the *seder* (SAY-der), a communal ceremonial meal with many symbolic forms of food and drink, all intended to remind Jews of their spiritual connection to God and their history.

    Pesach (pay-SOCH) is one of Judaism's most unifying rituals, bringing families and friends together in a reaffirmation of identity.

A Savage Foretelling

⚜ ⚜ ⚜ ⚜

This passage in Jeremiah is a prophecy—but of what?

Jeremiah 31:15 in the Old Testament reads, "Thus says the Lord: A voice is heard in Ramah, lamentation and bitter weeping. Rachel is weeping for her children; she refuses to be comforted for her children, because they are no more." Both Jews and Christians see this as a prophetic statement, but they disagree on what that statement is.

Who Was Rachel?

Rachel, who is introduced in the book of Genesis, was one of the four wives of Jacob, who was one of the three biblical patriarchs. She was the mother of Joseph and Benjamin. Joseph became the leader of Israel's tribes, and therefore the name "Rachel" has become almost a generic term for "Mother of Israel."

Jeremiah 31 is a chapter that is a promise by God that the Jews will always be his people and he will always be with them, no matter what atrocities they might face. Many Jews see the 15th verse as a prophecy of the many horrors their people had to live through after the Diaspora—the Crusades, the Inquisition, and of course, the Holocaust. But they take heart in God's assurance later in the chapter: "The days are surely coming, says the Lord, when I will make a new covenant with the house of Israel and the house of Judah."

For Christians, Jeremiah 31:15 is a prophecy of King Herod's Massacre of the Innocents. In Matthew 2:16–18, the Magi refuse to report the location of the infant Jesus to Herod, and in furious response, he orders the slaughter of all Jewish males under the age of two years. In describing the awful, bloody scenes that take place all across Israel, Matthew quotes Jeremiah and presents the nationwide tragedy as a brutal fulfillment of his prophecy.

The Least of Their Brothers

✤ ✤ ✤ ✤

Did the strong care for the weak in ancient Israel?

Orphans, the poor, the elderly, the disabled, the blind, lepers . . . We read about these people throughout the Bible. Sure, there was a miraculous cure here and there, but for the most part, they had to continue on in their pain and poverty. Did anyone help them? Or were they simply left to their own devices?

Society's Child

The weakest of the weak, of course, were the orphans of ancient Israel. These children were sometimes adopted into loving families. For example, if a Jewish man's wife was not able to give him a son, he might adopt an orphan boy to be his heir and mentor him in his craft. But for most orphans, life was far more sad and harsh. They were often used as slaves, or if girls, coerced into marriage or concubinage at a very young age. At the other end of the spectrum were the elderly. The large, extended families that were the norm in ancient Israel were an important safety net for most elderly people, whose care in late life was considered to be the responsibility of their eldest sons. Unfortunately, some elderly people did not have any relatives, which is why Bible passages such as James 1:27 exhort the faithful "to care for orphans and widows in their distress."

The blind and the disabled are also mentioned often in the Bible. In a society that was heavily dependent on manual labor, these people were almost always unable to find work. They were often forced to beg in the public square just to stay alive. It wasn't that the Israelites lacked compassion for such victims of fate; indeed, in Deuteronomy 27:18–19, they are warned by God: "Cursed be anyone who misleads a blind person on the road. . . . Cursed be anyone who deprives the alien, the orphan, and the widow of justice." The Jews took this seriously and did their best to care for the weak, but as a relatively impoverished people who were often under the oppression of others, it was not always easy.

Desperate Measures

If a Jewish man became so indebted that he just could not pay off the debt, his only choice was to sell himself—and sometimes his whole family—into slavery. Likewise, if a single woman had no male relative to take care of her and could not find a husband, she would often have to turn to indentured servitude, becoming a cook or governess for a well-off family. But what of those who were too weak to offer themselves as slaves? Some, like lepers, did not even have the option of begging, because their condition was contagious and they were quarantined from the rest of the community in leper colonies. They relied on kind-hearted people to bring food and clothing to the segregated areas where they lived.

Lepers are a good example of why tithing was so important to the Jews. Tithes and offerings were required of every able-bodied man, and by extension, his family. Ten percent was considered a fair tithe, but some devout Jews gave even more. The importance of charity is stressed over and over again throughout the Bible, in both the Old and New Testaments. In Deuteronomy 15:11, Jews are commanded: "Open your hand to the poor and needy neighbor in your land." In Leviticus 23:22, they are told to give the poor gifts not only of money but of food: "When you reap the harvest of your land, you shall not reap to the very edges of your field, or gather the gleanings of your harvest; you shall leave them for the poor and for the alien." In the New Testament, of course, Jesus repeatedly calls on his followers to care for one of "the least of these" (Matthew 25:45).

The lives of the poor, the orphaned, the elderly, and the disabled in ancient Israel were often cruel, but the light of compassion would at times shine into their world.

Books That Defile the Hands

For Jewish rabbis, books that were given by divine inspiration were ones that "defiled the hands" if they were touched. This idea prevented irreverent use of the scriptures. If people had to wash their hands every time they handled the scriptures, they would do so carefully and reverently.

David's Myrmidons

⚜ ⚜ ⚜ ⚜

In biblical times, a great king needed not only great advisors but also fearless champions: men of loyalty, might, and leadership.

Devoted to David

David, King of Israel, had 37 such valiant men about him, called the Thirty (not sure why). They were dedicated: When David commented out loud that he'd like some water from Philistine-occupied Bethlehem, three of these champions fought their way in, got the water, and brought it to him. Scripture (2 Samuel 23:8–18) points emphatically to three as his greatest: Eleazar, Shammah, and Josheb-Basshebeth. Second Samuel also names the chieftain of the Thirty, Abishai.

Eleazar: He was the son of Dodo (no, not the bird). Before one battle, the Philistines were gathered, and King David and Eleazar gave them some biblical trash talk. Perhaps they wanted to provoke rash action; maybe they just enjoyed insulting the Philistines. Whatever the motive, it worked too well. When the Philistines charged, Eleazar was the only Israelite who stood fast at King David's side. He fought until his hand froze clawlike about his sword, but he won a great victory.

Shammah: Son of Agee the Hararite, Shammah earned renown in a battle against King David's favorite enemies: the Philistines. Second Samuel 23 tells of a battle in a lentil field from which the entire Israelite fighting force fled in evident disorder. Except Shammah, that is, who stayed behind in the lentils clobbering the Philistines with God's help. He obviously feared nothing and no one, which says a great deal for his personal faith.

Josheb-Basshebeth: This legendary spearman was no one to mess with, given that he had once killed 800 enemies in a single battle with his spear. That should have taught someone a lesson.

Abishai: The Bible says he commanded the thirty without being a member. Put a spear in Abishai's hand and it was a bad day for the enemies of King David. He once killed 300 enemies with a spear.

David and Psalms

The story of King David is one of the Bible's most popular.
He also has a strong association with the book of Psalms.

King David is one of the central characters of the Old Testament. The youngest of Jesse's eight sons, he was a shepherd in his youth but went on to achieve fame by slaying a Philistine giant named Goliath, assuaging crazy King Saul with music, and eventually becoming the king of Israel. His story is revealed in 1 and 2 Samuel, 1 Kings, and 1 Chronicles.

A Man with Issues

David was a good man, but he was far from perfect. He was impulsive, committed adultery, failed to discipline his wayward children, and even arranged a murder. But at heart he was a man of God, repentant and honest in seeking the Lord's will. God loved David despite his faults, and David loved God.

This ancestor of Jesus was also the author of 73 psalms, which range from joyful songs of praise to soulful longings of lament. Perhaps his best known verses are Psalm 23. Psalm 51, verse 10, is also a popular favorite: "Create in me a clean heart, O God, and put a new and right spirit within me."

Based on Life Experience

Interestingly, several psalms can be linked to special events in David's life, as recounted in 1 Samuel, chapters 19 and 21–24, and 2 Samuel, chapters 12, 15, and 22. These psalms tell the story of David's spiritual awakening, his praise for God, and how God came to his aid during times of trouble and adversity. These psalms are, in chronological order, 59, 34, 56, 142, 52, 54, 57, 63, 18, 51, 3, and 7. They make for fascinating reading, if you haven't already.

David is a big kahuna within the history as laid out in the pages of the Old Testament, but we should never forget his remarkable contributions to the book of Psalms. Without them, we would be spiritually lacking.

Lamech, History's Second Killer

❧ ❧ ❧ ❧

A descendant of Cain, the first murderer,
Lamech becomes the second man on record
to kill another human being—and the first polygamist.

After Cain murders his brother, Abel, God tells him that he will no longer be able to farm the land, as he had been doing, for God was putting a curse on the land because it had absorbed the innocent blood of Abel. Instead of farming, Cain will lead a life of wandering. When Cain expresses fear that anyone he meets in the future will know him as a fratricide and kill him, God puts a mark on Cain to show that "Whoever kills Cain will suffer a sevenfold vengeance" (Genesis 4:15). Cain eventually marries and has children. Genesis completes Cain's story with a brief genealogy, ending with the birth of Lamech, Cain's great-great-great-grandson—of the seventh generation of humankind.

Lamech distinguishes himself by being the first to take two wives, named Adah and Zillah, making him the first polygamist. Each wife has significant sons. Adah gives birth to Jabal, the first animal herder (aside from the murdered Abel, whose career was cut short). According to Genesis, Jabal and his descendants live in tents and care for their cattle. Adah's other son, Jubal, is the world's first musician, or as Genesis puts it, "the ancestor of all those who play the lyre and pipe" (Genesis 4:21).

Zillah's son is Tubal-cain, the world's first metalworker; he "made all kinds of bronze and iron tools" (Genesis 4:22). Zillah also bears a daughter, named Naamah.

A Boast of Killing—in Verse!

Lamech's primary boast is not about his sons but about his heinous action. Apparently, he kills a man who gets into a fight with him and inflicts a minor wound. The injury Lamech receives can't be severe, as it doesn't keep him from killing his opponent. This defensive action far exceeds the original offense. If this imbalance is not enough,

Lamech then sings a boastful song to his wives about his crime. He says that he won't be satisfied with the seven-fold vengeance God granted his ancestor Cain. Instead, he'll take vengeance into his own hands and it will be more than ten times what God would do.

Lamech said to his wives:

> *Adah and Zillah, hear my voice;*
> *you wives of Lamech, listen to what I say:*
> *I have killed a man for wounding me,*
> *a young man for striking me.*
> *If Cain is avenged sevenfold,*
> *truly Lamech seventy-sevenfold*

(Genesis 4:23–24)

Lamech's song is one of the earliest surviving poems in Hebrew, but it already uses parallelism, the literary device found in much biblical verse. In parallelism, the second half of a line of verse repeats the first half in different words, contradicts it, or extends its meaning. Lamech's song itself seems to demonstrate the downward spiral morality has taken since the Fall. It will culminate in the flood and a subsequent renewal of life.

Another Lamech—No Relation

Lamech, the bigamist and boastful killer, is not the only Lamech in Genesis. Another Lamech is named as a descendant of Adam and Eve's third son, Seth. This other Lamech's claim to fame is that he is the son of Methuselah, who reaches the ripe old age of 969, making him the oldest man in the Bible. When Lamech is himself 182 years old, he gives Methuselah a grandson, Noah, and Lamech prophesies that Noah will bring relief from the curse God had put upon the earth when Cain killed Abel. Noah eventually fulfills that prophecy by rebooting civilization after the Great Flood. Lamech himself dies at the age of 777—a mere boy compared to his father.

Unlike the Lamech who was descended from Cain, the Lamech who was descended from Seth is peace-loving. Instead of bursting into song about his killing of a man who had only slightly injured him, he looks forward to the period of peace that his son Noah will initiate.

You've Been Owned

⚜ ⚜ ⚜ ⚜

In biblical times, how much you owned depended on who you were.

One of the biggest common misconceptions about ancient Israel and its neighbors is that the people of these regions were all transients who just pitched their tents on any old piece of land. While it's true that the Bedouins were a nomadic tribe at that time (as some of them still are today), many of the people in what we now call the Middle East preferred a more settled life. That meant holding property and the ownership of materials that were not easily transported.

Right from the Start

As soon as human beings appear in the Bible, they are described as being desirous of their own property. In Genesis 2:15–17, God didn't just hand over the ownership of the Garden of Eden to Adam. It was more like a landlord/tenant relationship: "The Lord God took the man and put him in the Garden of Eden to till it and keep it." It was a pretty sweet deal, with only one caveat: "And the Lord God commanded the man, 'You may freely eat of every tree of the garden; but of the tree of the knowledge of good and evil you shall not eat, for in the day that you eat of it you shall die.'" Obviously, the story of Eve and the serpent is about more than just property, but property is one of the things Eve wants and doesn't have. Why can't she have *that* tree as well as all the other trees in the garden? And though Adam has been a good boy up until that point, it only takes, oh, about two seconds for him to be convinced of her position. The innate greediness of human beings, and their desire for exclusive ownership, is clearly shown as the sin that led to the fall.

God knew that this acquisitiveness was something that humans would have to struggle against as long as they roamed the earth. So he set his rules about property and material things in stone when he gave Moses the Ten Commandments (Exodus 20:2–17). The eighth commandment is blunt and to the point: "You shall not steal." But, apparently foreseeing Clintonian arguments about what the word "steal" means, God goes on to elaborate in the tenth commandment: "You shall not covet your neighbor's house; you shall not covet your neighbor's wife, or male or female slave, or ox, or donkey, or anything that belongs to your neighbor." Seems pretty un-PC to us to throw people in there with houses and donkeys, but remember, there was no sensitivity training for patriarchs back in those days.

Location, Location, Location

Ownership of land in biblical times depended on location and status (sounds a lot like today, huh?). When the Israelites were in captivity—first under the Egyptians and then the Babylonians—they were not really allowed to own anything, property-wise. Sure, some of the more favored Jews who "went along to get along" were given comfortable—even luxurious—residences, but those residences were not theirs to keep. They could be taken away at a moment's notice by their overlords. And the number of Jews who enjoyed such privileges were tiny compared to the number living in very harsh circumstances, without even their own places to rest after long days of hard labor.

When the Old Testament Hebrews ruled themselves, such as in the times of King Solomon and King David, they did not extend the right to own property to women. In fact, women were considered property. A woman was first the property of her father, then of her husband. However, a man could delegate business duties to his wife. In Proverbs 31:16, for example, a woman "considers a field and buys it." Some widows managed to hold on to their property after their husbands died—but only if they had no sons. If a Hebrew couple had sons, the husband's property was divided between those sons at his death, with a double share going to the eldest son. This is because the eldest son was expected to take care of his mother. Indeed, many did live up to this responsibility. When they did not, the results were heartbreaking.

What Would Jesus Own?

By the time Jesus Christ began preaching, the Jews were under yet another oppressive regime: that of the Roman occupational government. Technically, Jews were allowed to own property at this time. Like the rich lad who approached Jesus in Matthew 19:16–22, some owned large tracts of land. Like the apostle Simon Peter, some owned boats or other equipment that allowed them to fish or farm. Like the apostle Matthew, some had stored up riches by betraying their people with shady professions. But again, whatever a Jew might own at this time—his home, his land, his boat, all his wordly possessions—could be taken away by the Roman authorities in the blink of an eye. And if he was allowed to keep those things, he was taxed to the breaking point.

This is why so many suffering Hebrews looked to Jesus as someone who might lead a political revolution and help them get the secure property rights and legal justice they felt they deserved. Jesus was a great disappointment to these people. He told them, "Do not store up for yourselves treasures on earth, where moth and rust consume and where thieves break in and steal; but store up for yourselves treasures in heaven, where neither moth nor rust consumes and where thieves do not break in and steal. For where your treasure is, there your heart will be also."

Few theologians would argue that Christ was telling his followers that they could never own property or have a few nice things around the house. But these things were so low on his priority list that it was hard for the majority of people who heard his sermons to understand. Still, those few who did understand would take his message about property far and wide.

The Sixth Sick Sheik's Sixth Sheep's Sick

The Hebrew language may not have any tongue twisters quite this difficult, but the use of assonance (successive words containing the same sounds) is common. One psalmist soothingly says, *"sha'alu shelom yerushalayim"* ("Pray for the peace Jerusalem," Psalm 122:6). Isaiah packs a powerful punch by preaching that *"pachad wapachat wapach"* ("terror and pit and snare") will come upon the wicked (Isaiah 24:17).

Great Bible Orators

Apostle of the British Empire

George Whitefield was one of the very first evangelists to take America by storm—and also one of the best.

George Whitefield was slight of build but a giant at the pulpit. He preached before huge crowds in his native England, then he brought his fiery oratory to the colonies, where he became known as the "apostle of the British Empire."

Whitefield was born in Gloucester, England, on December 16, 1714. His father, an innkeeper, died when Whitefield was just 2 years old, and his widowed mother worked hard to provide for her family. As a teenager, Whitefield briefly dropped out of school so he could help his mother manage the family inn. He eventually entered Pembroke College at Oxford, but he was forced to drop out due to illness. After a nine-month convalescence, Whitefield returned to finish his degree. His religious writings and other activities attracted the attention of the bishop of Gloucester, who later ordained Whitefield as a deacon and then a priest in the Church of England.

Man of Conviction

Whitefield's booming voice and personal conviction enthralled congregations, and as word spread, his sermons drew huge crowds in London. He then set his sights on America, traveling there a total of seven times to speak at revivals in the colonies.

Whitefield was also amazingly adept at reaching out and building relationships with different religious denominations. A member of the Church of England, he found support from a variety of callings, including Presbyterians, Congregationalists, and Baptists. Together with evangelists John and Charles Wesley, Whitefield was instrumental in nurturing the movement that came to be known as Methodism.

Whitefield died on September 30, 1770, and he remains venerated to this day.

Stormy Weather

✤ ✤ ✤ ✤

*Noah's ark is one of the best-known stories from
the book of Genesis. Could it have really happened?*

Shipbuilding is an important profession, yet most shipbuilders live
and die in anonymity. (Raise your hand if you know who designed
the *Titanic*. Yeah, didn't think so.) It's a different story, of course, if
your name is Noah and your boss is God—then your accomplishments will become one of the most fascinating tales in the Old
Testament.

Indeed, practically everyone is familiar with the story of Noah's
ark, perhaps the most famous floating menagerie in history. But
many people are a little light on the details, so let's take a closer look.

Wickedness Punished

The whole thing started because God was angry. He took a look
around and saw only wickedness and violence, so he decided to
wipe the earth clean with a global flood and basically start over. Not
everyone was wicked, however. God found one righteous man—
Noah—and instructed him to build a massive ship out of wood,
which he was then to fill with a mated pair of every kind of bird and
animal. Noah was also instructed to stock food for all the animals
as well as for himself and his family, which included his wife, three
sons, and their wives.

The ark itself, as designed
by God, was to be 300 cu-
bits long, 50 cubits wide,
and 30 cubits high. A cubit is
around 17.5 inches, though an
Egyptian royal cubit was a little
longer, around 20.5 inches.
(Noah went to school in Egypt,
so he may have used this
particular measurement.) As a

result, the ark was between 437 and 512 feet long and nearly three stories high—a pretty good-size vessel for the day.

Time-Consuming Project

Building the ark wasn't some weekend project. In fact, if one takes the Bible literally, Noah spent around 120 years constructing it—he was 480 years old when God first spoke to him and 600 when the flood finally occurred. (People lived a *lot* longer back then.)

The flood that followed was a horrifying event. God produced torrential rains for 40 days and 40 nights, enough to flood the entire planet past the mountaintops and kill everyone and everything on it. As the waters receded, the ark came to rest on the mountains of Ararat. However, it took several months more for the world to dry. When finally invited by God to exit the ark, Noah immediately built an altar and worshipped God with burnt offerings. God was pleased, and he promised never to destroy the earth by flood again.

It's a remarkable story, but one that begs a lot of questions. How did Noah fit thousands of birds and animals—plus their food—into the ark? And what about their waste? Feeding the animals and cleaning up after them must have been a Herculean task. The simplest answer, of course, is that God took care of it. After all, the entire event was supernatural in origin, from God instructing Noah on what to do and how to do it to the flood itself.

Fact or Fiction?

Whether the story of Noah's ark is true or not has been the subject of debate for centuries. Some theologians believe it literally, while others posit that the flood did occur, but that it was regional rather than global. And some believe the story is more allegory than fact—a fable designed to illustrate God's intolerance toward wickedness and sin.

Interestingly, some explorers believe that Noah's Ark still rests atop Mount Ararat in eastern Turkey. Over the years, several expeditions have searched the mountain looking for concrete proof of the vessel, though nothing conclusive has been found.

This is a remarkable tale, full of compelling characters and wild adventure, with a simple yet important moral: Righteousness always prevails over wickedness.

Bibles for the Masses

❧ ❧ ❧ ❧

*The Gutenberg Bible was the first to be printed using movable type,
a process that ultimately made the Good Book available to all.*

If it weren't for Johannes Gutenberg, the book you're holding in
your hands right now would not be possible. The German printer
developed the first functioning printing press to use movable type, a
process that eventually made books inexpensive enough for everyone to own.

Though the Bible wasn't Gutenberg's first project using his new
press, it's the one for which he would became most famous. Prior to
the development of the movable-type press, most mass-produced
books were created using engraved wood blocks, which were coated
with ink and pressed against a piece of paper. This was fine for printing pictures on a page, but it was unsuitable for books comprised
primarily of text. As a result, books such as the Bible had to be meticulously handwritten, a process that could take years to complete.

Man of Mystery

Little is known about Gutenberg's early life or how he came to actually invent the movable-type press. Once he had created a prototype,
he experimented by printing single sheets and small books, such as a
simple textbook of Latin grammar.

Gutenberg began work on the Bible in 1450, using quality paper
imported from Italy. Each page contains a unique watermark, which
is visible when held up to the light. Gutenberg also printed some
copies on a higher-grade material called vellum, which was made
from scraped calfskin. The ink he used was oil-based and deep black
in color due to its high metal composition.

Some historians speculate that Gutenberg had more than one
movable-type press in his shop due to the high number of Bible
pages he had to print. But even with movable type, it was a time-
consuming process. A typesetter had to carefully place the individual
pieces of type for each line of text within a frame, which was then
placed on the bed of the press and inked using balls stuffed with

horsehair. A sheet of paper was then lightly moistened and placed over the frame, which was then pressed to create the printed page.

Not Available at Barnes & Noble

The exact number of Bibles produced by Gutenberg is unknown, though it is believed to be around 180; there were 145 on paper and 35 on the more expensive vellum. The books were nearly finished by October 1454 and made available for sale by March 1455. Though movable type made publication easier than hand transcription, Gutenberg's Bibles were almost certainly beyond the wallets of even the period's wealthiest individuals and likely were purchased primarily by churches and monasteries.

Though printed via press, each copy of the Gutenberg Bible was unique. The Bible was sold in folded sheets and bound and decorated according to the instructions of the owner. As a result, each copy contained a number of distinctive features, such as the addition of red paint to capital letters and paragraph marks, painted decorations, and individual marks of ownership.

Though his new printing press changed the world, Johannes Gutenberg did not become rich as a result. In fact, he was forced to turn over some of his printing equipment to a wealthy benefactor who sued him for the return of a sizable loan. The benefactor, Johann Fust, then went into partnership with Gutenberg's assistant, Peter Schoffer, and started his own successful printing business.

A Revolutionary Invention

Nonetheless, Gutenberg's movable-type press revolutionized book publishing by making it possible to produce a large number of copies of any document in a relatively short period of time. The process quickly spread throughout Germany, then into Italy, France, and the rest of Europe. The first book to be printed in English on a Gutenberg press was *Recuyell of the Historyes of Troye* by Raoul Lefevre, published by William Caxton in 1473–74.

Only a handful of Gutenberg Bibles are known to still exist, including 48 complete copies on paper and 11 on vellum. If you'd like to see one, a fine copy can be found at the Harry Ransom Center, located at the University of Texas at Austin. Make sure you bring your German-to-English dictionary.

Plants of the Bible

✤ ✤ ✤ ✤

In an agricultural society, plants mean everything—whether as food for humans, animal fodder, construction material, or landscaping.

Farming

Palestine is relatively near to Mesopotamia, to which many edible grains are native. *Barley,* one of the most important, tended to be a crop of the poor. *Wheat,* of course, grew well when the weather cooperated—as it did in Exodus, when a hailstorm trashed the barley but spared the wheat because the latter wasn't up yet. *Beans,* especially *lentils,* provided nutritious sustenance to people who didn't eat a great deal of meat.

Biblical agriculture also produced two extremely valuable non-food crops: *papyrus* and *flax.* Papyrus is a grassy plant that can get very tall if it gets enough water; it still grows today in Israel. If you had writing to do—unless you wanted to write on parchment, which is animal hide—you did it on papyrus. If kept dry, papyrus would keep for a very long time—witness the fact that some of the Dead Sea Scrolls are on papyrus. Flax stems produce fibers, which were separated and woven into cloth. Probably every person mentioned in scripture wore flaxen clothing at some point.

Orchardry/Vintery

If properly cared for, some trees live for millennia. A few *olive* trees still survive from the time of Christ . . . maybe even from the time of the Exodus! To destroy an orchard was the height of scorched-earth scriptural warfare. Olives, of course, have always been a staple of Holy Land orchardry: The oil was delicious and healthy, and the fruit itself added to many meals. The olive branch has been a symbol of peace ever since a dove brought one to Noah. *Dates,* which come from date palm trees, are less prevalent today but were very important for their sweet fruit—plus, that's the tree whose branches were involved in Palm Sunday.

Nut trees, especially *almonds,* were very important in the Holy Land as a source of food and oil. When Aaron's staff produced almonds overnight in the Tent of the Covenant, the Lord ordered the fruitful staff placed in a special position to warn rebels. Probably those were the bitter almond variety, which can cause cyanide poisoning.

Fig trees not only produced leaves for wrapping (so the old idea about a fig leaf of protection isn't that big a joke) but a tasty fruit still popular today. Without *grapes,* of course, there wouldn't have been much wine. When Moses sent scouts ahead to the Promised Land, the grapes they brought back signified good things to come. Even the leaves made tasty wrappings, as anyone who enjoys stuffed grape leaves can attest. The emblem of the *pomegranate,* a fruit containing numerous juicy seed casings, adorned priestly robes and even the Temple of Solomon. While scripture refers to apples, we have good reason to believe they meant another fruit, quite probably *apricots,* which (unlike apples) thrive in the Holy Land and otherwise match biblical descriptions.

Gathering

Frankincense is a resin that was harvested from the tree of that name (somewhat like maple syrup is tapped—a frankincense tree can take a lot of punishment); the resin was burned for its rich, pleasant smell. *Myrrh,* at least the Palestinian version, came from Commiphora trees of various varieties; people also tapped these small trees for the myrrh. Of course, scripture records it as one of the gifts of the wise men at the birth of Jesus and as an embalming agent for him after the Crucifixion—so myrrh would seem special to Christians, as it was part of Christ's birth and death.

Exodus and Leviticus specify *hyssop* for ritual Israelite cleansing usage. Since it was good to plant between grapevines and attracted many bees, hyssop was a good companion crop—probably many Israelite farms grew a little. For building, the region's *cedars* remain famous today, just as they were specified for Solomon's Temple with their delightful fragrance and amazing mix of color patterns in lumber. Another important tree was the *acacia,* used to set up the tabernacle in the wilderness as specified in Exodus.

Judean Desert

The desert of Judea holds an important place in Jesus' life.
There he proved his dedication to his Father.

In Biblical Times
The desert of Judea lay in a long vertical strip east of Jerusalem, roughly between it and the Dead Sea. It was never very hospitable and of old was a common refuge for people on the run, bandits, religious fanatics, and rebels—plus a certain Messiah. Masada, the fortress where Jews committed suicide rather than be taken alive by the Romans, is located in the Judean Desert. There was some agriculture and grazing in the region, probably more so than today; the desert has become drier. We have no way of knowing exactly what parts Jesus visited, though anyplace near fresh-flowing water (there is some) is a reasonable bet.

Jesus' Connection
His fasting and temptation mainly occurred in the Judean Desert. Satan was in charge of the tempting, so Jesus was facing contractor-grade temptation that lasted 40 days. The Devil tempted him to break his fast by using his powers to turn rocks into bread. Satan then took Jesus to a pinnacle in Jerusalem and tried to provoke him to jump and wait for angels to catch him. That temptation didn't work either, of course. Finally, Satan flew Jesus to a mountaintop (the Judean Desert is flanked by mountains) and tempted him with the kingship of the world. Strike three! Jesus said, "Away with you, Satan! For it is written, 'Worship the Lord your God, and serve only him.'"

Judean Desert Today
It's a pretty desolate place, though it's not exactly the Sahara. On a map, if you imagine the Dead Sea as a hot dog, the Judean Desert is like a slightly larger, banana-shaped bun half flanking it on the west. Canyons crisscross it, and the scenery is gorgeous—parts of it look a lot like Utah or Arizona. It has numerous archaeological sites of interest, especially the site of the Jews' stand at Masada.

Israel's Neighbors

MOABITES

Moab was another nation produced by Lot's incest. While archaeology doesn't speak to that, it does describe this Israelite neighbor.

Who Were They?
The Moabites were a Semitic people, closely related to the Israelites and speaking almost the same language. Egyptian records note a conquest of Moab early in its independent existence. The Moabites lived just across the Dead Sea from Israel (modern Jordan) and south of the Ammonites. While often arid, the land of Moab was fertile enough for farming if the rain cooperated. It had some natural resources that facilitated trade, especially of salt and balsam. A relatively powerful nation by the region's standards, it maintained an independent existence from roughly the 13th century B.C. to 581 B.C., when the Babylonians conquered Moab. They worshipped multiple gods; the chief one was called Chemosh.

Where Are They Now?
After the Babylonian conquest, references to Moab become sparse to nonexistent. Over the next centuries, a proto-Arab Semitic people called the Nabateans moved northward into the area and absorbed the remnant Moabite culture into their own. To the extent that one can say modern descendants of the Moabites exist, they would be the region's Arab population. Most of what was once Moab is home to various Bedouin tribes.

Biblical Mentions
Genesis describes the beginning of Moab. Lot's oldest daughter got him drunk and effectively raped him, conceiving a son named Moab, who became the father of the people of that name. The Israelites didn't get on well with the Moabites; numerous Israelite kings declared war on Moab—something Moab feared, with cause, for the Israelites could be fierce and ruthless enemies. (Shades of the future, in which Jordan would not casually tangle with modern Israel.) God wanted the Israelites not to mingle with them, and he did not grant Moabite land to his people. When the Israelites displeased him, he strengthened the Moabites against them. One might say he used Moab to keep his people in line.

From Businessman to Man of God

*Former banking executive Luis Palau
now travels the world spreading the word of God.*

Some call Luis Palau the "Billy Graham of Latin America." While influenced by Graham, Palau set his own unique brand of preaching the Gospel.

Palau was born in Buenos Aires, Argentina, on November 27, 1934. His father, an affluent construction executive, died when Palau was 10. A few years later, Palau became his family's sole support. He was born again at age 12. Palau went to college and became a successful banker. On weekends, he preached to the poor on the streets of his hometown.

Palau journeyed to the United States. He studied at Multnomah Biblical Seminary in Oregon, and then he began a missionary crusade that took him throughout Latin America. He formed an evangelistic team and assisted other evangelists, including Billy Graham, for whom he sometimes worked as a translator during Graham's crusades. Impressed by Palau's work, Graham provided seed money for Palau's ministry.

New Approach to Evangelism

In the 1970s, Palau took his ministry to Europe and other parts of the world. In the 1990s, he placed his focus on the United States, an effort that culminated in a 15-city crusade in 1996. But Palau was dissatisfied, believing he could do more. In 1999, he kicked off an organizational model he called "festival evangelism," which offered an "open arms" approach to religion to appeal to younger people and families. Often held in sports stadiums, the free, interactive events typically feature contemporary musical performances, sports demonstrations by Christian athletes, and fair food, in addition to Palau's sermons.

Luis Palau has been preaching the word of God for more than 40 years, and he now employs more than 100 staff members on four continents. Not bad for a former banker from Buenos Aires.

Not Your Ordinary Tourist Traps

✤ ✤ ✤ ✤

*Biblically themed attractions bring the Good Book
to life in myriad ways.*

Tired of simply reading the Bible? Now you can experience the word of God up close and in person at many biblical theme parks!

One of the largest is The Holy Land Experience in Orlando, Florida. Touted as "a living, biblical museum that takes you 7,000 miles away and 2,000 years back in time to the land of the Bible," The Holy Land Experience aims to educate and inspire through attractions such as the Garden Tomb, Qumran Dead Sea Caves, Jerusalem Model, and Wilderness Tabernacle. In addition, Jesus gets crucified six days a week in a live recreation.

The Bible and Science

The Creation Museum in Petersburg, Kentucky, takes a different tack by incorporating a variety of science-based exhibits to demonstrate that creation is more fact than myth. Attractions include Natural Selection Is Not Evolution; Dinosaur's Den; Noah's Ark Construction Site; and A Walk Through Biblical History, which features "amazing scientific and biblical answers for the world we live in today."

Other smaller biblical attractions in the United States include:

Holy Land USA, Bedford, Virginia: Located on 200 acres in the foothills of the Blue Ridge Mountains, this attraction offers tours that follow the key events in the life of Jesus.

Palestine Park, Chautauqua, New York: Located on the grounds of The Chautauqua Institution, this park features a scale model of the Holy Land. Chautauqua Lake stands in for the Mediterranean Sea, and an artificial stream represents the River Jordan as it flows from the Sea of Galilee to the Dead Sea.

The Great Passion Play, Eureka Springs, Arkansas: Though not technically a theme park, The Great Passion Play has been inspiring audiences for more than 40 years. It incorporates a cast of hundreds to bring to life Christ's last days on earth.

Why Isn't the Bible in Chronological Order?

✤ ✤ ✤ ✤

If you've ever tried to read the Bible like a novel,
you've probably been frustrated or disappointed.

What's Up with That?

A lot of people who set out to read the Bible from cover to cover don't complete their goal. Why? Well, for one, the story keeps getting interrupted by long genealogical lists and ceremonial descriptions. And then there's the whole problem with one book not always picking up where the last one left off. What's up with that?

One simple answer is that the entire Bible is made up of 66 separate books, 39 of which comprise the Old (or Hebrew) Testament and 27 that make up the New (or Christian) Testament. It's not meant to be read as a novel, but as a collection of different types of literature with one overarching theme tying them together: God's interaction with humanity and his unfolding plan to bring his estranged creation back into fellowship with himself.

Outline of the Old Testament

This set of 39 books, which record much of Israel's early history, can be divided into 4 sections:

Section 1: The Pentateuch (or The Law)

The first five books of the Bible—Genesis through Deuteronomy—make up this section. The word Pentateuch is made up of two Greek words: *penta* meaning "five," and *teuchos* meaning "volume" or "book." A lot of content—the Creation, the Flood, the Patriarchs, and Israel's earliest history—is included in these "volumes." They also contain the covenant law God gave to Israel when Moses led them from Egypt into the wilderness and finally to the doorstep of the Promised Land.

Section 2: The Past (History)

While there's plenty of history recorded in the first five books of the Old Testament, the next 12 books—Joshua through Esther—record about 700 years' worth of Israel's history, once they began settling in the Promised Land. This section covers the leadership of a series of judges and priests and then the nation's transition to monarch rule. Ultimately the kingdom breaks apart and the people are carried into exile. First, inhabitants of the northern kingdom are hauled up to Assyria. Later, the southern kingdom is conquered by Babylon until the people are allowed to return home once the Medo-Persians are in charge.

Section 3: The Poetry (or Wisdom Literature)

The books of Job, Psalms, Proverbs, Ecclesiastes, and Song of Solomon make up this section that lies roughly at the middle of the Bible. Like a refreshing pause, they intervene between the hard facts of history and the powerful ministry of the prophets. In fact, the Bible contains some of the most exquisite poetry ever written.

Job, the title character of the book, inspires faith in the face of pain. Want encouragement and comfort? Check out the Psalms. For guiding principles in life, read through Proverbs: There are 31 chapters that can be read one at a time for a monthlong course in wisdom. Philosophers find Ecclesiastes an interesting read. Lovers might be surprised at how eloquent and explicit Song of Songs (or Song of Solomon) is in matters of romance. It's a rich section, especially for poetry lovers.

Section 4: The Prophets

This section is made up of 17 books. Isaiah, Jeremiah, Ezekiel, and Daniel account for the first five books (Jeremiah also wrote Lamentations), and these are called the "major prophets." Following these are 12 other books—Hosea through Malachi—written by what are called the "minor prophets," for a total of 17 books.

Throughout Israel's history, God gave prophets—messengers to his people—to remind them of his Word and his ways and to denounced idolatry while calling them to undivided devotion to himself. Having a timeline handy as you read the prophets (good study Bibles usually include them) can help you understand them in the correct historical setting.

Outline of the New Testament
What about the New Testament? It repeats itself! Well, yes, indeed it does . . . at first, but that also has to do with sections within the 27 books this smaller Testament contains. Here's what it's about.

Section 1: The Four Gospels
Here's the culprit for lots of repetition. In this section, the first three Gospels are called the "synoptic Gospels," meaning they're coming from similar perspectives. They are three accounts of Jesus' ministry, recorded by three different authors. Their overlap has to do with their collection of data from eyewitnesses, some of which came from the same sources or from sources who witnessed the same events. John's Gospel is different and stands out in a number of ways. If you read one of the first three Gospels and then read John's, you won't have the sense of reading the same material twice. (Note: Even the synoptic Gospels have unique content, though, so it's worthwhile to read them all.)

Section 2: Early Church History
The book of Acts, written by the Gospel writer Luke, gives an action-packed account of the start of Christianity and its growth. In this book, we discover how the apostle Paul went from persecuting early believers to propagating their faith.

Playing with Words

Hebrew writers often used words that sounded similar to illustrate their ideas. The prophet Isaiah made an effective point about conditions in the land with the following word play:

"And God looked for justice *(mishpat)*,
but he only found bloodshed *(mishpach)*;
he looked for righteousness *(tsedaqah)*,
but he only found a cry of distress *(tse'aqah)*!"

Section 3: The Apostle Paul's Letters to the Churches

Once Paul embraced Christianity, he traveled as an itinerant messenger—the first missionary, if you will. He was often imprisoned, and sometimes he remained in a place for a time, helping churches get established. While in one place, he often wrote letters to other places he'd been, to encourage believers, correct any wrong notions, and instruct in matters about which they inquired. His letters include Romans through Philemon (13 books), and some scholars attribute Hebrews to him, though the author of that book is not identified.

Section 4: The General Letters

This seven-book section is relatively brief compared with Paul's writings. The books—James through Jude—carry the names of their authors (while Paul's letters bear the names of their recipients). These messages were (for the most part) written to the church in general, not to a specific audience, thus the designation "general" letters.

Section 5: Revelation

This book stands alone in its own section for a reason. It uniquely describes the final outcome of God's redemptive plan and final judgment of evil. At the beginning of the Bible, Genesis describes a God-initiated beginning to the world. Here at the end, Revelation describes its consummation and a re-creation, in which there will be no pain, suffering, or sorrow. Evil will be a thing of the past. God's goodness will overcome and rule for eternity. It's called the Christian's "blessed hope" when Christ returns to establish his eternal kingdom of peace.

If You Still Hanker for Chronology...

OK, so that's the basic outline, and reading just one book or section at a time can be less daunting than trying to tackle the whole Bible at once. *However,* there *is* good news for fans of a more linear approach. You can find Bibles on the market now that orchestrate biblical content so that it flows in a chronological sense wherever possible. This approach places the writings of the prophets and poets alongside the places where they show up in the historical books. It synchronizes Paul's letter writing with his missionary journeys, and so on. It's a great way to read the Good Book.

10 Things

Shocking Bible Stories

It's surprising how much of scripture is . . . well, surprising.

1. Church Couple Drops Dead (Acts 5) In the early days of the Christian movement, people were selling their property and donating to the church. One couple, Ananias and Sapphira, decided to do the same . . . but they held back some of the proceeds. When Ananias made the donation, fudging the numbers, he was struck dead. A few hours later, his wife came in, repeated the lie, and she dropped dead too. The stern lesson for believers: *Don't lie to God.*

2. King David Falls Hard (2 Samuel 11—12) He was Israel's best king, "a man after God's own heart," and yet he spied a neighbor woman bathing and he wanted her. King David committed adultery with Bathsheba—but then things got even worse. In a desperate attempt at cover-up, the king arranged for her soldier-husband to be killed in battle. Then he took Bathsheba as his queen. The ruse would have worked—except for a prophet who challenged the king and provoked his repentance (see Psalm 51).

3. Helper Zapped by Ark (2 Samuel 6:6–8) The Ark of the Covenant was a sacred chest containing mementos of Israel's history. No one was to touch it, under penalty of death. For a time, the army carried it into battle, until it was captured . . . and then *given back* because it brought a curse on the enemy. King David finally decided to bring it to his new capital, Jerusalem, in a great celebration, but the ox pulling the cart stumbled. A man named Uzzah reached out to steady the Ark—and died on the spot. David was mad at God for that.

4. Adventures in Matchmaking (Hosea 1—3) God told the prophet Hosea to marry a prostitute. This instruction came with a warning that she would be unfaithful and bear illegitimate children. It was all a life-size object lesson for Israel. The nation had been unfaithful to God, following after idols, but God still loved them madly.

5. Moses Rocks Out (Numbers 20) As the Israelites wandered through the wilderness, they constantly needed to find sources of food and water. On occasion, God miraculously provided for them. Once, the Lord told Moses merely to speak to a rock and it would gush water. But, angry with the people's complaints, Moses struck the rock twice. As a result, the Lord prevented Moses from entering the Promised Land.

6. The Talking Donkey (Numbers 22) Balaam was a prophet hired by an enemy to curse Israel. The Lord didn't want him to go and sent an angel to block the road. The prophet didn't see the angel, but his donkey did, stopping in his tracks. When Balaam beat him, he moved on. This happened three times, until the donkey said, "What have I done to you, that you have struck me these three times?" After a brief conversation with the animal, Balaam saw the angel and turned around.

7. The Sun Stands Still (Joshua 10:12–14) Scholars still puzzle over this one. Israel's army was winning a battle, but there wasn't enough time in the day to complete the victory. Joshua prayed for the sun to stand still, and it did, for about a day.

8. Jonah's Bad Attitude (Jonah 1—4) When God told Jonah to preach to the most wicked city on earth, he went sailing in the opposite direction. Tossed overboard, swallowed by a big fish, and vomited onto the shore, the prophet finally realized he couldn't outrun God. So he preached in Nineveh, and they repented! It was a smashing success, except Jonah was angry about it. He didn't really want God to forgive the Ninevites.

9. Bad News Bears (2 Kings 2:23–25) The prophet Elisha was going about his own business when a gang of boys began jeering at him. "Go away, baldhead!" (Head-shaving was probably a ritual for prophets at this time, so they were mocking his religion, not his appearance.) He uttered a curse on them, and immediately two bears came out of the woods and mauled 42 of them.

10. Wall Fall (Joshua 6) When the Israelites entered the Promised Land, they immediately came up against the walled city of Jericho. How would they ever defeat it? The Lord gave Joshua a plan, and it sounded pretty crazy. March *around* the city each day for six days, and on the seventh day march seven times. Then blow your trumpets and the walls will fall. That's just what happened: *The walls came a-tumblin' down.*

From Arrogance to Babbling

✣ ✣ ✣ ✣

In primeval times, the people, who all speak one language,
begin to build a tower that will reach to the heavens. Affronted
by their arrogance, God stops the work by confusing the builders'
language, which results in what sounds like babbling.
The city is thereafter known as Babel.

Historians believe that some of the first cities in the world were built around 3000 B.C. in Sumer, which is situated on the southern plains along the Tigris and Euphrates Rivers. And the largest and most important of these first cities were Babylon, Nippur, and Ur, where Abraham would later be born. This history accords perfectly with the story of the Tower of Babel.

Overreaching City Planners

According to Genesis, in the era after the Great Flood, Noah's descendants settle on the plain of Shinar (Hebrew for "Sumer"). They all lived in peace and harmony and spoke the same language. As the population grew, some of the people said, "Come, let us build ourselves a city, and a tower with its top in the heavens, and let us make a name for ourselves" (Genesis 11:4). Such a grand structure, these planners said, would make them powerful and keep them from being scattered. And so they began making mud bricks and using them to build a city that centered on a skyscraper tower.

When God saw what the people were constructing, he was miffed. How could they be arrogant enough to believe they could build a tower that would reach to heaven? He realized that these people only wanted to please themselves, and they could accomplish almost anything because they were united by the same language.

God decided to "go down" (Genesis 11:7) and address the situation. The fact that he must go "down" to the city shows that the people were falling far short of their ambition to build a tower that reached into the heavens. Be that as it may, to make it more difficult for the builders to communicate and get things done, God decided to "confuse" their speech so that everyone spoke a different language. The Hebrew word for confuse is *balal,* and from then on the city was known as Babel (which sounds like *balal*). Even though the mixture of strange languages sounds like babbling to the people who have never before heard languages other than their own, the name Babel does not mean babbling, but confusion—which is close! Babel is the Hebrew name for Babylon.

Because the people no longer spoke a common language, they no longer understood one another, and the building of the tower came to an abrupt halt. God then scattered these proud people all over the world—the very thing they had tried to prevent by building their city. However, God, being merciful, later mitigated the punishment he inflicted on the arrogant builders of Babel by extending his grace to the descendants of Abraham.

Later Resonances

The Babylonians of later times would not have accepted Genesis' explanation of their city's name. In their own language the name is Babilu, which means "the gate of god," referring to the chief Babylonian god, Marduk. In the sixth century B.C., the Babylonians built a great nation and, ironically, reenacted their earlier story. They took entire nations into servitude, forcing them to build cities and monuments in order to spread their fame throughout the world—and history. They made a name for themselves, but once again they were stopped by God, who sent Cyrus the Great of Persia to conquer them.

The New Testament gives a kind of reversal of this story. In the Acts of the Apostles, Peter addressed people who spoke many different languages yet each person understood Peter in his own language. Other disciples spoke in tongues. All of them followed Jesus' instructions to scatter and spread the Gospel to all peoples. The difference between the stories is this: In the story of the tower, the multiple languages and scattering are used to punish people who were promoting their own agenda. In the New Testament, languages and scattering are used to promote God's agenda, spreading the Gospel, which will eventually result in world unity.

Quiz

Women I

Leaders, judges, mothers, teachers—they made things happen.

1. One judge of Israel sang a song extolling the heroism of *another* woman who tricked and killed an enemy commander. Who were these two women?
    - a. Miriam and Rahab
    - b. Deborah and Jael
    - c. Hannah and Abigail
    - d. Jezebel and Elisha

2. Jacob loved one sister, but he had to marry the other one first. Who were these two sisters?
    - a. Rachel and Leah
    - b. Dinah and Rebekah
    - c. Mary and Martha
    - d. Lydia and Dorcas

3. In the tabernacle, this woman prayed so fervently to have a son that Eli the priest thought she was drunk.
    - a. Delilah
    - b. Michal
    - c. Hannah
    - d. Mary Magdalene

4. The Christians were praying that Peter would be released from prison, and then there was a knock at the gate. Rhoda, the maid, answered and saw Peter there. What did she do next?
    - a. ran to tell the others, leaving him knocking at the gate
    - b. yelled for the soldiers to come and arrest him again
    - c. sang an improvisational song of praise, recorded in Acts 12
    - d. became a Christian herself

Fast Facts

- The hymn "Be Not Afraid" was inspired by the phrase "Do not be afraid," which is repeated in the Bible a total of 365 times. That's the same number of days in the year. Coincidence? You decide.

- Numbers are of great significance in the Bible. The number 7, for example, is often used as a symbol of completion, hence the superstition that 7 is a lucky number. The number 40 is also frequently mentioned in the Bible, and it is usually associated with a new beginning. For example, Jesus fasted for 40 days in the desert, the Great Flood was caused by 40 days and nights of rain, and Jonah warned Nineveh they had 40 days before being punished by God.

- Speaking of Jonah, it's unlikely that he was swallowed by a whale, as is commonly believed by many, because whales are rarely sighted in the Mediterranean Sea today and were probably unknown in biblical times. Many Bibles don't mention a whale at all, noting instead that Jonah was swallowed by a "great fish" or "large sea monster."

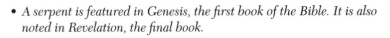

- A serpent is featured in Genesis, the first book of the Bible. It is also noted in Revelation, the final book.

- The star of Bethlehem, which guided the wise men to Jesus' birthplace, was likely not just a regional event. There are records of astronomers in China observing an unusually bright light in the sky at around the same time period. However, they thought little of it.

- The Old Testament contains three different types of books: 17 historical books, 5 poetical books, and 17 prophetic books.

- The dove is best remembered as the bird that informed Noah that the waters of the Great Flood were receding. However, the dove wasn't the first animal released from the ark—that honor goes to the raven, which angered Noah by flying back and forth rather than doing the job it was assigned. Good PR for doves, not so much for ravens.

Animated Theology

✤ ✤ ✤ ✤

*Several contemporary cartoon series have taken
satirical swipes at the Bible. But it's (mostly) all in good fun.*

Television cartoon series are well known for taking humorous jabs at almost all aspects of contemporary society. Until recently, however, one topic—religion—was strictly verboten. And for good reason: No one wanted to risk offending viewers and advertisers, regardless of faith.

Boy, how times have changed! Today, God, Jesus, and a host of other religious characters are regularly featured on shows such as *The Simpsons, South Park,* and *Family Guy.* Sometimes they're the focus of a story, other times they're the butt of a quick joke. Is it funny or offensive? That's for you to decide.

Homer Meets God

The Simpsons, which has never been afraid to poke gentle fun at all aspects of religion, was one of the first animated series to actually show God. In a season four episode titled "Homer the Heretic," Homer abandons his faith and starts his own religion. At the end of the episode, God visits Homer in a dream. God is shown only from the beard down and has five fingers, while every other cartoon character has four. While chatting with Homer, God scratches the Simpsons' cat on the head, and he admits that sometimes he'd rather spend Sundays watching football instead of being in church. This episode was well received by viewers, and God has been featured in several episodes since.

The *South Park* Perspective

Jesus is regularly featured in *South Park,* the irreverent series created by Trey Parker and Matt Stone. In fact, according to the show, Jesus actually lives in the small Colorado town, where he once hosted a public access call-in show titled "Jesus and Pals." Sadly, despite Jesus' good intentions, the residents of South Park rarely took his advice. Other biblical characters often featured on *South Park* include God, Satan, and Moses.

God, Jesus, and even Death also make frequent appearances on *Family Guy,* created by Seth MacFarlane. God is presented as a regular guy in a white robe who just happens to be omnipotent. In more than one episode, he has been shown using his powers to pick up women in bars. He also apparently drives an Escalade.

Jesus is portrayed with equal irreverence. In one episode it is alleged that most of his miracles were actually poorly performed magic tricks. In a 2008 episode, titled "I Dream of Jesus," Jesus returns to earth in the form of a record-store owner. After it is revealed that he has returned, fame goes to Jesus' head and he starts behaving badly, eventually landing in jail. At the episode's conclusion, Jesus acknowledges that the world isn't ready for him and he isn't ready for the world. He promises to return in another thousand years.

Thinking Man's Theology

Most cartoon biblical references are played just for laughs, but occasionally some genuinely thought-provoking theology presents itself. In a very popular episode of *Futurama,* titled "Godfellas," Bender the robot finds himself adrift in space as a civilization of tiny human-like creatures grows on his body and eventually comes to worship him as a god. At first, Bender treats the tiny people poorly, forcing them to do his bidding. Then he comes to love them, and feels badly when his attempts to help them fail. Eventually, Bender encounters an entity that he and the viewer assume to be God. Bender explains what has happened to him and expresses remorse at his inability to help in any meaningful way the little people who lived on him. Before returning Bender to earth, God tells him that he had a similar experience and has since stopped interfering in the lives of those who pray to him. "When you do things right," God explains, "people won't be sure you've done anything at all."

Not surprisingly, the cartoon portrayals of God, Jesus, and other biblical characters have received mixed reactions from viewers. Some have been warmly received ("Godfellas" won the first Writers Guild of America award for animation in 2003), while others have been criticized by various religious organizations. Ultimately, it all depends on your degree of faith—and your sense of humor.

Solomon's Temple

❧ ❧ ❧ ❧

Today, neither Solomon's temple nor the second temple exist.
The Western Wall (Wailing Wall) is all that remains of Herod's
expansion of the temple in 19 B.C. The site, however, remains
a holy place not just for Jews, but for Christians and Muslims
as well. The first temple began as a dream of King David.
It would take his son, Solomon, to realize it.

Judgment of Solomon

Solomon is best known for being a wise king with a knack for solving troublesome problems. He prayed to God not for strength or victory against his enemies but for wisdom. God granted it. With it, he famously judged a disagreement between two prostitutes. One woman's baby had died when she accidentally suffocated him in her sleep. She switched her dead son with another, then both mothers went to Solomon to settle the issue. Unable to determine whose son it really was, Solomon called for a sword and ordered the baby split in two, each woman receiving half. The mother of the dead son agreed, but the baby's real mother begged Solomon to spare the child and give him to the fake mother. Solomon knew the real mother would not allow her baby to be killed and gave her the boy.

Temple of Solomon

Solomon spearheaded many building projects during his reign, including fortifications, stables, and a palace. The most significant architectural achievement was the temple of Jerusalem.

Solomon's father, David, the king before him, planned to build a temple to house the Ark of the Covenant. David died before that could become a reality. Solomon enlisted the help of Hiram, a master builder, to construct it. During construction, God told Solomon that if he obeyed him, God would "not forsake" the people of Israel. Solomon, however, was caught up with his many wives and earthly pursuits. Solomon even worshipped other gods.

When Solomon died, because he had not kept his agreement with God, succession of power was not smooth. Israel was divided. Enemies rose up against her. Several hundred years later, in 597 B.C., Solomon's temple was destroyed by the Babylonians, sending the Israelites into exile.

Second Temple

The Persians supplanted Babylonian rule and provided aid to their Jewish subjects to build a new temple in 516 B.C. King Herod, a local king who ruled only at the permission of the Roman Empire, greatly expanded the second temple, largely as a monument to himself. Though historically he was an awful, forgettable king, his temple was an extraordinary sight so marvelous that 90 years later when Titus's army stormed Jerusalem to quell the Jewish rebellion in A.D. 70, he ordered the temple be preserved. Nevertheless, the temple did not survive the siege and was leveled.

A Muslim Caliph built the Dome of the Rock on the site; it was a shrine for religious pilgrims in the seventh century. The Caliph opened the city of Jerusalem to both Jews and Christians.

Beginning in the 11th century, the papacy called for a series of Crusades to capture the Holy Land. Though the Crusades are often associated with chivalry, there was nothing gallant about it. There are stories of victorious crusaders wading knee-deep in bodies around the Temple Mount. Killing was the order of the day. A cross was added to the Dome. The holy place that had once fallen into ruin prior to the erection of the Dome, was now a revered symbol of Christian might and right. The Knights Templar took residence in a nearby mosque, swearing to protect the roads to Jerusalem. The Muslim general Saladin retook Jerusalem in 1187, and several bloody campaigns followed.

The region has traded hands among Muslims, Christians, and Jews. Today, the Dome of the Rock sits in Israel-controlled Jerusalem, but the Dome itself remains under Islamic authority. There exist certain Jewish groups that wish to build a third temple, but this is complicated by political and religious realities.

Shofar Lessons, Anyone?

✤ ✤ ✤ ✤

*From these earliest designs of stringed, wind, and percussion
instruments, it's not hard to see the origins of our own
modern music-making devices.*

Strummin' on the Ol' Kinnor: Stringed Instruments

1. The *kinnor* is mentioned very early in the Bible—in Genesis 4—
and appears 40 times in the Old Testament. Various English Bible
translations use the words "lyre" and "harp" as nearest equiva-
lents. This little precursor to the modern harp was small enough
to be toted around and was made of a wood frame and sounding
box with camel-gut strings stretched between them.

2. The *nebel*—translated in various places as "harp," "lyre," "psal-
tery," and "viol"—gets 27 mentions in the Old Testament. Scholars surmise that this instrument was likely plucked and was the
bass of the harp world, with more and larger strings (made of
sheep gut) for a deeper sound. Frames of early versions of the *nebel* were made of cypress, but later almug was the wood of choice.

76 Shofars: Wind Instruments

1. The *khalil, ugab,* and *mashroquita* all refer to types of flutes
or musical pipes. It's not clear in any instance of these terms
whether the instrument in use is more like a flute, clarinet, oboe,
whistle, or pipe. It *is* clear, however, that wind instruments were
played for all kinds of occasions—in worship, at weddings, and for
funerals. For a sampling of flute music that may sound something
like what the Hebrew people played, one can listen to the local
shepherds of the modern Near East, playing their pipes as they
tend their flocks.

2. The *qeren,* a signaling trumpet, was made of metal, wood, or a
real animal's horn. It wasn't generally used in music ensembles,
though.

3. The *shofar* is made of a ram's horn and is usually translated "trumpet" in our English Bibles. Its distinctive shape isn't accidental:

The animal's horn is softened with steam, and the wide end is bent at a right angle to the rest of the horn. It was the instrument of choice for sounding war signals and alarms. It also had ceremonial distinctions, announcing sacred festivals, gatherings, and special occasions of national importance.

4. The *hatsotsera* are more like our modern trumpets and were made of metal. Moses had two of these made out of silver for signaling the camps of Israel when they were traveling in the wilderness.

The Beat of a Different Toph: Percussion

1. Percussion instruments seem to have been gender-specific in their use. The *toph* or *top* was a tambourinelike instrument that was generally used by women in all kinds of celebrations.

2. The *mesiltayim* or *selselim* were cymbals played only by menfolk. The words for these instruments sound a good deal like the hissing, clashing sound they made. These were two-piece instruments that were struck together, very much like our modern-day cymbals.

Toe-Tappin' Worship

Psalm 150—the final psalm—gives us a glimpse of Hebrew worshippers at their music:

Praise the Lord!
Praise God in his sanctuary;
praise him in his mighty firmament!
Praise him for his mighty deeds;
praise him according to his surpassing greatness!
Praise him with trumpet sound;
praise him with lute and harp!
Praise him with tambourine and dance;
praise him with strings and pipe!
Praise him with clanging cymbals;
praise him with loud clashing cymbals!
Let everything that breathes praise the Lord!
Praise the Lord!

Wow! Now *there's* a worship service you wouldn't want to miss!

A Great Enemy

❖ ❖ ❖ ❖

This ancient empire made life hell for the Jews of the Old Testament.

Babylonia was a cultural area in what is now known as Iraq. Its
capital city, Babylon, was probably founded about 2,300 years before
the birth of Christ. Situated on the banks of the Euphrates River, it
was about 50 miles south of modern Baghdad, and it was a monument to power, wealth, and luxury. The Babylonians themselves
spoke the Akkadian language and called their city "Babilu," or "the
gate of God," but that's not what the Hebrews called it. According
to Genesis 11:1–9, God cursed the Babylonians for their arrogance
and ambition when they tried to build a tower to heaven: "The Lord
came down to see the city and the tower, which mortals had built.
And the Lord said, 'Look, they are one people, and they have all one
language; and this is only the beginning of what they will do; nothing
that they propose to do will now be impossible for them. Come, let
us go down, and confuse their language there, so that they will not
understand one another's speech.' . . . Therefore it was called Babel,
because there the Lord confused the language of all the earth."

A Symbol as Well as a City

To the ancient Hebrews, Babylon was more than a city. It was a
symbol of evil. But an objective look at Babylonian culture reveals a
society that was constantly evolving and making great strides in the
areas of agriculture, architecture, astronomy, biology, chemistry, law,
mathematics, and medicine. Eight immense gates surrounded the
perimeter of Babylon, the greatest of them called the Ishtar Gate.
The Hanging Gardens of Babylon, one of the original Seven Wonders of the Ancient World, were built by King Nebuchadnezzar II
around 600 B.C. as a present for his homesick wife, Amytis of Media
(Amytis longed for the lush landscape of her native Persia). The
hanging gardens were 100 feet by 100 feet wide and built in tiers,
the highest of which was about 75 feet tall. A sophisticated system of
conduits and pumps was used to carry water from the Euphrates to

the top of the gardens. Inside the walls of Babylon, astronomers and mathematicians worked on books and maps that they hoped would explain the workings of the heavens and the earth. More practical scientists advised government leaders and farmers on how they could make their agricultural endeavors more efficient.

The Babylonians, along with the Egyptians, were extremely interested in medicine, and over the centuries they made many advances in the area. Physicians began to understand the value of regular examinations, and the concepts of diagnosis and prognosis were introduced to the general Babylonian public. Doctors were constantly developing new kinds of bandages, splints, creams, and pills with which to treat their patients. Many books were written on medicine, the most famous of all being Esagil-kin-apli's *Diagnostic Handbook,* but the Babylonians wrote books on all kinds of subjects. They were a relatively literate people, and most towns in the region had their own libraries, with scribes to take care of them and serve those who patronized them. Many girls, especially those in the upper class, were taught to read alongside their brothers.

The Other Side

There was a dark side to the Babylonian Empire, however, and the ancient Hebrews became its victims. In 587 B.C., the Babylonians, led by Nebuchadnezzar II, conquered the southern part of Israel, which was called Judah. They looted and burned Jerusalem and destroyed Solomon's temple. It is not known whether the Ark of the Covenant—the ornate chest that held the stone tablets on which the Ten Commandments were written—was destroyed, but it disappeared without a trace either at that time or soon after. When Jerusalem was sacked, thousands of upper-class Jews were kidnapped and forced to relocate to Babylon; this is now commonly referred to as the Exile.

One of the Hebrews who witnessed these events, Jeremiah, recorded his people's experiences during the Exile in the Bible. God spoke to Jeremiah through a Babylonian soldier: "The Lord your

God threatened this place with this disaster; and now the Lord has brought it about, and has done as he said, because all of you sinned against the Lord and did not obey his voice" (Jeremiah 40:2–3).

Jeremiah was lucky enough to escape captivity, but those (approximately) 14,600 Jews who were taken to Babylon in several deportations would endure 50 years of exile. Judah was no longer an independent kingdom but a province of Babylonia, and many of those Jews left behind were too scared to stay in their homeland. They instead chose to flee to surrounding lands such as Ammon, Edom, and Moab. This was the beginning of what would be called the Jewish Diaspora, or the scattering of the Jews across the earth.

New Place, Same Faith

The Jewish exiles in Babylon at first felt lost without the temple of Jerusalem as their spiritual center, but they quickly adapted and the Jewish religion was forced to evolve. No longer able to make animal sacrifices at the temple, the Jews began to focus on rituals such as the Sabbath, dietary laws, and circumcision. These were things that the Babylonians could not take away from them, a way to set themselves apart and remind their children that they were strangers in a strange land. Some Jewish exiles dreamed of the day when they would return to Jerusalem and rebuild the temple. They solidified their belief that their God was the one and only true God, and they began looking for an earthly messiah who would lead them back home.

Though Jewish life in Babylon during the Exile is portrayed in the Bible as slavery, when Persia's Cyrus the Great ended the Exile in 538 B.C., only a small number of Jews chose to return to Judah. Those who had profited financially or intermarried with the Babylonians saw no reason to leave the beautiful city they'd been forced to make their own.

"Abba, Father"

The Aramaic word *abba* is an intimate form of the word *ab*, which means "father." It was an informal term of intimacy and respect used by children, something like da-da or daddy. Jesus used this term in Mark 14:36 to describe the intimacy that believers could have with God the Father.

Where Jesus Walked

Capernaum

It was Jesus' home base—at least, until its members offended him.

In Biblical Times
Biblical Capernaum (or Capharnaum) was a relatively young city in Jesus' day, established sometime around 200 B.C. It lasted over a thousand years before dying out, ironically enough, just before the Crusader era (roughly A.D. 1050). Capernaum meant food; fishing and agriculture were the main activities. It was never a wealthy place, going by what archaeologists have found; it had few luxurious houses. It did have a Roman tax office, so it wasn't insignificant. If it weren't for Jesus, however, ancient Capernaum would be just another ancient ruin on the Sea of Galilee.

Jesus' Connection
After Christ got fed up with the Nazarenes, he moved to Capernaum. Shortly after arriving, he met some fishers and suggested they fish for people. Fortunately, Simon Peter and Andrew interpreted his words correctly—they became disciples. For some time, Jesus lived in Capernaum, and it was the site of several healing miracles in scripture. He walked on the Sea of Galilee to get there and preached an important sermon in which he foretold the Eucharist by describing his flesh and blood as the bread and drink of eternal life. Many followers deserted him at Capernaum for saying this, but the 12 disciples held on, even as Jesus pointed out that one of them (Judas, obviously) was a "devil." Jesus also got fed up with Capernaum for failing to repent of sin, warning its residents that Sodom would have a happier judgment day than Capernaum. Ouch.

Capernaum Today
Kfar Nachum (basically "Nahumville" in Hebrew) is an excavated ruin, located in northern Israel on the Sea of Galilee's north shore. The ruins of one of the world's oldest synagogues are in the ruins of Capernaum, which may be on the site of the one in which Jesus preached, though this is in dispute. The house of St. Peter, over which an octagonal church thrived for centuries, is a stone's throw from this synagogue.

A History That Asks Why

❧ ❧ ❧ ❧

In the 20th century, biblical scholars realized that the books of Deuteronomy through 2 Kings constitute a single history of Israel that begins just before the entrance into the Promised Land and ends with the Babylonian Exile. Known as the Deuteronomistic History, this long work brings together older histories and edits them in an attempt to understand why God let his people be taken into exile.

Jewish leaders couldn't figure out what had happened. They believed that God would protect them and his temple in Jerusalem, but both the temple and the city had been leveled and they were living in exile. Worst of all, their own culture was in danger of being lost. To preserve it and figure out what had happened, they sifted through ancient writings and reshaped them into a comprehensive history of their people.

History in a Nutshell

The Deuteronomistic History takes its title from the book of Deuteronomy, which introduces the collection. In it Moses addresses his people, retelling the history of the Exodus and the 40 years in the wilderness and reviewing—and updating—the commandments God had given him. Moses stresses the covenant the Israelites have made with God: In return for protection in their new land, the people must only worship Yahweh and obey his commandments. As the Israelites get ready to cross into the Promised Land, Moses dies.

The book of Joshua, which follows, tells how the Israelites enter the Promised Land of Canaan, conquer the people who live there, and settle the land, dividing it into 12 tribal areas—relating to the 12 sons of Jacob (Israel). The book of Judges tells how the tribes live separately under leaders called judges, who not only settle legal cases but also serve as military leaders. Unfortunately, the people frequently break God's covenant. Whenever this happens, they fall into trouble with local enemies; eventually they return to God, who forgives them. A cyclical pattern thus evolves.

The books of Samuel relate how the first two kings of Israel are anointed by Samuel, who is a prophet, priest, and Israel's last judge. Saul falls out of favor with God, but David, his successor, extends his kingdom, establishes Jerusalem as his capital, and prospers.

The books of Kings tell of the reigns of subsequent kings. David's son, Solomon, is noted for his wealth and wisdom, but he overburdens the people with taxes and forced labor in order to construct a temple, sumptuous palaces, and other buildings. When Solomon dies and his son Rehoboam refuses to soften Solomon's policies, the ten northern tribes break away and form their own kingdom, which they call Israel. David's heirs continue to rule the southern kingdom, called Judah. The remainder of the books of Kings shows how the northern kings frequently breach God's covenant until their kingdom is eventually conquered by the Assyrians. Although Judah prospers for some time after that, it is eventually decimated by the Babylonians, who take most of the people into exile.

A Theory Is Developed

For about 2,000 years, readers of the Bible had assumed that Deuteronomy was part of the Pentateuch (the first five books of the Bible) and that the books Joshua through 2 Kings had all been written by different authors at different times. In 1943, that changed. German biblical scholar Martin Noth showed that Joshua through 2 Kings (except for Ruth) had a uniform style and outlook. He then concluded that they constitute a single history. Furthermore, Noth claimed that Deuteronomy, which shares the same style and outlook, had been written as an introduction to the history, connecting the history to the Pentateuch. Today most scholars agree with Noth's evaluation, though most believe that the history evolved gradually.

A First Edition

Although the Deuteronomistic History as it appears in the Bible today was basically completed during the Babylonian Exile, an earlier edition may have been written centuries earlier. Soon after Israel was divided into two kingdoms, Jeroboam, the first ruler of the northern kingdom of Israel, scandalized orthodox believers by building shrines containing images of calves. This seemed to be a clear violation of the Law of Moses that forbids the making of images.

Jeroboam also appointed priests from among the people instead of using priests from the tribe of Levi as required by Mosaic Law.

It seems likely that the Levitic priests, who were replaced, joined to preserve their revered traditions by collecting materials for a kind of history. The descendants of these ousted priests continued the work and brought it to Jerusalem when they moved there sometime before the northern kingdom completely fell to the Assyrians in 721 B.C. Soon after, these so-called Deuteronomists may have written a history to explain why the northern kingdom had fallen.

The materials collected by the Deuteronomists included chronicles and court histories, military records, territorial lists, cycles of stories about the prophets Elijah and Elisha, and ancient songs (including the Song of Deborah). The first version of the history was probably completed during the reign of King Josiah of Judah.

Revisions Sorely Needed

The optimism of the Deuteronomists was dashed when Josiah was killed in battle. The next four kings were not good ones, and Jerusalem fell to the Babylonians, who took most of the Israelites into exile. To make the history understandable in the light of Jerusalem's fall, the Deuteronomists revised the history. They blamed Jerusalem's fall on Josiah's grandfather, King Manasseh, whom they painted in the darkest colors. But Manasseh's "evil" reign had preceded Josiah's golden reign, so the reasoning did not hold.

From exile, the Deuteronomists worked on a more thorough revision of their history. The changes show that it was not merely the kings who had done wrong, but the people as a whole. The history seems to end on a note of hope that if the people turn back to God during this time of exile, he will again forgive them and again restore them to his favor.

Final Touches

After the exile ended, the revised history was returned to Jerusalem, where it was joined to the Pentateuch, with more changes and additions being made to smooth out the fusion. The final text, which we have today, shows a loving God who continues to care for his people, even though they constantly move away from him. God is always seen as loving and faithful in the Deuteronomistic History.

Just How Many Zechariahs Are There in the Bible?

⚜ ⚜ ⚜ ⚜

Zechariah deserves a place in the record books as the most popular name in the Bible! Other names get used a lot too.

If you time-travel back into the biblical era and a man you don't recognize greets you as an old acquaintance, try addressing him as Zechariah. You may just get it right.

Even allowing for the possibility of confusing a single person for two different people, there are 33 Zechariahs in the Bible. Among them are a priest who is stoned to death for criticizing King Joash's idolatry, a short-lived king of Israel, and the minor prophet who urges the rebuilding of Jerusalem after the Babylonian exile. The sole New Testament Zechariah is the father of John the Baptist.

Many Among More
If you have trouble sorting out the New Testament's seven Marys, its five men named James, or if you keep confusing Jude (author of the New Testament letter) with the five men named Judas (traitor, disciple, both, or neither), you ain't seen nothin' yet. Happily, the Bible has only one Abraham and one Ichabod (the priest Eli's grandson), but many other biblical figures share names—often names that are difficult to pronounce. Just among the A's, there are eight Abijahs and eight Adaiahs (who?) and more than two dozen Azariahs (Zechariah's runner-up). There are also ten or more Josephs and more than a dozen Jonathans.

Jesus Too?
You're not even safe with the name Jesus. Did you think there was only one Jesus? Wrong! The thief Pilate releases in place of Jesus shares the Lord's name. He is Jesus Barabbas, which translates as Jesus, Son of the Father (Matthew 27:17). There is also a Jesus Justus, who works with Paul, and in the Old Testament there are more than a dozen Joshuas and Jeshuas—Hebrew forms of the name Jesus.

Quiz

Women II

More leaders, judges, mothers, teachers—they made things happen.

1. Who said, "Lord, already there is a stench because he has been dead four days"?
   - a. Sapphira
   - b. Jezebel
   - c. Martha
   - d. the widow of Nain

2. Rahab was a resident of Jericho who harbored two Israelite spies. What was her profession?
   - a. prostitute
   - b. poet
   - c. planter
   - d. prophetess

3. At the funeral of Dorcas (aka Tabitha), people were holding up items she had made. What were these items?
   - a. decorative stones of remembrance
   - b. clothing
   - c. household idols
   - d. scrolls of scripture

4. One biblical character is commended for the "faith that lived first in your grandmother Lois and your mother Eunice and now, I am sure, lives in you." Who was Lois's grandchild?
   - a. John the Baptist
   - b. Simon Peter
   - c. Timothy
   - d. the rich young ruler

Answers: 1. c (John 11:39); 2. a (Joshua 2:1); 3. b (Acts 9:39); 4. c (2 Timothy 1:5)

Fall from Grace

Jimmy Swaggart was the self-appointed judge of America's televangelists—until his own indiscretions brought him down.

One of the most successful "televangelists" was Jimmy Swaggart, a preacher known for his fire-and-brimstone sermons. He was one of the first to take advantage of what television had to offer—and was also one of the first to watch his ministry stumble as a result of personal scandal.

Child Preacher

Swaggart was born on March 15, 1935, in Ferriday, Louisiana. He began preaching on street corners at the age of nine, and he pursued evangelism full-time in 1955. His ministry slowly grew, and by the late 1960s, he had turned to television and radio to help him spread the word of God. A passionate speaker and vociferous social critic, Swaggart's sermons struck a popular nerve. By 1975, Swaggart's television ministry had expanded, and he soon found himself one of the most popular evangelists in the country.

Swaggart had exposed the foibles of a fellow evangelist, but he didn't keep his own house clean. In 1988, his ministry was rocked to the core when it was revealed that Swaggart had been seeing a New Orleans prostitute. Swaggart offered a tearful television apology and was suspended then defrocked by the national presbytery of the Assemblies of God.

Scandal Redux

Swaggart became a nondenominational Pentecostal minister and worked to repair the damage to his battered ministry. However, scandal hit once more when, in 1991, he was found in the presence of a prostitute during a visit to California. When the news became public, Swaggart temporarily stepped down as the head of Jimmy Swaggart Ministries to seek "healing and counseling."

Swaggart can still be seen on television and heard on the radio. His audience, while devoted, is not nearly as large as it once was.

Sing It Loud!

❧ ❧ ❧ ❧

Gospel music in its varied forms has inspired millions
of Christians since the genre's birth in the 1800s.

Music has long played an essential role in organized religion, and its place in Christianity is especially strong. Hymns, for example, have been an important part of most church services for generations, but a unique variation known as gospel music helped bring the Lord's message to a wider, more diverse audience.

Gospel music dates back to the Negro spirituals of the 1800s, which evolved from the hymns learned when slaves were often required by their owners to attend Christian church services. Later in the century, revival and camp meeting songs became popular, and it was from these musical declarations of praise and worship, sung with unreserved gusto, that contemporary gospel music was born.

In the Beginning

The word "gospel" in music is believed to have first been coined in the 1870s. At that time, the musical form was really starting to take shape, thanks to a number of especially talented pioneers such as Charles A. Tindley, George F. Root, P. P. Bliss, and Ira Sankey.

In the 1930s, composer/performer Thomas A. Dorsey, whose songs include such classics as "There Will Be Peace in the Valley" and "If you See My Savior," took gospel music to a whole new level. Originally a bluesman, Dorsey worked with some of the nation's all-time great blues singers, including Bessie Smith and Ma Rainey. Later, he turned to writing religious music that was heavily influenced in composition by the jazz and blues so popular in that era. At first, many conservative churchgoers didn't care for Dorsey's new gospel style, but it eventually caught on and today is considered a cornerstone of the genre.

Thanks in large part to Dorsey's fearless approach, other composers found themselves unrestricted and eager to push gospel in new and exciting directions. As a musical form, it evolved and stretched but never lost its spiritual heart and soul. Helping it along was the ever-growing popularity of radio, the only source of entertainment for many Americans.

National Respectability

By the 1950s, gospel had become established as a thriving musical force. So popular was gospel that singer Mahalia Jackson—one of the most celebrated gospel singers of her generation—produced several best-selling albums for Columbia Records and even performed on *The Ed Sullivan Show* and other national stages.

Today, gospel music remains as popular as ever. At first a predominantly African American musical form, it has become integrated to the point that race really isn't a factor. Numerous radio stations nationwide feature nothing but gospel, and many fans are excitedly rediscovering the genre's earliest stars. Meanwhile, gospel music continues to go in unique and varied directions as musicians and composers declare their love of God through their work.

Different Styles of Gospel

Modern students of gospel music like to divide the genre into various subcategories. Among them:

- Urban contemporary gospel, sometimes known as "black gospel."
- Christian country music, also known as country gospel, is characterized by a distinct country influence. It is sometimes also known as "inspirational country." In the 1990s, Christian country was so popular that many secular country musicians released gospel albums, including Larry Gatlin and Barbara Mandrell.
- Southern gospel, which typically describes how God helps people overcome daily problems and difficult times. It's a popular crossover style of music.
- Bluegrass gospel, which has its roots in traditional rural mountain music. If it ain't got a banjo and a whole lot of praisin', it ain't bluegrass gospel.
- Gospel blues, a hybrid of blues music with religious lyrics.

Gospel music has many different roots and influences, but one thing is certain—it's distinctly American music. It remains very popular inside church and out, and it never seems to go out of style. Indeed, as long as people feel the need to sing the praises of God and Jesus, gospel music will continue to be a major force in the arts.

Objects of Their Affection

❧ ❧ ❧ ❧

*Amulets and talismans allowed ancient peoples to feel
they had some control over their lives.*

Everyday life in biblical times could be a frightening experience.
Fear and superstition were widespread, and many people felt they
had no control over their own lives and the world around them.
They did not understand the viruses and genetic conditions that
caused plagues and ill health. They did not understand the mental
problems that caused some people to behave as though
they had "demons" inside them. They did not understand
the weather that affected their crops and livestock or
the construction of the solar system that controlled the
weather. All this ignorance led people to find comfort
and security in objects that they imbued with power;
these objects are called amulets and talismans.

Good Luck with That

The word "amulet" comes from the Latin *amuletum,* meaning "an
object that protects a person from trouble." In other words, a good
luck charm. The earliest recorded use of the word that historians
have been able to find is in *Naturalis Historia,* an encyclopedia published by Pliny the Elder in about A.D. 78. Pliny and other learned
people of the Roman Empire sought to banish the ignorance that
led people to use security objects, but they didn't have much luck.
Various peoples—Jews, Christians, and Muslims—had been using amulets for centuries, and old habits die hard. Educators could
lecture and scold, but where would they be when the next swarm of
locusts showed up? Blessed objects were believed to bring protection and healing, and those who put their trust in them did not want
to give them up.

Talismans are closely related to amulets, in that they are objects
that are considered to be protective. But talismans usually have a
more religious or sacred aspect to them. Perhaps the most obvious talisman is the *tallis,* the fringed and tasseled shawl that Jewish

men wear over their shoulders while praying. It is just a coincidence that the word "tallis" sounds so much like "talisman." They are not related, since "talisman" is Greek, not Hebrew, in origin. The Jews have other talismans, such as the mezuzah, a small case filled with scripture that is placed on one's doorpost, and the kimiyah, a similar case that is worn on the body. While many modern Reformed and Conservative Jews no longer use such talismans, most Orthodox cling to these sacred objects. For them, talismans are not a sign of ignorance but of faith in God and his Law. Because of the biblical prohibition against idols, Jewish amulets and talismans involve text and names rather than images of God or man.

Controversy That Rages On

While some Jews use amulets and talismans and some Jews do not, there is not much arguing over it amongst them. Most tend to have a "live and let live" attitude about it. Not so in Christianity. From the very earliest days of the Christian church, the issue of sacred objects, or *sacramentals,* has been a contentious one. Catholics (and some Anglicans) continue to use such sacramentals as crucifixes, rosaries, and holy water, but even many Catholics look askance when their co-religionists seem to be worshipping the dead body parts of saints or seeing images of the Virgin in windowpanes and tree bark.

During the Reformation, which swept across Europe approximately 500 years ago, men like Martin Luther and John Calvin raged against amulets and talismans as a vile form of idolatry. Luther despised the Jews, and felt that it was they who were originally responsible for luring Christians to their security objects. Both Luther and Calvin continually preached the doctrine of *sola scriptura,* the belief that the words of the Bible were all any person needed to lead a holy life.

Centuries after the Reformation, the argument rages on. Some Catholics take their amulets and talismans very seriously, and some Catholics wear things such as St. Christopher medals. Some Protestants wear crosses around their necks, while more reformed Protestants see even a simple cross as a form of idolatry. Whether powerful, harmless, or wicked, these objects don't seem to be going anywhere.

Israel's Neighbors

EDOMITES

Scripture tells us they are Esau's descendants. We know a little about them independent of the Bible, though not as much as we'd like.

Who Were They?
The Edomites were a Semitic people whose lands stretched from the southern tip of the Dead Sea to the Gulf of Aqaba (the modern Israeli port of Eilat, and the Jordanian port of Aqaba), divided neatly between modern Israel and Jordan. Depending on how one interprets the evidence, they existed as a nation and culture for roughly a thousand years beginning around 1000 B.C. (give or take a century or two—that's how vague the evidence is). Lacking much good cropland, the Edomites depended heavily on the caravan trade between Arabia, Mesopotamia (modern Iraq), the Mediterranean, and Egypt—much as the Nabateans would later do in the same region. In about 125 B.C., John Hyrcanus forced them to convert to Judaism, ending Edom's independent existence.

Where Are They Now?
Much of their land became part of the Nabatean kingdom, but by that time the Edomites had been absorbed into Jewish culture. Thus, Edomite blood surely runs in the veins of many with Jewish ethnic roots.

Biblical Mentions
In Genesis, Esau was Abraham's grandson and Jacob's twin brother. Esau was meant to inherit the Israelite leadership but decided he'd rather have a pot of red lentil stew. Later, the Edomite king refused to let the Israelites through his territory on their way to Canaan, but at least he didn't attack them. Evidently he was afraid they'd take over the neighborhood, and he wanted them to take someone else's, a fear perhaps later justified when David killed 18,000 Edomites in the Valley of Salt. Edom didn't fight the Israelites as often as some nations, but it created lasting enmity in Israel by helping Nebuchadnezzar II's Babylonians sack Jerusalem in 597 B.C. Herod, builder of the second temple, was an Edomite. Obadiah ranted against them at great length and with great fury.

Rosh Hashanah

*The Jewish New Year is a festive holiday
filled with good wishes and plenty of noise.*

Biblical Basis
In Leviticus, it is the festival of horns: specifically *shofarim* (rams' horns). On the first day of the seventh month (says the Torah, of which Leviticus is part), Jews are to do no work, to gather for worship, to present offerings by fire, and to blow rams' horns in celebration. The Bible does not call it *Rosh Hashanah* ("head of the year"; pronounce it ROASH ha-sha-NAH).

Biblical Practice
In addition to starting the economic year for the Israelites, ancient Rosh Hashanah's timing made it a harvest festival. The book of Numbers enumerates the correct burnt offerings: a young bull, a ram, and seven unblemished yearling lambs. Each was accompanied by offerings of specified quantities of grain. Though Judaism has another holiday shortly after Rosh Hashanah specifically devoted to atonement (*Yom Kippur*), Numbers makes clear that the sacrifices represent compensation for sins committed during the previous year.

Modern Practice
Rosh Hashanah begins at dusk of the first of Tishri, which falls in September or October. It's a two-day celebration. While a joyful event, it's not a time for drinking, football, or eating turkey. There are four different types of *shofar*-soundings in synagogue, totaling 100 notes. The liturgy of service in synagogues for Rosh Hashanah is longer than usual.

A popular food item is apples dipped in honey, to signify a sweet year to come; bread dipped in honey is another. Even Jews who speak little Hebrew exchange the good wishes in that language: *L'shana tovah!* ("to a good year!"). It is traditional (though not scripturally ordained) for Jews to go to a stream or creek on Rosh Hashanah and empty their pockets into it (usually of bread brought for this purpose) to symbolize rejection of sins and the resolution to lead a more righteous life in the coming year.

Finding Meaning in Biblical Names

⚜ ⚜ ⚜ ⚜

Many biblical names come from Hebrew. It may surprise you how much meaning you can decode with basic knowledge.

Morphed Letters

Hebrew's alphabet can confuse nonspeakers, because it has:

- two letter Ts (one of which is the TH you see in the Bible)
- a letter that can be B or V
- another letter that can be V, W, O, or U
- a letter that can be P or F
- a Y that modern Bibles reflect as a J
- two letter Ss, one of which doubles as an SH
- two letter Ks (or hard C; same sound), one of which doubles as a CH
- two letter CHs (a heavy H like German's Ch)
- a regular H, sometimes confused with the heavy CH letters
- two letter As, which can also represent other vowels or be silent (!)
- a letter TS that is often rendered, sloppily, as Z (Hebrew already has a Z and doesn't need an extra).

Knowing these, you can more easily spot meaning in Hebrew names. For example, if you see Zion as *Tsion* (the actual Hebrew), you'll guess correctly that it's the same word, just rendered differently in English. Most English renderings aren't very faithful to the Hebrew *alef-bet* (so called for its first two letters, just as in the Greek *alpha-bet*).

The Name(s) of God and Other Helpful Basics

In Hebrew letters, the name of God is spelled YHVH. No one today knows what its ancient pronunciation was, if it was pronounced at all. In Hebrew it has vowel marks that suit the word *Adonai,* which means "my Lord." This was a cue for synagogue-goers. Just like every regular churchgoer comes to know the regular order of service by heart, so Jews have long known that when they read YHVH, they are supposed to say *Adonai* rather than dare attempt to pronounce God's true name. While this differs from Christian usage, it is based upon a deep reverence that many Christians may appreciate.

"Jehovah" is a medieval scribe's mix of the *Adonai* vowel marks with YHVH, then spoken aloud, which is likely incorrect. It might have been *Yahweh,* or *Yahveh,* even *Yahoeah,* but it wasn't "Jehovah." Remember, Hebrew doesn't have a J, only a Y. Thus, when a J begins the modern version of a name, it often refers to God. Many ancient Hebrew names include God's name.

Another name of God is *Elohim.* When you see *El* in a biblical name, you can be 95 percent sure this refers to God. A common inclusion in biblical Hebrew is *Beit,* the modern name Beth. It means "house" in Hebrew. *Ben* is Hebrew for "son" or "son of," just as *Bat* (pronounced "baht," not like the flying mammal) means "daughter" or "daughter of."

Put on Your Thinking Israelite Headgear

Let's apply this to the name Jonathan, meaning "God gave" or "given by God." The J (Y) is attached to a verb, *Natan,* meaning "he gave." Modern Israelis pronounce the old TH as just T. In the name Nathan, of course, it means "he gave" but doesn't suggest that God was doing the giving.

Another example: Daniel. You see the EL immediately; *Dan* means "he judged," thus, "God judged." Raphael or Rafael is a good one: *Rafa* means "he healed"; *Rofeh,* for example, is modern Hebrew for "doctor." So you can gather that Rafael means "God healed."

How many Bethel Baptist Churches are there? There must be hundreds in the United States alone; if their founders meant to call their churches houses of God, they picked the right name. *Beit,* "house"; *El,* God (as *Elohim*).

Benjamin? Well, *Ben* is "son of"; in this case, "son of the south." But if someone describes biblical Jonathan as *Yonatan ben Shaul,* you know that Jonathan's the son and Saul's the dad. You aren't tripped up by the Y, because Hebrew doesn't really have that J, and you know that S and SH can be the same letter in Hebrew.

Even a little biblical Hebrew knowledge can enhance your reading of scripture.

A Messianic Age? Why Jews Do Not Consider Jesus the Jewish Messiah

✤ ✤ ✤ ✤

Mainstream Judaism most fundamentally disagrees with Christian theology over the status of a certain Jewish guy from Nazareth. Here we summarize the primary Jewish arguments.

What Constitutes a Jewish Messiah?

The Hebrew word *Moshiach* means "Anointed One." Jews believe that *Hashem* ("The Name," second syllable accented, a reverent Jewish way to refer to God) will send this Messiah to forever change the nature of human existence. Christianity accepts Jesus of Nazareth as this Messiah. Judaism does not.

Judaism bases its messianic teaching on Old Testament prophecies, which a prospective messiah must fulfill. The Old Testament says that the messiah will be a prophet. He will be a normal person, not a worker of miracles, descended through his father from King David. He will embrace and observe the Torah.

Problems

For Jews, the time of prophets ended around 300 B.C., when the Jews migrating back to Israel from Babylon didn't achieve a majority. Jews believe that Hashem's prophets can only appear when the majority of the world's Jews live in Israel. Thus, Jews can't accept Jesus as a prophet.

If Jesus was born to a virgin, it follows that he didn't descend through his father's line from King David. The New Testament attributes numerous supernatural events to Jesus, inconsistent with messianic prophecy. In Judaism, the Torah has no statute of limitations; it remains unalterably binding on humanity forever and denounces as false anyone (including Jesus) who proposes changing Torah. Christianity teaches that some of the Torah's requirements have been amended or discarded; furthermore, according to the New Testament, Jesus did not fully abide by the Torah.

Non-Achievements

Jews interpret Ezekiel 37 and Amos 9 to predict that the messiah will build the third temple. Isaiah 43 tells them that he will reunite all Jews in Israel. Isaiah 2 speaks of an end to all war—swords into ploughshares. In Zechariah 9, the prophet foretells that the faith of Hashem will unify humanity in its true faith. These messianic prophecies are central to the vision of a messianic age. An anointed king of Israel who brings them about will fulfill the prophecies.

No one argues that Jesus achieved them all, for no scriptural evidence indicates that he did. The temple isn't rebuilt, many Jews are scattered worldwide, Israel knows that all war has not ended, and Jews would laugh loudest at any claim that the world has adopted Judaism. Rather, Christianity teaches that Jesus will return to fulfill all of these, with the proviso that Christianity represents the new faith of Hashem to which all will gather. The Jewish rejoinder: Original prophecies do not speak of a Second Coming—just a single one.

Translation Issues

Judaism begins biblical study from the Hebrew of the Old Testament, which means that any disagreement or misunderstanding of the original leads one astray.

Christians believe Jesus was born to a virgin, in accordance with Isaiah 7. In that passage, however, Hebrew scholars contend that the term Christian scholars translate as "virgin" meant simply "young woman" in ancient Hebrew. Much would seem to hinge on this. Christian scholars see in Psalms 22 a reference to the Crucifixion, specifically to gouging the hands and feet, whereas Jewish scholarship translates the same passage as "like a lion." In Isaiah 53, Christians see a reference to Jesus in the suffering servant of Hashem. Jewish belief debates the context of this reference, interpreting it as referring to the nation of Israel (that would be themselves).

Shema

Perhaps the most fundamental disagreement has to do with the Trinity. The Shema, Judaism's basic expression of core faith, says: "Hear, O Israel: Hashem is our God, Hashem Alone." A triune deity—a Father, Son, and Holy Spirit—contradicts a tenet that Judaism specifies cannot be altered.

Abraham's Neglected Son

❖ ❖ ❖ ❖

Abraham had a son with a slave woman, but he was pressured into putting the boy out of the house when his wife, Sarah, got jealous of this rival of her own son, Isaac. The neglected son, Ishmael, ultimately became the father of a vast nation of people—the Arabs.

God has promised Abraham that he would have descendants as plentiful as the stars, but his wife, Sarah, couldn't get pregnant and was already in her seventies. Consequently, she tells Abraham to have a son with her slave-girl, an Egyptian named Hagar. Unwilling to trust that God will deliver on his promise without help, Abraham takes Sarah's suggestion. But when Hagar becomes pregnant, she lords it over Sarah, who in return treats Hagar so cruelly that Hagar runs away.

As Hagar sits near a well in the wilderness, an angel appears and convinces her to return to Abraham's home, submit to Sarah, and have her child, the first offspring of those that would be beyond counting. The angel (God in disguise) predicts that her son, Ishmael, "shall be a wild ass of a man, with his hand against everyone, and everyone's hand against him; and he shall live at odds with all his kin" (Genesis 16:12). Actually, this prediction is less about Ishmael himself than his descendants, the Ishmaelites.

Ishmael's Birth and Boyhood
When Abraham is 86 years old, Ishmael is born, and when Ishmael reaches 13, both he and Abraham are circumcised to seal Abraham's covenant with God. Abraham considers Ishmael his heir and loves him dearly. Then, against all odds, Sarah, at the age of 91, has a son of her own, Isaac. (Abraham himself is 100.)

When Isaac is weaned, Abraham throws a party for him. During the party, Sarah sees Ishmael "playing" with Isaac (probably mocking him) and panics. She insists that Abraham toss Hagar and her son out of the house, "for the son of this slave woman shall not inherit along with my son Isaac" (Genesis 21:10). Abraham is disturbed by the request, but God tells him to comply, "for it is through Isaac that offspring shall be named for you" (Genesis 21:12). God assures Abraham that he will also make of Ishmael a great nation because he is Abraham's offspring. So Abraham sadly sends Hagar and Ishmael away, giving them a good supply of bread and water for their trip into the wilderness.

When the water runs out, Hagar is in despair. She leaves the boy (who is now about 15 years old) and moves to another spot because she cannot bear to see her son die. And she weeps. Hearing her sobs, God returns in the form of an angel and tells her not to be afraid, but to hold the boy tight, "for I will make a great nation of him" (Genesis 21:18). Then God makes a water well appear before Hagar, and she draws water to sustain herself and her son.

Ishmael's Legacy

Ishmael grows up in the wilderness and becomes an expert with the bow and arrow. When he is old enough, his mother finds an Egyptian wife for him, and like Jacob, Abraham's grandson, Ishmael has 12 sons and a daughter. The daughter marries Jacob's twin brother, Esau, and the sons—"twelve princes according to their tribes" (Genesis 25:16)—become the ancestors of the Ishmaelites, who eventually scatter throughout the Near East and become the first central North Arabian tribal confederacy to appear in history. Ishmael himself dies at the age of 137.

All but one of Ishmael's 12 sons, as named in Genesis 25, are mentioned in the annals of the Assyrians, Babylonians, Persians, or Greeks, and the Roman Imperial Army even recruited archers from among the Itrureans (descendants of Ishmael's son Jetur).

Muhammad claimed to be descended from Ishmael, and Islam traces its connection to Abraham through Ishmael. According to a Muslim legend, both Ishmael and his mother, Hagar, are buried in the sacred Ka'aba in Mecca. The Ishmaelites are also considered the ancestors of today's Bedouins of Arabia. And so, ousted by his father, Ishmael became an independent man and, like his half-nephew Jacob (Israel), patriarch of 12 tribes of an independent people.

Stories of Psalms

*The book of Psalms is a favorite among many Christians
because it soothes during troubling times.*

Practically everyone is familiar with Psalms. It's the heart of the Good
Book, both figuratively and, in some versions, literally. But what is it?

In many way, Psalms is everything. It's a hymnal, a prayer book, a collection of poetry, and even a journal. It speaks to the human condition—
whether you were a troubled shepherd during biblical times or a harried
banker today—and offers solutions to problems of the heart and soul.

One Book That's Many

The book of Psalms is divided into five individual books and contains a
total of 150 psalms—many of which cover ground already discussed in
other books of the Bible. Book 1, for example, celebrates God's relationship to his creation, as noted in Genesis. Book 2 describes the story of
the chosen people of Israel and has certain parallels to Exodus. Book 3
illustrates the holiness of God and how he should be worshipped, a topic
also covered in Leviticus. Book 4 deals not only with the nation of Israel
and its place among neighboring nations but also the superior kingdom of
God, also noted in Leviticus. And Book 5 exalts the scriptures as the Word
of God, much like the book of Deuteronomy.

Interestingly, the psalms weren't written all at one time—they were
conceived over a long period, from about 1440 B.C. (the era of Moses) to
586 B.C. (the Babylonian captivity).

Multiple Authors

But where most books spring from the mind of a single author, not so
Psalms. Here, you'll find the wisdom of several contributors, including
David, who penned 73 psalms; Asaph, who wrote 12; and Solomon, who
wrote 2. Fifty-one psalms are anonymous, though Psalms 2 and 95 are
attributed to David in the New Testament books of Acts and Hebrews.

Psalms contains the answer to almost any dilemma you might face. All
you need is faith and the willingness to embrace God's love.

God's Love-Hate Relationship with Israel

✤ ✤ ✤ ✤

God loved Israel so much that he often referred to himself as its hus-band. Unfortunately, the "marriage" was a rocky one, as Israel was constantly breaking away and "committing adultery" by ignoring God and worshipping false idols. But God persevered. Although he had to discipline his beloved people, he never stopped loving them.

After freeing the Israelites from slavery in Egypt, God made a pact, or covenant, with Moses to adopt the Israelites as his people. In return, the people pledged to worship only him, Yahweh, and no other gods. The book of Deuteronomy stresses God's great love for his people and the obligation of the people to love him in return, as articulated in the prayer known as the Shema: "Hear, O Israel: The Lord is our God, the Lord alone. You shall love the Lord your God with all your heart, and with all your soul, and with all your might" (Deuteronomy 6:4–5).

God always remained faithful to his people even though they continually frustrated and angered him by worshipping the gods and goddesses of neighboring cultures. Foreign cults enticed the Israelites with sexual license, magic, and few demands. Because it was easier to follow Baal, the Canaanite fertility god, than to keep the commandments of Yahweh, the Israelites repeatedly abandoned the God who had done so much for them. God was wounded by this rejection.

Hosea Marries a Prostitute

A number of Israel's prophets looked upon the relationship be-tween Yahweh and Israel as a kind of spiritual marriage in which Israel was a totally unfaithful spouse. In the eighth century B.C., the prophet Hosea warned the people of the Northern Kingdom of Israel that the Assyrians would bring down their kingdom if they did not desist from idolatry and turn back to Yahweh, who as a loving spouse would save them. When the people failed to respond, God grew angry. In an attempt to let Hosea know how he felt, he ordered him: "Go, take for yourself a wife of whoredom and have children of whoredom, for the land commits great whoredom by forsaking the Lord" (Hosea 1:2). God himself was letting Hosea know that he was like a man with an unfaithful wife. Despite all he had done for the people of Israel, they had turned from him to worship false idols—they had taken other lovers.

Hosea does what God asks, marrying a woman named Gomer. As expected, Gomer takes other lovers and leaves her husband. But then, again prompted by God, Hosea buys Gomer back from her latest lover and takes her home, forgiving her unfaithfulness. God tells Hosea that he forgives Israel in the same way, for his love is unfailing. However, in the end Israel keeps falling away from God and the Assyrians sweep in and destroy the kingdom of Israel as God had warned. God then focuses his love on the southern kingdom of Judah.

Jeremiah Hears of God's Love

Jeremiah also describes Israel as God's unfaithful spouse. First he recalls the happy days Yahweh spent together with the Israelites in the wilderness during the time of Moses. As reported by Jeremiah, Yahweh muses: "I remember the devotion of your youth, your love as a bride, how you followed me in the wilderness, in a land not sown" (Jeremiah 2:2). That was a kind of honeymoon period. But when God reflects sadly on Israel's later unfaithfulness to him, he launches into an emotional speech that begins with his asking Israel, "What wrong did your ancestors find in me that they went far from me, and went after worthless things [idols], and became worthless themselves?" (Jeremiah 2:5).

After Israel splits into two kingdoms, the northern kingdom of Israel betrays Yahweh with so many idols that he proclaims a divorce. However, when the southern kingdom of Judah also engages in widespread idolatry, God is devastated. Why, he demands, couldn't Judah have learned from her sister Israel? In pouring out his soul-sickness, Yahweh bitterly tells Jeremiah that Judah is so good at finding lovers that she could give lessons to prostitutes (Jeremiah 2:33).

At this point Yahweh reconsiders his decree of divorce against Israel, which is a bold step. According to Deuteronomy 24:1–4, a man is not allowed to remarry a woman whom he has divorced if she'd had another man after leaving him. Despite this law, God orders Jeremiah to press the fickle people of Israel to return to him, for they were not as bad as the people of Judah. Yahweh is hurt, humiliated, and indignant, and he yearns for a renewed relationship with his people. Ultimately, he risks violating his own law in order to renew that relationship. He loves them so much that he will even violate his own divorce law for their sakes.

The invitation to return is motivated by pure mercy. If Israel returns home and acknowledges her wrongdoing, Yahweh will welcome her back with open arms. So intense is God's love for them that Israel's infidelity cannot extinguish the flame of his passionate love.

More Resistance, Then Capitulation

Israel does not to return to God and the nation is ultimately conquered by the Assyrians in 721 B.C. Over the next two centuries, God's prophets continue to beg the people of Judah to return to Yahweh, who forgives them over and over and keeps postponing their punishment. Finally, however, Yahweh stops trying and has the Babylonians destroy Jerusalem and take most of the people of Judah into exile.

While exiled in Babylon, the Jews finally reflect on their unfaithfulness to the one God who had given them everything. Realizing their own guilt, they return to him completely. From then on, most Jews accept only the loving Yahweh as their God and they worship no other.

God Is Love

Ultimately God sends the Messiah he had promised his people, in the person of Jesus Christ, and his great love spreads to the entire world. Jesus dies on the cross to save all people—not only his first chosen people, the Jews, but everyone who believes in him and keeps his commandments. For the long and the short of it is that God does not only love deeply, "God is love" (1 John 4:16).

Loony Laws in the Bible

✧ ✧ ✧ ✧

We all know and (we hope) still follow the Ten Commandments, refraining from stealing and killing and from committing adultery (unless we're politicians or sports stars). But the Ten Commandments are a drop in the bucket of Jewish laws.

There are more than 600 laws in the Bible—not to mention thousands of rules and regulations that were handed down by word of mouth (the so-called Oral Law). A large number of the written laws have to do with animal sacrifices and other cultic matters no longer practiced. But others relate to everyday life and range from common courtesy to downright weird. A dozen such laws follow:

- **Don't Eat That!:** We know that kosher laws forbid Jews to eat pork, shellfish, and the like, but some foods might have gone unmentioned as far as modern tastes are concerned. For example, do we really need laws that forbid us to eat lizards, mice, rats, owls, bats, or vultures (Leviticus 11:26, 29)?

- **Don't Attack a Robber During the Day:** "If a thief is found breaking in and is beaten to death, no bloodguilt is incurred; but if it happens after sunrise, bloodguilt is incurred" (Exodus 22:2–3).

- **Be a Good Boy—or Else!:** "If someone has a stubborn and rebellious son who will not obey his father and mother, who does not heed them when they discipline him, then his father and his mother shall take hold of him and bring him out to the elders of his town at the gate of that place. They shall say to the elders of his town, 'This son of ours is stubborn and rebellious. He will not obey us. He is a glutton and a drunkard.' Then all the men and women of the town shall stone him to death. So you shall purge the evil from your midst; and all Israel will hear, and be afraid" (Deuteronomy 21:18–21).

- **Be Sort of Kind to the Birds:** "If you come on a bird's nest, in any tree or on the ground, with fledglings or eggs, with the mother sitting on the fledglings or on the eggs, you shall not take the mother with the young. Let the mother go, taking only the young for yourself, in order that it may go well with you and you may live long" (Deuteronomy 22:6–7).

- **Be Kind to Animals, Even Those of Your Enemies:** "When you see the donkey of one who hates you lying under its burden and you would hold back from setting it free, you must help set it free" (Exodus 23:5).

- **Don't Sow More Than You Can Reap:** "You shall not sow your vineyard with a second kind of seed, or the whole yield will have to be forfeited, both the crop that you have sown and the yield of the vineyard itself" (Deuteronomy 22:9).

- **Don't Poach More Than You Can Eat:** "If you go into a neighbor's vineyard, you may eat your fill of grapes, as many as you wish, but you shall not put any in a container" (Deuteronomy 23:24).

- **Be a Leery Loaner:** "When you make your neighbor a loan of any kind, you shall not go into the house to take the pledge. You shall wait outside, while the person to whom you are making the loan brings the pledge out to you" (Deuteronomy 24:10–11).

- **Prevent Lawsuits:** "When you build a new house, you shall make a parapet for your roof; otherwise you might have bloodguilt on your house, if anyone should fall from it" (Deuteronomy 22:8).

- **Respect Your Elders:** "You shall rise before the aged, and defer to the old" (Leviticus 19:32). Although this law is more common courtesy than anything, you may want to cite it if you are an older person looking for a seat on the bus.

- **Don't Wear That:** "You shall not wear clothes made of wool and linen mixed together (Deuteronomy 22:11).

- **Hands Off!:** "If men get into a fight with one another, and the wife of one intervenes to rescue her husband from the grip of his opponent by reaching out and seizing his genitals, you shall cut off her hand; show no pity" (Deuteronomy 25:11–12).

Where Jesus Walked

Jerusalem

*It's one of the most storied cities in the world, pivotal
in Christ's life: Golden Jerusalem, as it is called in Hebrew.*

In Biblical Times
Jerusalem was greatly ancient even by the time of Christ, with known habitation at least back to 3000 B.C. Here King David reigned and Solomon built the temple. It had already been fought over, conquered, destroyed, and rebuilt numerous times. It was one of the Holy Land's most cosmopolitan cities and a center of Roman administration: in Latin it was called *Hierosolyma*. Its permanent population was somewhere between 30,000–50,000, with perhaps an equal number of pilgrims at any given time. Interestingly, guess who had restored the grandeur of the city with massive building projects? The hated King Herod.

Jesus' Connection
Jerusalem is thoroughly bound up with the life of Jesus. He went there for Passover, where to his disgust, a flea market was operating in the temple. He threw a fit, turning the tables over, and running out customers and vendors alike. Scripture recorded that his ministry would take him to Jerusalem several times. On his final visit, he prophesied its destruction. It was the site of the Last Supper, Jesus' sorrow as he prepared for the worst—his arrest, trial, and crucifixion.

Jerusalem Today
Incredibly, by A.D. 1800, Jerusalem had less than 10,000 people. How times change! Today, with nearly 800,000 residents, it is the capital of the state of Israel. It houses the Western (Wailing) Wall, the Church of the Holy Sepulchre, the Dome of the Rock, and Al-Aqsa Mosque.

One of the world's most important religious sites for all three faiths of the book, it's also a fairly modern city. Government employment and administration rank alongside tourism as the keys to modern Jerusalem's economics. It is 37 miles from the Mediterranean Sea. As Jerusalem is the major cause of disagreement between Muslims and Jews, the Arab-Israeli dilemma isn't going away until the Jerusalem issue is resolved.

The Shema

❦ ❦ ❦ ❦

"Hear, O Israel: The Lord is our God, the Lord alone."
Thus reads the Torah's fundamental statement of Jewish faith.

Scriptural Context

In Deuteronomy 5, Moses tells the Israelites what God expects of them according to their Covenant, beginning with the Ten Commandments. Moses next tells them the Shema (see above) and that they must love God with all in their power. They must teach this to their children, recite the words upon rising and laying down, bind them to their hands and foreheads, even put them on their doorposts and gates. If they swerved from this divine command, God would vent his rage upon them.

Implications

However one reads or prays this passage, it says the same thing: There is one God, period. No statement could be more monotheistic, which may explain why God became so infuriated any time Israelites backslid on the issue. Observant Jews obey Deuteronomy as literally as possible. When they die, they hope the Shema will be their last earthly words. They bind small boxes, called *tefillin,* to their heads and arms for prayers; these contain Torah verses handwritten on parchment in perfect Ashuri Hebrew script.

Christianity

Jesus, raised an observant Jew, affirmed the Shema as the foremost of God's commandments. When Paul wrote to the Corinthians, his interpretation was startling: "Indeed, even though there may be so-called gods in heaven or on earth—as in fact there are many gods and many lords—yet for us there is one God, the Father, from whom are all things and for whom we exist, and one Lord, Jesus Christ, through whom are all things and through whom we exist."

Was Paul affirming, amending, or contradicting the Shema? That would be something for each biblical scholar and reader to decide.

Who Was the Queen of Heaven?

✛ ✛ ✛ ✛

Many Christians, particularly Catholics, believe that Mary, the mother of Jesus, is the queen of heaven. But as far as the Bible is concerned, she's not. Even though Christians later gave Mary this title, the Bible never refers to her as queen of anything. The only biblical queen of heaven is a Canaanite goddess.

The queen of heaven appears in the Bible only as an object of scorn (in Jeremiah 7:18 and 44:17–25). Throughout his career, the prophet Jeremiah preached against idolatry, trying to drum it into his people's heads that if they continued to worship idols God would punish them and they would lose their land and go into exile. Unfortunately, Jeremiah's preaching was rarely effective, and idol worship flourished in Israel. In particular, women favored one special deity, the so-called queen of heaven, and they involved their entire families in her worship. In Jeremiah 7:17–18, God angrily points out these families to Jeremiah, saying: "Do you not see what they are doing in the cities of Judah and in the streets of Jerusalem? The children gather wood, the fathers kindle fire, and the women knead dough, to make cakes for the queen of heaven; and they pour out drink offerings to other gods, to provoke me to anger."

So Who Was She?

Although she is never named, the queen of heaven was probably Astarte, the Canaanite equivalent of Ishtar, the Assyrian-Babylonian goddess of the planet Venus. Ishtar was a fertility goddess who also oversaw childbirth. She was especially popular among women because sacrifices to her were said to assure safe and healthy children and her cult gave women a role in worship that they did not have at the Jerusalem temple. Offerings to the queen of heaven included wine and star-shaped or crescent-shaped cakes and figurines bearing the image of the goddess.

After Jeremiah had preached himself blue in the face against the worship of the queen of heaven, women seemed to have given it up, though this may not have been in response to the prophet. The cult may have been suppressed as part of King Josiah's religious reforms of 622 B.C. Whatever the reason, we hear nothing about the queen of heaven for a while.

Exile and Renewed Idolatry

After Josiah's death, the people of Israel again began worshipping various foreign idols and otherwise offending their one true God, Yahweh. In 586 B.C., the Babylonians invaded and destroyed Jerusalem and sent most of the people of Israel to Babylon as exiles. However, Jeremiah and some other Jews avoided capture and relocated to Egypt for safety.

In Egypt, much to Jeremiah's horror, his people revived the cult of the queen of heaven. When Jeremiah again preached against the cult, the guilty parties defended themselves by claiming that it is because they had stopped worshipping the queen of heaven that Jerusalem had been destroyed and they were in exile (Jeremiah 44:15–28). As long as they had worshipped this goddess in Judah, they told Jeremiah, they had prospered and suffered no evil.

In short, the Jews in Egypt truly believed that the queen of heaven had given them all they had, not Yahweh—the only God and Israel's true God and sole benefactor. With no way of countering this argument, Jeremiah simply tried to convince his people that things were actually the other way round. The queen of heaven did not punish them for terminating her worship in Judah. Yahweh punished them for worshipping the powerless queen of heaven.

Ending with a Twist

Jeremiah probably died in Egypt, agonizing over his failure to stop the people's idolatry, for he did fail. Not only did the cult of the queen of heaven survive him in Egypt, it seems to have continued well into the Christian era. However, it is possible that leaders of the early Syrian church transformed the cult of the queen of heaven into veneration of Jesus' mother Mary. If this is so, we do have a connection with Mary after all. By diverting believers away from a false goddess, the Syrians may have initiated devotion to Jesus' mother.

One God or Many?

✣ ✣ ✣ ✣

Every true Christian, Jew, and Muslim will insist
that there is and has always been only one God. Many
believe that this certainty goes back at least as far as
Abraham and that, since then, only "pagans" have ever
believed in more than one god. But the Bible says otherwise.

Monotheism, or belief in one God, came slowly, in halting stages.
Formal worship of the deity known as Yahweh probably started
when the patriarch Abraham took Yahweh as his personal God upon
moving to Canaan from Mesopotamia. But even though Abraham
chose Yahweh as the chief deity of his clan, he probably believed
that other gods existed. We know for sure that Laban, Abraham's
close relative, had idols in his house because Laban's daughter
Rachel stole them when she left home with her husband, Jacob
(Genesis 31:19).

   Some scholars hold that Moses, not Abraham, initiated the
practice of worshipping only one god. As we read in Exodus, God
appeared to Moses in a burning bush, commissioned him to free his
people (the Israelites) from slavery in Egypt, and revealed his name
as Yahweh. Moses soon succeeded in freeing his people with the
help of Yahweh, who parted the waters of the Red Sea to let them
escape the Egyptians. Moses then made a pact, or covenant, with
Yahweh at Mount Sinai. In return for following certain laws (notably,
the Ten Commandments), Yahweh would give the Israelites land
and protection.

First Commandment

The first commandment given to Moses reads: "I am the Lord your
God, who brought you out of the land of Egypt, out of the house of
slavery, you shall have no other gods before me" (Exodus 20:2–3).
Notice that the commandment does not claim that Yahweh is the
only god; nor does it say that anyone would be a fool to worship
other gods because they do not exist. On the contrary, even though

it forbids the Israelites to worship them, it seems to accept the fact that there are other gods (or at least the fact that people will continue to believe that they exist). As the God who freed them from slavery in Egypt, Yahweh demands that the Israelites worship him and him alone. Ironically, even while Moses is in the act of receiving this commandment, his people are breaking it by worshipping a calf made of gold.

Forty years later, as the Israelites are preparing to enter Canaan (the land God promised them), Moses begs his people to stay away from the Canaanites, who will lure them away from Yahweh and into idol worship. If they want Yahweh to support them in their new land, the Israelites must worship Yahweh alone. But the people ignore Moses' warnings, and in their new land they engage in a cycle of worshipping Yahweh, turning to other gods and goddesses, and returning to Yahweh when in trouble (Judges 2:11–22).

Influence of Kings

When David established the kingdom of Israel, he vigorously promoted the exclusive worship of Yahweh. But Solomon, David's son, grew lax in his old age and personally built shrines to foreign deities himself. He also married many foreign women, who introduced the cults of their own deities into Jerusalem (1 Kings 11:5–8).

In the divided kingdom, after Solomon's time, most of the people worshipped both Yahweh and other deities. In the southern kingdom of Judah, the kings, who were descendants of David, continued to promote the worship of Yahweh for the most part, but many of the kings of the northern kingdom of Israel let idolatry spread everywhere.

Yahweh Alone!

Several prophets rode herd, lambasting the people for idolatry and reminding them of the covenant they had with Yahweh. One of the first and most vigorous of these prophets was Elijah, who strove hard to abolish idolatry, taking especial aim at the cult of the god Baal, which was strongly promoted by Jezebel, the Phoenician wife of Israel's King Ahab. Some scholars believe that Elijah headed a small but enthusiastic Yahweh-alone movement that strenuously promoted the worship of Yahweh and only Yahweh. This group may even have been made up of the sons of the prophets—a kind of prophets' guild headed by Elijah that appears in 2 Kings. The Yahweh-alone movement continued with renewed force under Elijah's successor, Elisha, and may even have used terrorist activities to purify the religion of Israel. According to the Bible, God told Elijah to anoint Jehu as the next king of Israel and predicted that Jehu would overthrow the Ahab dynasty and kill all the Baal worshippers, "and whoever escapes from the sword of Jehu, Elisha shall kill" (1 Kings 19:17).

Hosea and Jeremiah

The situation did not improve. Both the kings and the people kept violating the first commandment and even practiced child sacrifice (Jeremiah 19:13).

The prophets Isaiah and Jeremiah preached against these violations, holding that it was foolish to worship human-made idols that had eyes that could not see and ears that could not hear and had no power to save anyone. Jeremiah also warned the Israelites that the Babylonians would conquer Jerusalem if they did not turn back to Yahweh and ask his help. But no one listened, and the Babylonians did destroy Jerusalem and take most of its people to Babylon as exiles.

At Last the Truth

In exile, some Jews believed that Jerusalem fell because Marduk, the Babylonian god, was more powerful than Yahweh. However, the prophets managed to convince most of them that Yahweh had simply used the Babylonians to punish his people for neglecting his worship. Isaiah then took the final step in establishing monotheism. He told his people that not only was Yahweh a powerful God who would continue to care for them once they returned home to the land he had given them, but that he is the only real God. Isaiah became the first to reveal that there is, in fact, only one God (Isaiah 45:14, 22).

After the return home from exile in Babylon, the Jews rebuilt Jerusalem. As the Bible does not report that Ezra and his followers were compelled to inveigh against the worship of idols, the Jews had probably come to fully accept the strict monotheism that all Jews, Christians, and Muslims hold dear today.

A Heritage from the Lord

❧ ❧ ❧ ❧

*Nothing was more important to the ancient Israelites
than the proper raising of their children.*

Psalm 127:3 states, "Sons are indeed a heritage from the Lord, the fruit of the womb a reward." It is far from the only biblical verse to stress the blessings of family life and child-rearing. In fact, from Eve's deliverance of Cain and Abel to the crucified Christ giving his mother, Mary, to the apostle John, the importance of the bond between parent and child is continually stressed throughout the Bible. The Chosen People believed that if they raised their children correctly, they would in turn be blessed in old age.

Baby Joy—and Sorrow

In Psalm 128:3, the faithful Jewish men of ancient Israel were told, "Your wife will be like a fruitful vine within your house; your children will be like olive shoots around your table." Jewish women were expected to bear many children, and infant and toddler care was almost entirely their responsibility. Male doctors were never involved in childbirth; female midwives attended laboring women, who were also supported by female relatives of their own and their husband's family. At birth, a baby was rubbed down with salt to toughen the skin and wrapped in swaddling clothes as the infant Jesus was in Luke 2:12. Each Jewish child would then be nursed until the age of two or three.

Mothers were usually given the honor of naming their children, and these names often reflected their personal joy or pain. For example, after a very difficult labor and birth, Rachel named her baby "Ben-Oni," which in Hebrew meant "son of my sorrow" (Genesis 35:18). Names were sometimes also the first step in educating a child, as when they described important events in the history of the Jewish people. In 1 Samuel 4:19–22, a heavily pregnant Jewish woman learned that the Ark of the Covenant had been captured in a battle in which both her husband and her father-in-law,

Eli, had been killed. The shock of the news sent her into early labor, but before she died after the birth, she named her son "Ichabod," meaning "the glory has departed from Israel."

School of the Soul

To the ancient Israelites, the most important part of a child's education was the religious aspect. Even as infants and toddlers, children would be exposed to the prayers and worship habits of their fathers and mothers. In the Old Testament, Proverbs 22:6 instructed parents to "Train children in the right way, and when old, they will not stray." The New Testament echoed this, as Ephesians 6:4 specifically spoke to fathers and warned them, "do not provoke your children to anger, but bring them up in the discipline and instruction of the Lord."

Young girls were taught to pray and become godly wives and mothers, but it was not generally thought important that they study scripture. They were to be submissive to their fathers, in training for the day when they would be submissive to their husbands. The older women in their families and villages were given the responsibility of being their role models, as in Titus 2:3–5: "Likewise, tell the older women to be reverent in behavior, not to be slanderers or slaves to drink; they are to teach what is good, so that they may encourage the young women to love their husbands, to love their children, to be self-controlled, chaste, good managers of the household, kind, being submissive to their husbands, so that the word of God may not be discredited." The repeated emphasis on submission may sound shocking to our post-feminist ears, but at the time it was not given a second thought by anyone, man or woman.

Boys were a different story, however. Just as the women were to be role models for the girls, the men were to show the boys how they were to behave: "Likewise, urge the younger men to be self-controlled. Show yourself in all respects a model of good works, and in your teaching show integrity, gravity, and sound speech that cannot be censured; then any opponent will be put to shame, having nothing evil to say of us" (Titus 2:6–8). It was considered absolutely essential for every Jewish man to know and understand scripture, so that he could lead his future wife and children in the ways of the Lord. Therefore, a boy was expected to digest much of the Law before his 13th birthday, at which time he would have a bar mitzvah. From that point on, he was no longer a boy, but a man, a "son of the law."

At Work and Play

Long before many boys were bar mitzvahed, they were taken to work with their fathers so that they could learn the trades of their families. We see this in the way that Joseph tutored Jesus in carpentry. Both boys and girls who lived in farm families would be expected to help in the fields during especially busy times of year, such as planting and harvest times. Families often also worked in the marketplace together, selling either the crops they had harvested or the products, such as woven blankets or clay pots, that they had made at home. Children who came from wealthy or rabbinical families lived a softer life that was focused on studying the Law.

Almost all Israeli children, rich or poor, made time for leisure and games. Balls and dolls were the most common toys for youngsters. No racquets or bats have been found from this time, so apparently only the hands were used to swing at balls. Some dolls were quite intricate, with jointed limbs and strings attached so the doll could be manipulated as a puppet. Small versions of furniture and tools were made for the dolls. A version of backgammon was played in ancient Israel, and dice were thrown by both adults and children. Kids enjoyed jumping over hopscotch squares, but only until it was time to jump back to work.

Strange Meditations

The Hebrew word for "meditation" (*hagah*) is also used to describe the coo of a dove, the growl of a lion, the plotting of evil rulers, as well as the reading of the Bible. These things are all done audibly. Thus, when Jews were instructed to "meditate" on God's Word (Psalm 1:2), this meant that they should recite it aloud to themselves.

Religious Shocker

Jim Bakker created one of the most successful ministries in the United States—then lost it all to his own avarice.

In the late 1970s and early '80s, Jim and Tammy Faye Bakker's national teleministry was a model of success, with an estimated 13 million viewers. It seemed that the Bakkers could do no wrong, until Jim Bakker found himself trapped in a financial and moral scandal that ultimately landed him in prison.

Born in Muskegon, Michigan, on January 2, 1940, Bakker met his future partner, Tammy Faye LaValley, when they were students at North Central University in Minneapolis. They married in 1961 and received their first big break in 1966 when they joined Pat Robertson's fledgling Christian Broadcasting Network. *The Jim and Tammy Show* demonstrated the couple's talent for reaching and holding an audience, and it was instrumental in turning CBN into an evangelistic powerhouse.

Charismatic Hosts

The Bakkers went off on their own in the early 1970s, joining forces with Paul and Jan Crouch to create the Trinity Broadcasting Network. From the start, the new network's most popular show was *Praise the Lord* (aka PTL), hosted by the charismatic Bakkers. When the couple split from the Crouches after about a year, they took the show with them to their new digs in Charlotte, North Carolina. There, they started *The PTL Club*, which proved so popular that it led the Bakkers to start the PTL Television Network.

The Bakkers' success was predicated on a number of factors, including their decision to embrace members of all faiths and backgrounds. Perhaps most important, however, was the Bakkers themselves, a loving couple who loved Jesus even more and weren't afraid to show it. It was not uncommon for the Bakkers to burst into tears of joy while discussing God's love and bounty with their viewers, a phenomenon that later bordered on parody.

The PTL Television Network gave the Bakkers a platform upon which to let their ministry grow. First up: the construction of Heritage USA in

Fort Mill, South Carolina. A religious theme park of sorts, Heritage USA was, for a brief period, the third most successful attraction of its type in the nation. The Bakkers also established a satellite system that allowed them to broadcast their shows nonstop throughout the country.

Legal Problems

With money literally pouring in, the Bakkers indulged in material excess to an embarrassing degree. Unsurprisingly, the press soon started digging into the couple's business dealings, which ultimately led to criminal charges against Jim Bakker for fraud.

In March 1987, a scandal of a different sort hit the organization when it was revealed that Bakker had been buying the silence of a New York church secretary named Jessica Hahn, who alleged that Bakker had tried to rape her. Bakker acknowledged having a one-time liaison with Hahn, but he denied attacking her. Bakker resigned as the head of PTL in the face of a public outcry and turned the running of the organization over to evangelist Jerry Falwell.

In 1988, following a federal grand jury probe, Bakker was indicted on eight counts of mail fraud, fifteen counts of wire fraud, and one count of conspiracy. He was found guilty on all charges and sentenced to 45 years in prison and a $500,000 fine. In 1992, his sentence was reduced to eight years and the fine waived.

Bakker was granted parole in 1994, but he came out of prison with almost nothing. Tammy Faye divorced him while he was behind bars, and he still owed considerable money to the government and others.

The Road Back

Finally free, Bakker began the arduous process of self-redemption. He publicly condemned the prosperity theology that had gotten him into so much trouble, and he went to work for an urban ministry in Los Angeles. In 1996, he published his memoir, *I Was Wrong,* and in 1998 authored another book, *Prosperity and the Coming Apocalypse.*

Today, Jim Bakker is back behind the pulpit. In 2003, he moved to Branson, Missouri, where he began broadcasting *The Jim Bakker Show* with his wife, Lori Bakker. It's a far cry from the glory days of *The PTL Club,* but Bakker considers himself lucky: At least he still has an audience eager to hear him preach God's good word.

Why Did Jesus Die?

✤ ✤ ✤ ✤

It's a fair question. Why should God's Son be martyred for human-ity's salvation? What meaning underlies the crosses and crucifixes Christians wear, emblems of suffering and sacrifice?

The Bigger Plan

Christians believe that Jesus' death was part of God's plan, basing this view on numerous Old Testament prophetic references. Zecha-riah refers to the Savior's betrayal by a friend, even specifying the price of 30 silver shekels (a number Judas would come to know all too well). Other passages foretell his silent conduct and acceptance of his fate at trial, even his captors divvying his clothing. In Psalms, we read that his bones would not be broken; again in Zechariah, that a wound would pierce his side. Isaiah 53 gives a vivid description of a divine servant sent to endure suffering, abuse, and death: "But he was wounded for our transgressions, crushed for our iniquities; upon him was the punishment that made us whole, and by his bruises we are healed." The Lord, it seems, was giving his people advance notice of what would happen to him.

Foresight and Acceptance

Shortly after Peter stated that Jesus was the Christ, Jesus began preparing his disciples for his inevitable death. No one was taking his life, he said. He was giving it as an act of free will, expressing his love for humanity (even the parts of humanity that treated him shabbily). Jesus confirmed this submission to his Father's will at Gethsemane. Let's be realistic: Does any believer suppose that an all-powerful God couldn't have sent a squadron of angels to slap the Roman police around, preventing his Son's arrest? The trial and cru-cifixion could therefore only occur with the consent of Father and Son. As scripture describes, they knew these events were coming, yet they did nothing to alter them.

Not that others couldn't have foreseen it as well, of course. Jesus was a great irritant to the Pharisees, the Jewish religious/political party that is the ancestor of modern rabbinic Judaism. He didn't follow Jewish law (at least not to the Mosaic letter), and he heaped scorn on the Pharisees. In Matthew 23, he gave them both barrels—it's worth opening up your Bible for a read. He accused them of locking people out of heaven and ignoring justice, mercy, and faith. He called them numerous insulting names: hypocrites, children of hell, blind guides, vipers. Jesus' tongue could leave impressive blisters when he cut loose.

The Pharisees were a powerful force in Israelite society. It didn't take prophecy to foresee that they would remember Jesus' fierce critique; common sense would have told anyone that. Common sense also tells us that Jesus realized this, yet he did it anyway. If one believes Christ sane and intelligent, as believers surely do, one has to believe he expected a severe backlash.

What Did It Mean?

Remember the Old Testament concept of substitute sacrifices? So that humans wouldn't have to pay for their sins in blood, the Israelites would sacrifice an animal. On the Day of Atonement, the high priest sprinkled the sacrificial goat's blood on the Ark of the Covenant. He then laid hands on the goat to transfer Israel's sin into the creature, thus the term "scapegoat." Driving the scapegoat into the wilderness drove out the accumulated sin. In Romans 3, Paul uses this analogy to explain Jesus' death as atonement "by his blood" for all human sin, thus restoring the judicial balance between God and humanity.

Had this not occurred, humanity lay under God's judgment. The Old Testament abounds with references to people turning away from his law and God's great frustration with this ongoing backsliding. It would seem that he felt humanity had strayed so far afield from his expectations that they couldn't possibly make full restitution. Imagine a terrorist who kills 2,000 people. Murdering one person can earn a life sentence or even death; how can one person pay 2,000 life sentences or 2,000 deaths? It's not possible. Christ's sacrifice balanced the books of divine justice.

Considering that it wasn't God who had sinned, it was pretty generous of him to offer such a precious sacrifice—but then again, as we've seen, God and his Son knew this would come.

10 Things

Great Prayers of Jesus

He taught us to pray and then modeled it in several conversations.

1. The Lord's Prayer (Matthew 6:5–13) After criticizing the way hypocrites prayed (showing off) and the way pagans prayed (babbling), Jesus gave his disciples a template: *Our Father in heaven.* This prayer includes praise and petition, confession and commitment. If, as a child, you practiced reciting this prayer as quickly as possible, you missed the point. That would be both showing off and babbling.

2. Hide and seek (Luke 10:21) Jesus had regular run-ins with the religious intelligentsia, those who knew everything except their own need for God's grace. After sending out his ragtag band of disciples to extend his own preaching-and-healing ministry, he prayed, "I thank you, Father, Lord of heaven and earth, because you have hidden these things from the wise and the intelligent and have revealed them to infants."

3. Very public prayer (John 11:41–42) At the raising of Lazarus, Jesus uttered a rather strange prayer for the benefit of the crowd of mourners. Perhaps he had just prayed silently for Lazarus to be resurrected, or maybe that part of the prayer was not recorded, but then Jesus said, "Father, I thank you for having heard me. I knew that you always hear me, but I have said this for the sake of the crowd standing here, so that they may believe that you sent me." This miracle was a demonstration of his identity, and this prayer makes that clear.

4. A prayer answered... audibly (John 12:27–30) Jesus moved from teaching to prayer and back again, as if he had an "always on" connection with his Father. Talking about his impending suffering, he wondered whether he should ask to avoid them but concluded, "No, it is for this reason that I have come..." And then he prayed: "Father, glorify your name." A voice from heaven replied, "I have glorified it, and I will glorify it again." Some thought it was just thunder, but Jesus explained, "This voice has come for your sake, not for mine."

5. Do not sift (Luke 22:31–32) Simon Peter frequently bragged about his loyalty, which is why it was so stunning when Jesus predicted that Peter would deny him. "Simon, Simon, listen!" said Jesus, probably at the Last Supper. "Satan has demanded to sift all of you like wheat, but I have prayed for you that your own faith may not fail."

6. A prayer for us (John 17) John's Gospel contains a lengthy account of Jesus' teaching and conversation during the Last Supper. He also includes a prayer Jesus prayed at that time. At one point he even prays for *us*, specifically. "I ask not only on behalf of these, but also on behalf of those who will believe in me through their word."

7. While you were sleeping (Matthew 26:36–42) Jesus had warned his disciples about his "cup of suffering." As his arrest neared, he was troubled about this. Taking his disciples to the Garden of Gethsemane, he withdrew from them a bit and prayed while they slept. "My Father, if it is possible, let this cup pass from me; yet not what I want but what you want." It remains a model of surrender to God's desires.

8. Famous last words: Forsaken (Matthew 27:46) While on the cross, Jesus cried, *"Eli, Eli, lema sabachthani?"* This is Hebrew for "My God, my God, why have you forsaken me?" Some bystanders thought he was calling for Elijah, but this is the first verse of Psalm 22, which contains an eerily accurate description of the process of crucifixion (though it was written centuries before the Romans invented crucifixion).

9. Famous last words: Forgiven (Luke 23:34) Jesus had been criticized for offering forgiveness when only God could forgive sins, so it's fitting that he forgave his tormentors with one of his dying statements. "Father, forgive them; for they do not know what they are doing." The Romans, well-practiced in crucifixion, knew exactly what they were doing. But they didn't grasp the full impact of this death.

10. Famous last words: Into Your Hands (Luke 23:46) Earlier, Jesus had made the point that no one would take his life from him, but he would "lay it down" (John 10:18). Just before he breathed his last, he did so. "Father, into your hands I commend my spirit." When the soldiers came by to break his bones (a standard practice to hasten death), they found him already dead (John 19:33). One wonders if anyone remembered the full content of his earlier quote: "I lay down my life in order to take it up again" (John 10:17).

What Is the Purpose of Prayer?

✤ ✤ ✤ ✤

All through the Bible, God's people—
and Jesus himself—are praying. Why pray?

That might seem an odd question in a believing context, but arguments *against* praying exist. For example:

- God has far more important matters than an individual's needs.
- All that happens is God's plan, so praying won't change it.

These arguments were old hat to early Christian scholars. They prayed anyway. Why? Because God said they should. Why would he want that? Even though it's hard for the human mind to fathom divine wisdom, surely we can grasp some of the logic.

Christians believe that the Bible's central message is about getting to know God personally. Despite his divinity, God desires human friendship. Friends confide in each other, and prayer is an expression of friendship, opening one's heart and life to him.

The Lord's Prayer

Jesus' disciples saw him praying and asked that he teach them. The Lord's Prayer starts with worship, then it identifies with God's concerns: his reputation, reign, and will. Then come the praying person's concerns, be they great or small: sustenance, forgiveness, and protection. Neither Matthew nor Luke cite Jesus as using the traditional ending: "For the kingdom and the power and the glory are yours forever. Amen." However, this conclusion honors God's lordship and divine might. Afterward, Christ emphasized that if Christians hadn't first forgiven others, God wouldn't forgive them.

Jesus advised the apostles not to make a show of public prayer, nor to "heap up empty phrases." He made clear that when one prays the Lord's Prayer, one should think about and mean the words.

Nearness to God

The theme of prayer is simple enough: Everything about it brings the praying person nearer to God. That God would command humans to pray expresses his desire for humans to draw nearer to him.

A New Look at Old Icons

✤ ✤ ✤ ✤

*Archaeologists have uncovered the earliest known icons
of the apostles Peter and Paul.*

Timeless treasures often turn up where you least expect them. Such was the case in 2009 and 2010 when Vatican archaeologists announced the discovery and restoration of the earliest known icons of the apostles Paul and Peter on a ceiling in a catacomb beneath a modern eight-story office building in Rome.

A Significant Find

The remarkable images are believed to date from the second half of the 4th century A.D. and were found on the ceiling of a tomb belonging to a Roman noblewoman in the famous St. Thekla catacomb, located near the Basilica of St. Paul. The square ceiling painting also included the earliest known images of the apostles John and Andrew, as well as a painting of Jesus as the Good Shepherd.

It took two years and cost an estimated 60,000 euros to restore the frescoes and paintings in the catacomb. A new laser technique was used to meticulously burn away several centimeters of white calcium carbonate deposits without harming the original artwork beneath it. The restoration is considered a triumph because the damp conditions within most ancient catacombs typically make the restoration and preservation of paintings within them extremely difficult.

St. Paul Restored

"The result was exceptional because from underneath all the dirt and grime we saw for the first time in 1,600 years the face of Saint Paul in a very good condition," Barbara Mazzei, who directed the work at the catacomb, told a British newspaper.

More than 40 catacombs—underground Christian burial places—are known to exist throughout Rome. They fall under the jurisdiction of Pontifical Commission of Sacred Archaeology because of their unique religious significance.

Israel's Neighbors

ASSYRIANS

"The Assyrian came down like a wolf on the fold..." So goes The
Destruction of Sennacherib, *Lord Byron's classic poem based on
2 Kings 18–19. The Israelites, however, were far from the only
people of the region with reason to despise and fear Assyria.*

Who Were They?
Assyrians were a Semitic people, thus distant kin to the Israelites and
their neighbors, living in the environs of modern northern Iraq. They wrote
in Akkadian (an early Semitic tongue), then Aramaic; they worshipped
multiple gods, sometimes counting their own rulers as god-kings. The
two principal cities were Ashur (the source of "Assyria") and Nineveh.
History identifies three separate phases of Assyrian imperial power: the
Old, Middle, and New Assyrian Empires, spanning the era from about
2000 B.C. to 612 B.C. Assyrian laws were brutal, especially toward
women; punishments leaned heavily toward mutilation and death. Assyrian
conquest generally meant disaster for any nation that resisted or rebelled.

Where Are They Now?
Assyria fell under Babylonian dominion in 605 B.C., then Persian, then
Macedonian dominion. The Akkadian language fell out of use. By Christ's
time, the Assyrians were merely a series of minor client kingdoms. There
are still millions of Assyrians, mostly Christian, who claim ancestral ties to
Assyria of old.

Biblical Mentions
For much of the period covered by scripture, Assyria was a major power
feared by every neighboring nation. King Menahem of Samaria extorted
tribute money from wealthy Israelites to pay off Assyria. It didn't last;
King Hoshea of Assyria carted the Israelites of Samaria into exile, which
was God's punishment for sins. However, God didn't always side with the
Assyrians, as seen when God sent an angel to kill 185,000 of them—at
which point Sennacherib went back to Nineveh. Isaiah and other prophets
had a lot to say about Assyria, making it one of their great bogeymen.

Fast Facts

- *The Bible is an exercise in dichotomy. For example, various passages talk of Jesus as God, such as John 1:1 and Romans 9:5, while others specifically address his humanity. Among the latter: John 1:14, Luke 2:7, and Hebrews 4:15.*

- *The Bible is peppered with a wide variety of prayers. They include: confession (Psalm 51); praise (1 Chronicles 29:10–13); thanksgiving (Psalm 105:1–7); petition (Acts 1:24–26); confidence (Luke 2:29–32); intercession (Exodus 32:11–13); commitment (1 Kings 8:56–61); and benediction (Numbers 6:24–26).*

- *The word "Christian" appears only three times in some versions of the Bible.*

- *Baptism is big in the Bible. The very first such act was performed by Moses, who used ox blood to anoint his people. Luckily, water—which is a whole lot less messy—later took its place.*

- *Can you name the one domesticated animal that is NOT mentioned in the Bible? There's a pretty good chance you own one—it's the cat. (Dogs are mentioned several times, often in less than flattering terms.)*

- *Two books in the Bible make no mention of God at all: Song of Solomon and the book of Esther.*

- *Contrary to the belief of some, Christ is not Jesus' last name. It's the English translation of the Greek word for "anointed one," as well as the transliteration of the Hebrew word for "savior."*

- *John is the most commonly shared name among popes.*

- *Can you name the nation with the highest number of Catholics? Nope, it's not Vatican City. (Good guess, though!) It's Brazil. The place is teeming with 'em.*

- *If you look closely at Leonardo da Vinci's famous painting of* The Last Supper, *you'll see oranges. Turns out da Vinci took some creative license. According to horticultural experts, oranges weren't grown in the Holy Land until long after Jesus' time.*

Elijah Fights Four Hundred

❦ ❦ ❦ ❦

The prophet Elijah was quite a showman, and in fighting foreign prophets he put on a spectacular display of attitude and action that would put Friday Night SmackDown *to shame. Swaggering and shouting like a boastful wrestler, Elijah single-handedly faced 450 opponents—and won!*

When the notorious Jezebel came from Phoenicia to Israel as the bride of King Ahab, she went all out to promote the cult of the Canaanite rain god Baal in her new home. Drawing on Israel's state funds, Jezebel managed to support hundreds of prophets of Baal and his consort, Asherah. Although Ahab did little, if anything, to stop her, she encountered fierce resistance from Elijah, who won a significant victory over her prophets on Mount Carmel.

One Against Hundreds

At that time a drought was devastating Israel, which Elijah characterized as punishment for the Israelites who persisted in worshipping both the Lord and Baal. So Elijah called the people together and asked: "How long will you go limping with different opinions? If the Lord is God, follow him; but if Baal, follow him" (1 Kings 18:21). When he received no answer, Elijah called in 450 of Jezebel's prophets and proposed a test to determine whose god was the more powerful and thus end the drought. Both he and the Baalists prepared an animal for sacrifice, cutting it up and placing it on wood. Then, instead of lighting a fire, the prophets prayed to their gods to supply the fire to burn the sacrifice.

The prophets of Baal went first, but when they called for Baal to send down fire, nothing happened. From morning to noon they danced around the altar, crying out, "'O Baal, answer us,' But there was no voice, and no answer" (1 Kings 18:26). Elijah stood by watching and, dripping with sarcasm, he urged the frantic prophets to call louder, telling them that Baal may be meditating. He also insinuated that Baal had wandered off to relieve himself. Try as they might, the followers of Baal could not get the wood to burn.

Elijah Takes Charge

In the afternoon, after disdainfully pushing the Baalists aside, Elijah single-handedly set up his own altar using 12 stones (one for each of the tribes of Israel). He dug a trench around the altar and set the wood and the prepared animal on the altar. In an act of sheer bravado, Elijah then made the proposed sacrifice virtually impossible to burn by pouring water over it three times. In fact, he used so much water that it covered the entire surface of the altar and ran down and filled the trench. Elijah told the people that he was the Lord's servant and had acted at the Lord's bidding. He then asked the Lord to send down fire to prove to the Israelites that he is their God. Fire immediately fell from the sky, consuming "the burnt offering, the wood, the stones, and the dust, and even licked up the water that was in the trench" (1 Kings 18:38). After this victory, Elijah had all 450 of the false prophets seized and put to death, obeying God's law that any prophet who speaks in the name of other gods shall die (Deuteronomy 18:20).

So Where's the Rain?

To make the test complete, Elijah needed to produce rain. At the top of Mount Carmel, he bowed down and prayed, then sent a servant to look out toward the sea for a cloud. There was none. God had quickly sent the fire Elijah asked for, but at this point he seemed to want to check the prophet's arrogance. Elijah had to repeat his prayer seven times before he got results. After the seventh, the servant spotted a cloud the size of a human hand. Elijah sent Ahab back to his capital with a promise of rain. But Elijah, on foot, outran Ahab's horse and arrived there first. Soon after, the sky grew dark, the wind rose, and heavy rain began to fall. Of course, when Jezebel heard what Elijah had done, she went on the warpath and tried to have the prophet killed, but God protected him.

The Other Psalmists

King David wrote many of the psalms, but he wasn't the only author.

A lot of individuals contributed to the book of Psalms. Some, such as King David, are fairly well known; others, not so much. So let's take a moment to get to know the less-famous psalmists and what they brought to the party.

Asaph, who wrote Psalms 50, 73, 75—77, 79, 80, 82, and 83, was the Justin Timberlake of his day. A descendent of Levi, he was chosen by the chief priests to be a leading singer when the Ark of the Covenant was brought to Jerusalem. Later, David made him leader of the choral worship. The sons of Asaph became the top family of musicians—sort of like the Osmonds.

Sing Those Psalms!
The Sons of Korah, responsible for Psalms 42, 47—49, 84, 85, 87, and 88, were also singers and musicians. In fact, the Korahites were appointed by David to be choir leaders and were temple musicians and assistants for centuries. Talk about a sweet gig!

Ethan was a leader of the Levites and was likely an important temple musician. Wise and well known among his people, he wrote a 52-verse psalm that celebrates God's promises to David and his descendants. (It's Psalm 89, in case you're curious.) Heman is best known for writing an achingly honest psalm that implores God for help in time of great misery (Psalm 88).

The Oldest Psalm
Moses, who is perhaps best known for his chat with a burning bush and jotting down the Ten Commandments, is also credited with penning the oldest psalm (Psalm 90). It's a prayer that praises God as "our dwelling place in all generations" and asks for "compassion on your servants."

Solomon, the third king of Israel, made a name for himself by building a temple for God. In addition to two psalms of the canon, he also wrote much of Proverbs and Ecclesiastes, not to mention the popular Song of Solomon.

Seeing God—Sort of

❧ ❧ ❧ ❧

The Bible tells us that if you see God you will die. Yet a number of Old Testament figures purportedly do see God without immediately keeling over. Why? The answers vary.

On Mount Sinai, when Moses asks if he may see the Lord's "glory," God tells him plainly: "You cannot see my face, for no one shall see me and live" (Exodus 33:18–20). Here, as elsewhere, the terms "glory of God" and "face of God" are used interchangeably for "God in all his radiance."

Although the Old Testament recounts that God "appeared" to a number of people, few actually "see" him with their eyes, and no one sees him in his full "glory." On the other hand, numerous Old Testament figures do hear God. After eating the forbidden fruit, Adam and Eve "heard the sound of the Lord God walking in the garden at the time of the evening breeze" (Genesis 3:8). They also hear God talking to them, as do Cain and Noah. But seeing God is another matter.

Humans cannot look at God in his full glory, for the sight would be too exhilarating to endure. Consequently, when God "appears" to someone, he does so in a vision or in a lesser form—such as an angel or a human. God sometimes appears in a storm, and he leads the exodus procession in a pillar of cloud by day and in a pillar of fire by night" (Numbers 14:14).

Visions of God

In Genesis and Exodus, God appears to Abraham, Isaac, and Jacob, but seemingly in visions or dreams. Exodus 24:9–11 states that Moses and the elders actually "saw the God of Israel," but what they see is not a realistic image of God but a strange spectacle that seems to be a kind of hallucination or vision. Furthermore, the Hebrew verb used here for "see" often means having a vision. But even this secondary sight of God frightens the elders, who seem surprised when no harm comes to them.

These visions continue in later Old Testament books. For example, when Isaiah and Ezekiel are called to be prophets they have visions of God that are filled with hallucinogenic images of fire and winged creatures. Ezekiel's view of God is twice removed, for it is merely "the appearance of the likeness of the glory of God" (Ezekiel 1:28).

God in Other Guises

God sometimes appears in the form of human beings or angels. When he comes to tell the aged Abraham and Sarah that they will have a son, he takes the form of three men. (Some Christians see this as a foreshadowing of the Trinity.) When Hagar, soon to be the mother of Ishmael, runs away from home, God—in the guise of an angel—appears to her and convinces her to return to Abraham's home. Hagar also expresses amazement, "Have I really seen God and remained alive after seeing him?" (Genesis 16:13). She had, but again she had seen God in the guise of a lesser being, not in his full glory. Similarly, Gideon is called to be a military leader by God, who comes to him in the shape of an angel. When Gideon realizes he is with God, he panics and cries out: "Help me, Lord, for I have seen the angel of the Lord face to face" (Judges 6:22). But God assures Gideon that he will live and complete his mission.

Jacob's Wrestling Partner

In a rather bizarre passage from Genesis, after Jacob has wrestled all night with a mysterious "man," the man gives him a new name—Israel, which means "the one who strives with God." Jacob reacts in amazement: "I have seen God face to face, and yet my life is preserved" (Genesis 32:30). But even though Jacob claims to have seen God's face, he has not encountered God in all his glory. The Hebrew term "face" is often used to convey an awareness or direct knowledge of someone's presence, without using a mediator—in other words, to describe a close encounter of a personal kind. So even though Jacob did not look directly into the face of God, he is still relieved to be alive, though we are not told why. Perhaps God is granting the father of the future 12 tribes of Israel a special grace, or perhaps Jacob lives on because he has not seen the full glory of God but merely God disguised as a human being.

Moses Sees God's Back

Moses first encounters God in a burning bush. At another time, "The Lord descended in the cloud and stood with him there" (Exodus 34:5). In addition: "The Lord used to speak to Moses face to face as one speaks to a friend" (Exodus 33:11). But the face to face cannot be taken literally here, for soon after God tells Moses: "You cannot see my face; for no one shall see me and live" (Exodus 33:20).

But God makes a concession, telling Moses: "See, there is place by me where you shall stand on the rock, and while my glory passes by I will put you in a cleft of the rock, and I will cover you with my hand until I have passed by; then I will take away my hand, and you shall see my back; but my face shall not be seen" (Exodus 33:21–23). God equates his face here with his glory. When Moses returns to his people they see that "the skin of his face shone because he had been talking with God" (Exodus 34:29). From then on Moses wears a veil over his face when not in God's presence.

God Among Us

In the olden days, sour disciplinarians used to mutter that children should be seen but not heard. The Old Testament seems to say, in a much more positive way, that God should be heard (by all means) but not seen—for the full sight of him is more than any of us could take. Ultimately, of course, God bypasses this problem by coming to earth in the form of a human being, Jesus Christ, who is God made human: "And the Word became flesh and lived among us, and we have seen his glory, the glory as of a father's only son, full of grace and truth" (John 1:14).

Where Jesus Walked

𝕸𝖆𝖌𝖉𝖆𝖑𝖆

Mary of Magdala, best known as Mary Magdalene,
presumably came from this small town.

In Biblical Times

Mary Magdalene was a small-town girl. Scripture only mentions the town once by a name like the one we know (Matthew 15), and the New Revised Standard Version renders it as "Magadan." Another reference in Mark to "Dalmanutha" almost surely describes the same place, given that Mark is describing the same miracle. Magdala was a very small fishing village on the northwestern shore of the Sea of Galilee, known for quality boatbuilding. A couple of generations after Christ's time on earth ended (A.D. 67), it was evidently a holdout of the Jewish Revolt. A Roman army under Titus recaptured Magdala, slaughtering thousands and selling more into slavery. Somehow the town revived thereafter, but it eventually faded to abandonment in the Middle Ages.

Jesus' Connection

The Bible documents one visit by Jesus, after the miracle of loaves and fishes. His primary connection to the place is because some of his most devoted followers lived there. A common belief, now challenged by scholarship, is that Mary Magdalene was a prostitute. The Bible credits Jesus with casting seven demons from her. While most would agree that being rid of demons is a good thing, scripture doesn't elaborate on whether the demons were causing sin or disease. In any event, Mary Magdalene was better off for meeting Jesus, and she showed her gratitude with loyalty. It seems fitting she was the first to see the risen Christ.

Magdala Today

The ruins lie along the Sea of Galilee some four miles northeast of *Tverya* (Tiberias) in modern Israel, very near the modest farm town of Migdal (population 1,500). One can see the remnants of a Byzantine monastery there, and with a little imagination, one can imagine the fishing docks now buried somewhere in the beach. Like any town in its position, Migdal thrives on tourism.

Quiz

Water I

Thirsting for more Bible knowledge? It's right here.

1. Genesis tells us that a river flowed out of the Garden of Eden and broke into four branches. Two of these were Pishon and Gihon. What were the other two?
   - a. Cygon and Milon
   - b. Jordan and Nile
   - c. River of Dreams and Crystal Sea
   - d. Tigris and Euphrates

2. Three warriors in the service of this king crept through enemy lines to get him a drink of water from the well of Bethlehem. Who was the recipient of this brave act?
   - a. Gideon
   - b. Saul
   - c. David
   - d. Herod

3. When Jesus asked the "woman at the well" for a drink, she was surprised. Why?
   - a. the well was dry
   - b. he was Jewish and she was Samaritan
   - c. it was improper for men to speak with women
   - d. he wasn't even there a moment earlier

4. When the Israelites needed water in the wilderness, Moses struck a rock and it gushed forth with water. Why was God upset about this?
   - a. it was the wrong rock
   - b. God had told Moses merely to speak to the rock
   - c. God opposed violence in any form
   - d. Moses cursed as he did this

Answers: 1. d (Genesis 2:10–14); 2. c (2 Samuel 23:13–19); 3. b (John 4:9); 4. b (Numbers 20:8–12)

217

Chariots of Fire

✤ ✤ ✤ ✤

In war and peace, these vehicles served the ancient world well.

About 3,000 years before the birth of Jesus Christ, the Mesopotamians invented the ox cart as a means of conveyance. The four-wheeled ox cart was useful for transporting both people and products, but it was slow—certainly too slow to be effective for other uses, such as active warfare. While ox carts could be used to carry weapons from one place to the next, they could not be used in actual battle. Frustration led to invention, and over the centuries, the ancient peoples of the Middle East refined their vehicles until the chariot was born.

Triumph of Human Ingenuity

Before the chariot could be invented, humans had to invent something else: the spoked wheel. Spokes are the rods that radiate from the center of a wheel, allowing for more weight, greater pressure, and faster movement. Archaeologists date the first spoke-wheeled chariots to about 2000 B.C., and within the next 700 years, they were ubiquitous in the ancient world, especially for use in warfare. The solid, wooden wheels that had been both helping and hampering armies were now a thing of the past, and warriors relished the opportunity to use lighter, faster vehicles. But in addition to the invention of the spoked wheel, horses had to be tamed and trained. Once these two things were accomplished, the chariot was inevitable.

In biblical times, chariots were used by the Hebrews, Romans, Greeks, Hittites, and Egyptians. Most chariots were two- or four-wheeled vehicles with a floor to stand on and a waist-high, semicircular guard to protect the lower half of the driver. A driver could lean against this guard while moving or attach himself to it in order to leave his hands free to carry a shield and/or sword. Though most chariots were designed to hold only the driver, others were big enough to accommodate one or two riders as well. The Latin word for chariot is *carrus,* from which we take the name for our modern-day cars. A two-horse chariot was called a *biga,* a three-horse chariot was called a *triga,* and a four-horse chariot was called a *quadriga.*

Battle for the Mediterranean

Once the chariot had been invented, it quickly became a common sight throughout the Middle East and factored into almost every battle until about the 4th century B.C. Some of the greatest chari-oteers of ancient times were the Hittites. An ancient Anatolian people, the Hittites conquered much of Syria and Mesopotamia with their fierce, chariot-powered army. Indeed, it was the Hittites who fought and won what was probably the largest chariot battle ever: the 1299 B.C. Battle of Kadesh, in which 3,500 to 5,000 chari-ots (exact number unknown) clashed in a bloody fight for regional dominion. The Egyptians, Assyrians, and Hurrians were put in their place—for a time.

Though the Egyptians lost the Battle of Kadesh, they won many other battles with their brilliantly designed and beautifully orna-mented chariots. It was the Egyptians who invented the yolk saddle for their horses, and as the Romans did, they enjoyed making their chariots works of art as well as practical. It was not unusual for wealthy warriors to use fine leather and gold trim on their chariots. But while ancient chariots were often beautiful, they were rarely comfortable due to the lack of suspension. Though military engi-neers of the time attempted to make a primitive form of springs for chariots, they had little success in this area. Suspension in horse-drawn vehicles would not be perfected until the 19th century. Still, compared to the ox- and ass-drawn vehicles that came before them, chariots seemed positively revolutionary and modern to the peoples of the Bible.

The Word on Chariots

Chariots are mentioned many times in the Bible, especially in the Old Testament. First referred to in Genesis 50:9, they are often used as symbols of power, glory, and dominance. The great Hebrew King Solomon had a huge army that was described in 2 Chronicles 1:14: "Solomon gathered together chariots and horses; he had fourteen hundred chariots and twelve thousand horses, which he stationed in the chariot cities and with the king in Jerusalem."

When the prophet Elijah died and left his mantle to Elisha, "a chariot of fire and horses of fire separated the two of them, and Elijah ascended in a whirlwind into heaven. Elisha kept watching and crying out, 'Father, father! The chariots of Israel and its horsemen!'" (2 Kings 2:11–12). But chariots could also be used in biblical metaphors of a more tender sort; for example, in Song of Solomon 1:9: "I compare you, my love, to a mare among Pharaoh's chariots." Might not sound too "hot" to us today, but back then, it was quite a sexy compliment.

By the time Jesus Christ was around, chariots were no longer used in warfare. Why? Because horses were bred to be bigger and stronger so that warriors could use them alone in battle, without having to attach them to chariots. Chariots were still used in Jesus' time for other reasons, and chariot races were still quite popular, as was shown in the iconic chariot race scene in the 1959 film *Ben-Hur,* starring Charlton Heston. This spectacular action sequence is still considered one of the greatest and most authentic historical scenes ever filmed. Using the largest film set to that time (it took five months to build on 18 acres) and 15,000 extras, it was a grueling five weeks of work for Heston and the other actors, who drove nine chariots that were each pulled by four horses.

Though chariots had been retired as war transportation by Jesus' time, they were still a part of everyday life, as was made clear in Acts 8:38, when the disciple Philip meets an Ethiopian eunuch on the road to Gaza: "He commanded the chariot to stop, and both of them, Philip and the eunuch, went down into the water, and Philip baptized him." In Revelation 9:9, chariots are used as symbols of God's wrath. So from beginning to end, the Bible features chariots, both physical and supernatural.

Chanukah

Many assume Chanukah to be a Jewish Christmas equivalent. That assumption is false; Chanukah isn't even in the Bible.

Biblical Basis
Chanukah isn't in the Old or New Testament, though it may have been mentioned in John 10:22, called the Feast of Dedication. Its sources are the Apocrypha (considered canon by Roman Catholics and Orthodox Christians) and the Talmud. Before the Romans occupied Palestine, Alexander the Great's Greek and Macedonian successors ruled Israel. In 175 B.C., Seleucid Emperor Antiochus IV decided to suppress Judaism, leading to the Maccabean Revolt. By 165, the revolt had ejected the Greeks and they recaptured Jerusalem's temple. The Jews wanted to light the temple's lamp, but they had only enough oil for one day. You make do with what you have, so they lit it, and it miraculously lasted eight days (by which time they had found more oil). So Chanukah began as an eight-day celebration of Jewish victory, liberation, and faith. While scripture does not record Christ commenting on Chanukah, as a Jew, he likely celebrated it.

Biblical Practice
Obviously, there is none. However, Jews have joyfully celebrated Chanukah for more than two millennia since biblical times.

Modern Practice
Why spell it *Chanukah*? Because the first H is a heavy H, as in German "Ach." Chanukah begins on the 25th of Kislev (normally early to mid-December) and lasts eight days. Each night, the woman of the house lights another candle, with all present reciting special prayers. The feasting part honors the miracle of oil by concentrating on fried foods.

The traditional gift is small amounts of money, called *Chanukah gelt,* though many modern Jews give their children other gifts so they aren't left out of the Christmas gift frenzy. Jews spin a top called a *dreidel* (DRAY-del) bearing the Hebrew initials for "A Great Miracle Happened There." A traditional greeting is *"Chag sameach!"* (KHAG sa-MAY-akh), "happy holiday."

Original Raiders of the Not-Yet Lost Ark

✤ ✤ ✤ ✤

Harrison Ford wasn't the first to have adventures as a result of the Ark of the Covenant (the chest containing the Ten Commandments). During their 40 years in the wilderness, the Israelites carried it with them wherever they went—and one man even dropped dead from touching it. They also took it into battle to assure God's protection—but it was captured by the enemy!

After Moses received the stone tablets inscribed with the Ten Commandments, he had skilled craftsmen build an elaborate chest in which to keep them. In the Bible, this chest is variously called the Ark of the Covenant, the Ark of God (or Yahweh), the Ark of Testimony, or simply the Ark. It is a chest that measured just over four feet long and a little under three feet wide and high. The chest had a solid gold lid over which were carvings of two cherubim that faced each other with their wings extended forward and meeting at the center of the Ark. Four rings attached to the sides of the chest accommodated two poles (made of gold-plated acacia wood like the chest). The poles were used for carrying the Ark. However, the Ark was considered sacred and could only be handled by priests or by Levites (other men of the priestly clan).

The Presence of God

The Israelites took the Ark with them everywhere they went during their 40 years in the wilderness, carrying it in procession as the people moved from one location to another. For them it represented the presence of God himself, and the tablets of the law inside the Ark represented the covenant, or contract, that the Israelites had made with God. He would protect them and bring them into their own land in return for their undivided allegiance and their obedience to the laws enclosed in the Ark. When the Israelites were in camp, they kept the Ark in a special tent, known as the tabernacle, and it was to that tent that Moses went to consult God, who spoke to him from between the gold cherubim that hovered over the Ark.

Although the Israelites by no means believed that God was physically contained within the Ark or its tent, they saw the chest as a representation of his presence among them, a symbol of his protection. In some fanciful way, they also envisioned the Ark as the footstool used by God as he sits enthroned in the heavens. As the Israelites moved toward the land that God had promised them, they marched behind the Ark itself, which was carried by Levites. Moses even formulated a ritual to initiate and end a leg in their journey. "Whenever the Ark set out, Moses would say, 'Arise, O Lord, let your enemies be scattered, and your foes flee before you.' And whenever it came to rest, he would say, 'Return, O Lord of the ten thousands of Israel'" (Numbers 10:35–36).

Crossing Jordan

When the Israelites reached the Jordan River after 40 years in the wilderness, the Ark played a significant role. The priests led a grand procession, reverently carrying the Ark of the Covenant, and the people followed at a respectful distance. As the priests waded into the river, Joshua, following Yahweh's instructions, had them stand still. The powerful presence of God in the Ark caused the flow of the river to stop, and all the people of Israel crossed the river as though "on dry land" (Joshua 3:17)—just as their parents and grandparents had passed through the Red Sea 40 years earlier. This clearly shows that God is with Joshua and with his people.

Once safely across the Jordan and in the Promised Land, the Israelites continued to carry the Ark when they went to war to oust the resident Canaanites. In their very first battle, the Ark played a significant role. During the siege of the city of Jericho, the Israelites paraded around the city walls for seven days, shouting and blowing trumpets. But the most significant part of the parade was the Ark of the Covenant, which was carried behind the priests who were blowing the trumpets (ram's horns). The Israelites never raised a weapon, and even though they blew trumpets and shouted, the mere noise was not enough to bring them victory. It was God, whose presence was proudly represented in the Ark, who caused the walls to come tumbling down. From that time on, the Israelites never went into battle without the Ark—or almost never.

The Ark Narrative

Even after the Israelites had taken possession of their land, they had to fight off troublesome neighbors, particularly the Philistines, who had settled along the Mediterranean coast. During one battle with the Philistines, the Israelites failed to carry the Ark with them and they lost, suffering 4,000 casualties. Resolved to correct their grievous error, they again fought the Philistines, but this time they decided to carry the Ark with them. When the Ark was brought into the Israelite camp, the soldiers "gave a mighty shout, so that the earth resounded" (1 Samuel 4:5). When the Philistines heard the noise of the shouting, they began to express fear of this "god" (the Ark) and recalled how Yahweh had saved the Israelites in Egypt. Despite their fear, the Philistines fought hard and won the battle, killing 30,000 Israelite foot soldiers and capturing the Ark.

The Israelites were stunned. They felt that God had deserted them. Meanwhile, in the city of Ashdod, the Philistines placed the Ark of the Covenant in their temple beside a statue of their own god, Dagon, contemptuously offering this weak foreign god of the Israelites (as they saw the Ark) to their own more powerful god. However, when the Philistines returned to their temple in the morning, they found the Dagon idol lying face down before the Ark, assuming a penitential posture. They were shocked but tried to reason it away. Then, on another morning, they found their precious idol with its hands and head cut off. Later, the Philistines were stricken with boils that were attributed to the Ark.

Totally terrified, the Philistines realized that Yahweh wielded great power and that no one should mess with his Ark. They frantically looked for a way of returning the Ark safely. Finally, they packed the Ark into a cart, together with many rich peace offerings to placate Yahweh. Then they put the cart on a road and yoked it to two milk cows, hoping that the cows would pull the cart to the Israelites. And indeed they did, lowing all the way. In a kind of reenactment of the Exodus, the Ark returned home. In this story, commonly known as the Ark Narrative (1 Samuel 4–6), God at first seemed powerless (enduring capture and mocking) but was soon shown as powerful again. After being defeated, Yahweh rose again much as Jesus would do later.

What Happened to the Ark?

The Ark continued to be kept in its tent. When King David decided to bring it into Jerusalem, the Ark tipped over during transport and Uzzah, one of the oxcart drivers, reached up to steady it. But when he touched the sacred Ark, he was instantly struck dead. David was then afraid to bring the Ark into the city, and so he left it in the care of a man from Gath named Obed-edom. When David later discovered that Obed-edom and his entire family had been blessed because of the Ark, he decided to bring the Ark into the city after all, and he did so amid great rejoicing. When Solomon built his temple, he placed the Ark in its innermost room, known as the Holy of Holies, where only the high priest could enter.

Sometime just before the Babylonians destroyed the temple in 586 B.C., the Ark disappeared—no one knows where. After the Babylonian Exile, the Holy of Holies remained empty. According to one early tradition, the prophet Jeremiah hid the Ark as the Babylonians were advancing on Jerusalem, meaning to rescue it at a later time. However, Jeremiah was soon taken off to Egypt (against his will) and never had the opportunity to let anyone in charge know where the Ark was hidden. According to the book of Revelation, however, the Ark of the Covenant will be seen again in the temple of the New Jerusalem at the end of time.

> ### Numbers: Censuses, Laws, and Journeys
>
> The book of Numbers is about preparations for Israel to enter the land of Canaan. The people are numbered, more instructions are given, and the starts and stops of their journey to the Promised Land are detailed, including the 38 years of wandering in the wilderness.

10 Things

Odd Transportation

Bible characters got around, sometimes in weird ways.

1. Chariot of Fire/Whirlwind (2 Kings 2:11) Elijah knew it was time to leave this earthly existence, so he took Elisha across the Jordan River. "As they continued walking and talking, a chariot of fire and horses of fire separated the two of them, and Elijah ascended in a whirlwind into heaven." It's not clear whether the prophet rode the chariot or the whirlwind, but either certainly qualifies as an unusual mode of transport.

2. Wheel Within a Wheel (Ezekiel 10:9–13) The prophet Ezekiel had some strange visions. In one, he saw four heavenly creatures (cherubim) moving together, accompanied by "something like a wheel within a wheel. When they moved, they moved in any of the four directions without veering as they moved; but in whatever direction the front wheel faced, the others followed without veering as they moved." Some readers have suggested that Ezekiel was looking at a scene of modern helicopters, but we'll let you be the judge of that.

3. River Basket (Exodus 2:1–10) The Egyptians were killing the male infants of the Israelites. So, after Moses was born, his mother "got a papyrus basket for him, and plastered it with bitumen and pitch; she put the child in it and placed it among the reeds on the bank of the river." Pharaoh's daughter found the boy in the basket and adopted him.

4. Wall Basket (Acts 9:23–25) Saul, an opponent of the church, was on his way to arrest Christians in Damascus, but he was converted. Now his former colleagues were plotting to kill him. Normal escape routes were too dangerous; the gates were being watched. Saul's new friends "took him by night and let him down through an opening in the wall, lowering him in a basket." After that, Saul (later known as Paul) rushed off to Jerusalem and decades of effective ministry.

5. Fish's Belly (Jonah 1:17; 2:10) The Lord had a job for Jonah, but he didn't want it. The prophet boarded a ship going the opposite way. God sent a storm, and Jonah knew he was responsible. At his request, the crew threw him overboard—and he was swallowed by a "large fish," which swam back and "spewed Jonah out upon the dry land."

6. Walking on Water (Matthew 14:23–33) Leaving Jesus in prayer, his disciples sailed across Lake Galilee, but the wind was against them. Suddenly, Jesus "came walking toward them on the sea." Most were afraid of this "ghost," but Peter "got out of the boat, started walking on the water, and came toward Jesus." Distracted, Peter began to sink, but Jesus picked him up, and they both got back in the boat.

7. Stairway to Heaven (Genesis 28:11–17) Jacob, on the run, stopped for the night. He used a stone for a pillow and had an odd dream: "There was a ladder set up on the earth, the top of it reaching to heaven; and the angels of God were ascending and descending on it." Then the Lord was standing beside him, promising to be with him. Jacob awoke ecstatic. "Surely the Lord is in this place—and I did not know it!" he said. "How awesome is this place!"

8. Mobile Menagerie (Genesis 6:14–22) God was about to punish a wicked world, but he wanted to save one family—and lots of animals. He told Noah, "Make yourself an ark of cypress wood; make rooms in the ark, and cover it inside and out with pitch." This boat was 450 feet long, 75 feet wide, and 45 feet high, with a roof and three decks.

9. The Spirit (Acts 8:26–40) The Spirit told Philip to leave his ministry in Samaria and move to a "desert road." When he did, he encountered an Ethiopian official sitting in his chariot puzzling over the scriptures. Philip told him about Jesus and baptized him. Then, "when they came up out of the water, the Spirit of the Lord snatched Philip away." The evangelist "appeared" at another town and continued his ministry.

10. Jehu's Chariot (2 Kings 9:16–20) General Jehu, anointed the next king of Israel, drove his chariot to the capital city to seize control of the government. A sentinel marked the progress of the army, with a chariot leading. Apparently Jehu's road habits were known, because the watchman reported, "It looks like the driving of Jehu . . . for he drives like a maniac."

Units of Measure

✤ ✤ ✤ ✤

Weight, surface area, land, volume, money, time—all these have been around for a long time. The terms we use, however, have changed. That's why it's important to measure your words.

In the words of Noah (as portrayed by Bill Cosby), after God conveyed the dimensions of the ark: "Right.... What's a cubit?"

How Long? How Far?

Linear measurements:

- **Cubit:** *about 18 inches, the length of adult's forearm. It was the ruler of Bible times, the standard measurement of length*
- **Handbreadth:** *3 fingers' width, about 3 inches*
- **Span:** *a half-cubit, about 9 inches*
- **Reed:** *6 cubits, or 8 feet 9 inches*

Distance:

- **Fathom (or orgyia):** *6 feet*
- **Furlong (stadium):** *100 fathoms, or 202 yards*
- **Mile (milion):** *8 furlongs, or 1,618 yards*

Long-distance measurements were given in terms of about how many days' journey it was to the destination. Miles traveled per day: walking, 20; donkey, 20; horse, 25–30; camel, 30 as pack animal but up to 100 with rider.

The Weighting Game

Dry goods:

- **Cor:** *about 6 bushels, the standard for measuring wheat, flour, and the like*
- **Ephah:** *about three-fifths of a bushel*
- **Cab:** *about 1 quart*

- **Omer (translated as "measure" in NRSV):** *about 2 quarts*
- **Seah:** *about 7 quarts of dry goods*

Liquids:

- **Bath:** *6 gallons, which was a typical amount carried in a jar from a well*
- **Log:** *about one-third quart*
- **Hin:** *about 1 quart*

Keep Current with Currency

Weighing pure silver and gold:

- **Pim:** *about one-third ounce*
- **Shekel:** *about two-fifths ounce (To earn 1 shekel, the average person worked about 4 days.)*
- **Mina:** *60 shekels, about 1.25 pounds (To earn 1 mina, about 3 months.)*
- **Talent:** *60 minas, weighing approximately 75 pounds (To earn 1 talent, about 15 years.)*

Using actual silver and gold as currency was the standard until the Persian Empire introduced coins in about 538 B.C.

> **FUN FACT:**
>
> ✝ *Noah's ark's dimensions make it just over half the size of the* Titanic.

Coins:

- **As:** *usually bronze, the basic Roman coin (Often translated in English as "penny.")*
- **Lepta:** *small and copper, a Jewish coin worth about one-eighth of an as coin (This was the poor widow's "mite" in Mark 12:42.)*
- **Denarius:** *silver, worth 16 as coins (The most common Roman coin, it equaled one day's wage. This is the coin Jesus held up when questioned about paying taxes in Luke 20:24.)*
- **Drachma:** *a silver Greek coin, about equal to the denarius (It appears only in Jesus' parable about the woman who found a lost coin in Luke 15:8–10.)*
- **Stater:** *worth 4 drachmas (It is the Greek coin Peter found in the mouth of a fish in Matthew 17:27.)*

Psalms of Ascents

Certain psalms, meant to be sung, helped the ancient Hebrews through adversity during lengthy journeys.

During biblical times, Hebrews were encouraged to make the trip to Jerusalem for one or more of the three major annual festivals: Passover, Weeks, and Tents, also known as Booths or Tabernacles. Because of where Jerusalem was located, such a trek could be both physically and spiritually challenging, so Psalms 120—134 were recited to make the journey a little easier.

Known as "Pilgrim Psalms" or "Songs of Ascents," four are attributed to David and one to Solomon. The rest are anonymous, though some scholars believe they may have been written by Hezekiah, a king of Judah.

On the Road Again

Each of the 15 Psalms of Ascents represents a step in the journey to the holy city of Jerusalem. They begin with Psalm 120, which notes the pilgrims' distress at the fact that they live far from Jerusalem. Psalm 121 promises God's protection through lonely and dangerous country.

Psalm 122 celebrates the pilgrims' arrival in Jerusalem ("Our feet are standing within your gates, O Jerusalem"), while Psalms 123—126 praise God for his goodness and remind everyone to be thankful.

A visit to the temple follows. The first temple to God was built by Solomon, who is credited with Psalm 127: "Unless the Lord builds the house, those who build it labor in vain. Unless the Lord guards the city, the guard keeps watch in vain."

Encouraging Words

Psalms 128—133 encourage the Israelites to remain faithful to God, while Psalm 134 notes their arrival at the temple and calls for all to worship God: "Lift up your hands to the holy place, and bless the Lord."

The Psalms of Ascents don't hold quite the importance they did eons ago (today we just hop on a plane), but back in biblical times, they helped ease the burden of a truly arduous trek.

Books You'll Never See

❧ ❧ ❧ ❧

There are many more books of the Bible than those found in the New and Old Testaments. Why are they missing?

To the faithful, the Bible is the literal word of God, perfect in every way. But all is not as it seems. There are 39 books in the Old Testament and 27 books in the New Testament—yet many more books have been uncovered, including some mentioned in the Bible but not found there.

Before we examine this phenomenon, it's important to note that the Bible as we know it today is based on texts written many, many years after the events they chronicle. The books that compose the Old Testament canon, for example, are believed to have been written over several centuries beginning sometime in the 10th century B.C., though certain parts, carried forward through oral tradition, may go as far back as the 18th century B.C. Similarly, the books that compose the New Testament were compiled long after the life of Jesus. The oldest surviving complete text of the New Testament is the Codex Sinaiticus, which dates back to the 4th century A.D.

What's Not There

The books contained in the Old Testament mention several other books that, for reasons that remain unclear, are not part of the Bible. Joshua 10:13, for example, mentions the book of Jashar. So does 2 Samuel 1:18. And yet, the book of Jashar is nowhere to be found.

There are numerous other examples. 1 Kings 11:41 mentions the book of the Acts of Solomon, while 1 Chronicles 29:29 mentions the books of Nathan the Prophet and Gad the Seer. Additional books mentioned but not found in the Bible include:

2 Chronicles 12:15: The book of Shemaiah the Prophet. ("Now

the acts of Rehoboam, first to last, are they not written in the records of the prophet Shemaiah and of the seer Iddo, recorded by genealogy?")

2 Chronicles 20:34: The book of Jehu. ("Now the rest of the acts of Jehoshaphat, first to last, are written in the Annals of Jehu son of Hanani, which are recorded in the Book of the Kings of Israel.")

2 Chronicles 33:18–19: The book of the Kings of Israel. ("Now the rest of the acts of Manasseh, and his words of the seers who spoke to him in the name of the Lord God of Israel, these are written in the Annals of the Kings of Israel. His prayer, and how God received his entreaty, all his sin and his faithlessness, the sites on which he built high places and set up the sacred poles and the images, before he humbled himself, these are written in the records of the seers.")

Jude 14: The Book of the Prophesies of Enoch. ("It was also about these that Enoch, in the seventh generation from Adam, prophesied, saying, 'See, the Lord is coming with ten thousands of his holy ones.'")

The Apocrypha

A discussion of the missing books of the Bible must also address the Apocrypha—dozens of books dating from both Old and New Testament eras that have been left out of the official Bible for various reasons. (Some editions of the Bible contain the Apocrypha, but not all of the associated books.) Certain elements of the early church considered many of these books to be inspired by God and the apostles, but in the end they simply didn't make the editorial cut, so to speak. Others, however, were and remain controversial, even heretical in the eyes of many.

The Infancy Gospel of Thomas is a good example. It supposedly describes Jesus' childhood and paints him as a show-off and, for lack of a better word, a vengeful bully. According to this book, which many biblical scholars consider a fraud, young Jesus performed a variety of bizarre miracles in his youth, such as returning to human form a man who had been transformed into a mule by a bewitching spell, bringing to life clay birds and animals, and lengthening a wood throne built by his father that was too short. It also alleges that Jesus killed some boys who had opposed him.

It is believed that the Infancy Gospel of Thomas originated in the mid 2nd century A.D. It shares certain stories also found in the book of Luke, but apparently was never seriously considered for inclusion in the official Bible. Not surprisingly, many of the earliest Christian writers considered its contents heresy because of its bizarre portrayal of Jesus as a child.

Needless to say, the Infancy Gospel of Thomas and many other books that are a part of the Apocrypha have always been regarded as illegitimate by many mainstream churches. However, that didn't stop these missing books from finding an audience.

Publication of the Apocrypha

In 1820, several books of the Apocrypha were collected into a volume called *The Apocryphal New Testament,* a sort of alternative to the mainstream Bible that was a collection two English translations originally published in 1736 and 1738. The book was reissued in 1926 as *The Lost Books of the Bible,* and it was reprinted in 1979. According to some experts, the earliest publications of these missing books were an effort to further biblical study. Subsequent editions, however, were less scholarly and put into print because they were considered so scandalous.

Though the Bible has been altered, edited, and updated through the centuries, its most basic canons have remained set and resolute from the very beginning. The issue of "missing" books is just one of the mysteries surrounding its history, but one shouldn't place too much emphasis on their importance. The books it does contain have served believers well since the earliest days of both Judaism and Christianity.

Duplicate Psalms

Some psalms appear more than once in the Bible. David's song of praise when God delivered him from the hands of Saul appears as 2 Samuel 22 and also as Psalm 18. The psalm beginning, "The fool says in his heart, 'There is no God,'" appears as both Psalm 14 and 53.

Quiz

Water II

Still thirsting for Bible knowledge? Here's more.

1. Who, besides Jesus, walked on water?
    a. John the Baptist
    b. Moses and Aaron
    c. Elijah and Elisha
    d. Peter

2. What biblical figure, thrown overboard, was "spewed" onto dry land?
    a. Paul
    b. Peter
    c. Jonah
    d. Jeremiah

3. What future wife did Jacob meet at a well?
    a. Rachel
    b. Leah
    c. Rebekah
    d. Zipporah

4. What prisoner was shipwrecked on the Mediterranean island of Malta?
    a. Joseph
    b. Jeremiah
    c. John the Baptist
    d. Paul

Answers: 1. d (Matthew 14:29); 2. c (Jonah 2:10); 3. a (Genesis 29:1–12); 4. d (Acts 27:41–28:1)

Healing Heart

A gifted healer, evangelist Ruth Carter Stapleton's most memorable legacy may be the (brief) conversion of a porn icon.

During Jimmy Carter's four years in the White House, his family became as well known to the American public as the president himself. Especially notable was Carter's younger sister, Ruth, a talented healer who helped the ailing through a combination of prayer and psychotherapy.

Ruth Carter was born in Plains, Georgia, on August 7, 1929. She attended Georgia State College for Women for two years, then left to marry Robert Stapleton, a veterinarian. The couple moved to North Carolina, where Ruth earned her bachelor's degree in English from the University of North Carolina. She later earned a degree in theology.

God's Guidance

Afflicted with severe depression, Ruth sought recovery through group therapy supplemented with spiritual guidance received through an interdenominational religious retreat. It was there, she later recalled, that she "experienced God as a God of love." She became a member of the Pentecostal Church.

Based on her own recovery, Ruth developed a novel psychological healing technique in which Jesus was used to neutralize emotionally devastating memories. In 1976, Ruth published *The Gift of Inner Healing* and spoke at numerous spiritual workshops.

The Pious Pornographer

In 1977, Ruth found herself in the media spotlight as the woman who helped Larry Flynt, the infamous publisher of *Hustler* magazine, find God. Flynt publicly claimed to have experienced a religious conversion as a result of a conversation with Ruth, and he vowed to introduce an element of religion into his magazine and turn his publishing empire into a nonprofit religious foundation. However, Flynt failed to follow through with his promise and the magazine remained relatively unchanged.

Ruth died on September 26, 1983.

Bibles and Bullets

❀ ❀ ❀ ❀

The Bible is great at saving souls. It's also pretty good at saving lives.

Many people carry a Bible with them for solace during troubling times. On more than a few occasions, however, a Bible has also proved quite helpful at stopping a bullet. Following are the stories of several lucky men and women who owe their lives to the Good Book.

In April 1862, Sam Houston Jr., the son of renowned Texas governor Sam Houston, was fighting on the side of the Union at the Battle of Shiloh in southwestern Tennessee when he was struck in the chest by a Confederate bullet. Luckily, the bullet hit the Bible that Houston carried in the breast pocket of his coat, stopping at Psalm 70. Wounded, Houston was taken prisoner and held at Camp Douglas. He studied medicine after the war but later gave up his practice to become a writer.

Corporal Frank Richards of the 6th Liverpool Rifles, a British regiment, was fighting the Germans in northern France during World War I when an enemy bullet struck him. Richards would have died instantly had the bullet not been deflected by the YMCA Bible and metal tin he carried in his jacket. As a result, Richards walked away with only a couple of bruised ribs. The life-saving Bible is now part of the King's Regiment collections at the former Museum of Liverpool Life in England.

Richards wasn't the only soldier in World War I to have his life saved by a Bible. Nineteen-year-old William R. Wilson of New Castle, Pennsylvania, was fighting in France when he too was struck in the chest by a German sharpshooter. Like Richards, Wilson was saved by the Bible he kept in his breast pocket, which absorbed the brunt of the shot. He survived with only minor injuries.

In August 2007, PFC Brendan Schweigart was working to retrieve a tank outside Baghdad, Iraq, when a sniper shot him. The bullet hit him in the side and exited through his chest, landing in his Bible. The impact knocked Schweigart off his feet as if hit by a sledgehammer, but his life was saved by the Bible he carried over his heart. According to Schweigart, if not for the Bible, the bullet would have richocheted off his armor and back into his body, probably killing him.

In March 2008, a hunter's bullet tore through several walls of the Milks family home in Hambden Township, Ohio, before embedding in a Bible stored in a bedroom closet. Luckily, no one was injured during the incident, and the 17-year-old shooter visited the family to apologize for the errant shot. No charges were filed.

A stray bullet from a shoot-out on an Indianapolis street almost took the lives of two young girls sitting in a car at a stoplight in July 2008. Amazingly, a Bible sitting between the youngsters slowed the projectile so that no one died. One of the girls, age 10, was struck in the stomach but survived. The bullet then went through the Bible and finally came to rest in a watermelon held by the other child.

A Bible saved the life of a minister in Argentina's Mendoza province in May 2009, when he was shot point blank by an enraged mugger because he didn't have enough money. The terrified pastor instinctively held up the Bible as a shield as the gun went off, and the book's hardcover stopped the bullet. The minister escaped with only minor injuries.

Going the Extra Mile

In the Sermon on the Mount, Jesus spoke repeatedly about going beyond the minimal requirements of law or social courtesy in order to show true generosity of spirit. One vivid illustration was when he said, "if anyone forces you to go one mile, go with him two miles" (Matthew 5:41). This referred to the detested Roman practice of forcing civilians into service carrying military baggage for a prescribed distance, one Roman mile.

The Gideon Bibles

✤ ✤ ✤ ✤

*The year 2008 marked the 100th anniversary of
the "Bible Project," the Gideons International practice of placing
special Bible editions in every hotel room in the United States.*

That the Gideons would choose hotel rooms to spread their faith is
not surprising. The organization was formed by three travelers who
met in a Wisconsin hotel in 1898, and the majority of the group's
early membership consisted of traveling salesmen—somewhat fitting
considering that Jesus and the apostles are sometimes referred to
as the greatest traveling salesmen of all time. Here are a few facts
about the book you'll probably find at your next hotel stay.

1.3 billion: Number of Gideon Bibles distributed by Gideons International since 1908

140,000: Number of Gideons International members

56 million: Number of Bibles distributed per year

400 per year: Number of Bibles distributed per member

6,410: Number of Bibles distributed per hour

17: Minimum number of rock songs referencing Gideon Bible in the lyrics

Parts of the Gideon Bible

- **Preface:** *The front matter of the Gideon's Bible consists of a preface exhorting the reader to "read it slowly, frequently, and prayerfully."*

- **John 3:16:** *The Bible's most famous verse* ("For God so loved the world that he gave his only Son, so that everyone who believes in him may not perish but may have eternal life") *is translated into dozens of languages.*

- **"Bible Helps"**: *Suggested Bible verses depending on the need.*

- *The text of the Bible, without any kind of commentary or notes.*

- *A place for the reader to sign and date his confession and acceptance of Christ as his Savior.*

In Good Company
The Gideons' practice of placing Bibles in hotel rooms must have seemed like a good idea, because other religious groups soon followed suit. By the mid-1990s, Gideon Bibles across the country shared hotel drawer space with Buddhist texts, Christian Science literature, and the Book of Mormon. Why not the Qu'ran? Islamic leaders were worried that people might bring the holy book into unclean places, such as the bathroom. Or, you know, the average motel room in the United States.

The Namesake
The Gideons International take their name from Judges 7, in which Gideon agrees to do whatever God commands. However, they conveniently ignore other aspects of Gideon's story, such as the fact that he demanded reward in the form of a gold earring from each of the 300 warriors who helped him defeat the Midianites. Gideon melted this gold into an "ephod," a sort of ceremonial vest, which became an object of idolatry and would ultimately lead to a renewal of God's wrath against the Israelites.

World's Oldest Bible Publisher

The longest-running publisher of Bibles is the Cambridge University Press. The Press began in 1591 with the Geneva Version of the Bible, and it has continued ever since. Today, it still has a reputation for producing fine-quality Bibles.

Ishmael the Assassin

✤ ✤ ✤ ✤

*When the Babylonians destroyed Jerusalem and took most
of the people into exile, some stayed behind under the
governorship of a man named Gedaliah. But when a hot-headed
royalist named Ishmael (not Abraham's son) assassinated
Gedaliah, the remaining Jews were forced into exile
in Egypt along with the prophet Jeremiah.*

Abraham's first son, born of a slave woman, was named Ishmael,
and though he was "a wild ass of a man," he managed to become
the patriarch of a large powerful nation, the Arabs. Another Ishmael
was no more than a crazed zealot and an assassin who made a late
entrance into the drama of the fall of Jerusalem.

Out of the Rubble

In 589 B.C., totally ignoring the prophet Jeremiah's council,
King Zedekiah of Judah rebelled against King Nebuchadnezzar of
Babylon, wrongfully believing that Babylonian power was declining.
Nebuchadnezzar besieged Jerusalem and finally broke through into
the city in 586 B.C. He captured Zedekiah and forced him to watch
the execution of his sons, then he blinded him and deported him
to Babylon with hundreds of others. Only the poor and unskilled
and a few others were left behind. Among those few others was
Ishmael, a member of the royal family who had managed to escape
the Babylonians but foolishly continued to resist their power and
consort with the king of Ammon, a neighboring land. Many of the
other Jews who escaped the Babylonians took refuge in other surrounding lands. Meanwhile, the Babylonians tore down Jerusalem's
walls; burned the temple, the palace, and other major buildings; and
took the remaining treasures of Jerusalem to Babylon.

   With Jerusalem being totally uninhabitable, Nebuchadnezzar
set up a provisional government in the nearby town of Mizpah and
appointed a respected Jewish leader named Gedaliah as governor.
Once Gedaliah was established in Mizpah, many of the poor Jews

who remained in the land gather there. The prophet Jeremiah also chose to remain in Mizpah and support Gedaliah, who was his friend. As word spread, Jews who had dispersed to Moab, Ammon, Edom, and other nearby lands returned to join the remnant that had been left in the land by the Babylonians.

Gedaliah encouraged the people to cooperate with the Babylonians, as Jeremiah had often done in the past, and assured them that he would act as mediator between them and the Babylonian officials. This no doubt rankled Ishmael, who resented the Babylonians for what they had done to him and his own family. He probably considered Gedaliah a traitor who was collaborating with the enemy (Babylon) and betraying his own people. He may have resented that Nebuchadnezzar had appointed a lesser nobleman to govern Judah and overlooked Ishmael himself—who was, after all, of royal blood!

But the opinions of Ishmael and his cohorts seemed to have been in a minority, for most of the Jews responded positively to Gedaliah, who told them: "Stay in the land and serve the king of Babylon, and it shall go well with you" (Jeremiah 40:9). Encouraged by Gedaliah, the people of Judah planted and harvested their crops and prospered.

Ishmael Does His Thing

The prosperous times lasted only about two years, however, before chaos erupted. Johanan, one of the local Jewish leaders who patrolled the open company, came to Gedaliah and warned him that Ishmael had been conspiring against him with Baalis, the king of Ammon (just east of the Jordan). At Baalis's urging, Ishmael was planning to assassinate Gedaliah. Johanan then took Gedaliah aside and quietly asked his permission to stop Ishmael by killing him. No one need know, Johanan told Gedaliah, but if Ishmael is allowed to live, he will kill you, then the people will be scattered and what little there is left of Judah will perish. Gedaliah couldn't believe that Ishmael would harm him, and so he said: "Do not do such a thing, for you are telling a lie about Ishmael" (Jeremiah 40:16).

Unfortunately, Johanan was not lying. Ishmael and ten others arrived in Mizpah and went to Gedaliah, who invited them to dinner. While dining, Ishmael and his men murdered Gedaliah. They also killed everyone else in the dining hall, including some visiting Babylonian soldiers. But they were still not satisfied.

The next day, Ishmael and his cronies met 80 Jewish pilgrims who were coming to Jerusalem from the north to offer sacrifices in the temple—apparently they didn't realize that the Babylonians had leveled the temple. Ishmael greeted the pilgrims at the city gates, weeping and imploring them to come to Gedaliah. He led them into the center of the city, and he and his men slaughtered them, sparing only ten pilgrims who offered large bribes. After tossing the murdered corpses into a large cistern (a pit for storing water), Ishmael took all the remaining people in Mizpah captive and started leading them to Ammon.

Civil War and Its Aftermath

At this point civil war erupted. Johanan heard about what had happened and quickly gathered together a militia (with the help of other local leaders). The militia, under Johanan's command, set out to overtake Ishmael and his captives and eventually caught up with them. When Ishmael's captives saw Johanan, they shouted for joy, broke away from Ishmael, rushed to join Johanan's troops, and helped them fight Ishmael and his men. Facing sure defeat, Ishmael escaped with eight of his men and returned to Ammon and the king who had conspired with him against Gedaliah.

Having won the battle, Johanan and his people had to worry about losing the war. Knowing that Nebuchadnezzar would seek retaliation for the assassination of Gedaliah, the man he had appointed governor of Judah (not to mention the Babylonian soldiers who were included in the dining-hall massacre), they banded together and headed for safety in Egypt, taking the prophet Jeremiah and his scribe Baruch with them. They left Judah virtually deserted.

The people under Johanan settled in Egypt, where Jeremiah continued to preach to them, and the community apparently prospered. History tells us that a community of Jews thrived in Egypt for centuries, and by the time of Jesus, Egypt was a major center of Jewish life.

Nothing further is known of Ishmael, however.

> ## Is He a Nimrod?
>
> Nimrod is often a pejorative term today, but the biblical Nimrod was the first warrior (Genesis 10:8, 9). The Bible says he built Nineveh.

Where Jesus Walked

Sea of Galilee

In most cases, the person under discussion would not have actually walked on the sea, but around its edges. This was a special case.

In Biblical Times
The Sea of Galilee Christ walked around (and on) was a very important source of fish for all the towns ringing it. The Jordan fed it from the north and passed out of its southern tip, just as it does today. Tiberias and Bethsaida Julias were probably the largest towns fronting the sea, but Capernaum, Gennasaret, and Magdala were also situated along its edges. It was subject to terrific and violent storms but offered bountiful catches of fish.

Jesus' Connection
Much of Christ's ministry occurred along the Sea of Galilee. He resided at Capernaum, though he was on the road a lot. He called Simon Peter and Andrew, Galilee fishers plying their nets, to be his disciples. James and John soon followed. He cast out an evil spirit in Capernaum, healed a disabled man, and ate with sinners and tax collectors (some would say that's redundant). In one public address along the Sea of Galilee, he had to have a boat ready so that all the sick people seeking healing wouldn't trample him. The miracle of loaves and fishes occurred along the Galilee and the Beatitudes may have been given here (Luke's level place could be near the Sea). Shortly after the loaves and fishes, Christ walked on the waters of the Galilee. In short, anywhere on the western and northern shores of the Sea of Galilee may have been trod on by Jesus.

Sea of Galilee Today
Called *Yam Kinneret* in Hebrew, the entire Sea of Galilee is in northern Israel. It's not very deep, no more than 150 feet at the lowest point; it's 13 miles long and 7 miles wide. Storm surges can send huge waves crashing onto the coastline. The water level is lower than in biblical times, not surprising given how precious and scarce water is in the region. It is 700 feet below sea level. A recent ban prohibits fishing.

Who Was the First Woman?

✤ ✤ ✤ ✤

*Eve is firmly believed to have been the first woman, created to be
Adam's companion and helper. If that's the case, who is Lilith, who
was supposedly Adam's first wife until she demanded equality?*

In the opening chapter of Genesis, God creates humans in his own
image: "male and female he created them" (Genesis 1:27). God
seems here to be creating the first human man and woman simultaneously, making them equal, and giving them all the surrounding
vegetables and fruits for food—with no restrictions. Then, in the
second chapter of Genesis, there is another account of how God
created the first humans. In that version, God creates the man from
dust and tells him that he may eat any fruit or vegetable except for
what grows on the tree of the knowledge of good and evil. Only later
does God create a woman, forming her out of the man's side, to be
his helper and his partner (Genesis 2:18–22).

Adam's First Wife

From these accounts we surmise that Eve was Adam's first wife, yet
according to ancient folktales recorded by revered Jewish rabbis, she
was not. These tales accord that privilege to a woman called Lilith.
But Lilith soon left Adam because he tried to dominate her and
she refused to submit to him, correctly claiming that they had been
created as equals. Adam appealed to God, who sent three angels to
find Lilith and force her to return. But Lilith had mated with a great
demon, and when the angels found her she was bearing children in a
cave. When she refused to come back to the garden, the angels told
her they would kill a hundred of her children every day as punishment for her disobedience. In revenge, Lilith committed herself to
the mission of causing stillbirths and crib deaths. Male children are
at risk of Lilith's wrath for 8 days after birth (until circumcision) and
girls are at risk for 20 days. However, Lilith reluctantly agreed not
to kill any children who had amulets bearing the names of the three
angels: Sanoy, Sansanoy, and Samangelof.

Because no proper name is ever given to the woman created along with Adam in chapter 1 of Genesis, it is tempting to conjecture that she was Lilith. Once Lilith left, God may have created a second wife, this time out of Adam's side, and taken the precaution of placing a restriction on the new couple, forbidding them to eat from the one tree. Unfortunately, they did eat from it and it is only after doing so that Adam gave his new wife a name, Eve. But that's another story.

Lilith in the Bible and Beyond

Lilith's name appears only once in the Bible—in Isaiah's description of the coming destruction of Edom, the land to the south and east of Israel where the descendants of Jacob's brother Esau had settled. After its destruction, Edom will be a place where wild beasts and goat-demons roam, and "there too Lilith shall repose" (Isaiah 34:14).

Lilith probably entered Jewish folklore from Assyria about 700 B.C., coming from a class of Mesopotamian demons called Lilitu. Several centuries after Isaiah, we find Jewish writings that describe Lilith as a seductive she-demon with wings and long hair (signifying wantonness). Her story as Adam's wife is told at length in a ninth-century narrative called *The Alphabet of Ben-Sira.* A cult devoted to Lilith survived until at least the 7th century, and even today some Jewish parents hang red ribbons or red yarn from their infant's crib to keep Lilith away. (Because red is the color of blood, it is looked upon as life-giving.)

> ## Mother of Life
>
> Eve's name in Hebrew means "life" (*chavvah*). Adam called her this because she was the mother of all living things (see Genesis 3:20).

Lilith Today

The specter of Lilith is a persistent one, and it has even been used in politics. Because of her self-assertiveness as Adam's first wife (and despite her reputation as a baby-killer!), some feminist groups have adopted Lilith as an emblem. Many Christians, on the other hand, are quick to point out that the story of Lilith as a predecessor of Eve is not in the Bible, but is merely a folktale, even though it was reported in the Middle Ages by reputable and pious Jewish rabbis.

Lost Sources of the Bible

✿ ✿ ✿ ✿

When the biblical authors sat down to write their books, what did they have to go on? Did they rely solely on memory? Or did they refer to earlier writings as modern historians do? The Bible itself tells us that the authors of the historical books of the Old Testament did indeed rely on earlier sources. Some of them are even named in the Bible itself, though sadly they are now lost.

Many of the stories in the Old Testament books, especially those covering the time before King David, were probably passed along verbally from generation to generation by professional storytellers. Most of the material was transmitted in the form of simple prose tales, but often major historical events were immortalized in poetry. Both prose and verse accounts were later incorporated into the Bible—and occasionally the Bible refers to these sources by title.

Royal Records

When David established his capital in Jerusalem, he championed literacy and began keeping court records. Along with statistics and inventories, these records included annals or chronicles of what was done by the individual kings from David on. The annals provided an invaluable source for the authors of 1 and 2 Kings and Nehemiah, who cite them. Because the biblical authors were concerned with examining the relationship that existed between Yahweh and the king, they often left out material that would ordinarily be included in a history. To compensate for what was missing, the authors of these books often end their accounts of a king by stating that other (secular) information on that ruler can be found in the book of the Acts of Solomon (1 Kings 11:41) or, more frequently, in the annals of the Kings of Israel or Judah. For example, 1 Kings 14:19 reads: "Now the rest of the acts of Jeroboam, how he warred and how he reigned, are written in the Book of the Annals of the Kings of Israel." Because of these references, we know the biblical authors consulted the court records, undoubtedly using them as research materials.

The author of the books of Chronicles used the books of Samuel and Kings to retell and update Israel's history—although he seems to have used a different version of those books than the one in the Bible today. The chronicler also cites the court records plus accounts of the words and actions of various prophets. Finally, in 2 Chronicles 24:27, he cites the commentary on the Book of the Kings. Even though its title suggests an interpretive volume, this otherwise unknown book may be the court records under another name.

Early Poetry

Two poetic works constitute the most interesting of all the cited source material in the Old Testament. The first of these is either a long poem or a collection of poems about the wars fought by the Israelites when they took possession of the Promised Land of Canaan. Numbers 21:14–15 cites two lines from the poem and identifies the verses as coming from the book of the Wars of the Lord. The archaic nature of the language in the cited passage suggests that the poem may have originated around the time of the war. Although they are difficult to translate, the verses seem to describe Yahweh as he leads the Israelite warriors into battle against the Canaanites.

The other poetic source is the book of Jashar, which is first cited in Joshua 10:12–13 as the source of Joshua's prayer for the sun to stand still long enough for him to win the battle at Gibeon. After giving the text of the short poem, the author asks: "Is this not written in the Book of Jashar?" In 2 Samuel 1:18 the book of Jashar is again given as a source—for David's lament over the deaths of Saul and Jonathan, which contains the refrain, "How the mighty have fallen!" The rest of the book of Jashar is lost to us, but if the other poems in the book were of as high quality as the two we have, the loss is great indeed.

Did They Wear Kilts Too?

Daniel 3:7 mentions the bagpipe along with many other musical instruments that were played when people fell down and worshipped Nebuchadnezzar's golden statue. This bagpipe would have been made of goatskin, with two pipes protruding.

Tidbits and Trivia

No matter how much you read the Bible,
there's probably a lot you still don't know about Psalms.

Psalms is one of the most fascinating books of the Bible from both a historical and insightful perspective. Scholars and theologians have been poring over it for centuries and have come up with a wealth of amazing fun facts.

For example, did you know that Psalms is the longest book in Bible, with 150 "chapters"? The longest psalm is 119, which contains 176 verses; the shortest is Psalm 117, which has just two verses. Interestingly, the Bible used by most Orthodox churches contains one more psalm than Bibles used by Jews, Roman Catholics, and Protestants.

Praise for Psalms

A lot of important people in early Christianity found much to like in Psalms. Saint Ambrose, the bishop of Milan, for example, wrote: "Although all Scripture breatheth the grace of God, yet sweet beyond all others is the Book of Psalms." Later, Martin Luther called Psalms "a Bible in miniature."

Psalms take a variety of forms. Some are meant to be sung to musical accompaniment, while others are essentially instructional poems, known as maskils. Examples of instructional poems include Psalms 42, 45, 52—55, and 74.

The apostles cherished the book of Psalms and used its literary treasures to spread the Gospel following Jesus' crucifixion. Psalm 2:1–6, in particular, inspired them and kept them motivated during a period of terrible persecution by nonbelievers.

And speaking of Jesus, several psalms make mention of a messiah, which Christians believe to be Jesus. References can be found to Jesus' lineage through David and events of Holy Week and the crucifixion.

The book of Psalms is rich in history, insight, and advice. Read it, and you'll always learn something.

Quiz

First Impressions

*First impressions are vital.
So let's see how some books of the Bible raise our interest.*

Which Bible book begins...?

1. "In the beginning was the Word, and the Word was with God, and the Word was God."

2. "Paul, a servant of Jesus Christ, called to be an apostle, set apart for the gospel of God."

3. "How lonely sits the city that once was full of people! How like a widow she has become, she that was great among the nations! She that was a princess among the provinces has become a vassal."

4. "Happy are those who do not follow the advice of the wicked, or take the path that sinners tread, or sit in the seat of scoffers."

5. "In the days when the judges ruled, there was a famine in the land, and a certain man of Bethlehem in Judah, went to live for a while in the country of Moab, he and his wife and two sons."

6. "In the first book, Theophilus, I wrote about all that Jesus did and taught from the beginning."

7. "The elder to the beloved Gaius, whom I love in truth."

8. "Long ago God spoke to our ancestors in many and various ways by the prophets."

9. "In the beginning God created the heavens and the earth."

10. "In the thirtieth year, in the fourth month, on the fifth day of the month, as I was among the exiles by the River Chebar, the heavens were opened, and I saw visions of God."

11. "The beginning of the good news of Jesus Christ, the Son of God."

12. "After the death of Moses the servant of the Lord..."

Answers: 1. John; 2. Romans; 3. Lamentations; 4. Psalms; 5. Ruth; 6. Acts; 7. 3 John; 8. Hebrews; 9. Genesis; 10. Ezekiel; 11. Mark; 12. Joshua

Why Is the Song of Songs in the Bible?

❧ ❧ ❧ ❧

The Song of Songs seems to be a love song that has nothing to do with religion. And its language is so erotic that many perplexed interpreters have endeavored to find more pious meanings in the book. Some have even questioned why it is in the Bible.

A beautifully poetic book, the Song of Songs celebrates the mutual, unwavering love of a man and a woman, now meeting, now parting, now seeking, and now finding each other. Although it seems entirely secular, never so much as mentioning God, it was accepted as part of the Hebrew Bible sometime before the time of Christ, presumably without offending anyone. By the end of the first century, however, rabbis began to react to the sexual nature of the text and question its place in the Bible. Eminent first-century Jewish scholar Rabbi Akiba defended it as "the holiest of the holy," but then went on to condemn those who profane it by singing it in banquet houses. He did not see the texts as profane songs of sexual love—but others did.

From then on, the jig was up. Both Jews and Christians went to great lengths to interpret the Song of Songs in any way they could to avoid admitting it was sexual (though by no means pornographic). Jews saw it as describing God's love for the Jews or even the marriage of God and Israel. The prophets Hosea and Jeremiah had described Israel as God's bride, but in their prophecies Israel is condemned as an adulterous wife, while there is no hint that the woman in the Song of Songs is unfaithful. Others saw the book as an allegory of the love between God and the Synagogue or Church or between God and the Christian soul, or even between Mary and her son Jesus, though this came shudderingly close to suggesting incest.

One offbeat interpretation insists that the Song of Songs was originally written in Egyptian hieroglyphics and is solely about Jesus' death and believers who long for Jesus' return.

The Song as History

The Song of Songs was also often seen as a history of Israel or of the Christian Church, though ending in different eras. Jews saw it as ending with the Jews returning from exile in Babylon. One commentator sees the "city" the woman goes through in search of her lover in verse 3:2 as the desert the Jews crossed, noting that 600,000 Jews in the desert would constitute a city. For Christians, the history ended variously with the founding of the Church, the Reformation, or the Last Judgment.

Some Verse Readings

Verse-by-verse readings also went far afield to avoid the erotic, and they often had little to do with the text. For example, the lovers' kiss has been interpreted as the oral law (Jewish laws passed down by word of mouth). "Your belly is a heap of wheat, encircled with lilies" (7:2) was said to refer to the book of Leviticus, for just as the belly is situated between the heart above and the legs below, so Leviticus has two books before it and two after it.

The woman's breasts are the tablets of the Ten Commandments or the Old and New Testaments, which produce the milk that nourishes Christians. Or, in one anti-Semitic view, the Jews have the two breasts of the she-goat (the tablets of the Ten Commandments), but Christians, like cows, have the four breasts of the Gospels—full of the sweet milk of wisdom.

So What's It All About?

Today the Song of Songs is generally accepted as love poetry, but it is love poetry with a purpose—to teach what ideal love is all about. The relationship between lovers in the Song of Songs is unwavering, faithful, strong, and selfless. It dissolves the boundaries set between male and female by ancient Near Eastern society. The woman is seen as a whole character, an individual with her own opinions and desires—and with her own will. The man supplements the woman rather than dominating her. She in turn complements him. Together, they make a perfect whole. So there's no need to blush or toss the book out of the Bible. It's a beautiful lesson on how to love—and we can learn much from it.

Sukkot

A holiday where you camp? Precisely. The roots of Sukkot go back to Leviticus, and it commemorates the Israelites' escape from Egypt.

Biblical Basis
The biblical heart and soul of *Sukkot* (suh-COAT), which means "booths" (singular is *sukkah*), is the twofold significance of harvest festival and Mosaic migration. When God brought the Israelites out of Egypt, they had to camp out (obviously there were no bed-and-breakfasts in the Sinai peninsula back then). Thus, when they reached Israel, God told Moses: "Tell my people that every year, they have to live in booths for a week, to remember how I got them out of Egypt."

Biblical Practice
In scripture, Sukkot was a time when devout Israelites gave thanks to God for a good harvest, showing their joy and appreciation with a big feast. Yet it meant far more, because having to spend seven nights in a booth served as a lasting reminder of God's deliverance from having to perform slave labor in Egypt.

Modern Practice
Coming only five days after the quiet contemplation of Yom Kippur—on the 15th of Tishrei, usually in early October—Sukkot is a very upbeat holiday. Most Jewish families at least build some form of sukkah, and devout families camp out in the sukkah for the full week of the feast. It is a *mitzvah* (righteous deed) to help construct a sukkah. There are certain rules for the sukkah: It has to have at least 2.5 walls, and it has to stand up to the wind. (Now you know why there aren't many Jews in Kansas.)

It is customary to hang corn and squash in the sukkah, which honors the harvest tradition. Just as Christian families enjoy setting up and decorating a tree together at Christmas, so an observant Jewish family will make a happy team project out of building their sukkah. Some even claim that the pilgrims of Massachusetts got the idea of a Thanksgiving feast from Sukkot, though that is highly debatable.

Israel's Neighbors

EGYPTIANS

*The Egyptian civilization was one of world history's great cultures—
and a player in some of the Bible's best-known stories.*

Who Were They?
As early as 6000 B.C., the Nile Delta's lush fertility drew Stone Age
hunter-gatherers. Around 3200 B.C., the upper and lower Nile Egyptian
communities united into the monarchy whose successors Moses and his
people would later flee. During Old Testament times, Egypt was often
invaded and sometimes conquered, but it always reasserted itself. As the
breadbasket of the eastern Mediterranean and a gateway to African trade,
geography guaranteed that major powers would covet Egypt. Egyptian
religion revolved around dozens of gods, often part animal. In the first
century A.D., Christian belief gained momentum in Egypt and would remain
ascendant until the Muslim conquest in 639 A.D. Egyptian architecture,
writing, burial customs, and history have fascinated scholars for millennia.

Where Are They Now?
In 343 B.C., the Persian Empire ended Egypt's independence. First,
Macedonian/Greek, then Roman, Byzantine, and Arab conquerors seized
the valuable prize in sequence, all adding their genetics and cultural
overlays. The descendants of the ancient Egyptians are still present; they
simply consider themselves Arabs. Some believe Egyptian Arabic is the
nearest thing to a modern Arabic standard dialect.

Biblical Mentions
Abram went to Egypt during famine times with his beautiful wife, Sarai.
Joseph was sent against his will to Egypt, but he became an important
vizier once there. The Israelites went to Egypt and lived peacefully for
years until pharaoh used them for too much forced labor; God sent the
famous plagues until pharaoh told Moses to get out. One nonbiblical
aspect of Egypt of interest to biblical scholars is the country's flirtation
with monotheism under Akhenaten (1350–1334 B.C.). Inspired by God? We
can't know, but anything's possible!

The Fruit of the Vine in Ancient Times

✤ ✤ ✤ ✤

Wine, wine, wine. Seems like everybody is constantly drinking wine in the Bible. What's up with that?

Yes, it does seem as though wine is mentioned constantly in the Bible, but there were plenty of Hebrews who abstained from the drink. All rabbis who performed the services of the temple were forbidden to drink wine on the days they were "on duty." Men who had taken the Nazirite vow went even further—they refused at any time to eat or drink anything that was "produced by the grapevine, not even the seeds or the skins" (Numbers 6:3–4). Still, for most Israelites, wine was not only a part of everyday life but an important component of their religious rituals.

Noah's Hangover

The first time wine is mentioned in the Bible is when Noah blows off some steam after the whole "ark thing" (Genesis 9:20–25). He plants the world's very first vineyard, makes some wine from the grapes, gets wasted, and passes out naked in his tent. Noah's son Ham sees his father naked, but his two other sons, Shem and Japheth, are mortified and cover their father's nude body. Noah wakes up feeling like the bottom of someone's shoe and puts a curse on Ham. This is not just the story of a man and his sons, however; it also marks the Hebrews' transition from a nomadic people to a settled agricultural people, and their very first crop was grapes that were made into wine.

The ancient Israelites were famous for their hospitality; indeed, hospitality was considered to be one of a patriarch's most important duties. In all Hebrew homes but the very poorest, wine was kept on hand at all times and offered to friend and stranger alike. Wine was also an integral part of Jewish religious life. At the Passover meal, for example, four cups of wine are drunk by each participant (though the wine is often watered down for reasons of propriety). In the New Testament, wine becomes the symbol of Christ's blood sacrifice. At the Last Supper, Jesus offers his apostles wine as a symbol of the blood of the new Covenant (Matthew 26:27, Mark 14:23–25, Luke 22:19–20). "Do this in remembrance of me," he tells them, and millions of Christians to this day follow their example.

A Pressing Concern

The ancient Israelites made wine with wine-presses that were at their vineyards. This usually happened around the end of September or the beginning of October, when the vintage season came to an end and the grapes were fully ripe. A wine press consisted of two troughs cut next to each other in solid rock. One of the troughs was at a higher level than the other, and a partition of a few inches with a small opening separated them. The grapes were put into the upper trough and mashed by the feet of men, women, and  children. The juice flowed either into the lower trough or directly into some kind of collection vessel, usually a "bottle" made of animal skin. The Hebrews made both red and white wine in this way, although sometimes grape juice was consumed before fermentation. Families lived together at their vineyards and worked as teams against locusts, wild animals, bad weather, and human intruders who would rob them.

There are many warnings against drunkenness in both the Old and New Testaments, though alcoholism does not seem to have been as much of a hereditary problem among the Jews as it was among those in certain other ethnic groups. Wine was often used for medicinal purposes, not only internally but as an external antiseptic. In the crude, primitive surgical procedures of the day, wine would be offered to the patient to dull the sometimes agonizing pain. So, we see that wine represented all the elements of life, both bitter and sweet, and was a constant presence in ancient Israelite culture.

Which Son Did Abraham Not Sacrifice?

❧ ❧ ❧ ❧

God tested Abraham by ordering him to sacrifice his son, only to let the patriarch off the hook at the last minute. Jews and Christians believe that son was Isaac, but many Muslims identify him as Isaac's older half-brother, Ishmael, ancestor of the Arab peoples.

According to Genesis, God tested Abraham's faith in a harsh manner, telling him: "Take your son, your only son Isaac, whom you love" and offer him up to me as a burnt sacrifice on a mountain in the land of Moriah (Genesis 22:2). Straining against every fiber in his being, Abraham determined to obey this awful command without protest. He cut some wood, loaded it onto a donkey, and set out with Isaac and two servants. After walking for three days, the party came to the mountain in Moriah. (According to tradition, it was the place

where Solomon later built his temple.) Abraham told the servants to stay behind, and he and Isaac climbed the slope. Isaac carried the wood (much as Jesus would later carry his cross), and Abraham carried a torch and a knife. When Isaac noticed that there was no animal to sacrifice, he questioned his father, who replied, "God himself will provide the lamb for a burnt offering, my son" (Genesis 22:8).

The Sacrifice

On the hilltop, Abraham built a rock altar and covered it with wood. Then he bound Isaac, who offered no resistance, laid him on the wood, and raised the knife to kill him. Suddenly an angel called out, stopping Abraham because he had proved his complete faith in God.

When Abraham looked up, he saw a ram caught by its curved horns in some bushes. This was the "lamb" that Abraham had said God would provide. After Abraham had sacrificed the ram, the angel again addressed him, saying: "Because you have . . . not withheld your son, your only son . . . I will make your offspring as numerous as the stars of heaven and the sand that is on the seashore" (Genesis 22:16–17).

The only glitch in this story is that Isaac was never Abraham's "only" son, as Genesis twice calls him. Although Isaac was the only son of Abraham's wife, Sarah, about 15 years earlier Abraham had had a son, named Ishmael, with Sarah's maidservant, Hagar. And so Ishmael was Abraham's only son for some 15 years before Isaac was born.

Isaac or Ishmael?

The Qur'an (the holy writ of Islam) tells the story about Abraham being commanded to sacrifice his son, but it leaves out the name of the son. Today many Muslims believe that the son featured in the story was not Isaac, but Ishmael, Abraham's firstborn son and their own ancestor. The story in the Qur'an is found in a section that tells various stories of men who prove their fidelity to God's will, and it is not chronologically tied to the story of Abraham. It could easily have occurred before Isaac's birth, making Ishmael Abraham's only son at the time. With only one son, there was little need to name him. Furthermore, there is nothing in the Qur'an to indicate that Ishmael and Hagar became alienated from Abraham and Sarah, as Genesis tells us. Consequently, Muslims see Ishmael and Isaac as equally important sons of Abraham and recognize both as links in the chain of prophets that extends from Abraham to Jesus and Muhammed. Following this line of thought, then the brotherhood of Isaac and Ishmael should unite Jews, Christians, and Muslims into a single spiritual family.

Whichever son was intended, the story of Abraham's near sacrifice of his son is not as cruel as it may sound to us today. God was not sadistically torturing Abraham but was presenting him as a model of unshakable faith for all to follow. In addition, it is likely that the story was meant to signal God's disapproval of human sacrifices, which were common in Abraham's day.

Worst Man for the Job

✤ ✤ ✤ ✤

God chose Gideon to head a fighting force to deal with bands of raiders who were swooping down on local farmers every year at harvest time and stealing their crops. But God didn't pick Gideon because he showed the most potential for stopping the raids. He picked him because he was the worst man for the job.

The story of Gideon takes place around 1140 B.C. It is the time when each of the 12 tribes of Israel was being ruled by a separate leader, or judge. There was no centralized government or military force, and so the farmers were helpless to stop organized troops of raiders. However, instead of entreating their God, Yahweh, for help, they offered sacrifices to local idols. Yahweh wanted to help them, but he had to first make them fully aware of how powerful he is and how empty of power were the stone and wood idols the people of Israel were honoring.

Terrorized by Camels

The raiders that were making life so difficult for the Israelites were said to be Midianites, Amalekites, and others from the east, but their exact background is debated. Suffice it to say they were well-organized bands of foreigners who traveled large distances across the southern and eastern deserts to raid the Israelites and then disappeared with their booty until their return for more the following year. The threat they posed was no joke. They were mean and numerous— "as thick as locusts" (Judges 6:5)—and they rode in on large, aggressive camels.

The poor farmers in Israel had probably never seen these huge, unruly, bad-tempered animals before. The camel had only recently been domesticated, and the raiders were putting them to good effect, using them to traverse desert lands and carry large amounts of booty. Furthermore, the raiders could ride the camels furiously in the direction of the farmers, who quickly took to the hills and hid in caves until the invaders left—with their precious crops. Something had to be done about them, but what?

Gideon's Unlikely Commission

One day Gideon, a simple farmer, was hiding inside a winepress (a large vat used for making wine) where he was beating out his grain, hoping to salvage at least part of his crop by keeping it out of sight. Suddenly, an angel appeared and told him: "The Lord is with you, you mighty warrior" (Judges 6:12). Completely flummoxed, Gideon asked how God could be with him when so many bad things were happening to him and his people. Gideon had heard tell of the many wonderful deeds God had done for the Israelites in the past, but he had seen no evidence of such works lately.

The angel then completely blew Gideon's mind by commissioning him to "go in this might of yours" and defeat the raiders. Gideon sarcastically pointed out that he was the least qualified man in his family and that his family was the least of all the families in the tribe of Manasseh. Gideon demanded a sign, but first he went off to prepare a meal for his guest.

With the meal came a sign. The angel made the food vanish in flames, making it clear that he was from God. The angel then ordered Gideon to destroy the altar to the god Baal that his father had built and to erect an altar to Yahweh in its place. That night he did. When the townspeople wanted to punish Gideon for destroying the altar to Baal, his father said that Baal is a powerful god and can defend himself. Let Baal punish Gideon. But, of course, Baal did nothing because he was powerless.

Gideon then sent out calls for fighting men from the northern tribes, but the situation was so bizarre that Gideon was still not completely convinced he was doing the right thing. Consequently, he asked for two further signs from Yahweh, involving the formation of dew in different specified places on successive nights. He got his signs, and his doubts were dismissed.

Assembling an Army of Misfits

Gideon managed to muster 32,000 men to fight the Midianites. Then God ordered Gideon to reduce the number of men by weeding out the best men and fighting with the dregs.

Accordingly, Gideon sent home all the men who were afraid—good riddance some might say. This left 10,000 men. Then God told Gideon to take the men to a lake or stream and let them drink. Most of the men drank by kneeling and bringing the water to their lips in their hands so they wouldn't take their eyes off the enemy. But 300 men lapped up the water like dogs. Most readers think God would tell Gideon to use the first group of men, but no. He told Gideon, "With the three hundred that lapped I will deliver you, and give the Midianites into your hand. Let all the others go to their homes" (Judges 7:7).

The Noise of Battle

At this point, Gideon was left with a puny force of 300 men, and these men did engage in the battle, but not in the expected way. (Surprised?) Instead, each man was given a trumpet and a jar with a lighted torch in it. Late at night, the men surrounded the enemy, blowing their 300 trumpets, smashing their 300 jars, and shouting, "A sword for the Lord and for Gideon!" (Judges 7:20). The Midianites believed that a gigantic force was closing in on them, and they fled in all directions and even killed each other in the confusion. Gideon and his men pursued them and killed the two princes of Midian, intensifying the panic of the Midianites, who went back to their own lands never to return.

After the success of the battle, the people wanted to make Gideon king, but Gideon refused, saying that God alone is the king of Israel. And it was certainly God who defeated the camel-riding raiders—not the pathetic assembly of troops led by Gideon. Baal could not punish Gideon for destroying his altar because he was totally powerless, but Yahweh is all-powerful and was fully committed to saving his people, the Israelites.

Color Commentary

❧ ❧ ❧ ❧

*The Bible is filled with colorful characters and colorful language.
But that's not all! Discover more hues on the scriptural palette.*

- **Red:** "When Pharaoh let the people go, God did not lead them by way of the land of the Philistines, although that was nearer; for God thought, 'If the people face war, they may change their minds and return to Egypt.' So God led the people by the roundabout way of the wilderness toward the Red Sea" (Exodus 13:17–18).
- **Black:** "I am black and beautiful, O daughters of Jerusalem, like the tents of Kedar, like the curtains of Solomon" (Song of Solomon 1:5).
- **Amber:** "As I looked, a stormy wind came out of the north: a great cloud with brightness around it and fire flashing forth continually, and in the middle of the fire, something like gleaming amber" (Ezekiel 1:4).
- **Purple:** "On the sabbath day we went outside the gate by the river, where we supposed there was a place of prayer; and we sat down and spoke to the women who had gathered there. A certain woman named Lydia, a worshiper of God, was listening to us; she was from the city of Thyatira and a dealer in purple cloth" (Acts 16:13–14).
- **Blue (and White and Purple):** "Then Mordecai went out from the presence of the king, wearing royal robes of blue and white, with a great golden crown and a mantle of fine linen and purple, while the city of Susa shouted and rejoiced" (Esther 8:15).
- **Green:** "The Lord is my shepherd, I shall not want. He makes me lie down in green pastures; he leads me beside still waters; he restores my soul" (Psalm 23:1–3).
- **White:** "Then I saw heaven opened, and there was a white horse! Its rider is called Faithful and True, and in righteousness he judges and makes war.... And the armies of heaven, wearing fine linen, white and pure, were following him on white horses" (Revelation 19:11–14).

Truth Be Told

Freed slave Sojourner Truth was a vocal advocate of social justice, and her love of God carried her through trying times.

Sojourner Truth was unique among 19th-century preachers—she was a former slave who fought for women's rights and other social causes, and she steadfastly refused to back down in the face of adversity. Her life was rife with abuse and heartache, but she always found comfort in the Bible.

Truth was born into slavery as Isabella Baumfree in 1797, in a Dutch enclave in upstate New York. She was sold around age 9 for $100 (which also included a flock of sheep) and endured physical abuse at the hands of her new master because she spoke limited English, her first language being Dutch. It was during this period that Truth first sought solace in religion, praying loudly whenever she was frightened or hurt.

Finding Freedom
Truth was sold several more times in the ensuing years. She married another slave in 1817 and bore four children. Freedom seemed at hand when the State of New York enacted legislation that called for the end of slavery within the state on July 4, 1827. Her owner promised to set her free a year early, but he reneged at the last minute. Angry and bitter at being lied to, Truth worked until she felt she had paid off her debt then walked away. She arrived at the home of Isaac and Maria Van Wagenen, who agreed to buy her services for the rest of the year for $20. The Van Wagenens treated Truth well and insisted she call them by their given names.

It was while working for the Van Wagenens that Truth experienced a religious epiphany that inspired her to become a preacher. She began attending a local Methodist church, and in 1829, she left to travel in the company of a white female evangelical teacher. Truth began preaching at regional churches and developed a reputation as an inspiring speaker.

She later joined a religious reformer named Elijah Pierson, who became her mentor until his death in 1834.

Truth moved to New York City, where she decided to become a traveling minister. She changed her name from Isabella Baumfree to Sojourner Truth and set out on the road, relying on the kindness of strangers to make her way. In 1844, Truth joined a Massachusetts commune known as the Northampton Association of Education and Industry, which had been founded by a group of abolitionists who espoused women's rights and religious tolerance. She left when the collective disbanded in 1846.

Literary Success
Truth began dictating her autobiography, *The Narrative of Sojourner Truth: A Northern Slave,* shortly after, and renowned abolitionist William Lloyd Garrison privately published the book in 1850. The memoir was a success and brought Truth both a needed income and promotion as a public speaker. Soon, Truth found herself in great demand, speaking about women's rights and the evils of slavery, often turning to her own experiences as illustration. In 1854, she gave one of her most famous lectures, titled "Ain't I A Woman?" at the Ohio Woman's Rights Convention in Akron.

Through everything, religion was Truth's personal mainstay. She was very active during the Civil War, enlisting black troops for the Union and helping runaway slaves. In 1864, she worked at a government refugee camp for freed slaves on an island off the coast of Virginia, and she even met President Abraham Lincoln. Following the war, she continued her efforts to help newly freed slaves through the Freedman's Relief Association.

"Religion without humanity is very poor human stuff."
—Sojourner Truth

Truth pursued her work on behalf of freed blacks until her death on November 26, 1883, from complications related to leg ulcers. She was buried next to her grandson, Sammy Banks, in Oak Hill Cemetery in Battle Creek, Michigan.

A Lasting Legacy
Sojourner Truth's legacy of spiritual pursuit and social activism resulted in numerous honors in the decades following her death. Among them were a memorial stone in the Stone History Tower in downtown Battle Creek; a portion of Michigan state highway M-66 designated the Sojourner Truth Memorial Highway; induction into the national Women's Hall of Fame in Seneca Falls, New York; and a commemorative postage stamp.

Rahab Saves the Day

✣ ✣ ✣ ✣

*When Joshua's men were scouting the city of Jericho to plan
the battle that would bring down its walls, a prostitute named
Rahab saved their lives by hiding them from her own people.
Did this make Rahab a traitor or a heroine?*

Soon after Moses' death, Joshua planned to cross the Jordan River
and lead the Israelites in an invasion of Canaan, the land the Lord
had promised to give them and their descendants. But first he sent
two spies to scout out the land and report back on the nature and
number of the enemy.

The spies sneak into
the town and take refuge
in the house of the pros-
titute Rahab. When the
king of Jericho gets news
of the spies, he sends
soldiers to Rahab, who
demand that she sur-
render the spies to them.
But hearing the soldiers approach, the wily Rahab quickly hides the
spies under some stalks of flax that were drying on the roof. She tells
the soldiers that the men they were looking for had indeed been
there, but that she had not known who they were and that they had
left when the time came to close the city gates for the night. Rahab
then cleverly tells the soldiers that if they hurry they can probably
still catch them.

Saved by a Crimson Cord

Having sent the soldiers of her own king on a wild goose chase,
Rahab goes to the spies on the roof. She tells them that everyone
in Jericho is terrified of the Israelites because they have heard how
the God Yahweh parted the waters of the Red Sea and performed
many subsequent wonders for them: "As soon as we heard it," Rahab

says, "our hearts melted, and there was no courage left in any of us because of you." Rahab agrees to help the Israelites because she is convinced that Yahweh has given the Israelites their land, for "The Lord your God is indeed God in heaven above and on earth below" (Joshua 2:11). In return for her help, Rahab asks that the Israelites spare her and her family when they invade Jericho. The spies enthusiastically respond: "Our life for yours!" (Joshua 2:14).

Rahab advises the spies on how to evade Jericho's military men, "then she let them down by a rope through her window, for her house was on the outer side of the city wall and she resided within the wall itself" (Joshua 2:15). During the invasion of Jericho she will hang a "crimson cord" from her window, presumably the rope the spies had climbed down, as a sign for the Israelite soldiers to spare the people inside.

The spies, who seem to be a couple of wimps, follow Rahab's instructions exactly and safely make their way back to Joshua. Their report to Joshua simply repeats what Rahab had told them: "Truly the Lord has given all the land into our hands; moreover all the inhabitants of the land melt in fear before us" (Joshua 2:24). The spies, who are never named, have done no real spying but have merely followed a prostitute's instructions and repeated what she told them. Rahab has single-handedly done the work of the spies. She has betrayed her people to save her own skin and the lives of her family, though she claims to have done it because of her faith in Yahweh. Later, when the Israelites bring down the walls of Jericho and kill all the other people in the city, they see the crimson cord hanging from the window and spare the house of Rahab. And "her family has lived in Israel ever since" (Joshua 6:25).

What to Make of Rahab

Far from being a model of the upstanding woman, Rahab had several strikes against her: She was a prostitute, a foreigner, and a woman. Even though the book of Joshua refers several times to Rahab's family using the respectable term "house of the father," her family's claim to honor is thoroughly undercut by both Rahab's profession and the fact that, though a woman, she is making political and religious decisions for her family, a role reserved for the father in the patriarchal societies of Bible times. Behind the statement that

Rahab's family continued to live among the Israelites after the fall of Jericho lurks an imputation of second-class status of her descendants. Rahab's story hides within it an ethnic slur.

Nevertheless, Rahab's story succeeded in reversing expectations. Rahab the prostitute has paradoxically always impressed both Jewish and Christian readers as brave, quick-witted, and decisive, even though her people would have seen her as a traitor. Most ancient Jewish and Christian interpreters begin with the assumption that after surviving the fall of Jericho, Rahab repudiated her sinful profession and lived the life of a proselyte and converted to Judaism.

Christian Views of Rahab

According to Matthew 1:5, Rahab is an ancestor of Jesus. In fact, she is one of only four women in the genealogy of Jesus given in that Gospel. The letter to the Hebrews in the New Testament holds that Rahab survived only because of her great faith. The letter of James holds Rahab up as an example of justification by both good works and faith (James 2:25). The church fathers also commended Rahab. Clement of Rome asserts that she was a sinner saved by her faith, providing a prototype of the reformed prostitute that was later applied to Mary Magdalene. Justin Martyr interprets Rahab's crimson cord as a "symbol of the blood of Christ, by which those who were at one time harlots and unrighteous persons out of all nations are saved." In his sermon "Against Lying," Augustine minimizes Rahab's deceit in order to praise her heroism.

Today, feminist theologians view Rahab as a rarity in the Bible, which is generally patriarchal. They see her as a female hero who displayed a prophetic spirit when she proclaims: "The Lord your God is indeed God in heaven above and on earth below" (Joshua 2:11).

> # Nurses in Israel
>
> The midwife was the Israelite equivalent of a visiting nurse or public health worker. The Hebrews had professional midwives when they lived in Egypt who refused to obey the pharaoh's orders to kill Hebrew baby boys (Exodus 1). A midwife also helped Tamar when she had trouble giving birth to twins (Genesis 38).

Biblical Names in the Real World

❧ ❧ ❧ ❧

Anxious parents often turn to the Bible for naming possibilities.

Here's a quick overview of some of the most popular biblical names.

Most Popular Boys' Biblical Names, 2009:
1. Jacob (Esau's twin brother)
2. Ethan (author of Psalm 89)
3. Michael (the archangel)
4. Alexander (son of Simon of Cyrene)
5. Joshua (subject of the book of Joshua)

Most Popular Girls' Biblical Names, 2009:
1. Isabella (from Elizabeth, mother of John the Baptist)
2. Olivia (from the olive tree, a common symbol in the Bible)
3. Sophia (from *sophos*, the Greek term for "wise men")
4. Ava (city in Assyria where the Assyrians populated Samaria)
5. Madison (from Magdalene, as in Mary Magdalene)

Second Coming
Old biblical names are making a comeback. These 19th and early 20th century biblical names are enjoying a resurgence:
1. Ezekiel (boy)
2. Hezekiah (boy)
3. Noah (boy)
4. Elijah (boy)
5. Abigail (girl)
6. Caleb (boy)
7. Elisha (boy or girl)

. . . and a Few Names Left Behind
1. Enoch. Enoch was the eldest son of Cain. The name was popular for hundreds of years, but virtually died out in the 20th century.
2. Hephzibah. Though Hephzibah's husband, Hezekiah, is enjoying a resurgence, Hephzibah, the mother of King Manasseh, is not.
3. Job. Even the cult popularity of the television show *Arrested Development* hasn't boosted the long-suffering Job back into the nation's naming consciousness.

Doing Time

✤ ✤ ✤ ✤

In ancient Israel, "crime" and "prison" were very flexible words.

In our age, we think of prison as a place of shame; a secure area in which to hold those who have done "bad" things. In biblical times, however, imprisonment was a much more complicated subject, especially for the Hebrews. While prison could mean disgrace, it could just as easily mean glory. Among the murderers, thieves, and cons, there was always a healthy minority made up of patriotic soldiers, political activists, and religious advocates, and for these types of "criminals," prison was not a stigma but a badge of honor.

Psychology of a People

By the time New Testament figures such as Jesus Christ and Paul were imprisoned, the Jews had suffered through thousands of years of being persecuted simply for existing. While enslaved in Egypt, they were often treated no differently from working animals such as donkeys. Then there was the captivity in Babylon, during which they had to struggle constantly to hold on to the remnants of their faith and their identity as a people. So, while they weren't really "in prison" per se, they were also far from being free. These experiences left deep psychological scars in the Jewish people as a whole and taught them to have a mistrust of authority. Never again would they believe something just because those "in charge" told them it was true. They owed their obedience to God, not any human.

There can be no doubt that prisons in the time of the Old Testament were horrible places, but most prisoners did not languish in jail for long periods. This is not because their captors were kind or concerned about justice; it was a simple matter of practicality. There were no guns in biblical times. There were no effective metal handcuffs. Taxes were harder to collect and allocate. The types of maximum-security procedures taken by law enforcement today were quite impossible back then. It was just much, much harder to hold a group of prisoners in those times. The same enslavement that had built the pyramids had built the Hebrews into strong, sometimes dangerous captives. They often took chances to rebel, riot, and escape, and many times they were successful.

Hard to Hold

The difficulty of keeping prisoners is reflected in the laws of the Old Testament. In Exodus 22:1–3, for example, the punishment for stealing is not jail time but restitution: "When someone steals an ox or a sheep, and slaughters it or sells it, the thief shall pay five oxen for an ox, and four sheep for a sheep. The thief shall make restitution, but if unable to do so, shall be sold for the theft." In other words, the authorities would only hold this thief until they could sell him as a slave to whoever had the money to buy him; then he'd be that person's problem, not the state's problem. In both Exodus and Deuteronomy, the length of this type of imprisonment was given as six to seven years; then the criminal would go free and try to straighten up and fly right. His master was not to just dump him out on the streets, however: "And when you send a male slave out from you a free person, you shall not send him out empty-handed. Provide liberally out of your flock, your threshing-floor, and your wine press, thus giving to him some of the bounty with which the Lord your God has blessed you" (Deuteronomy 15:13–14).

In this way, the state was able to deal with minor and nonviolent crimes without having to organize and rely on a large, federal prison system. But what of violent, dangerous criminals such as murderers? Well, of course, they were imprisoned immediately. But justice was swift and the punishment was almost always death. Exodus 21:12 makes God's view on murder perfectly clear: "Whoever strikes a person mortally shall be put to death." Indeed, the Old Testament calls for the death penalty for many actions: striking or cursing at one's mother or father, kidnapping, adultery, bestiality, being a false prophet, prostitution, and rape. It is easy to see why the locally run prisons rarely suffered from inefficiency or overcrowding.

Roman "Justice"

Under the Roman occupation, all this changed. Though the Romans executed many Jews for crimes ranging from thievery to murder, they were quite organized and bureaucratic, and every person had his day in court. That meant long prison sentences for countless Jews. Crimes the Romans considered too petty to bother with would be handed over to the local Jewish authorities, as in John 8:3–7: "The scribes and the Pharisees brought a woman who had been caught in adultery; and making her stand before all of them, they said to [Jesus], 'Teacher, this woman was caught in the very act of committing adultery. Now in the law Moses commanded us to stone such women. Now what do you say?'... When they kept on questioning him, he straightened up and said to them, 'Let anyone among you who is without sin be the first to throw a stone at her.'"

As we know, neither Jesus nor many of his followers were so lucky. They were imprisoned, sometimes tortured, and often executed. John the Baptist was kept in a filthy cell for months before he was beheaded, and Paul spent five to six years in Roman prisons, where he wrote his letters, or epistles, to Christian communities throughout the Mediterranean. And Jesus himself explicitly linked prisoners to the poor and oppressed in Matthew 25:34–36: "Come, you that are blessed by my Father, inherit the kingdom prepared for you from the foundation of the world; for I was hungry and you gave me food, I was thirsty and you gave me something to drink, I was a stranger and you welcomed me, I was naked and you gave me clothing, I was sick and you took care of me, I was in prison and you visited me."

Barefoot Priests

Israelite priests performed many, if not all, of their duties in the tabernacle and temple barefooted. This was because of the sacredness of the ground on which they walked. God told Moses to remove his sandals at the burning bush because he stood on holy ground.

Israel's Neighbors

PHILISTINES

Today we call someone a "philistine" if she or he can't appreciate beauty and quality. The label is simply unfair, as any ancient Israelite who ever owned a fine Philistine iron sword could attest.

Who Were They?
The Philistines came to Palestine (named for them) as the "sea peoples," fierce invaders who poured in from Crete and Asia Minor around 1200 B.C. They crushed the Hittites and stormed southward, finally halted in the Holy Land by Egyptian arms. The Egyptians made them settle in a tiny strip of the modern Israeli coast just north of the Gaza strip, in five cities: Gaza, Ashkelon, Gath, Ekron, and Ashdod, all called Philistia. While history has painted them in barbarian colors (mainly for fighting regularly with the tribes of Israel), the Philistines were a sophisticated society of traders, ironsmiths, and warriors. As polytheists, they did not worship God.

Where Are They Now?
Philistine independence was finished with their conquest by Assyrian forces in 732 B.C., and with it they lost their cultural identity. By 400 B.C., Philistia identified a region but not a people, and their cities had become mainly Jewish. Israelite culture absorbed them well before Jesus' day.

Biblical Mentions
Abraham lived among the Philistines for a time. When the Israelites slipped into paganism, as described in Judges, God let the Philistines (among others) oppress his people until they repented. When the Israelites did the same thing again, God let the Philistines have at the Israelites for another 40 years. Samson delivered the Israelites from Philistine domination by torching Philistine crops and killing a thousand Philistines with a donkey jawbone. Philistine Delilah was his downfall; she cut his hair and he lost his power. The Philistines captured the holy Ark of the Covenant, but they sent it back after God dumped plagues on their cities. Goliath of Gath, slain by David, was a Philistine champion. Scripture characterizes the Philistines as Israel's archenemies.

Simchat Torah

After Sukkot (Feast of Booths) comes Simchat Torah: a spiritual holiday to rejoice in the law of Torah and in what it means to be Jewish.

Biblical Basis
In a sense, there is no biblical basis for *Simchat Torah* (sim-KHAT tor-AH), which means "rejoicing/joy in the Law/Torah." There certainly is for *Shemini Atzeret* ("eighth day assembly"; the holy convocation specified by Leviticus to end Sukkot), which immediately precedes Simchat Torah. Yet in another sense, Simchat Torah encompasses the biblical basis for Jewish faith and practice. The first five books of the Old Testament represent the holy Jewish scripture called *Torah,* the law given by God to Jews with the expectation of willing obedience. By rejoicing in the Torah, observant Jews demonstrate this devotion.

Biblical Practice
Except for Shemini Atzeret, the scriptural references pertinent to Simchat Torah actually refer to Sukkot. Jews spend part of Shemini Atzeret in the *sukkah* (booth) they built for Sukkot.

Modern Practice
Shemini Atzeret and Simchat Torah occur on the same day in Israel but on two days (22nd and 23rd of Tishrei, typically in early October) outside the Jewish state. No work is done. Synagogues read through the Torah scrolls each year, a piece at a time, and on Simchat Torah congregants read Deuteronomy 34 (the final chapter), then Genesis 1 to begin the new cycle. As many people as possible help carry the Torah scrolls around the synagogue, with lots of singing and dancing (and sometimes drinking). Children participate by carrying small toy Torahs in the procession.

Simchat Torah arose in medieval Europe, when Jews could expect persecution. By about A.D. 1700, Simchat Torah had achieved a form much like that observed today. During the Soviet era, to the Politburo's annoyance, Simchat Torah often took on a defiant tone in Moscow—a reminder that Jews who wanted to leave for Israel were not giving up.

Young David Arouses King Saul's Jealousy

✤ ✤ ✤ ✤

*After killing the giant Goliath with a slingshot,
young David is invited to the court of King Saul, where he
often soothes the king's mood swings by playing the harp. But
when David wins renown as a military leader, he unwisely
shows up his king, rousing him to murderous jealousy.*

When God becomes displeased with King Saul, he has the prophet
Samuel secretly anoint David, the son of Jesse, a Bethlehem shepherd, as Israel's next king—even though David is still a mere shepherd boy. Shortly thereafter, David's brothers are called to fight
in Saul's armies against invading Philistines. One day, Jesse sends
David with food for his brothers, and when the boy reaches the
battlefield, he sees a towering figure swathed in bronze armor. This
giant, Goliath, is proposing that the war between the Israelites and
Philistines be settled in one-on-one combat. Goliath will fight Israel's fiercest warrior, and the winner will claim victory for his people.
The Israelites are in despair, for no one could overpower this giant.

David Fells Goliath

When David discovers what is going on, he takes up Goliath's challenge. His brothers try to stop him, scolding him for abandoning
the family's sheep. Saul himself tries to dissuade David, saying, "you
are just a boy, and he has been a warrior from his youth" (1 Samuel
17:33). David responds that as a shepherd he has often killed lions
and bears that threaten his sheep. So Saul dresses David in his own
helmet and armor and gives him his sword. But the boy can't walk
with all that heavy equipment, so he throws it off and advances toward Goliath in his simple shepherd's garb, with five smooth stones
in his shoulder pouch and only a slingshot in his hand.

Goliath scoffs that he will feed the boy to the birds, but David
counters with a typical warrior's boast: Goliath has it wrong. Even

though the giant comes against him fully armed, he, David, will vanquish him in the name of the Lord. Not only will David kill the giant, he will also cut off his head and feed him and all the other Philistines to the (carrion-eating) birds and beasts.

David then takes a stone out of his pouch, loads it into the sling he has used to kill wolves and bears, and sends the stone flying into Goliath's forehead. The giant topples like a felled tree, and David uses the giant's sword to cut off Goliath's head. The other Philistines flee in terror.

David in Saul's Court

Impressed by the boy, Saul brings him to live in his court, where David sometimes plays the lyre to soothe the king during his frequent bouts of depression. Meanwhile, David's popularity with the people grows to almost epic proportions. Women dance in the streets and sing: "Saul has killed his thousands, and David his ten thousands" (1 Samuel 18:7).

Already moody, Saul becomes insanely jealous of David. One day, while David is playing the lyre, Saul throws his spear at him twice, but David eludes the weapon. (He apparently had good reflexes, thank goodness.) To get David out of the palace, Saul makes him military commander of 1,000 men. He also offers his daughter Merab as David's wife, but he then marries her to another man. Soon after, Saul offers David the hand of another daughter, Michal, who loves David dearly. However, in return for the right to marry Michal, David must give him the foreskins of 100 Philistines. Saul is hoping that David will be killed in his attempt to acquire the foreskins, but David goes into battle, kills 200 Philistines, and brings the king twice the number of foreskins he had demanded.

David and Michal

Saul begrudgingly gives Michal to David as a wife, realizing that the Lord is no longer with him, but with David. Saul becomes more afraid of David than ever. After David goes to war and wins even more battles, Saul falls into a deep depression and again throws his spear at David, but it sticks into the wall and David hurries home.

His fury building, Saul orders some men to hide overnight outside David's house and kill him the next morning. But when it gets dark, Michal helps her husband climb out the window, and to gain extra time for David to flee, she places an idol in the bed and covers it with blankets to make it look like David is sleeping. The next morning, when Saul's men come inside, Michal sends them away, saying David is too sick to see anyone. Saul is furious that his men have failed and orders them to bring David, in his bed if necessary, so that he himself can kill him. But by then, David is long gone.

Don't Prophesy! Arrest Him!

David goes to Samuel, who had earlier anointed him as the next king, and confides in him about Saul's behavior. Saul discovers David's whereabouts and sends three sets of messengers to arrest him. But in all three cases the messengers meet a group of prophets led by Samuel, who are prophesying in a frenzy and "the Spirit of God came upon the messengers of Saul, and they also fell into a prophetic frenzy" (1 Samuel 19:20). Biblical prophets often worked themselves into frenzies when delivering God's word, but the frenzy here keeps the messengers from doing what they came to do—arrest David. Finally, Saul is so angry that he goes in person, but he too is caught up in frenzied prophesying.

David Spares Saul's Life—Twice

Saul eventually tracks David down at the oasis of En Gedi on the Dead Sea. When Saul stops to relieve himself in the very cave where David and his men are hiding, David sneaks up behind him, cuts off a piece of Saul's garment, and slinks away. Although he has ample opportunity, David refuses to kill the king, telling his men: "The Lord forbid that I should . . . raise my hand against him; for he is the Lord's anointed" (1 Samuel 24:6).

Instead, David calls out to Saul from a safe distance. Boastfully waving the cloth he had cut from Saul's garment, David demonstrates that he might have killed Saul if he had wished to do so. David assures Saul that he had never meant to harm him. Shaken, Saul concedes David's good intentions, adding: "I know that you shall surely be king, and that the kingdom of Israel shall be established in your hand" (1 Samuel 24:20). Saul then asks David not to wipe out his family when he becomes king, and David swears he won't.

That is one of two stories in which David has a chance to kill Saul and refuses to do so. In the other story (1 Samuel 26), David sneaks into Saul's camp at night and takes Saul's spear and water jug from beside his sleeping form—again refusing to kill the Lord's anointed king. Again he goes off to a safe distance and calls to Saul, showing that he has been near enough to kill him but did not do so. Saul responds to David in tones of reconciliation, but David wonders if Saul is sincere. He never finds out, for soon after, while David is far away, Saul is killed in battle with the Philistines.

David Mourns Saul's Death

David learns of Saul's death from a foreigner, who claims that he had wandered onto the battlefield to find Saul near death and afraid of being captured. The stranger claims that Saul had begged him to give the final blow that would end the king's life, and the foreigner complies. He then gives Saul's crown and armlet to David, hoping to be rewarded for his deed. However, the foreigner is probably lying because his story is full of holes and a different account of Saul's death has already been reported in the Bible. David asks the foreigner, "How is it that you were not afraid to put forth your hand to destroy the Lord's anointed?" (2 Samuel 1:14). The foreigner does receive a reward, but not one he expected. Because (according to his own story) he had raised his hand against Yahweh's anointed (something even David himself would not risk), he is rewarded with instant death.

David then sings a lament in honor of Saul. Their conflict has finally come to an end.

Fast Facts

- There are more than 2,000 registered saints, two-thirds of which are claimed by Italy and France. Among the handful of saints from the United States, Saint Frances Xavier Cabrini, known during her life as Mother Cabrini, was the first American citizen to be canonized by the Roman Catholic Church.

- The word "amen" appears 773,692 times in the King James Bible.

- Babylon—home of the famous Hanging Gardens—was located on the Euphrates River about 55 miles south of Baghdad.

- A lot of animals are referenced frequently throughout the Old and New Testaments. The critter mentioned most often, however, is the sheep.

- Only one nation on earth can correctly claim to be 100 percent Christian—Vatican City.

- *Bible brings big box office!* The Ten Commandments, *starring Charlton Heston as Moses and Yul Brynner as the Pharoah Ramesses II, was the top-grossing movie of 1956 and one of the top five highest grossing movies of the 1950s. Gross to date: $80 million. Cost to produce: A little over $13 million.*

- Noah's Ark was a remarkable architectural achievement, and God even told Noah how to make it waterproof—by sealing it inside and out with pitch.

- Though scholars aren't 100 percent certain, it is commonly believed that Jesus spoke Aramaic.

- The entrance to heaven is often referred to as the Pearly Gates, and according to the Bible (Revelation 21:12–21) there are twelve gates—three each on the east, west, north, and south walls.

- The Bible may be Holy Scripture, but it still contains many contradictions. For example, in Genesis, it first says that man was created after the other animals (Genesis 1:25–27), then it says man was created before the other animals (Genesis 2:18–19). In Exodus, it first says that all of the (non-Hebrew) cattle and horses in Egypt died (Exodus 9:3–6), but later it is suggested that all of the pharaoh's horses did not die (Exodus 14:9).

Four-Color Theology

❧ ❧ ❧ ❧

Not all comic books star muscle-bound guys in spandex and capes.
Some find their heroes in Holy Scripture.

Mention comic books and most people think of Superman or Spider-Man, not biblical figures. Yet, the Bible has been a wellspring of ideas for comic book writers since the medium's humble beginnings in the mid-1930s. Even before that, church groups and specialty publishers were producing educational Bible-themed cartoon books for young churchgoers. One of the earliest was *Christian Cartoons* (1922), a 96-page compilation of cartoon panels and strips written and drawn by Dr. E. J. Pace and published by the Sunday School Times Company and the Bible Institute Colportage Association. In 1937, Polzin Press of Chicago published *Gospel Cartoons,* a 28-page collection of U. S. Abell's cartoon panels and sequential stories originally created for *Moody Monthly.*

A New Trend

The 1940s saw a proliferation of biblical comic books, such as The Standard Publishing Company's *The Life of... Visualized* series. In 1942 and 1943, *The Life of Jesus Visualized* was published in three soft-cover books, and subsequent editions covered everything from *The Life of Joseph Visualized* to *Parables Jesus Told.* But these books were far from alone. A variety of Bible comics and books from other publishers was offered to churches throughout the decade.

In 1942, M. C. "Max" Gaines, the acknowledged father of the comic book as we know it, introduced *Picture Stories From the Bible,* published first by DC Comics, then later through Gaines's own company, Educational Comics. Gaines felt that comic books were the perfect medium to teach children about important topics, but the *Picture Stories* series was never a strong seller. When Gaines died in 1947, his son, William, took over the company, changed the name to Entertaining Comics, and killed the *Picture Stories* line to make room for more mainstream titles. A few years later, Gaines made a fortune as the publisher of *MAD* magazine.

Billy Graham Jumps In

In the 1950s, the Billy Graham Evangelistic Association and Grayson Publishing got into the comics biz with the *Billy Graham Presents* series, which were often distributed during Graham's evangelistic crusades. Titles included "The Story of Naaman the Leper" and "The Story of David and Goliath."

Graham's contemporary, Oral Roberts, also waded into the comic book game in the 1950s with *Oral Roberts' True Stories*, which ran for 19 issues. From 1959 through 1961, the Oral Roberts Evangelistic Association also published the *Oral Roberts' Junior Partners* series, which ran for 29 issues.

Religious comic books, most of which were distributed by church groups, thrived through the 1960s, '70s, and '80s, and some publishers are still going strong today. Many of these comics were competently illustrated at best, but a few managed to stand out by securing the services of some genuinely talented comic book professionals.

Interesting Adaptations

Following the demise of Max Gaines's *Picture Stories From the Bible,* which were killed because of poor sales, mainstream comic book publishers featured biblical stories only occasionally. Most commonly, such comics were adaptations of then-popular biblical books or movies, such as *Moses and the Ten Commandments* and *Ben-Hur.*

Today, however, a growing number of contemporary comic book creators are turning to the Bible for inspiration, with interesting results. One intriguing example is *The Bible: Eden,* a lush adaptation of the book of Genesis by Dave Elliot and Keith Griffen and painter Scott Hampton that was collected in hardcover in 2003; it was recently released in a soft-cover edition. The book is faithful to the Old Testament story, and as a result features some nudity.

Other contemporary comic books with biblical themes include *Testament* by Douglas Rushkoff, which juxtaposes the Old Testament with futuristic tales; *King David* by cartoonist Kyle Baker; and *Marked* by Steve Ross, a unique adaptation of the book of Mark.

Biblical comic books have long been hit or miss in both storytelling and sales, and yet they keep on coming. Some creators use the Bible as a springboard, while others attempt faithful adaptations. The result is comic books for every theological school of thought.

Where Jesus Walked

Tyre and Sidon

*Two great Phoenician trading cities figured briefly
but importantly in Christ's ministry: Tyre and Sidon.*

In Biblical Times

Tyre's history extends back nearly three millennia before the time
of Christ. A great deal of Mediterranean commerce passed through
Tyre, strategically placed with one of the finest harbors in the eastern
Mediterranean. Sidon, about 20 miles south of Tyre, is even older; it may
have had Stone Age settlements. The two grew into commercial rivals for
Phoenician bragging rights. The Phoenician alphabet was the ancestor of
many, if not all, western phonetic alphabets. Like all of the modern Holy
Land, Tyre and Sidon were under Roman rule during Jesus' day. Scripture
acidly notes the general corruption of both cities.

Jesus' Connection

Christ went to Tyre and Sidon after straightening out some Pharisees in
Genasseret. A Canaanite (or Syro-Phoenician; depends which Gospel you
read) woman came to him at Tyre; the disciples tried to brush her off, but
the power of her faith convinced Jesus to hear her plea for her daughter.
He healed her of a demon before heading back to Galilee. This was his
only recorded visit in the Bible.

Tyre and Sidon Today

If you value their histories, pray for peace in Lebanon, because Tyre
(Arabic, *Sur*) and Sidon (*Saida*) are within its borders. Sidon is some
50 kilometers south of Beirut, with Tyre almost halfway in between; Tyre
might have 120,000 people, Sidon not quite double that. (Lebanon's
semi-functional government does not always get a precise census.) Both
are wonderful places to visit in peacetime, with mixed Arab Christian and
Muslim populations and covered with archaeological sites from prebiblical
Roman and Crusader times. Both are known for the cosmopolitan welcome one would expect from cities of vastly ancient heritage that depend
heavily on tourism.

Quiz

Enemies

Outscore your opponents on this challenging test.

1. We all know young David killed the enemy giant Goliath. But why was this shepherd boy in the Israelite army camp?
    - a. he was running away from home
    - b. he was trying to win the hand of the king's daughter
    - c. he was bringing food to his brothers
    - d. he was composing an epic song about the Israelite army

2. What enemy nation was Goliath fighting for?
    - a. Philistines
    - b. Moabites
    - c. land of Sheba
    - d. Assyrians

3. In what Bible verse would you find the words, "Love your enemies"?
    - a. Deuteronomy 6:4
    - b. Psalms 23:1
    - c. Matthew 5:44
    - d. John 3:16

4. What were the weapons with which Gideon's army defeated the Midianites?
    - a. plowshares, rocks, and reins
    - b. slings and arrows
    - c. trumpets, torches, and pitchers
    - d. catapults and siege ramps

Answers: 1. c (1 Samuel 17:17–18); 2. a (1 Samuel 17); 3. c; 4. c (Judges 7)

David and Jonathan—Best Friends

❧ ❧ ❧ ❧

*Although King Saul turned against David and wanted to kill him,
Saul's own son Jonathan never failed in his devotion to David,
who remained his best friend until the day he died.*

Jonathan appeared in the Bible before David was introduced. The
oldest son of Israel's King Saul, Jonathan was not only heir to the
throne but also a fearless commander-in-chief of Israel's army. Chapter 14 of 1 Samuel tells how Jonathan led an attack on an enemy
Philistine force that was far larger and better equipped than that of
the Israelites—and won! He was clearly the right man to succeed his
father as king.

Jonathan as Hero

In a later bold move, Jonathan, helped only by his armor bearer,
launched a surprise attack on a unit of Philistines. He killed about
20 of them and threw the rest into such a panic that they were
defeated by Saul and his troops. Unfortunately, Jonathan's heroic
attack, though successful, proved to have regrettable results for both
him and his father.

Earlier that day, Saul, hoping that fasting would buy God's help,

had ordered his
men to eat nothing
until the Philistines
were defeated. The
penalty for breaking
the fast was death.
But Jonathan had
not heard the order;
during a pause in the
fighting he ate some
wild honey, which
restored his energy.
When a soldier told

him of Saul's decree, Jonathan was puzzled and angry. It made no sense, for he saw that the Israelites were weak from hunger, as he had been.

When Saul discovered that Jonathan had violated the fast, he was shocked but felt he had to enforce the death penalty. Although Jonathan seemed ready to accept his fate, his soldiers called out: "As the Lord lives, there shall not one hair of his head fall to the ground" (1 Samuel 14:45).

Saul relented and freed his son, but his rash, ill-advised command to fast that day showed impulsiveness and poor judgment. In contrast to Saul, his son Jonathan showed superior leadership qualities. He was practical, decisive, brave, and considerate, and Israel's fighting men responded to him even to the point of opposing their king. But even though Jonathan was an ideal successor to Saul, he would never be king, as he had inadvertently fallen under his father's curse. For after Saul demonstrated further lapses in judgment and impudently took over duties permitted only to priests, God rejected Saul's kingship and had the prophet Samuel travel to Bethlehem and secretly anoint David, the son of the shepherd Jesse, as the next king. Although David was still little more than a boy, he suddenly became a superstar by single-handedly killing the Philistine giant Goliath with his slingshot.

David as Hero

After the victory over Goliath, Saul kept David at court and Jonathan bonded with David, forming a covenant, a kind of blood-brotherhood pact. In fact, the Bible tells us, "the soul of Jonathan was bound to the soul of David, and Jonathan loved him as his own soul" (1 Samuel 18:1). Jonathan loved David so much that he gave him his royal robe to wear and his armor and sword to use when he went out to battle. With this gesture, Jonathan seemed to be symbolically ceding his right of kingship to David.

The attention paid to David by his own son angered Saul, whose sourness deepened when David's popularity reached epic proportions. Already moody, Saul became insanely jealous, and while David was playing the lyre for him one day, Saul threw his spear at David twice—but fortunately missed. His anger unabated, Saul confided to Jonathan that he would kill David. Jonathan alerted David to lay low and then managed to talk Saul into forgiving David. Jonathan accompanied David back to court, and all went well for a while. However, when war broke out again and David won more battles, Saul again threw a spear at David, who fled.

Plot and Counterplot

While in hiding, David told his ever-loyal friend Jonathan that Saul was planning to kill him as soon as he could get his hands on him, but Jonathan protested: "Far from it! You shall not die. My father does nothing either great or small without disclosing it to me; and why hide this from me? Never!" (1 Samuel 20:2). After David pointed out that Saul knew of their friendship and was unlikely to tell Jonathan of any plot against David, the two friends contrived a plot to discern Saul's true intentions.

The Feast of the New Moon was starting, and David would be expected to sit at the king's table for meals over the next three days. If Saul asked why David was not at the table, Jonathan would tell him that he had given David permission to go to Bethlehem to celebrate the annual festival with his family. If the king said, "Good," David was safe, but if the king became angry it meant that he had wanted David there because he had planned to harm him. David would not really be in Bethlehem but would hide in a field, and Jonathan would get word to David by a prearranged signal whether to return to court or flee.

> ## A Poor Father
>
> The Bible states that David did not practice good discipline with at least one of his sons. His son Adonijah rebelliously proclaimed himself king. In 1 Kings 1:6, it says David never asked Adonijah, "Why have you done thus and so?" David never held him accountable for his bad actions.

Jonathan was devastated at the thought that his father really may have wanted to kill David, but he remained convinced that David was meant to succeed his father as king. Worried that he himself might die before this happened, Jonathan begged David to remain loyal to his family when he became king. David later honored this plea by bringing Jonathan's lame son, Mephibosheth, to live with him after all of Saul's other descendants were massacred. For the moment, though, the friends again swore loyalty to one another and proceeded to put their plot into effect.

During the second day of the feast, Saul asked why David was absent, and when Jonathan gave him the concocted excuse, Saul howled at his son: "You son of a perverse, rebellious woman! Do I not know that you have chosen the son of Jesse to your own shame? . . . For as long as the son of Jesse lives upon the earth, neither you nor your kingdom shall be established. Now send and bring him to me, for he shall surely die" (1 Samuel 20:30–31). When Jonathan asked his father why David should die, the enraged king threw his spear at his own son. Fortunately, his aim was once again poor and he missed—perhaps his poor aim was a sign of the paucity of his rule. Horrified, Jonathan used the prearranged signal to get word to David to flee. Once again Jonathan had proven that his loyalty to David was greater than even his filial loyalty and that he valued David more than a royal throne.

A New Covenant and a Sad Parting

David took refuge in the Wilderness of Ziph, and Jonathan met him there at Horesh. The two friends agreed that David would be the next king of Israel and Jonathan would be his second in command. Jonathan confided in David that even Saul realized that this was what was meant to be. And so "the two of them made a covenant before the Lord; David remained at Horesh, and Jonathan went home" (1 Samuel 23:18). This was the last time the friends would see each other. Soon after, both Saul and Jonathan were killed in a battle with the Philistines, and David sang a lament over their deaths, ending with an emotional farewell to his best friend (2 Samuel 1:25–27):

> *How are the mighty fallen in the midst of the battle!*
> *Jonathan lies slain upon thy high places.*
> *I am distressed for you, my brother Jonathan;*
> *greatly beloved were you to me;*
> > *your love to me was wonderful,*
> > *passing the love of women.*
> *How are the mighty fallen,*
> > *and the weapons of war perished!*

10 Things

Key Finds in Bible Archaeology

What have scholars dug up in the last century?

1. The Dead Sea Scrolls In 1947, some shepherds accidentally found scrolls in a desert cave. Soon archaeologists were going through all the caves in the area, finding more than 800 ancient documents. Many of these are portions of the Hebrew scriptures from about the time of Christ.

2. The Amulet Scroll from Hinnom In 1979, an Israeli archaeologist found a collection of jewelry and other ancient artifacts in an ancient burial cave in Jerusalem's Hinnom Valley. One silver amulet, dating to about 600 B.C., has an inscription bearing part of the priestly blessing found in Numbers 6:24–26, the earliest evidence of biblical wording that has been found.

3. The "House of David" Inscription Cleaning up a site in northern Israel in 1993, at the foot of Mount Hermon, workers found a basalt fragment with an ancient inscription that mentions the "house [or dynasty] of David." Two other fragments were found later, and archaeologists have surmised that this was from the 8th century B.C., a victory boast of an Aramean king (Hazael or Ben-hadad?). It seems the Israelites had intentionally smashed the monument.

4. "Peter's House" Earlier excavations had found a 5th century church in Capernaum, but in 1968 the remains of another church were found *underneath* it. And that church had been built around a private house. The names of Jesus and Peter have been found etched in the walls. Some think this was actually Peter's house (where Jesus stayed?), used as a house church, then expanded and built over.

5. The Baruch Bulla In ancient times, important documents were folded, tied, and sealed with a glob of clay, which was then stamped with an official seal. The impression in clay is called a *bulla*. Thousands have been preserved, but in the 1970s one of these was discovered bearing the name of "Berechiah, son of Neriah, the scribe." Scholars believe this is a form of the name Baruch, who worked as secretary to the prophet Jeremiah.

6. The Galilee Boat When a 1985–86 drought dropped the level of the Sea of Galilee, an ancient boat emerged on the exposed shoreline. Experts have dated it to the time of Christ. The 30-foot by 8-foot craft could have been propelled by sail or oars and could have fit as many as 15 people. Was it a boat like this that Jesus and his disciples used?

7. The Bone-Box of Caiaphas An errant dump truck did an accidental excavation in Jerusalem in 1990, uncovering an ancient ossuary, or bone-box, belonging to the Caiaphas family. A burial site would be owned by a particular family, which would collect the bones of ancestors in decorative chests. Dating to the first centuries B.C. and A.D., this bone-box bears the name "Caiaphas" and includes (among others) the bones of a 60-year-old male, thought to be the high priest who questioned Jesus.

8. Pilate's Inscription Various Jewish and Roman historians mentioned Pontius Pilate, but if there was any doubt about him, it was answered in 1961 when a stone plaque was found in Caesarea bearing his name, with the title "prefect of Judea."

9. The Ebla Collection Beginning in 1964, excavations at the Syrian site of Ebla have produced a treasure trove of ancient tablets in a cuneiform text. As these have been translated, they have provided insight into the ordinary trade and social life of a civilization from the second and third millennia B.C. While the connection of these texts to biblical references has been disputed, they still help us understand the world of Abraham's time and earlier.

10. Ugarit Another accidental discovery: In 1928, a peasant plowing a field found an old tomb. Ensuing digs uncovered the remains of a civilization that thrived from the 16th to 13th centuries B.C. The ancient city was called Ugarit, named in a few other ancient inscriptions and documents, but now its own cuneiform tablets bore witness to a rich Canaanite culture—giving us insight into the world into which the biblical Israelites migrated.

Bitter Old Testament Prophets

✣ ✣ ✣ ✣

The Hebrew scriptures brim over with prophets mad at someone: Jews, persecutors of Jews, non-Jews. Let's review the grievances of some of the loudest and/or most pessimistic.

Moses: His primary complaint was against pharaoh, of course. The treacherous Egyptian monarch broke deal after deal with the Israelites, deliberately making their forced labor more difficult. Moses conveyed God's prophecies and wishes to the Israelites, leading them out of Egyptian servitude toward the Promised Land and establishing the Jewish faith.

Elijah: This prominent prophet railed against the worship of other gods. He challenged the priests of Baal to a sacrifice-off: Elijah predicted that his God could burn a sacrificial altar at will, and he challenged Baal's priests to do the same. Elijah and God won the challenge (go figure). Later Elijah prophesied a very unpleasant end for King Ahab and Jezebel, his wife, over their foul plot to seize Naboth's vineyard. In Jezebel's case, it was unpleasant indeed—she was chucked out a window and eaten by dogs.

Elisha: Receiving Elijah's prophetic mantle in a literal sense, Elisha was sensitive about his bald head. When some boys mocked him over the shiny scalp, Elisha cursed them in God's name, causing 2 bears to maul 42 of the bratty kids. This prophet had few kind words for Syria; his last prediction was a victory for Israel over Syria (kind of like 1948, 1967, and 1973).

Isaiah: Many things got under Isaiah's skin: church and government corruption, rich people exploiting the poor, any foreign entanglements that trusted in alliances and deals (rather than God) to protect Israel, and especially worship of gods who were not the one God. He foretold the defeat of Sennacherib's Assyrian army, which worked out pretty well for the Israelites when an angel showed up and killed 185,000 Assyrians, causing Sennacherib to hightail it back to Nineveh. (He wasn't stupid, it seems.)

Jeremiah: This prophet saw that Israel had been unfaithful to God and foretold that Israel would experience another round of foreign captivity in which to reflect—this time in Babylon, and they'd better learn from it. One of Jeremiah's favorite metaphors was to compare God to a husband and Judah to an unfaithful wife who slept around. He made some enemies this way, but what self-respecting prophet didn't? In Lamentations, Jeremiah expressed his sorrow over how far the Israelites had fallen away from God.

Hosea: He was married to Gomer, who was unfaithful to him, and this colored Hosea's rhetoric. He indicted Israel in language that involved prostitution and loose morals. As with most other prophets, Hosea demanded that Israel repent, threatened it with terrible fates otherwise, and predicted deliverance if it did—a theme Israel would get rather used to.

Joel: Joel's theme was disaster and judgment day. If the Israelites didn't return to worship the true God, Joel foretold devastation, pain, earthquakes, gloom, and fire. If they did, however, they would receive many blessings. What sets Joel apart is not so much his theme of repentance (hard to find a prophet not preaching repentance), but the exaltation and joy he foretold if Israel heeded his words.

Amos: A farmer, Amos called for social justice, never a strong point with the Israelite religious hierarchy of his day. He preached against many nations: Damascus, Gaza, Tyre, Edom, Ammon, Moab, Judah, even Israel (why leave out the home team?). It got Amos kicked out of the Bethel religious sanctuary, but he evidently felt the prophetic truth was worth it.

Obadiah: His rant was specific to the Edomites, Israel's southeastern neighbors and general targets of scorn. Obadiah calls the Edomites overly proud and accuses them of aiding and abetting the Babylonian invasion of Judah. It's amazing how much yelling he packs into 21 verses, the gist of which is that Edom is *really* going to get it.

Jonah: His is an interesting case because Jonah didn't want to go lecture Nineveh, a city badly in need of lecturing. After sailing away—and sailors pitching him overboard to appease a storm—and a big fish barfing him up on the beach, Jonah began to see things

God's way. When Jonah threatened Nineveh with destruction, the place actually repented. God had second thoughts and didn't blast Nineveh, whereupon Jonah got mad at God. Jonah, it seems, tended to act first and think second.

Micah: He was deeply annoyed with both Judah and Samaria. He compared the latter to a prostitute (a favorite curse of OT prophets) and foretold the former's conquest (the people would have to shave off all their hair). Like many other frothing prophets, Micah saved special dislike for those who oppressed the poor or tried to confiscate others' property. He prophesied the ruin of deeply corrupt Jerusalem.

Nahum: As a rule, annoyed prophets were either angry with the Israelites or with their enemies. Nahum fell into category #2, and his chosen enemies were the much-despised Assyrians. This prophet went into exact detail about the fall, which actually occurred in 612 B.C. He finishes with words too choice not to quote: "There is no assuaging your hurt, your wound is mortal. All who hear the news about you clap their hands over you. For who has ever escaped your endless cruelty?"

Zephaniah: This man was absolutely disgusted with God's people in Jerusalem. The strong oppressed the weak at will. As Zephaniah saw it, they had backslid, dabbled in idolatry, distrusted the Lord, profaned sacred things, and scoffed at God's law. Zephaniah was mad at other nations too, so at least he didn't single out Israel: God would destroy Assyria, for example. (Nahum, one supposes, would gladly have hung out with Zeph.)

Haggai: His book is short but memorable. The Jews had not gotten on with rebuilding the temple, and God (via Haggai) wanted them to get their act together. The sooner they got it squared away, the sooner Haggai prophesied that God would bless them. Sometimes God used the stick, other times the carrot.

Malachi: This prophet, whose book appears last (though it may not be the last written) in the Old Testament, took God's people to task when they questioned their faith in his covenant. In fairness to them, they were stuck in Babylon at the time, but Malachi was deafer to excuses than a Marine gunnery sergeant. He urged people not to divorce and assured the Israelites of the return of Elijah.

Shakespeare and the 46th Psalm

❧ ❧ ❧ ❧

It was April 1610, the 46th birthday of William Shakespeare, already England's most acclaimed actor-playwright. He had already written and produced Romeo and Juliet, Hamlet, A Midsummer Night's Dream, *and dozens of other masterpieces.*

Meanwhile, King James I had decided to authorize a new English translation of the Bible, gathering an impressive crew of scholars and wordsmiths to do so. They had been working on the project since 1607. It would be published in 1611.

Surely these translators were familiar with Shakespeare's work. As literary men themselves, they probably admired his ability to turn a phrase. So, as the story goes (and there's no proof of this), for Shakespeare's 46th birthday some of the translators decide to slip a verbal homage into the text of Psalm 46. It begins:

God is our refuge and strength, a very present help in trouble. Therefore will not we fear, though the earth be removed, and though the mountains be carried into the midst of the sea; Though the waters thereof roar and be troubled, though the mountains **shake** *with the swelling thereof.*

The 46th word is *shake.*
And here are the last three verses:

He maketh wars to cease unto the end of the earth; he breaketh the bow, and cutteth the **spear** *in sunder; he burneth the chariot in the fire. Be still, and know that I am God: I will be exalted among the heathen, I will be exalted in the earth. The* LORD *of hosts is with us; the God of Jacob is our refuge.*

The 46th word from the end is *spear.* Count 'em up yourself. *Shake ... spear.*

Coincidence? Maybe. Or perhaps a really cool birthday gift.

Six Aramaic Words or Phrases from the Bible You Should Know

❧ ❧ ❧ ❧

A third biblical language pops up here and there.

The New Testament was written in Greek, and the Old Testament in Hebrew... mostly. A third ancient language was seen occasionally: Aramaic. This was a common trade language spoken throughout the Middle East in the millennium before Christ. Several chapters of Ezra and Daniel were written in Aramaic, and it was probably the everyday language spoken by Jesus and the disciples. A few Aramaic words and phrases are preserved within the Greek text of the New Testament.

1. *Abba*—"Father" (Mark 14:36)

It was a critical moment for Jesus, praying in the Garden of Gethsemane on the eve of his crucifixion. He removed himself a short distance from his disciples and spoke earnestly to his Father. Mark records that he said, "*Abba,* Father, for you all things are possible; remove this cup from me; yet, not what I want, but what you want." This form of address was picked up by the apostle Paul, who wrote, "God has sent the Spirit of his Son into our hearts, crying, "Abba! Father!" (Galatians 4:6; see also Romans 8:15).

2. *Mammon*—"Wealth" (Matthew 6:24)

This was one of Jesus' gentle witticisms. "No one can serve two masters," he said in the Sermon on the Mount. His hearers understood this as a matter of common sense. There would always be a question of ultimate loyalty. "You cannot serve God and Mammon." The Aramaic word for wealth, *mamona,* seems to be used as a proper name, almost as some wannabe deity, the "other master" who's challenging our exclusive service to God.

3. *Maranatha*—"Come, Lord Jesus" (1 Corinthians 16:22)

The apostle Paul ends his first epistle to Corinth with this Aramaic term, suggesting that it was a very early catchphrase among Christians. Scholars disagree on its best translation. *Mar* clearly means "Lord," and *an* or *ana* means "our," but the verb tense is up for grabs. Does it mean the Lord *has* come, or that the Lord *will* come again? Some cite a similar phrase at the end of Revelation and consider this a prayer asking the Lord to return quickly.

4. *Raca*—"Dimwit" (Matthew 5:22)

In the Sermon on the Mount, Jesus was making the point that true morality is in the heart, not just the actions. So don't be too self-satisfied if you've avoided murdering anyone. Have you *wanted* to murder anyone? "Again, anyone who says to his brother, '*Raca*,' is answerable to the [court]." This uncommon word has all the markings of a vulgar insult. Apparently it was Aramaic for a stupid person. Choose your own modern version of it.

5. *Talitha kum*—"Little girl, get up" (Mark 5:41)

A synagogue leader begged Jesus to come to his 12-year-old daughter's deathbed and heal her. By the time Jesus arrived, mourners had assembled, bewailing the girl's death. The anguished father was about to send Jesus away, but Jesus announced that the girl was only sleeping. Some scoffed, but Jesus took her by the hand and said, "*Talitha kum*." Immediately she got up and walked around.

6. *Ephphatha*—"Be opened" (Mark 7:34)

In the Ten Cities region of Galilee, Jesus encountered a deaf man who also had a speech impediment. Taking him aside, Jesus put his fingers in the man's ears, and he "spat and touched his tongue." Looking upward, Jesus said something that sounded like "Effatha." The Aramaic word for "open" is *pthah*, and its passive imperative would have been *ethpthah*. "And immediately his ears were opened, his tongue was released, and he spoke plainly" (Mark 7:35).

Great Bible Orators

Religious Pioneer!

Church founder Aimee Semple McPherson was an evangelical innovator who pulled out all the stops to broaden her audience.

Though little remembered today, Aimee Semple McPherson was one of the most famous Americans of the 1920s. She was an evangelistic pioneer who courted the press with the savvy of a Hollywood press agent and was the driving force behind the establishment of the Foursquare Gospel Church.

McPherson was born Beth Kennedy near Ingersoll, Ontario, on October 9, 1890. Because her mother was active in the Salvation Army, religion was an important aspect of her life starting in childhood. At age 17, she married Robert Semple, and together they traveled to Hong Kong to become missionaries in China. When her husband died of typhoid fever, McPherson went to New York with her infant daughter and rejoined her mother. Together, they traveled the country, speaking at revival meetings.

Religious Road Trip
She married Harold McPherson, a sales-man, in 1912, and gave birth to a son a year later. In 1916, McPherson conducted a cross-country lecture tour in her "Full Gospel Car," which had religious slogans painted on it. A couple of years later, she settled in Los Angeles but continued to travel the country to speak at revival meetings. Harold McPherson couldn't handle her time away, and he filed for divorce in 1921, charging her with desertion.

The divorce freed her to continue her evangelical work unencumbered, and in 1923, she raised enough money to build the 5,000-seat Angelus Temple in Los Angeles. Later that year, she opened a Bible school, which became the Lighthouse of International Foursquare Evangelism.

Quick to tap anything that would help her reach more people, she began broadcasting her sermons from the church via radio. She was a charismatic speaker who sometimes used costumes, music, and other tools to grab and hold her audiences. During this time, she also developed a reputation as a faith healer, which drew even more people.

Mysterious Disappearance

In May 1926, McPherson went swimming in the ocean and simply disappeared. It was believed at first that she had drowned. The national media reported her apparent death, and her mother mourned her passing. But no body was recovered.

On June 23, she reappeared in Mexico with a wild story of being kidnapped and held captive. A few days before her reappearance, her mother had received a note threatening to sell McPherson into "white slavery" if a ransom was not paid.

There were several holes in the story, and it was widely believed that she had run off with Kenneth Ormiston, a radio operator for the the church who had gone missing at the same time she had. There had been rumors of an affair between McPherson and Ormiston before the couple's bizarre disappearance, and Ormiston's wife had stated that the couple was romantically involved before she left Ormiston and returned to Australia.

Criminal Charges

Suspicions of wrongdoing were so strong that a grand jury investigation led to charges against McPherson and Ormiston of perjury and manufacturing evidence, but the charges were dropped the following year without explanation.

She returned to her church, where the publicity from her disappearance attracted even more followers. Behind closed doors, however, insiders were troubled, and McPherson's mother left the organization. In the years that followed, the church was plagued by financial difficulties, but she continued with her radio show and other activities, including a variety of charity work. At the height of the Great Depression, for example, the Angelus Temple's commissary distributed food and clothing to those in need. By the 1940s, most of the church's money problems had been resolved, and she began touring the country as a revival speaker yet again.

McPherson died of a sedative overdose on September 27, 1944. Her death was reported as accidental, but some within the church believed she had committed suicide. More than 50,000 people attended her viewing.

The International Church of the Foursquare Gospel, which McPherson founded, continues today, with an estimated 30,000 churches worldwide. It remains Aimee Semple McPherson's lasting legacy.

In the Footsteps of Their Fathers

✤ ✤ ✤ ✤

*Though Jesus would later be considered a dangerous radical,
his professional choice was quite conventional.*

Everyone knows that Jesus was a carpenter, just like his earthly
father, Joseph (Matthew 13:55). Ancient Israel was a patriarchal
society, and most sons went into the same business as their fathers,
though it was not unheard of for a son to develop his own interest and be apprenticed out to another man in another field. Jesus,
however, took the more conventional route and learned carpentry
from his own dad. Long before he became a famous religious leader
who was known throughout the entire country, he lived in obscurity
with his family and worked hard at his humble yet respectable trade.
What was his all-but-anonymous life like in those early years? What
were his workdays like?

Skills and Scarcity

Though carpenters were vital in ancient Israel and always in demand, the trade was not without its hardships. The work was in-
tensely physical, and since there was a scarcity of timber in urban
areas such as Jerusalem, much time could be eaten up in gathering
and hauling. Because of this shortage of wood, Hebrew carpenters did less work on houses, which were
constructed of stone by masons,
than did carpenters in many
other places in the world.
A carpenter would add the
finishing touches, such as
a wooden door, window shut-
ters, or decorative latticework, but
his handiwork was more likely to
be seen inside. The Bible speaks
many times of the tables and chairs
made by carpenters, but furniture

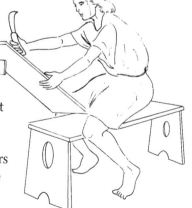

was mostly a luxury for the wealthy. Peasants simply sat on the floor when resting or eating.

Luckily for carpenters, there were some places in Israel that were full of trees. Oak, fir, olive, fig, cedar, acacia, cypress, and pomegranate—these are just some of the trees that provided lumber for the carpenter's work. Carpenters especially loved working with the cedar tree. The cedar was (and is) a beautiful red color, and the sap from its trunk and cones is tantalizingly fragrant.

Location was crucial to a carpenter's professional focus. If he lived in a coastal area, he might specialize in the construction of boats, which were of great importance to the large fishing industry. If his neighbors were farmers, his specialty might be ploughs or ox carts for hauling produce. If he was well-connected in religious circles, he might concentrate on creating intricate and beautiful interior decorations for synagogues. In ancient Israel, as today, who you knew was as important as what you knew.

Thinking Outside the Toolbox

Also just like today, it was necessary for skilled workers such as carpenters to adapt to changing times and trends. Archaeologists have discovered that during biblical times, improvements were made in the tools of carpentry: saws, hammers, awls, nails, chisels, bow drills, and adzes (the last is an instrument that looks like a combination ax/hoe and is used to shape and gouge wood). The successful carpenter would have made it his business to keep abreast of these improvements through communication with others in his trade.

In Old Testament times, a carpenter was likely to be paid in barter, for example with livestock, flour, wine, dry goods, or even land if the job was big enough. By the time of Jesus, however, coinage had become standardized in Israel, and it is likely that Jesus and Joseph were paid for their work in a mixture of coins and barter. In their neck of the woods—Nazareth—the most bartered items would probably have been pickled fish, wool, olive oil, and dried figs. Of course, however a carpenter in ancient Israel was paid, it would not be long until the taxman came looking for his cut. After leaving carpentry and devoting himself full time to spreading God's Word, Jesus would make one of those taxmen, Matthew, one of his beloved apostles (Matthew 9:9, 10:3).

The Once and Future Elijah

❧ ❧ ❧ ❧

*Because the colorful prophet Elijah was taken up to heaven
in a fiery chariot, it was presumed that he didn't die. Soon enough
word got around (egged on by a couple of later prophecies) that
he would return to earth someday.*

At first, the prophet Elijah's followers have difficulty believing that
their beloved leader is gone, despite the fact that Elijah's successor,
the prophet Elisha, tells them plainly that he had seen a whirlwind
draw the beloved Elijah up to heaven in a fiery chariot. Even though
Elijah's disciples believe that his spirit has come to rest on Elisha,
they still beg Elisha to let them send out a search party, saying: "See
now, we have fifty strong men among your servants; please let them
go and seek your master [Elijah]; it may be that the Lord has caught
him up and thrown him down on some mountain or in some valley"
(2 Kings 2:16). At first Elisha resists, but finally he lets the 50 men
go in search of Elijah, knowing they won't find him.

After three days of looking everywhere with no results, the
search party reluctantly gives up. But Elijah's dramatic departure
from this earth, like that of Enoch before him, continues to haunt
them. They cannot believe that the prophet has left them forever.
They and their descendants continue to believe that God must have
special plans for Elijah—and since he still retained his human body,
Elijah must have been set aside to do something more here on
earth.

Biblical Prophecies of Elijah's Return

According to Jewish tradition, Elijah is neither dead nor in heaven,
but wandering the earth undetected. At some time in the future,
he will step out of obscurity to usher in the Messiah and the final
redemption of humankind. This tradition is firmly rooted in scripture. Centuries after Elijah's ascension, the prophet Malachi reports
that God himself promised Elijah's return: "Lo, I will send you the
prophet Elijah before the great and terrible day of the Lord comes.

He will turn the hearts of children to their parents, so that I will not come and strike the land with a curse" (Malachi 4:5–6). According to Malachi, Elijah would return to earth to reconcile his people and save them from incurring punishment at the hands of God, who was angered by their flaunting of his laws. Malachi depicts the coming reconciliation by saying that children would again begin respecting their parents, as required by Mosaic Law, but he surely meant that God's other laws would also be respected as well. These are the final words of the Christian Old Testament. In the Apocrypha, the learned Jewish scribe and teacher Jesus Ben Sira backs Malachi up by announcing that in the future Elijah would reconcile the people of Israel to God (Sirach 48:10).

Later Jewish Traditions

Based on the prophecies of Malachi and Ben Sira, as well as their own oral traditions, Jews continue to await the return of Elijah. Even today, at the Passover Seder (meal) an extra cup of wine, Elijah's Cup, is always placed on the table in anticipation of his return. And in some Jewish homes, a place at the table is reserved for Elijah and a door is flung open to admit him. In addition, most Jews still reserve a chair for Elijah at circumcisions.

Elijah and the New Testament

Just as the promise of Elijah's return ends the Old Testament, allusions to the prophet abound at the start of the New Testament, where he appears at least symbolically in the person of John the Baptist. First, in predicting the birth of John, the angel Gabriel tells the bewildered father, Zechariah, that his future son will turn many people to the Lord and "with the spirit and power of Elijah he will go before him [Jesus] to turn the hearts of parents to their children, and the disobedient to the wisdom of the righteous, to make ready a people prepared

for the Lord" (Luke 1:17). Later, rumors claim that Jesus himself is Elijah come back to earth, but Jesus denies it. When speaking about John the Baptist, Jesus says: "He is Elijah who is to come" (Matthew 11:14).

Later, when Jesus is transfigured before his three closest disciples on a mountaintop, Elijah and Moses appear and converse with Jesus. Elijah is probably there to represent the prophets of the past, while Moses represents God's laws. On the way down the mountain, the disciples ask Jesus why the scribes (Jewish religious authorities) say that Elijah must return before the Messiah appears. Jesus answers: "I tell you that Elijah has already come, and they did not recognize him, but they did to him whatever they pleased" (Matthew 17:11–12). Jesus is referring to John the Baptist, who had been put to death, reminding Jesus that he too will be put to death.

Elijah at the End of Time

Just as Elijah was expected to usher in the Messiah at his first coming, he is also expected to appear at the end of time to introduce

Jesus' second coming. In the early Christian era, Elijah was named as the author of a number of nonbiblical books in which he is described as predicting the events at the end of time. However, these works, called apocalypses, seem more suited to Enoch or even Ezekiel than Elijah and may have been assigned to Elijah only because he plays a key role in one incident that is included in all of these books. The same incident is also vividly recorded in the book of Revelation.

Just before the end of time, seven seals are broken and seven trumpet blasts are blown to release and announce the final woes that will afflict the world in those dark final days. But before the final trumpet blast, God announces from the heavens: "I will grant my two witnesses authority to prophesy for one thousand two hundred sixty days, wearing sackcloth" (Revelation 11:3). God gives these witnesses extra protection: "If anyone wants to harm them, fire pours from their mouth and consumes their foes" (Revelation 11:5). The witnesses are generally believed to be (once again) Elijah and Moses, for the next verse tells us that the men will have the power to cause droughts—something Elijah had done during his first time on earth—and they will be able to turn the waters to blood and call down plagues at will, which Moses had done in Egypt.

Despite fiery breaths, however, Elijah and Moses will not have it easy. According to the vision recorded in Revelation, once the duo completes their prophesying, they will battle a great beast that will rise from the abyss—the Antichrist in his first appearance in Revelation. The beast will attack the prophets and kill them, and their corpses will be left to rot in the open. Instead of burying them, people "will gloat over them and celebrate and exchange presents, because these two prophets had been a torment to the inhabitants of the earth" (Revelation 11:9–10). The gloaters envisioned here are probably unbelievers whom the prophets had angered by constantly preaching at them to reform, which was the last thing they wanted to do.

This Is the End—I Can See It All Now

Despite all the merrymaking, the witnesses will have the last laugh. After Elijah and Moses lie dead for three and a half days, "the breath of life from God entered them, and they stood on their feet, and those who saw them were terrified. Then they heard a loud voice from heaven saying to them, 'Come up here!' And they went up to heaven in a cloud, while their enemies watched them" (Revelation 11:11–12). At that moment in the vision a great earthquake destroys the mockers and others, and the seventh trumpet blast announces the defeat of all evil and the second coming of the Lord Jesus Christ.

And so, as Malachi had prophesied, Elijah did return to earth before the Messiah—in the person of John the Baptist to prepare the people for Jesus' ministry. He will also appear at the end of time to prepare for Jesus' second coming. Fittingly, Elijah will once again be taken up to heaven alive, but this time in a cloud rather than in a whirlwind propelled by a fiery chariot.

Israel's Neighbors

PERSIANS

It was one of the most tolerant and cosmopolitan empires in world history—until it was conquered by thugs from Macedonia.

Who Were They?
The Persians, also known as the Achaemenids during the part of their history in which they interact with biblical affairs, lived in modern Iran. While the region was inhabited and civilized as far back as Egypt, Persia achieved its glory days between 625–331 B.C. As overlords, the Persians permitted nearly all forms of religion, and their own was mainly Zoroastrianism—a one-god faith bearing some likeness to Judaism. They ruled an empire stretching from India to modern Turkey to Egypt to central Asia. The Persians forbade slavery; they asked only that subject peoples pay taxes, obey laws, and contribute troops. Beyond that, they could live as they chose.

Where Are They Now?
They are in the same place, but the faith is different today. The Achaemenid Empire fell to Alexander the Great's Greeks and Macedonians in 331 B.C., but Persian culture heavily infiltrated the conquerors and their successors. As Persia (also called Parthia), the country would be a thorn in Rome's side for all the Empire's days—like Germania or Dacia (Romania). With the rise of Islam in the A.D. 600s, Persia mainly converted to the Shi'a version, which dominates the nation today.

Biblical Mentions
Emperor Cyrus of Persia not only let the Jews leave Babylonian captivity to go home to Israel and rebuild their temple, he flat-out told them to. Emperor Ahasuerus, of the story of Esther, was in reality Xerxes I—the same emperor whose army the Spartans fought at Thermopylae and whose navy the Athenians sank at Salamis. The Persians were perhaps the ideal ruling country from a Jewish standpoint, thanks to their liberal stance on religion and ability to prevent too much infighting between client states. Nearly all scriptural mentions of Persia are favorable.

The Twelve Tribes of Israel

✤ ✤ ✤ ✤

*God promised Jacob that an entire nation would spring from him.
Jacob, later renamed Israel, fathered 12 sons. On his deathbed,
he gathered his sons and blessed them, announcing, "All these
are the twelve tribes of Israel" (Genesis 49:28).*

Jacob had sons by four different women—his first wife, Leah; his favorite wife, Rachel; Leah's maid, Zilpah; and Rachel's maid, Bilhah.

Leah was the mother of Reuben, Simeon, Levi, Judah, Zebulun, and Issachar. Rachel was the mother of Joseph and Benjamin. Zilpah was the mother of Gad and Asher. Bilhah was the mother of Dan and Naphtali.

The Tribes in History

Little is known of most of Jacob's 12 sons, but the tribes made up of their descendants played vital roles in Israelite history. First, Moses appointed a leader for each tribe, and these leaders guided the people during the 40-year sojourn in the wilderness. When the Israelites entered Canaan, each tribe—except the tribe of Levi—was given its own land. The Levites, who served as priests for all the tribes, were supported by the tithes of the people. However, to keep the number of tribal lands at 12, the descendants of Joseph were split in two tribes, descended from Joseph's sons Ephraim and Manasseh.

Under David and Solomon, all 12 tribes were brought together in a single great kingdom. After Solomon's death, however, the kingdom split, with ten of the tribes forming the northern kingdom of Israel, while the tribes of Judah and Benjamin formed the southern kingdom of Judah. In 721 B.C., the Assyrians invaded the northern kingdom and permanently dispersed the people. Consequently, they are often referred to as the Ten Lost Tribes of Israel. Only Judah and Benjamin remained in the south, and Benjamin was slowly absorbed by Judah and foreign powers.

Most Jews today trace their ancestry to the tribe of Judah. And, in fact, the word *Jew* is taken from the name of this tribe. Jacob had indeed become a nation.

10 Things

Misquoted (or Misunderstood) Bible Verses

Sometimes it doesn't say what we think it says.

1. Judge Not: *"Do not judge, so that you may not be judged"* *(Matthew 7:1).*

This text, spoken by Jesus, is no diatribe against all discernment. It's a warning against hypocrisy, criticizing others for the things we're doing.

2. Working Together for Good: *"We know that all things work together for good for those who love God, who are called according to his purpose" (Romans 8:28).*

Too many believers edit this verse to "all things work together for good." When we consider the verse within its chapter, we find that it's far more than a pep talk. It's a powerful truth rooted in God's eternal purposes. The Lord is working on a greater plan—and it's often different from our plans.

3. The Forbidden Fruit: *"God said, 'You shall not eat of the fruit of the tree that is in the middle of the garden'" (Genesis 3:3).*

A lot of people think the "forbidden fruit" in the Garden of Eden was an apple. The fact is, no specific fruit is mentioned.

4. Killing: *"Thou shalt not kill" (Exodus 20:13, KJV).*

In old translations, the sixth of the Ten Commandments seems to forbid all killing, and pacifists and vegetarians have found support. But the Hebrew word deals with murder—causing the wrongful death of another person.

5. The Root of All Evil: *"For the love of money is a root of all kinds of evil" (1 Timothy 6:10).*

You may have heard that "money is the root of all evil." Not exactly. It's the *love of* money, and modern translations rightly note that it's the root of all *kinds of* evil. You can have money, as long as you don't love it.

6. The Three Wise Men: *"After Jesus was born in Bethlehem of Judea, wise men from the East came to Jerusalem" (Matthew 2:1).*

Everyone thinks there were three wise men in the Christmas story, but that's not necessarily true. They brought three *gifts*—gold, frankincense, and myrrh—but the Bible doesn't say how many wise men there were.

7. The Innkeeper and the Stable: *"And she gave birth to her firstborn son and wrapped him in bands of cloth, and laid him in a manger, because there was no place for them in the inn" (Luke 2:7).*

There is no stable or innkeeper in the nativity story. The Greek word for "inn" usually referred to the guest room of a house. It's likely that the animals were kept in an adjoining room or perhaps in a courtyard under the guest room, and the manger would be there.

8. Mary Magdalene: *"The twelve were with him, as well as some women who had been cured of evil spirits and infirmities: Mary, called Magdalene, from whom seven demons had gone out...and many others" (Luke 8:1–3).*

There's little about Mary from Magdala in the Bible. We know only that she had been possessed by seven demons, which Jesus exorcised. She was also a devout disciple of Jesus, present at the cross and the tomb.

9. The Lion and the Lamb: *"The wolf and the lamb shall feed together, the lion shall eat straw like the ox" (Isaiah 65:25).*

Familiar with the idyllic image of the peaceable kingdom of God—"the lion shall lie down with the lamb"? That's not the way scripture puts it. The wolf was a more common predator in Bible lands, and the prophet Isaiah twice mentions the future détente between wolves and lambs.

10. Spare the Rod: *"Those who spare the rod hate their children, but those who love them are diligent to discipline them" (Proverbs 13:24).*

"Spare the rod, spoil the child" is a common parenting aphorism. The biblical maxim has a similar point, but adds a positive angle. Good discipline is an expression of parental love.

Bible Prophecies Fulfilled

✤ ✤ ✤ ✤

Bible prophecy is a major field of Christian study—and big business, with millions of dollars in books and articles about biblical prophecy sold each year.

3 Prophecies Related to the People of Israel

1. The people of Israel will never disappear. Despite thousands of years of persecution, exile, and wholesale slaughter, the Jews have survived as a people, as prophesied in Leviticus 26:44. "Yet in spite of this, when they are in the land of their enemies, I will not reject them or abhor them so as to destroy them completely, breaking my covenant with them. I am the Lord their God."

2. Zion would be plowed under. Micah 3:12 says, "Therefore because of you, Zion will be plowed like a field, Jerusalem will become a heap of rubble, the temple hill a mound overgrown with thickets." Around A.D. 135, Roman authorities ran a plow over parts of Jerusalem in preparation for founding a new Roman city.

3. Jews would be exiled after Jesus' death. In Luke 21:24, Jesus claims of the Jews that "They will fall by the sword and will be taken as prisoners to all the nations. Jerusalem will be trampled on by the Gentiles until the times of the Gentiles are fulfilled." A few decades after Jesus' death, the Romans began the persecution of the Jews that would last for two millennia.

5 Prophecies Related to the Life of Jesus Christ

1. Jesus would be born in Bethlehem. Micah 5:2 says, "But you, Bethlehem Ephrathah, though you are small among the clans of Judah, out of you will come for me one who will be ruler over Israel, whose origins are from of old, from ancient times."

2. Jesus would be born to a virgin mother. Isaiah 7:14 states "Therefore the Lord himself will give you a sign: The virgin will be with child and will give birth to a son, and will call him Immanuel."

3. Herod would kill the children of Bethlehem. Jeremiah 31:15, "This is what the Lord says: 'A cry of anguish is heard in

Ramah—mourning and weeping unrestrained. Rachel weeps for her children, refusing to be comforted—for her children are dead.'" Matthew 2 describes Herod's execution of the infants of Bethlehem and notes that this fulfills Jeremiah's prophecy.

4. Jesus would cure the deaf and blind. Isaiah 35:5–6 says, "And when he comes, he will open the eyes of the blind and unstop the ears of the deaf. The lame will leap like a deer, and those who cannot speak will shout and sing!"

5. Jesus would be crucified for others' transgressions. Isaiah 53 described how Jesus would be rejected by his peers, bear others' iniquities, and ultimately be "pierced" for others' sins.

Specific Prophecy About the Founding of Israel

According to one school of thought, the book of Ezekiel correctly prophesied to within the month the date of Israel's 1948 establishment. Fitting the prophecy into history takes a little work, though. In 537 B.C., about 70 years into the Babylonian captivity, Ezekiel prophesied that Israel would not return to nationhood until they had fulfilled a period of servitude: "Now lie on your left side and place the sins of Israel on yourself. You are to bear their sins for the number of days you lie there on your side. You will bear Israel's sins for 390 days—one day for each year of their sin. After that, turn over and lie on your right side for 40 days—one day for each year of Judah's sin" (Ezekiel 4:4–6).

Only after this servitude of 430 years would Israel re-establish its nation. Seventy years of the sentence had been served in Babylon, leaving 360 of servitude remaining. Simple math shows that Israel should have been re-established in 176 B.C. Right? Sorry, but that's the wrong answer.

God warned the Jews on multiple occasions that a failure to repent would increase their punishment "seven-fold." Though King Cyrus sent the Jews back to their homeland to rebuild Jerusalem in 537 B.C., the Jews were not immediately repentant. Which meant that those 360 years left of servitude were multiplied by seven—to 2,520 years. That's 2,520 biblical years, which consisted of 360 days each. Accounting for this difference, the prophecy seems to indicate that the time of servitude would end in May 1948. Israel declared its independence on May 14, 1948.

Tunneling to Water—and Safety

❖ ❖ ❖ ❖

When the Assyrians were threatening to capture Jerusalem,
King Hezekiah acted quickly to fend off the attack.
He ended by tunneling his way to invulnerability.

After the Assyrians defeated the northern kingdom of Israel in
721 B.C., they returned in 701 to conquer the southern kingdom of
Judah. As the invaders approached Jerusalem, brutally destroying
several other cities of Judah along the way, King Hezekiah of Judah
built up Jerusalem's defenses to better fend them off. And it worked.

When the Assyrians finally reached Jerusalem, they surrounded
and besieged the city but were unable to break through its walls.
The Assyrians settled in, assuming that even if they couldn't get in,
the people of Jerusalem wouldn't be able to get out to reach their
water supply. The people of Jerusalem would surrender when they
got thirsty enough. But the Assyrians were in for a surprise.

While the Assyrians were brutalizing other Judean cities, King
Hezekiah had exhibited great foresight. Until then, all of Jerusalem's
fresh water had come from the underground Gihon Spring outside
the city walls and flowed through unprotected canals into storage
pools inside the city. Because these canals could be blocked by the
enemy, cutting off the city's water supply, Hezekiah had workers
close off the canals and dig a six-foot-high tunnel under the city
walls through 1,749 feet of solid bedrock. The work was done mainly
with hand tools by two sets of men who worked from opposite directions and met in the middle. Hezekiah then used the completed
tunnel to divert the water from the spring through the tunnel, which
sloped gently downward, allowing the water to flow naturally into a
large reservoir, called the Pool of Siloam, inside the city walls.

And so the people of Jerusalem weren't trapped without water.
The Assyrian siege failed. Archaeologists have found remains of this
tunnel, including a plaque written by its engineers that describes
the meeting of the two groups of workers as they completed their
gargantuan task. It is a monument to Jewish ingenuity.

Where Jesus Walked

Bethsaida Julias

The home of Peter, Andrew, and Philip,
Bethsaida Julias was part of the walk of Christ on earth.

In Biblical Times

Bethsaida was easy to find: From Capernaum on the Sea of Galilee's north coast, go clockwise a few miles around the lake. Named for Julia, believed to be the wife of Roman Emperor Augustus, it had been an insignificant fishing village until just before the time of Jesus when Herod II expanded it. The Bible may actually refer to two different Bethsaidas; since we aren't sure of its modern site, it's hard to determine whether the differing descriptions refer to the same or different places.

Jesus' Connection

The miracle of loaves and fishes occurred near Bethsaida, if not in it. Shortly thereafter, Jesus sent his disciples across the water (in boats) to that city. Since this occurred just before the water-walking incident on the Galilee, we may presume this happened near Bethsaida Julias as well. Jesus restored a blind man's sight outside Bethsaida and ranted at its people for not believing more in him. He said that if he'd done the kind of miracles at Tyre and Sidon (implying that these were two of the sleaziest places in the Levant, probably a fair description) that he had done at Bethsaida, both cities long before would have repented in sackcloth and ashes (perhaps a little optimistic on his part).

Bethsaida Julias Today

Not only are we unsure where it is, as mentioned earlier, it is possible there were two Bethsaidas. The best candidate is the modern archaeological site just north of the Sea of Galilee named *et-Tell* ("the ruin mound" in Arabic), which is in the correct general area but slightly back from the Galilee. Theories exist to explain that, but don't confuse this et-Tell with another that lies much further south, close to Jerusalem. In any case, if you want to seek the et-Tell associated with Bethsaida Julias and make up your own mind, it's easy to visit both it and Capernaum on the same day.

Those Despised Samaritans

✣ ✣ ✣ ✣

The origin of the Jewish-Samaritan schism isn't entirely clear,
but by Jesus' time, the controversy was full blown.

A Little Background

The golden years of Israel's United Kingdom era came to an end
when King Solomon's young son Rehoboam listened to the foolish
counsel of his young friends. Upon Rehoboam's ascent to the throne,
the people came to appeal to him to lift the heavy labor burdens
Solomon had imposed. Instead of listening to the counsel of his
father's senior staff members, who coached him to be merciful,
he chose to play the role of macho king and threatened to be a far
harsher taskmaster than his father had ever been.

At this juncture, the kingdom split into the northern kingdom,
known as Israel, with ten tribes who rallied around a guy named
Jeroboam, and the southern kingdom, known as Judah, made up of
the tribes of Benjamin and Judah, who remained loyal to Rehoboam.

All that to say this: The region where the northern tribes were
concentrated was known as the district of Samaria.

Samaria Meets Assyria

Despite many warnings by God through his prophets, the northern
tribes of Israel persisted in their idolatry, introduced by Jeroboam
and perpetuated by a suc-
cession of kings. Sadly, Israel
met her end through a series
of Assyrian invasions, about
which God had forewarned
them. After a while, all that
was left of the northern
kingdom was its capital city,
Samaria, and some outlying
villages. In 722 B.C., Assyria's

King Shalmaneser V took Samaria and populated it with other settlers. Later, Alexander the Great sent Greek colonists there.

While the newcomers to Samaria sought to learn the rites and customs of the "local God," they also brought along with them their idols; they worshipped both the God of Israel and their own gods. Of course, intermarriage occurred between these various peoples.

Three Strikes, You're Out!

While relations between Israel and Judah had been somewhat strained before their respective exiles (Israel exiled by Assyria, then Judah by Babylon), irreconcilable differences began to accumulate when Judah returned from her exile to rebuild the walls of Jerusalem.

Strike one against the Samaritans was likely their intermarriage with the idol-worshipping colonists. Jews returning from Babylon had learned their lesson about idolatry and were bent on worshipping only their God. As a result, when Nehemiah got permission from the Medo-Persian king to rebuild the walls of Jerusalem and the temple, he rejected some folks from Samaria who offered to help. The Samaritans retaliated by petitioning the Assyrian king to stop the work Nehemiah was doing. And so the pot of hostility began to boil.

Strike two consisted in the Samaritans' contention that Shechem was the original capital of Israel (which it was) and should therefore be the rightful place of worship, rather than Jerusalem. In 409 B.C., Manasseh (a priest who had been "defrocked" in Jerusalem) obtained permission from the Persian king to build a temple on Mount Gerizim, where Samaritans sought to worship according to the Law of Moses. This became the main quarrel between Jews and Samaritans: Which one had the true holy temple of God?

Strike three might well be chalked up to the ongoing false claims made by Samaritans. For example, they tried to secure certain Jewish tax exemptions from Alexander the Great, claiming to be Jews. Their claims were examined and found to be false.

Manasseh, the one who spearheaded the temple construction on Gerizim, made a copy of the Law—the books Genesis through Deuteronomy—and claimed that it was the oldest copy in existence.

Then there was the ongoing claim that their temple was the true place of worship. Such claims piqued traditional Jewish sensibilities and flew in the face of what they knew God had directed regarding the place of worship.

Over time, the antagonism between the Jews and Samaritans persisted and grew more hostile. In Jesus' day it was so pronounced that Jews often skirted Samaria when traveling back and forth between the regions of Judea and Galilee (Samaria lay between them), choosing the long way around rather than encounter the despised Samaritan locals.

What's an Apostle?

The Greek word *apostolos* ("apostle") comes from *apostello,* which means "to send." In secular Greek usage, it often meant "ship," "fleet," or "naval expedition" (something sent out), but almost never a person. In the New Testament, the meaning was attached to people.

Jesus: Breaking Down the Barriers

In Jesus' era, the Samaritan temple on Gerizim was just a heap of rubble. (The Jewish king Hyrcanus destroyed it in 128 B.C.) It was near these ruins that Jesus had a conversation with a Samaritan woman—something quite socially unconventional. When she got over her initial surprise, the woman brought up the differences in worship between the Jews and Samaritans. Jesus set the record straight: Jerusalem was the proper place of worship, but only for a while longer. True worshippers—as Jesus would unite them—would be ones who worshipped God in truth through the Holy Spirit. As the conversation progressed, Jesus revealed himself as the Messiah—for whom the Samaritans were also waiting—and her village received Jesus' message with joy (see John 4:1–42).

Jesus also elevated the Samaritans, much to his opponents' chagrin, in a parable he told—well known through the ages as the parable of the good Samaritan. This was just after Jesus himself had been rejected by some Samaritans, which highlights Jesus' own benevolence in telling the story the way he did (see Luke 10:25–37).

Jesus' response to the Samaritan people revealed that he had come to bring salvation to all of humanity, just as his Father had said he would do, just as he promised throughout the pages of the Old Testament scriptures.

Quiz

Music I

Name that tune . . . and some of the tunesmiths of scripture.

1. Who was playing the harp to soothe the nerves of King Saul when a spear was thrown at him?
    - a. Asaph
    - b. Jonathan
    - c. Samuel
    - d. David

2. Who led the women of Israel, with tambourines and dancing, in a song of triumph: "horse and rider he has thrown into the sea"?
    - a. Jacob's wife, Leah
    - b. Moses' sister, Miriam
    - c. Samuel's mother, Hannah
    - d. Mary's cousin, Elizabeth

3. Who compared his generation to children who complained, "We played the flute for you, and you did not dance; we sang a dirge, and you did not mourn"?
    - a. Elijah
    - b. Jeremiah
    - c. Jesus
    - d. James

4. In what book of the Bible would we find the song of the "living creatures and the elders"?
    - a. Deuteronomy
    - b. Psalms
    - c. Song of Songs
    - d. Revelation

Answers: 1. d (1 Samuel 18:10–11); 2. b (Exodus 15:20–21); 3. c (Matthew 11:16–17, NIV); 4. d (Revelation 4)

4 Bible Prophecies Still Unfulfilled

❧ ❧ ❧ ❧

According to some who study the Bible, just about every bit of prophecy in the Bible that could possibly have come true until the present has done so. Indeed, the only prophecies not yet fulfilled are those concerning the "end times." However, the books of Daniel, Ezekiel, and Revelation all make very distinct— and somewhat terrifying—prophecies of what will happen when the end draws nigh. Here are four prophecies that have yet to be fulfilled. When they are, get ready.

1. Revival of the Roman Empire: According to Daniel 2:38–43, there will be a succession of five empires; later, in Revelation, this is amended to seven empires. According to prophecy scholars, these seven empires, in order, are: Egypt, Assyria, Babylonia, Persia, Greece, Rome, and finally, a second Roman Empire. That multiple empires have risen and fallen between Roman times and today has led many critics to argue this prophecy will never be fulfilled. Considering the current state of Italy, they may be right.

2. The Rise of a Single Global Leader: Throughout the Bible, especially in Daniel and Revelation, scripture refers to a single, evil dictator who rules the world on the eve of the Apocalypse. This dictator will be a megalomaniac—greedy, consumed by power, and godless. He will exterminate "two-thirds" of the Jews and will also launch an attack on Christians. He will be the Antichrist.

Attempting to identify this dictator is one of the favorite pastimes of end-time scholars. Throughout the past two millennia, various world leaders have been identified as the Antichrist—Titus of Rome, Adolf Hitler, Saddam Hussein, etc.—but clearly none of them fit all the biblical criteria. But it doesn't stop people from trying to find out who it is. In the *Left Behind* series, Tim LaHaye depicts the leader of the United Nations as the Antichrist, while more than one right-wing commentator has suggested Barack Obama fits the mold. That he doesn't even remotely fit the description provided by scripture just shows another way in which politics and religion don't mesh.

3. The Appearance of Two Witnesses: According to Revelation 11, God will send two witnesses to prophesy during the Tribulation, the seven-year period before Jesus' Second Coming. "'And I will grant my two witnesses authority to prophesy for one thousand two hundred sixty days, wearing sackcloth.' These are the two olive trees and the two lampstands that stand before the Lord of the earth. And if anyone wants to harm them, fire pours from their mouth and consumes their foes; anyone who wants to harm them must be killed in this manner. They have authority to shut the sky, so that no rain may fall during the days of their prophesying, and they have authority over the waters to turn them into blood, and to strike the earth with every kind of plague, as often as they desire."

It is unclear who these two witnesses are, though many scholars believe the witnesses are Elijah and Moses. Two who definitely were *not* the witnesses: Marshall Applewhite and Bonnie Nettles. While recovering from a heart attack, Applewhite had a vision that he and Nettles, who was his nurse, were the two witnesses described in Revelation. The two went on to found the Heaven's Gate cult.

4. A Massive Rebellion Against God: Throughout the Bible, particularly in 2 Thessalonians 2, Revelation, and Daniel 8, scripture refers to a time when a leader gathers his godless followers en masse in an attempt to overthrow the kingdom of heaven. Some think this revolt will be quashed without mercy by Jesus during the time of his Second Coming, after which he will establish a 1,000-year kingdom for his followers.

Dove's Dung? Ewww!

In 2 Kings 6:25, the New Revised Standard Version mentions "dove's dung" selling for a good price during a siege of Samaria. Other versions have translated the same thing as "locust beans" (New English Bible) or "wild onions" (New American Bible). They're all talking about a bulb that was roasted or boiled before eating. Today, the plant is known as the star-of-Bethlehem.

Great Bible Orators

Promoter of Prosperity

Wealth wasn't a sin in the eyes of Oral Roberts, one of the best-known—and richest—religious leaders of the 20th century.

Preachers often warn that the love of money is the root of all evil, but not Oral Roberts. A child of poverty, it was his long-held belief that God wanted everyone to prosper, both spiritually and financially.

Roberts was born in Pontotoc County, Oklahoma, on January 24, 1918. His father, Ellis Roberts, was a minister who instilled in young Oral a love of God that carried him through the rest of his life.

After finishing high school, Roberts attended Oklahoma Baptist University and Phillips University but left without a degree. He became a traveling faith healer, preaching to audiences and fervently soliciting God's help in curing their ailments. Faith healing became an integral part of his ministry, a phenomenon that drew both parishioners and controversy.

Pursuit of Wealth
In 1947, at age 29, Roberts was at a crossroads. He loved preaching but disliked the poverty that seemed inherent in the job. He would later recall dropping a Bible and having it fall open to the Third Epistle of John (verse 2, KJV), which contained the passage: "I wish above all things that thou mayest prosper and be in health, even as thy soul prospereth." Roberts knew instantly what that meant: God wanted him to be rich.

Driven to better himself, Roberts left his ministry with the Pentecostal Holiness Church to found the Oral Roberts Evangelistic Association. He traveled the country putting on crusades that almost always featured sessions of faith healing, which drew hundreds people desperate to be cured of their myriad problems. Many people claimed to have been cured by Roberts's healing touch, but there were also reports of people actually dying while standing in line.

A Growing Organization

As Roberts's ministry grew both nationally and internationally, so did his personal wealth. A flamboyant showman, he wore the finest clothes, drove the latest cars, and lived a life of luxury. God wanted it that way, he told his audiences—there was no shame in making money. By the 1980s, Roberts was the head of a $120 million-a-year organization that included Oral Roberts University, founded in 1963, and the City of Faith Medical and Research Center in Oklahoma, a facility that Roberts claimed Jesus himself told him to build. Unfortunately, the medical facility never really took off and was forced to close its doors in 1989.

Roberts was sometimes criticized for his fundraising methods. His frequent direct-mail appeals for "seed-faith," for example, directly targeted poor ethnic minorities. And in 1987, he was roundly condemned for telling his television audience that God would "call him home" if he didn't raise $8 million within three months. Many laughed, but just as many dug deep, helping Roberts exceed his goal by $1.1 million.

Over the years, Roberts made many outrageous claims specific to his faith-healing abilities. In 1987, he announced that God had raised the dead through his ministry, and later in the year, Roberts's son Richard told *Time* magazine that he had seen his father resurrect a child who had passed away.

In the years that followed, it was revealed that huge sums raised by Roberts's organization had been used to purchase property in Beverly Hills, California (ostensibly so Roberts would have a West Coast office), as well as a pricey country club membership. The extravagances became so outrageous that some board members resigned.

A Preacher to the End

Oral Roberts's ministry lost some of its sheen toward the latter part of Roberts's life, but he continued preaching and touting the good life right up until the end. He may have loved money almost as much as he loved God, but Roberts was clean in ways that many of his fellow evangelists were not. For example, he was never tainted by a sex scandal. In fact, his loving marriage to wife Evelyn lasted nearly 67 years, until her death in 2005.

As a result of Roberts's good work over the years, the Oklahoma Senate adopted a resolution honoring him in 2009. Roberts accepted the accolade in person, standing tall and still looking righteous at age 91. He passed away seven months later from complications of pneumonia, but he left a remarkable legacy.

Divine Inspiration

✤ ✤ ✤ ✤

*For hundreds of years, the Bible has inspired some of the
most beautiful artwork the world has ever seen.*

Few phenomena in world history have inspired as many artists as the
Bible. From the first words of Genesis in the Old Testament to the
last words of Revelation in the New, almost every important event in
Holy Scripture has been depicted in a wide range of media, including paintings, frescoes, sculptures, and tapestries. Some of it has
been controversial, all of it thought-provoking.

The earliest known biblical paintings date back to around A.D. 70,
literally the very beginnings of Christianity, and the earliest sculptures can be found on sarcophagi created at the beginning of the
2nd century A.D.

Not surprisingly, much of the earliest biblically themed art—
including paintings found in the catacombs of Rome—depict events
in the life of Jesus. What's most interesting are the varied depictions
of Christ, a sort of artistic evolution that wasn't officially set until
around the 6th century A.D., after which such images became fairly
homogenous.

Church Collections

With the fall of the Roman Empire, much of the art that survived
throughout Europe was Christian in theme, primarily because
churches worked extremely hard to retain and preserve the varied
works within their walls. The Roman Catholic Church was especially
involved in funding and collecting works from a variety of talented
artists, much of which remains today.

The depiction of biblical events in art went through a variety of
phases over the decades, though the themes remained relatively
constant. During the era of the Byzantine Empire, images tended to
be more surrealistic because the artists of the day were driven more
by religious meaning than realism. Only later, especially during the
Renaissance, did artists place a greater focus on the accurate depic-

tion of biblical figures, places, and events as they attempted to bring the Bible to life through their works.

Numerous Renaissance artists remain famous as a result of the biblical- and Christian-themed art that they produced over their careers. Michelangelo, for example, is best known for decorating the ceiling of the Sistine Chapel with biblical depictions that remain as evocative as the day they were created. (Certainly the most iconic of Michelangelo's Sistine Chapel paintings is that of God giving life to Adam—almost everyone has seen it, even if they didn't know who created it.) Other celebrated artists who worked on the Sistine Chapel include Sandro Botticelli, Pietro Perugino, and Raphael, who created several large tapestries that chronicle much of the doctrine of the Catholic Church.

Leonardo da Vinci's Most Famous

Equally famous, of course, is Leonardo da Vinci, who, just a decade before Michelangelo first set up scaffolding in the Sistine Chapel, created one of the best-known works of Christian art in the world: *The Last Supper,* which graces the back wall of the dining hall at the monastery of Santa Maria delle Grazie in Milan, Italy. It equals, if not surpasses, the *Mona Lisa* as Leonardo da Vinci's most revered artistic work.

The Renaissance saw the production of a tremendous amount of biblical/Christian art, including notable works by most of the great masters, including sculptors Alessandro Algardi and Giovanni Pisano and painters Federico Barocci, Giovanni Bellini, and Piero della Francesca. Indeed, practically every Italian artist of the period created works based on the Bible when not working on better-paying portraits of nobles and church leaders.

Biblical art became less common starting in the 1800s, as mainstream artists turned to other areas for their subject matter.

As a result, the religious art of centuries came to be viewed more for its aesthetics than its symbolism. That's not to say the Bible disappeared as an inspirational source in the decades that followed; many well-known secular artists created stunning works of biblical beauty, including Eric Gill, Marc Chagall, and Henri Matisse.

Controversial Art

Religious art remains popular today, though its public exhibition is not nearly as common as in years past. In certain instances, however, contemporary artists have found themselves in the middle of controversy as a result of their work. One of the most infamous is photographer Andres Serrano, the creator of a piece titled *Piss Christ*, which is nothing more than a photograph of a small plastic crucifix submerged in a bottle of Serrano's urine. The work won the Southeastern Center for Contemporary Art's Awards in the Visual Arts competition in 1988, but it generated a firestorm of protest from outraged Christians who understandably found the piece offensive.

Controversy has also followed British painter Chris Ofili, whose painting titled *The Holy Virgin Mary* featured an African representation of the Virgin Mary surrounded by images from blaxploitation movies, photos of female genitalia cut from pornographic magazines, and dried elephant dung in the shapes of cherubim and seraphim.

Rudy v. The First Amendment

When *The Holy Virgin Mary* was exhibited at the Brooklyn Museum in New York in 1999, New York Mayor Rudy Giuliani threatened to cut off public funding to the facility if it and certain other pieces were not removed. Such works, the mayor said, were nothing more than a government-funded attack on Christianity. The museum fought back by filing suit against Giuliani for violating its First Amendment right to freedom of speech. The suit was successful, and Giuliani was ordered to restore funding to the facility.

More recently, in Glasgow, Scotland, the city's Gallery of Modern Art received more than its share of criticism for a 2009 exhibit in which visitors were encouraged to write comments on the pages of a Bible and a later exhibit in which artists Craig Little and Blake Whitehead battered and deep-fried a 200-year-old Bible. Needless to say, local church officials were not amused.

Isaiah 1, 2, 3

✤ ✤ ✤ ✤

The book of Isaiah is presented as a collection of oracles by a single prophet. However, the prophecies in the book span some 200 years, so most biblical scholars believe that two or even three Isaiahs were responsible for the contents of the book.

Isaiah is one of the most widely discussed books of the Old Testament. It is particularly known for the comforting words of its later chapters, which hold that God accepts all people instead of a chosen few. These chapters anticipate Jesus' teachings. Isaiah also contains the Servant Songs that describe a messianic hero who will suffer and die for the people—Jesus Christ, in the view of Christians.

How Many Isaiahs Were There?

As revered as it is, the book of Isaiah constitutes a puzzle because it seemingly presents the life and teachings of a single prophet, Isaiah, yet spans more than 200 years of history. Could one man have lived so long? Or did an early prophet foresee the events of the distant future? Some Christians accept the latter theory, but most biblical scholars are skeptical. Because they believe it to be unlikely that the prophet of the book's early chapters predicted events that were to occur two centuries later, they hold that the book of Isaiah was written by two, three, or even more persons over a period of time.

Generally, three Isaiahs are posited. The first is Isaiah of Jerusalem, the real-life Isaiah, who lived in the eighth century B.C. His life and teachings are found in chapters 1—39 of the book. Second Isaiah (or Deutero-Isaiah) would have prophesied from Babylon just before the end of the Exile (539 B.C.). His teachings, for the most part, are found in chapters 40—55. Finally, Third Isaiah (or Trito-Isaiah) would probably have prophesied in Jerusalem after the return from the Exile, and his views are recorded in chapters 56—66.

That's a simple breakdown of the three Isaiahs theory. In fact, scholars believe that the situation is much more complicated and that the writings of the three prophets may have been mixed together by later editors. It's possible that even parts of Isaiah of Jerusalem's writings may appear in the later chapters along with the writings of second or third Isaiah or vice versa. It's a tangled web best left to the experts.

Isaiah's Prophetic School

Perhaps there's a simple solution to this puzzle. It seems likely that after Isaiah of Jerusalem's death, the revered prophet's teachings may have been taken up and extended not by independent prophets but by prophets who had been Isaiah's disciples and who possibly even studied in a school or guild of prophets that Isaiah ran. We

know that such organizations existed, as Elijah and Elisha headed one called the Sons of the Prophets. Consequently, a school/guild of Isaiah may have continued to operate for centuries, preserving and adding to the original teachings of the historic Isaiah of Jerusalem. These disciples and their later disciples could have written the later chapters of the book now known as Isaiah, and some of them may have collected and edited these writings to give them the form found in the Bible today.

Will the Real Isaiah Please Stand Up

The original prophet Isaiah proclaimed his message to Jerusalem and the rest of Judah from 742 until about 701 B.C. Nothing is known about the early life of Isaiah, though it has been conjectured from certain passages in his book that he may have been a priest.

In 742 B.C., Isaiah had a vision in which God commissioned him to be a prophet but warned him that the people wouldn't believe him. This turned out to be the story of Isaiah's life. For four decades, Isaiah preached tirelessly against the wrongs done by the rich and by Judah's government officials. "Your princes are rebels and companions of slaves," he said. "Everyone loves a bribe and runs after gifts. They do not defend the orphan, and the widow's cause does not come before them" (Isaiah 1:23).

Isaiah told the people that because they didn't trust in God, Israel would be invaded. At first he didn't name the enemy, but later he predicted that the Assyrians would conquer Israel. In 722 B.C., the Assyrians did conquer Israel and the people were scattered. The nation never recovered. Isaiah then predicted that in the future Judah too would fall as a punishment for the sins of the rich and powerful, who continued to live well while the poor suffered.

In his day, Isaiah preached not only to the people but to four different kings of Judah. He was rarely heeded. Among the kings, only Hezekiah took Isaiah seriously. Soon after Hezekiah's death, Isaiah, as a living person, is heard of no more.

Isaiah After Isaiah

Even though Isaiah was almost certainly dead, prophecies continued to be made in his name. Most of the prophecies contained in chapters 40—55 of the book of Isaiah were written in Babylon, where the Israelites had been taken as captives after the Babylonians destroyed Jerusalem in 586 B.C. These oracles offer the exiles hope for the future and speak of a mysterious servant who will suffer and die for them. This second Isaiah also predicts that Persia's King Cyrus the Great will overthrow the Babylonians and free the Israelites, who have suffered enough for their sins.

Chapters 56—65 (the third Isaiah) were probably written in Jerusalem after the Israelites had returned from exile to rebuild the city. In these chapters, the prophet encourages his people, telling them that God's salvation will come not only to them but to all the world.

Isaiah's Legacy

Because Christians believe that the promises Isaiah made were fulfilled in the Gospels, his book is often called the fifth Gospel. Jerome, who translated the Bible into Latin in the late fourth century, said Isaiah "should be called an evangelist rather than a prophet because he describes all the mysteries of Christ and the Church so clearly that you would think he is composing a history of what has already happened rather than prophesying about what is to come."

Finally, the New Testament itself is a champion of Isaiah's, citing him 419 times!

Fast Facts

- Ramses II, the Egyptian pharaoh believed by many historians to be the guy who gave Moses and the Hebrews such a hard time in Exodus, also had a good side. He ruled for an amazing 67 years and built several massive temples, including a temple complex carved into the cliffs at Abu Simbel on the Nile River. In the 1960s, the temples were physically cut out and relocated so they wouldn't be damaged by the construction of the Aswan Dam.

- In 1642, a man named John Lightfoot calculated that human creation began on September 12, 3928 B.C. Whether he was correct, we'll never know.

- Everyone is familiar with the story of how God parted the Red Sea so Moses and his followers could flee from the approaching Egyptians. But that wasn't the only time waters were miraculously parted in the Bible. The Jordan River, in fact, parted on three separate occasions, including one instance in which Joshua needed to cross so he could enter the promised holy land.

- In many biblical lands, priests and prophets practiced divination of omens by examining animal entrails and the markings of their livers. The liver was so important for this that detailed clay models were made, with various lobes and lines marked and sometimes even inscribed with omens and magical formulas.

- Long before Christ, the revered Jewish rabbi Hillel was asked by a skeptic to teach him the entire Torah while standing on one leg. Hillel did exactly that, stating, "What is hateful to yourself do not do to another. This is the whole Torah; go and study it; the rest is commentary."

- Blood represented life in the Bible, and shed blood represented death. The sacrifice for sin required the shedding of blood. This was true whether the victim was an innocent animal or the ultimate sacrificial lamb, Jesus. Because of its special significance, Jews were to drain blood from meat before eating it. This is required for a kosher diet.

A Host of Angels!

❧ ❧ ❧ ❧

*From warrior to messenger, the Bible shows
that angels serve many important functions.*

Angels appear frequently in the Bible. They act as God's messengers
and are fearless defenders of God's righteousness. Here's a rundown
of the four angels actually named in the Old and New Testaments:

Spreading the Word: Gabriel

Gabriel is mentioned four times in the Bible. In the Old Testament,
he appears twice before Daniel to help him understand things beyond his comprehension. In the New Testament, Gabriel announces
to Zechariah that his wife, Elizabeth, will give birth to John the
Baptist. Gabriel also tells Mary that she will give birth to Jesus.

Leading God's Army: Michael

Archangel Michael is a warrior. According to Jude, Michael rebuked
Satan—but did not judge him, leaving that up to God. Revelation
tells us that Michael will lead an army of angels against the forces of
Satan when the end times come.

Keeper of the Pit: Apollyon

In Revelation, Apollyon is referred to as the angel of the bottomless
pit and the king of an army of locusts that appear as fearsome war
horses with human faces, lion's teeth, and scalelike breast plates.
There has been some debate among theologians as to whether
Apollyon is good or evil.

Overseer of Evil: Satan

It's easy to forget that Satan was an angel before God cast him down
for being prideful. Now he rules in hell and lords over the wicked,
though according to Revelation, there eventually will be a reckoning.

   These certainly aren't the only angels referred to in the Bible.
Many, many others are mentioned throughout for their work as messengers, warriors, and good-deed doers.

Goal: Bibles in Every Language

✤ ✤ ✤ ✤

While the Christian missionary William Cameron Townsend was working with the Cakchiquel Indians in Guatemala in the 1930s, a local man asked: "If your God is so great, why doesn't he speak my language?" Flummoxed, Townsend thought deeply about the problem and soon established the Wycliffe Translators, an organization devoted to translating the Bible into every language in the world.

Convinced that every person should be able to read God's Word in his or her own language, William Cameron Townsend established a linguistics school for Bible translators in 1934 and named it for John Wycliffe, the 14th-century reformer who was the first to translate the Bible into English. Once students completed training, Townsend sent them into the field to develop alphabets for languages that had none so they could translate scripture into that language.

One of the first to go into the field was Kenneth Pike. In 1935, Pike traveled to Mexico, where he committed himself to learning Mixtec, an Indian dialect, with the help of an old Mixtec man. Pike's efforts were almost foiled from the start when he discovered that the words for "one" and "nine" differed only in pitch and sounded exactly alike to his ears. At a loss to master the tone problem, Pike sought help from former linguistics professor Edward Sapir, who explained his own system for analyzing the tones of Navajo. Using Sapir's technique, Pike cracked the Mixtec system, but it took him ten years. Today, computers are often used to chart and organize sounds and find symbols to represent them. If Sapir had only had a computer, how much easier his work would have been! His Mixtec New Testament was published in 1951. It was the first of hundreds of Wycliffe translations.

Forming Two Corporations

Wycliffe Bible Translators was incorporated in 1942, as was its affiliate, the Summer Institute of Linguistics, which operates as a secular society in order to gain admission into countries that prohibit missionary activity. Wycliffe translators work hard to identify cultures that have no written language, develop writing systems for them, and translate scripture into those languages. Sometimes requests for help come from the people themselves, but more often, needy people are identified through surveys. Young people trained by Wycliffe drive and hike through remote areas of the world for days or weeks at a time, combating foul weather, loathsome leeches, and bombarding insects. On their travels they interview dozens of people to determine which groups truly need scripture in their own language. The groups that seem most in need are later visited by translators who first develop writing systems, then ultimately publish the Bible in the language of the people.

Numbers Are Staggering

Since incorporating in 1942, Wycliffe Bible Translators and the Summer Institute of Linguistics have been involved in translating 24 complete Bibles and 735 New Testaments, potentially reaching some 107 million people. Yet this is only the tip of the iceberg. About 6,900 languages are spoken by the 6.9 billion people on earth. At the start of 2010, only 459 of these languages had decent versions of the full Bible and only 1,213 had adequate New Testaments, though scripture portions appeared in another 836 languages.

Wycliffe forges on and continues to be a leader in producing scripture in obscure languages. Though other organizations, most notably the United Bible Societies, have produced Bibles in many languages, Wycliffe has an impressive track record. At the start of 2010, Wycliffe translators were involved in rendering scripture into 1,363 languages, which are spoken by about 939 million people. This constitutes some 68 percent of the 1,990 active Bible-translating programs in the world. But there's still a long way to go.

Future Plans

In 1999, Wycliffe International initiated a campaign called Vision 2025, determining that by the year 2025 they will have translation projects started—though not necessarily completed—in every language that needs one. It's an ambitious program. Current estimates suggest that about 353 million people, speaking 2,252 languages, may have a need for a Bible translation. The Wycliffe translators will need all the stamina they can muster—and lots of help from on high.

Purim

While the Jews were stuck in Babylonian exile, they escaped a bloodbath. Purim, the Festival of Lots, celebrates the deliverance.

Biblical Basis

The events that brought on Purim occurred well before Jesus' time but long after Moses led the Israelites out of Egypt. When the Achaemenid (Persian) Empire captured Babylon in 538 B.C., it inherited thousands of Jewish exiles whose forebears had been hauled off by Nebuchadnezzar II beginning in 597 B.C. The book of Esther tells the story of Haman, a wicked advisor to the Achaemenid emperor Ahasuerus (Xerxes), who connived to have his sovereign wipe out the Jews. Esther, a Jewish woman who kept her heritage and faith secret, had become Ahasuerus's queen. She ruined Haman's plot so thoroughly that Ahasuerus hanged him and let the Jews crush their enemies. Soon after, the Jews were allowed to return to Israel.

Biblical Practice

Because the wicked advisor was drawing lots to decide when to go after the Jews, *Purim*'s Hebrew meaning ("lots") remembers this close shave. Esther tells us that Jews thereafter celebrated by feasting and giving alms to the poor. Unlike some Jewish holidays, Purim was ordained not by God but by Esther and the other survivors.

Modern Practice

Purim is party time, sometimes called the Jewish Mardi Gras. It occurs on the 14th of Adar, normally in March. Jews gather to hear the reading of the book of Esther, and every time Haman's name comes up, everyone boos, hisses, and/or rattles noisemakers to drown it out. It is not only okay for adults to drink alcohol, it is encouraged—with the exception of health reasons, recovering alcoholism, or anything that would lead to breaking Jewish or civil law. Jews send gifts of food to their friends and donate to charity as part of the festivities. Purim has been a triumphant, joyful holiday for 25 centuries.

Quiz

Music II

Name more tunes . . . and some of the tunesmiths of scripture.

1. Genesis 4:21 describes a man named Jubal as "the ancestor of all those who play the lyre and pipe." He was a sixth-generation descendant of a biblical character you might know. Who is it?

    a. Cain   c. Noah
    b. Abel   d. Moses

2. Paul and Silas were singing hymns when an earthquake damaged the building they were in. What was that building?

    a. a synagogue
    b. a prison
    c. the Parthenon
    d. a Greek amphitheater

3. In what book of the Bible would we find: "Praise him with trumpet sound; praise him with lute and harp! Praise him with tambourine and dance"?

    a. Leviticus   c. Ecclesiastes
    b. Psalms   d. Jude

4. In Amos 5:23–24, the Lord says, "Take away from me the noise of your songs; I will not listen to the melody of your harps." Instead, he wanted *something* to "roll down like waters." *What?*

    a. harmony   c. justice
    b. prayer   d. rainPharisees—Good and Bad

⚜ ⚜ ⚜ ⚜

Answers: 1. a; 2. b (Acts 16:25–26); 3. b (Psalms 150:3–4); 4. c

Pharisees—Good and Bad

❖ ❖ ❖ ❖

The Pharisees were Jewish leaders who regarded Jesus as an upstart
hick and a danger to all they stood for. Undaunted, Jesus admon-
ished them with a ferocity that could make one's spine tingle. Yet
most Pharisees were pious men, and some even followed Jesus.

As experts in the Jewish law, the Pharisees governed their people on
a daily basis. On the other hand, even though some Pharisees served
on the Sanhedrin, Judea's highest court, the chief priests were the
ultimate Jewish authorities. Pharisees who resented their secondary status vied for more control by rigidly enforcing regulations
concerning ritual cleansing, fasting, and observance of the Sabbath.
They especially insisted on separating themselves from the presence
of sinners. (The word Pharisee means "separate").

Jesus as Opponent

So along comes Jesus, the son of a carpenter from a hick town.
Without presenting any credentials, Jesus has the gall to mix with
and teach sinners and virtuous Jews alike, assuming authority that
the Pharisees regard as theirs alone. And to make matters worse,
Jesus allows his followers to disregard fasting laws and such rituals
as washing before eating. To cap it all off, Jesus heals the sick on the
Sabbath—a clear violation of the law.

Jesus respects the authority of the Pharisees and tells his followers to do what the Pharisees tell them to, but he adds, "do not do as
they do, for they do not practice what they teach" (Matthew 23:3).
The battle is engaged, and Jesus and the Pharisees denounce each
other until the Pharisees finally manage to get Jesus arrested.

Jesus is not afraid to speak out against these men. When a
Pharisee criticizes Jesus for not observing the prescribed ritual of
washing before a meal, Jesus responds: "Now you Pharisees clean
the outside of the cup and of the dish, but inside you are full of
greed and wickedness" (Luke 11:39). This story does not show that
Jesus is an unwashed slob but only that he has little patience with
Pharisees, who are so concerned with carrying out the minutiae of

the law that they forget to observe its chief tenets—to love God and neighbor.

In his most vicious tirade against Pharisees (Matthew 23:13–36), Jesus berates them for imposing impossible regulations on others while they themselves ignore the spirit of the law. He calls them hypocrites, blind guides, snakes, and killers of prophets. He compares them to tombs that are clean and white on the outside but full of rot and stench on the inside.

Jesus also tells parables that criticize Pharisees. In one, he favors a humble tax collector who stands near the rear of the temple, humbly begging God to forgive him. This man is better than the pompous Pharisee who stands proudly in the temple, boasting of all the good he has done and thanking God that he isn't "like other people: thieves, rogues, adulterers, or even like this tax collector" (Luke 18:11). Jesus doesn't condemn Pharisees as such in these parables, he merely makes examples of prideful Pharisees (who should know better), showing them to be arrogant, self-righteous people who lord it over others while constantly finding fault with everyone else.

Pharisees as Good Guys

In contrast, the Gospels include a few Pharisees who live according to their teachings. In Chapter 3 of John's Gospel, the Pharisee Nicodemus comes to Jesus at night, open to learning from Jesus but afraid of being mocked by other Pharisees.

The apostle Paul starts out as a Pharisee. As an interpreter of the Jewish law, he initially persecutes the followers of Jesus. After experiencing a vision of Jesus, however, Paul becomes his most vigorous promoter. His own teacher, Gamaliel, acts wisely when the apostles are arrested for teaching about Jesus. At the trial, Gamaliel advises his fellow Pharisees to let the apostles go. If this Jesus movement is a fake, like others before it, he reasons, it will die out on its own, but if it is of God, you may end up "fighting against God!" (Acts 5:39).

Did the Ark of the Covenant Break God's Law?

✤ ✤ ✤ ✤

Fanciful winged figures, called cherubim, were carved into the lid of the Ark of the Covenant. But the commandments seem to outlaw such images. Did the chest that contained God's commandments break one of them?

On Mount Sinai, God instructed Moses to construct a chest, or ark, to hold the tablets of the Ten Commandments and to fashion its lid with two cherubim facing each other. The lid would represent God's throne, and the chest itself, God's footstool (Exodus 25:10–22). Now the second commandment (part of the first for Jews and Catholics) forbids making images of living things. What's going on here?

It seems the commandment originally applied only to idols, and because the cherubim were servants of God, their depiction was legitimate. As idolatry increased, however, religious leaders narrowed the prohibition against images. Trouble began as soon as Moses came down from Mount Sinai carrying the law tablets and erupted when he found people worshipping a calf made from melted gold.

The cherubim were positioned above the Ark, and later in Solomon's temple, two cherubs were placed over the Ark in the Holy of Holies, though they were not seen by the public. Still, idol making continued to increase, compelling the prophets to preach against it.

More Calves

Things reached a climax after Solomon's death, when his kingdom split in two and the king of the northern kingdom of Israel built shrines—adorned with golden calves—to serve as footstools for God. Unfortunately, these calves reminded the priests of Jerusalem, in the southern kingdom of Judah, of the idol of Moses' time. Although the calves followed the idea of the cherubim over the Ark, the priests of Jerusalem were outraged, calling the calves idols, and from then on the commandment against making any images of living things was strictly enforced. No more cherubim.

Where Jesus Walked

Caesarea Philippi

It was as far north as scripture records Christ traveling and such a pleasant location overall that one supposes he must have had urgent reason not to remain there longer. (Even the Savior needs to relax.)

In Biblical Times
Caesarea Philippi was some 30 miles north of the Sea of Galilee, adjoining Mount Hermon. The home of a luscious freshwater spring in antiquity, it probably had human habitation of some sort back into the Stone Age. In Old Testament times, it first housed a temple of the Canaanite god Baal. Later (roughly 190 B.C.), the Seleucids built a pagan temple to Pan on the site, which was then called Paneas or Panium. Right around the time of Jesus' birth, Philip the Tetrarch founded a city there, naming it in honor of Augustus Caesar. Caesarea Philippi shouldn't be confused with a couple of other Caesareas in the Holy Land.

Jesus' Connection
Christ's brief time at Caesarea Philippi produced some of his most famous utterances. Shortly after giving the disciples a minor chewing-out for failure to grasp the fine points of his comments on the Pharisees and Sadducees (Hint: He wasn't impressed with them), Jesus came to this former pagan holy place. There he asked his disciples the famous question: "Who do people say that the Son of Man is?" Simon Peter got it right: "You are the Messiah, the Son of the living God." Christ praised Simon Peter with great enthusiasm, promising him the keys to the kingdom of heaven. However, thereafter he ordered his disciples to keep the Messiah part under their hats for the moment. Shortly after that, he began to warn them about his eventual martyrdom.

Caesarea Philippi Today
In the Golan Heights (under Israeli occupation, technically still Syria's), modern *Banias* (in Hebrew) is part of the Mount Hermon National Park. The ancient pagan grotto can still be seen, as can the town's ruins. It is one of Israel's most pleasant places, lush and beautiful.

Jericho: The Archaeological Record

❧ ❧ ❧ ❧

It's one of the greatest ancient cities, and what a story it has to tell!

How We Know

Several mid-20th-century digs uncovered the history of Jericho, which lies just north of the Dead Sea and about a mile from its modern incarnation, the Arab town of Ariha. One method archaeologists use—and the one that revealed a great deal at Jericho—was the deep-trench technique, which enables scientists to study the layers of habitation. In the 1950s, Dame Kathleen Kenyon, one of Britain's most accomplished archaeologists, dug all the way to the most ancient human evidence at Jericho.

Stone Age: 10,800–8500 B.C.

Jericho's earliest people were hunter-gatherers. To place this in context, the most ancient evidence of the rise of civilization in Sumer dates back before 5000 B.C., and the last Ice Age was still winding down in 10,000 B.C. The people at that time in Jericho were part of the Natufian culture, a rough grouping of humanity that left its markings all over what is now Israel.

For meat, they hunted gazelle, deer, wild cattle, wild pigs, and presumably whatever else they could bring down. They supplemented this food with wild-growing wheat, barley, and tree nuts. Natufians lived in half-sunken huts. They may have had dogs as pets or helpers; another Natufian site holds the oldest-known instance of a human buried with a puppy. Jericho had fertile soil and a steady water supply, which would prove central to its place in history.

Late Stone Age: 8500–3100 B.C.

The first people to make Jericho a year-round permanent home lived like the Natufians, for the most part, but with a more sophisticated city and social structure. We infer this because in the early part of this period there is what appears to be a temple or religious shrine at Jericho—such a building requires and implies that the people are organized and are staying put. One of the most interesting bits from this period entails skulls, plastered and painted to look like people, with shells for eyes. Did descendants keep these in their huts to remember the deceased? Whatever the reason, this is the oldest known human evidence of portraiture.

Jericho also had walls (though not the ones Joshua knocked down in the Old Testament) and a tower in this time frame. This tells us that not only were they organized, they felt the need for watchfulness and defense—probably against invaders or raiders. These walls were rebuilt multiple times, possibly after earthquake damage. As the Stone Age wound down, evidence gets sparser at Jericho, and at times the site seems to have been empty.

Bronze Age: 3100–1400 B.C.

This was Jericho's glory era, when its people built major defensive walls connected by towers. It was also Jericho's biblical phase, in which it grew into a Canaanite city of great importance. Joshua was leading the Israelites to claim their Promised Land, and Jericho looked like a formidable obstacle. He didn't have to settle in for a long siege, though. The Israelite army marched around the walls for a week with the Ark of the Covenant, blowing *shofarim* (rams' horns). On day seven, down came the walls, and the Israelite army slaughtered almost the entire Canaanite population.

While archaeologists have debated evidence for the walls' fall, there is evidence for an assault some time between 1600–1400 B.C. This is directly connected evidence of earth and stone for Joshua's siege. The Israelites moved on their path of conquest.

Shadows of Glory

The site of Jericho was reoccupied after 1000 B.C., but the town never again mattered much. It became something of a resort town for bigwigs, especially Herod, who built a winter palace at Jericho shortly before Christ's time. For the next 3,500 years—indeed, until and including today—Jericho was a minor town taking orders from a series of overlords: Assyrian, Babylonian, Persian, Macedonian, Roman, Muslim, Christian, Ottoman, British, Jordanian, and Israeli.

Today, as you may imagine, in addition to agriculture, Ariha makes a living off Jericho's past.

Israel's Neighbors

HITTITES

*An Old Testament major power, Hittite culture was
virtually gone by the time of Christ. Let's meet them.*

Who Were They?
Hittites were a people of Asia Minor (modern Turkey) whose era of power
stretched from the 1600s B.C. to about 1180 B.C., until the "sea peoples"
came ravaging across Asia Minor to trample Hittite civilization. Hittites
spoke an Indo-European language written in cuneiform. Their capital was
Hattuša, near modern Boğazkale, not far from Turkey's capital at Ankara.
They may have been history's first constitutional monarchy, a strong military power that contended with Mitannian and Egyptian armies for control
of Syria and Palestine. The Hittites may have been the first to master iron-
work. They were polytheistic and inclusive, adopting conquered peoples'
gods into their worship.

Where Are They Now?
After centralized Hittite power crumpled, a few neo-Hittite kingdoms
hung on in Asia Minor for several hundred years. All eventually fell into
the bronze manacles of Assyrian domination. The rise of Phoenician-
developed alphabetic writing superceded Hittite language, which gradually
ebbed away. By 700 B.C. or so, little remained of Hittite culture. If they
have a modern heritage at all, it is a drop in the Turkish sea—albeit a
proud one cherished by modern Turks.

Biblical Mentions
There is reasonable debate whether some Old Testament Hittite references refer to the same people as the archaeological record. According
to Genesis, the Hittites (from "Heth") were distant descendants of Ham
via Canaan, thus the Israelites equated them with Canaanites. Hittite
overlords sold Abraham a fine burial plot for Sarah. God promised to push
the Hittites (among others) out of the Promised Land. Hittites served in
David's army; out of lust for Bathsheba, wife of Uriah the Hittite, David
committed a grave sin by deliberately sending Uriah out to his death.

4 Sects and Cults Based on Bizarre Readings of the Bible

✤ ✤ ✤ ✤

The Bible is filled with prophetic, poetic, and at times inscrutable prose.

It's understandable that certain people might misinterpret a chapter or verse here or there. In some cases, though, these readings have led to bizarre consequences. Here is a look at some of the sects and cults based on odd interpretation of scripture.

1. Heaven's Gate: Considering that heaven is traditionally depicted as being somewhere up in the firmament, it is perhaps not surprising that an entire group of religious sects has sprung up connecting scripture with outer space. Heaven's Gate, perhaps the most famous religious cult in history, is also one of the most mysterious. The Heaven's Gate cult was founded by Marshall Applewhite and his one-time nurse Bonnie Nettles, who believed they were the "two witnesses" referenced in chapter 11 of the book of Revelation. They believed themselves to be prophets who were to spread the Word of God on the eve of the Apocalypse.

And when exactly was the Apocalypse? Applewhite and his followers believed it to be in the spring of 1997, signified by the appearance of the Hale-Bopp comet in that year. They believed the comet meant certain doom for the planet, but Heaven's Gate members were to be saved by a spaceship traveling in the comet's tail. To prepare for this, on March 26, 1997, the 39 members of the Heaven's Gate cult dressed in identical black shirts, sweatpants, and running shoes, and armed themselves with five dollars and three quarters. They then committed suicide.

2. Branch Davidians: Few people who followed the news in 1993 can forget the drama surrounding the Branch Davidians and their leader, David Koresh. Dubbed the "Wacko in Waco" by the media, Koresh led a splinter group of Seventh-Day Adventists who lived in a compound in Waco, Texas. Like many cult leaders, Koresh proclaimed himself the Son of God and the Second Coming of Christ.

Koresh also had a fondness for women, especially young women. Through an elaborate and bizarre reading of the Song of Solomon, he constructed a theological argument justifying polygamy. Conveniently, this polygamous lifestyle only applied to him (not to other men of the group), and it was reported that he sired more than a dozen children with various members of the sect.

In 1993, following up on reports of child abuse and illegal firearms at the compound, the United States government decided to get involved, with tragic consequences. After a 51-day siege,

> Number of self-proclaimed messiahs in United States, approximate:
> **3,000**
>
> Number of biblical cults in United States, approximate:
> **5,000**

on April 19, ATF agents began their final assault. In the ensuing raid, a fire broke out, trapping the cult members inside. Meanwhile, federal agents were met with a hail of gunfire, which they returned. When all was said and done, David Koresh and between 70 and 75 other sect members were killed, including more than 20 children.

3. Snake-handling Pentecostal Sects: In describing the casting out of devils, the speaking in tongues, and the healing of the sick by the laying on of hands, Mark 16:17–18 is a veritable mother lode of guidelines for fundamentalist Christian sects throughout America. But it is another claim of those verses that has led to perhaps the most bizarre and dangerous of the Christian sects: the admonition that followers "shall take up serpents." These four words, considered symbolic by most Christian scholars, are considered the literal command of God by a small number of snake-handling Pentecostal sects, mostly located in the rural Appalachia region of the southeastern United States.

Snake-handling rituals have been around for the better part of a century, and they show no signs of disappearing. According to Pentecostal leaders, handling poisonous snakes is ordained by scripture, and practitioners are fully aware of the dangers involved. There have been more than 100 fatalities attributed to the practice, with thousands more injured.

4. Millerites: Daniel 8:14 states: "And he said unto me, 'Unto two thousand and three hundred days; then shall the sanctuary be cleansed.'" For most, these verses merely describe one of the many numerical obscurities in the Bible. For William Miller, it was a clue.

Miller, a 19th-century Adventist and student of the Bible, would go on to found the Millerites, one of the first American doomsday cults. Based on the verses from Daniel and some serious calculating, Miller prophesied that the Second Coming of Jesus Christ would be around 1843. Despite little evidence for this, Millerism spread quickly throughout the American northeast in the 1840s. When 1843 passed without a visit from the Lord, members of the sect established definitively that the end date would be not in 1843, but on October 22 of the following year.

On October 22, 1844, a large group of Millerites gathered in open fields and on rooftops to wait for the Second Coming. Needless to say, it didn't happen. The event, surely one of the biggest blow-offs in history, became known as "The Great Disappointment."

What! No Tattoos?

Leviticus 19:28 prohibits self-mutilation of any sort: "You shall not make any cuttings in your flesh on account of the dead or tattoo any marks upon you." This prohibition was mainly because such self-mutilation was practiced in several pagan cultures. A good illustration of this comes from the prophets of Baal, who cut themselves with knives while they were trying to get Baal to send fire down from heaven (1 Kings 18:29).

Great Bible Orators

Archbishop of the Airwaves

For nearly 40 years, Archbishop Fulton J. Sheen was a comforting presence on both radio and television.

Generally speaking, the Catholic Church has not engaged in televangelism to the degree that other religions have. The Catholic Church has had a presence on television, to be sure, but early on only one Catholic leader—Archbishop Fulton J. Sheen—actively used the broadcast media to spread the word of God. As a result, Sheen became one the best known Catholic officials of the 20th century.

Sheen was born in El Paso, Illinois, on May 8, 1895. His family members were devoted, practicing Catholics, and Sheen chose to follow the church at an early age. He was ordained a priest in the Diocese of Peoria in 1919, and he developed a reputation as an expert theologian, earning the Cardinal Mercier Prize for International Philosophy in 1923.

Sheen taught theology and philosophy and acted as a parish priest until being appointed Auxiliary Bishop of New York in 1951, a position he held until 1966. He was later appointed the Bishop of Rochester, New York.

Master of Mass Media

Sheen understood the value of the broadcast media in spreading the Gospel, and he took advantage of it. Good looking and with a pleasant, soothing voice, he hosted a nighttime radio program called *The Catholic Hour* from 1930 to 1950, then moved on to television in 1951 with *Life Is Worth Living,* which he hosted until 1957. His final television show was a syndicated series titled *The Fulton Sheen Program,* which ran from 1961 to 1968. Sheen was recognized for this television work with an Emmy Award for Most Outstanding Television Personality, and many of his shows are still being rerun on various religious cable networks.

Sheen took his television appearances very seriously and spent hours preparing his material and how he would present it. He typically wore the full regalia of a bishop and never relied on notes or cue cards. *Life Is Worth Living* appeared on the small Dumont Network, often opposite such television powerhouses as Milton Berle, but Sheen still managed to find a devoted audience.

In addition to his television work, Sheen was a prolific author. Over the course of his career, he penned scores of books, many of them best-sellers. Among his most popular books were *The Eternal Galilean* (1934), *Peace of Soul* (1949), *Way to Happiness* (1953), *Way to Inner Peace* (1954), and *Treasure in Clay: The Autobiography of Fulton J. Sheen* (1980). He also wrote numerous magazine and newspaper articles.

Popular Speaker

Willingly thrust into the public spotlight, Sheen used his popularity to advance the church and Christianity in general. He found himself in great demand as a public speaker, and he traveled the nation and the world giving talks on a wide variety of topics. He was comfortable before large crowds and proved himself a masterful lecturer who had an astounding ability to educate while simultaneously putting his audiences at ease.

Sheen owed much of his early success to Cardinal Francis Spellman of New York. A powerful figure within the Catholic Church, Spellman admired Sheen for his intellect and way with people, and in 1950, he made Sheen the head of the American branch of the Society for the Propagation of the Faith, which was the church's primary source of missionary funds. Sadly, the two men later engaged in a bitter feud over dispersal of Society funds that ultimately led to a joint audience with Pope Pius XII, who sided with Sheen. The relationship between Spellman and Sheen was never the same after that.

Advocate of Reform

Sheen was an advocate of reform within the Catholic Church, and he participated in the Vatican II sessions in Rome. In the mid-1960s, he worked to incorporate sweeping reform within his own diocese in Rochester, New York, but met with resistance from parishioners. He eventually stepped down and returned to New York City.

Fulton J. Sheen suffered from heart disease during the final years of his life, but he didn't let that stop him from traveling, lecturing, and writing. He died on December 9, 1979, in his chapel, just two months after meeting Pope John Paul II in the sanctuary of St. Patrick's Cathedral. In 2002, the Catholic Church began an effort to have Sheen canonized.

Jesus Wasn't the First?

❀ ❀ ❀ ❀

The prophets Elijah and Elisha had their own flair, and because
they did such good work among the poor, God gave them the
ability to work wonders through him. Consequently, the two
men anticipated Jesus in performing some awesome feats.
So Jesus wasn't the first to work some of the miracles so closely
associated with him—including raising the dead!

In the 9th century B.C., groups of men known as the Sons of the
Prophets lived simply, learned the craft of prophesying, and worked
with the needy. In addition to their work as prophets to the kings,
Elijah and Elisha headed the Sons of the Prophets and sometimes,
to help them as well as others, they called upon God and worked
wonders, some of which anticipated Jesus' miracles.

Caring for the Needy
Most of the miracles worked by Elijah and Elisha were designed
to help those in need and occasionally amounted to no more than
simple courtesy. For example, when one of the Sons of the Prophets,
a poor man, is using a borrowed ax, the head of the tool flies off into
the river. Unable to replace the borrowed ax, the man is devastated.
Elisha simply causes the ax head to float to the surface of the water
for easy retrieval.

Much more seriously, the creditors of a widow of one of the Sons
of the Prophets threaten to sell her sons into slavery to satisfy her
debts. All she has to her name is a single jar of oil. Elisha has her
collect a lot of empty jars and fill them with the oil from her jar. She
ends up with enough oil to sell and pay off all her debts.

Miracles with Food and Water
After predicting a famine sent from God, Elijah hides from the
wrath of King Ahab in Sidon, a center for the worship of the god
Baal. There he asks a local woman for bread and water. The woman
tells the prophet that she is a widow with a young son and has only

enough grain and oil to prepare one last meal for her son and herself "that we may eat it, and die" (1 Kings 17:12). Elijah tells her to make the cake and share it with him and God will sustain her. She complies and the woman, her son, and Elijah have enough to eat until the drought ends.

Years later at Jericho, when the water supply is polluted, Elisha freshens it by adding salt. Similarly, during a famine, the Sons of the Prophets at Gilgal make pottage from unknown herbs, which turn out to be poisonous. When someone calls out, "There is death in the pot!" (2 Kings 4:40), Elisha neutralizes the poison by adding flour to the pottage.

But the most significant miracle of this sort occurs during another famine, when a friend brings Elisha 20 barley loaves and some fresh grain. As Elisha prepares to feed the people with them, someone asks how he can feed a hundred men with so little. Elisha does, and there are even leftovers. Jesus would later feed thousands of people with a few loaves and two fish.

Miracles of Self-Defense

Sometimes the miracles wrought in the name of the prophets were not for the benefit of the needy but to protect themselves. When King Ahaziah of Israel learns that Elijah has predicted his death, he sends a captain and 50 soldiers to arrest Elijah (an arrest that would probably have ended in the prophet's death). Elijah tells the captain: "If I am a man of God, let fire come down from heaven and consume you and your fifty" (2 Kings 1:10). Fire does consume the soldiers, and the same thing happens to a second delegation of 50. However, when a third delegation arrives, God tells Elijah to go with them, and when he does the king listens without harming the prophet.

Elisha's situation was not quite as perilous. One day a group of boys mock Elisha, calling out, "Go away, baldhead!" (2 Kings 2:23). When Elisha curses them in the name of the Lord, two bears come out of the woods and maul 42 of the youngsters. A revered rabbi of ancient times called this miracle a double one, for there were no trees in the area and no bears! While the initial picture of the bad boys being pursued by bears is funny, the outcome of the chase is not. However, God's prophets were considered sacred people in biblical times, and both the bad boys and King Ahaziah had violated the dignity of the Lord's spokesmen.

Elisha Heals a Leper

Jesus was not the first to heal lepers. Elisha beat him to the punch. When Naaman, a Syrian army commander, is stricken with leprosy and no one in his own country can cure him, a servant girl from Israel advises him to go to Elisha. Naaman arrives pridefully at Elisha's door with his horses and chariots. Instead of seeing him, Elisha sends out a messenger, telling Namaan that if he washes in the Jordan seven times he will be healed. Naaman is angry because Elisha does not personally come to pray over him, and he storms off, saying there are rivers in Syria that are better than the Jordan. But Naaman's servants convince him to do what Elisha had told him. And, of course, he is instantly cured. Acknowledging the power of the God of Israel, Naaman offers Elisha gifts, which Elisha refuses. When Naaman departs, however, Elisha's wily servant, Gehazi, runs after him and pretends that Elisha had sent to ask him for provisions for two Sons of the Prophets who had just come to him in need. Naaman gladly grants the gifts, which Gehazi plans to keep for himself. But Elisha knows what Gehazi has done, and the servant is himself struck with leprosy as punishment for his crime.

Raising the Dead

Anticipating Jesus' greatest miracles, both Elijah and Elisha raise the dead through God's power. Elijah does so while staying with the widow whose supply of grain and oil he had miraculously made to last through a drought. When the widow's son dies, Elijah stretches himself out on the boy's body three times, crying out: "Oh, Lord my God, let this child's life come into him again" (1 Kings 17:21). God listens and revives the child.

Elisha works his miracle over death for a wealthy foreign woman he had befriended. Through Elisha's prayers, the woman bears a son, though she is advanced in age. When the boy gets older, trouble comes. While out in the field at harvest time, he says to his father, "Oh, my head, my head!" (2 Kings 4:18–19). The boy soon dies in his mother's lap. The mother calls for Elisha, who sends a servant to lay his staff on the dead boy—to no effect. Then the woman takes Elisha himself to the dead boy. Elisha lies full length over the boy's body with his mouth on the boy's mouth and his eyes upon the boy's eyes, bringing him back to life.

Jesus would also raise the son of a widow from the dead (at Nain), as well as his friend Lazarus and the daughter of the synagogue leader Jairus. And, of course, more importantly he would rise from the dead himself.

Although Elisha does not rise from the dead, he doesn't lose his grip even in his grave. Sometime after Elisha's death, foreign raiders interrupt a local funeral and the mourners hastily hide the corpse of their loved one in Elisha's grave. When the body contacts Elisha's bones, the dead man comes back to life. There was just no stopping Elisha!

A Longview

In working some of these miracles, Elijah and Elisha seem to have anticipated Jesus. Biblical scholars seize on such foreshadowings and call the persons or events that anticipate others in New Testament "types." And so Elijah and Elisha in many ways are seen as types of Jesus. Their miracles are types of Jesus' feeding the multitudes and raising the dead. In most cases, the miracles of all three figures serve to make people believe in God. For Elijah and Elisha, and even Jesus, acknowledge that it is through the power of the one God that these wonders are wrought.

> # What Is Winnowing?
>
> Winnowing is throwing the threshed grain into the air so the wind could blow away the straw (or chaff). The heavier grains fall to the ground and are saved, after which the grain is ready for storing or selling. Psalm 1 speaks of the insignificance of the wicked in God's sight as "chaff which the wind drives away."

10 Things

Important Visions and Dreams

God often communicated with Bible characters in strange ways.

1. Marry Mary (Matthew 1:20–21) Joseph was engaged to Mary when he learned she was pregnant. He was planning to avoid scandal by quietly breaking the engagement, but the Lord spoke to him in a dream: "Do not be afraid to take Mary as your wife." He did so, taking on the role of stepfather to the Savior.

2. Take a Bow (Genesis 37:5–11) A different Joseph told his 11 brothers what he dreamt: their stars bowing down to his; their bundles of grain paying homage to his. This didn't make the boy popular. His jealous brothers staged his death and sold him as a slave.

3. Have a Cow (Genesis 41) As a slave in Egypt, Joseph continued his saga of survival. Falsely accused of rape, he was tossed in prison— where he interpreted dreams for fellow prisoners. When the pharaoh had a strange dream about fat cows and skinny cows, he was told of Joseph's skill at explaining dreams. Brought out of jail to face the pharaoh, Joseph told of upcoming years of plenty and then famine. For this, he was immediately hired to manage the nation's response.

4. Up on the Roof (Acts 10) Peter was meditating on a rooftop when the Lord gave him a vision of nonkosher animals. A voice said, "Kill and eat." When he protested, the voice reminded him that *God* decides what's kosher. Just then there were messengers at the door, asking him to preach in the home of a gentile—a "nonkosher" *person*. Peter got the message, and he went with them.

5. Holy, Holy, Holy (Isaiah 6) The prophet Isaiah had a vision of the Lord sitting on a high throne, surrounded by seraphim—fiery angels that sang, "Holy, holy, holy is the LORD of hosts; the whole earth is full of his glory." This was Isaiah's calling as a prophet. When he worried about his "unclean lips," an angel took a coal from the altar and touched his lips with it, cleansing them. "Who will go for us?" the Lord asked, and Isaiah offered a response that many have echoed since: "Here am I; send me!"

6. Word to the Wise (1 Kings 3:3–15) Solomon didn't feel ready to succeed David as king. So God appeared to him in a dream, offering him what he wanted. Acknowledging that he was "only a little child; I do not know how to go out or come in," Solomon asked for wisdom. "Give your servant therefore an understanding mind to govern your people."

7. Come and Help Us (Acts 16:9–10) Paul was on his second mission trip, revisiting areas throughout Asia Minor (modern Turkey). Suddenly he and his team didn't know where to go next. It seemed that the Lord was thwarting all their plans. But then, in a dream, Paul saw a man saying, "Come over to Macedonia and help us." This meant crossing into the European continent, but Paul boldly did so, continuing his successful ministry.

8. Dry Bones (Ezekiel 37:1–14) The prophet Ezekiel did some crazy stuff, and he saw some odd visions too. One of his most dramatic visions was a valley of dry bones. As he watched, the bones reassembled into skeletons and added sinews and flesh. He prayed that God would breathe new life into them, and that's what happened. "I am going to open your graves," God said, "and bring you up from your graves, O my people."

9. Feet of Clay (Daniel 2) Daniel had a Josephlike experience as one of the Jewish exiles in Babylon. King Nebuchadnezzar had a troubling dream, but he couldn't remember what it was. Of all his advisors, only Daniel could reveal what he dreamt and what it meant. It was a vision of a huge statue, head of gold, chest of silver, and inferior metals down to the feet of clay and iron. Daniel announced that this foretold a series of kingdoms, progressively inferior, that would follow Babylon.

10. Sevens Are Wild (Revelation) John was exiled to the island of Patmos when the Lord gave him the remarkable vision that we know as the book of Revelation. It starts as a series of divine messages to seven churches in Asia Minor but continues with a vivid depiction of events in heaven and on earth—seven seals sealing the scroll, seven angels proclaiming events, with seven trumpets. The images are highly symbolic, allowing for all sorts of interpretations. The key fact, through all these supernatural struggles, is that *God wins!*

Quiz

Miracles I

*The Bible is full of bizarre happenings.
How much do you know about them?*

1. The name of this miraculous thing is a Hebrew phrase meaning "what is it?" What is it?
 - a. chariot of fire
 - b. manna
 - c. Aaron's rod
 - d. gefilte fish

2. When the Israelites were dying of a plague borne by snakes, Moses put up a pole with an image on it, telling the people to look at it and be healed. What was the image on the pole?
 - a. pyramid
 - b. stone tablet
 - c. lamb
 - d. snake

3. Something fell into the river, and the prophet Elisha miraculously made it float. What was it?
 - a. oar
 - b. scroll
 - c. ax head
 - d. stone tablet

4. While Paul was preaching, a young man named Eutychus fell three stories from of a window and died, but Paul raised him back to life. What was he doing just before he fell?
 - a. looking out for soldiers
 - b. translating Paul's words for the overflow crowd
 - c. prophesying
 - d. sleeping

Answers: 1. b (Exodus 16:15); 2. d (Numbers 21:8–9); 3. c (2 Kings 6:5–6); 4. d (Acts 20:9–12)

From Simon to Peter

✤ ✤ ✤ ✤

Jesus renamed his apostle to make an important statement.

Jesus Christ revealed himself gradually to his disciples, giving them time to slowly come to grips with his divinity. He knew that until they had witnessed him healing and performing miracles, they would not be ready to take the next step: accepting Christ as their Lord and Savior.

In Matthew 16:13–20, Jesus decides that the time is right to reveal all to the 12 apostles, but rather than flat-out telling them himself, he wants them to come to the realization of his godliness on their own and say it aloud. Jesus uses the gossip that has been going around the district of Caesarea Philippi as a starting point, asking the apostles, "Who do people say that the Son of Man is?"

The apostles reply, "Some say John the Baptist, but others Elijah, and still others Jeremiah or one of the prophets." Jesus presses them further: "But who do you say I am?" Simon alone replies, "You are the Messiah, the son of the living God."

The First of Many

At this moment, Simon, by being the first human being on earth to profess his belief in Jesus Christ as God's son, both created the Christian Church and became its leader. To stress the significance of this occasion, Jesus renamed Simon: "Blessed are you, Simon son of Jonah! For flesh and blood has not revealed this to you, but my Father in heaven. And I tell you, you are Peter, and on this rock I will build my church, and the gates of Hades will not prevail against it. I will give you the keys of the kingdom of heaven, and whatever you bind on earth will be bound in heaven, and whatever you loose on earth will be loosed in heaven."

As Peter, this apostle would face many more challenges before assuming his place at the heavenly gates.

Naked Man Running

❀ ❀ ❀ ❀

Mark's Gospel tells us that at the time of Jesus' arrest,
soldiers grab a young man by his garment, but the man manages
to disengage and run off naked. Who is this guy?

Two puzzling verses in the Gospel of Mark present a person who is
not otherwise mentioned in the Bible—or so it seems. When Jesus
is arrested in the Garden of Gethsemane, his followers desert him.
According to a brief passage in the Gospel of Mark, this includes an
unidentified young man. The passage reads: "A certain young man
was following him [Jesus], wearing nothing but a linen cloth. They
caught hold of him, but he left the linen cloth and ran off naked"
(Mark 14:51–52). Who is this young man and why is he in the garden wearing nothing but a linen cloth? It's an intriguing puzzle with
intriguing possible solutions.

What's It All About?
The first thing the situation brings to mind is how the patriarch
Joseph, while a young slave, escaped the sexual advances of his master's wife by running from her and losing his garment in the process.
But Joseph was acting heroically, while the young man in the garden was not. It is hard to see why Mark would have introduced the
memory of Joseph here. Clearly the answer lies elsewhere. Some
scholars see the incident as an allusion to an Old Testament end-
time prophecy: "And those who are stout of heart among the mighty
shall flee away naked in that day, says the Lord" (Amos 2:16). Others
speculate that the young man is either the Gospel's author or someone he knows, and he is adding a personal recollection here. Still
others see the young man as a negative counterpart to the ideal disciple, who leaves everything to follow Jesus. But this seems unlikely,
as Jesus' true disciples also leave Jesus at this time.

A Secret Gospel
Possibly the most interesting theory about the young man involves
an earlier edition of Mark's Gospel. There is good reason to believe

that Mark's Gospel went through several editions before reaching the revered text now in the Bible.

In addition, one of the earlier editions was known as the Secret Gospel of Mark because it contained material that was meant only for mature Christians—material that may be misunderstood by spiritual neophytes. In order to make the Gospel safe for all Christians, this material was later excised and all of it was lost—well, maybe not all.

Surviving Fragments

Some of the lost material appears in an 18th century copy of a letter from the Church Father Clement of Alexandria. In his letter, Clement defends the authenticity of both the canonical Gospel and the Secret Gospel against a falsified version. When Mark died, the letter claims, he left the Secret Gospel to the church at Alexandria, Egypt, where it is "read only to those being initiated into the greater mysteries." In discussing the Secret Gospel, Clement reproduces passages about a rich young man from Bethany who brings to mind both the naked man in Gethsemane and Lazarus, whom Jesus had earlier raised from the dead.

According to the cited passages, when the young man dies, Jesus raises him from the dead at the request of the man's sister. At his rising, the young man looks upon Jesus and loves him. Six days later, he comes to Jesus, wearing only a linen cloth on his naked body (possibly as a baptismal garment). Jesus then teaches him the mystery of the kingdom of God.

Conclusions

Scholars who have studied the passages in Clement's letter believe they predate the Gospel we know. If this is so, they may preserve an early telling of the story of the raising of Lazarus, as later told in John's Gospel. In addition, the texts bring to mind the young man who runs off naked at Jesus' arrest. If the Secret Gospel passages are authentic, then the young man at Gethsemane may be a part of the story of the young man in the Secret Gospel. It is possible that the editor charged with deleting this story from the Gospel overlooked these two brief verses, which then remained in the final text of Mark's Gospel to mystify us.

The Devil Made Me Do It

✤ ✤ ✤ ✤

When God confronted Adam and Eve about eating the forbidden fruit, Adam quickly copped out and blamed Eve for putting him up to it. Eve, in turn, countered with, "The serpent tricked me and I ate it." Was Eve, in effect, saying "the devil made me do it?" Was the serpent in the Garden of Eden really Satan or some other form of the devil? Perhaps not. Many scholars believe that the devil does not appear in the Bible until the New Testament.

Although most people think of the serpent in the Garden of Eden as Satan, the Bible doesn't say so. The serpent is merely a wild creature that stands out from the other newly created animals only because of its cleverness. In fact, the serpent is almost incidental, introduced simply to tempt Adam and Eve without introducing a supernatural agent. The focus of the story is the guilt of the humans, not the role of the tempter. Adam and Eve knew they were doing wrong, but they did it anyhow. Blaming the serpent is as foolish as blaming the tree. If Eve had climbed a ladder to reach the fruit, the ladder would not have been guilty. Like the serpent, it would merely have made the sin easier to commit.

Satan Before and After Jesus

In Old Testament times, Jews had no idea of an evil counterpart to God. God was the sole cause of everything that happened. Since God is good, when bad things happened a human cause was suspected, and an accuser or adversary sometimes pointed out human faults. The Hebrew word used for such a finger-pointer was *satan*. When David joins the Philistines to avoid King Saul, who is trying to kill him, some of the Philistines worry that he may turn out to be a *satan*, an adversary (1 Samuel 29:4). *Satan* is not a proper name in the Old Testament; with one exception, it is always preceded by the definite article "the." The exception comes in the prophet Zechariah's vision of a high priest standing trial in heaven with "Satan standing at his right hand to accuse him" (Zechariah 3:1). Because there is no definite article here, Satan may be intended as a proper name, though it may merely be meant as a kind of generic name, such as Mr. Prosecutor.

The most famous *satan* in the Old Testament appears in the book of Job, where he is called *the* accuser (*satan*), though the term is often translated as Satan. When God convenes his heavenly court and praises the virtues of the man Job, the *satan* scoffs that Job is virtuous only because he enjoys good health and prosperity. God allows the *satan* to wreak havoc in Job's life to test his virtue. This *satan* is not the devil or he would not be in heaven. He is merely used as a device (like the serpent in Genesis) to get the story going. No matter what sufferings the *satan* inflicts on Job, the good man refuses to curse God. But once the *satan* does inflict suffering on Job (in chapter 2), he disappears, no longer needed, though the book continues with a 40-chapter discussion about why bad things happen to good people.

What About Lucifer?

No matter how diligently you search through the Bible, you will probably not find the name Lucifer, though most Christians consider Lucifer to be the Prince of Darkness, Devil No. 1, the entity who entered the serpent in Eden, or simply the supernatural being behind every diabolic act in history. In fact, the word "Lucifer" appears only once in the Bible and only in one translation. "Lucifer," from the Latin for "light bringer," was often used for the morning star. In Isaiah 14:12, the prophet refers to the king of Babylon as the Day Star when mocking his great fall from power:

> *How you are fallen from heaven,*
> *O Day Star, son of Dawn!*
> *How you are cut down to the ground,*
> *you who have laid the nations low.*

The King James Version of the Bible uses "Lucifer" in place of "Day Star." Later, because Christians associated this passage with Jesus' saying "I watched Satan fall from heaven like a flash of lightning" (Luke 10:18), the name Lucifer became another name for Satan. But most Christians have heard that before Adam and Eve sinned, Lucifer and a band of angels waged war against God only to be cast down into the fiery pit of hell. Where did that story come from if it's not in the Bible? Actually, it all started with a brief Old Testament passage, Genesis 6:1–4, which tells how a group of angels (curiously called "sons of God") defied God by marrying human women. Much later, in the two centuries before Jesus' birth, demonic figures began to appear in nonbiblical Jewish books, including a volume that tells an elaborate story involving these "sons of God."

The Watchers

Chapters 6–7 of the First Book of Enoch tells about the "Holy Watchers," a corps of angels who are also referred to as "sons of God" (as in Genesis). Two hundred Watchers band together under a leader named Semyaza and rebel against God by having sexual intercourse with mortal women. Then, one of the angels, Azazel, reveals the secrets of metallurgy to humans, who abuse the craft by making weapons that lead to war and jewelry and cosmetics that lead to sexual excesses. Vice runs rampant, and God decides to send down a flood to destroy evil and leave the earth clear for restoration.

When they are told of the planned flood, the offending Watchers realize that they cannot defeat God, but they refuse to repent. Consequently, God sends word to Noah to build his ark and sends Raphael, a good angel, to bind Azazel hand and foot and throw him into the darkness. God also condemns Semyaza and his other rebels to die in the flood. At the Last Judgment, all of the rebel Watchers will be cast into eternal fire.

Enoch's tales fired the imaginations of Christians in the Middle Ages, and they elaborated upon them to tell the story of a great war in heaven in which a prideful angel (Lucifer) declares war on God and is defeated and cast out of heaven into a lake of fire—hell. Later, Lucifer emerged from hell long enough to tempt Eve, as told by the English poet John Milton in the epic poem *Paradise Lost* (1667).

Jesus and the Devil

In the New Testament, which is written in Greek, the Hebrew word *satan* is translated as *diabolos*—devil in English. However, the Hebrew Satan is frequently used as the devil's proper name. In Jesus' time, the devil was considered the supernatural force responsible for much of the world's evil and a being who seeks to turn humans against God. Satan is no longer a mere adversary or accuser, but a force that opposes God. Throughout his ministry, Jesus is depicted as fighting the devil and all he stands for.

That fight starts early. At the beginning of his ministry, Jesus spends 40 days fasting in the desert. There he is tempted by the devil to break his fast, to leap from the top of the temple to force God to send angels to bear him up, and to worship the devil in return for worldly power.

Who Was Belial?

Belial was not originally a name, but it develped into a name for Satan in Jewish literature in the period between the Testaments.

Jesus counters each of these temptations with an appropriate quotation from scripture. After three years of fighting, Jesus finally defeats the devil by offering himself on the cross.

End to the Devil

In the book of Revelation, the book's author describes a vision he has had of a future war between God and Satan. In that war, Michael the archangel fights for God, leading forces of good angels against troops of renegade angels led by Satan (appearing as a seven-headed red dragon). In the vision, the devil loses the war and is imprisoned for a thousand years; he then returns to power but God again defeats him, and the devil is "thrown into the lake of fire and sulfur" where he "will be tormented day and night forever and ever" (Revelation 20:10). Whatever else Revelation has to tell us, one thing is clear. In the end God will triumph over the forces of evil that are represented by Satan, and the devil will no longer make anyone do anything.

Where Jesus Walked

Rural Galilee

*Christ spent most of his ministry traipsing about Galilee—
a hilly and scenic region in his time, just as it is in ours.*

In Biblical Times
A border region between powerful empires, Galilee changed hands a lot. Stretching roughly from the Sea of Galilee to the Mediterranean near Mount Carmel, it had many small towns rather than a few large cities, and it was Canaanite property before the Hebrews came along. Solomon had ruled it, even giving a part of it away as a reward for help in building the temple. The Assyrians ruled the land of Galilee, then the Persians, then Alexander's successors, then the Romans or their vassals. Agriculture flourished in Galilee, as it does today. The number of synagogues built in the centuries after Christ testify to the region's Jewish roots.

Jesus' Connection
Since his steps took him across the Galilee countryside quite often, Jesus did much of his teaching on the way from one town of Galilee to another: Cana, Tiberias, Nazareth, Capernaum. Very probably, he knew Galilee like you know your home county. All his walks along the western shore of the Sea of Galilee passed through the Galilean fishing villages where he performed some of his best-known miracles. He raised a widow's son at Nain, and he got on the Pharisees' nerves. They returned the favor, accusing him of casting out demons in the devil's name. (The Pharisees never seemed to ask why Satan would want demons cast *out*.)

Rural Galilee Today
This region has a large Arab population (despite the Israeli government's best efforts to get more Jews to move there), and it has many Druze, a religious and cultural minority who enjoy special status in Israel. It has numerous *kibbutzim* (collective farms) and produces lots of olives and wine grapes. During troubled times, unfortunately, nearly any part of Galilee is vulnerable to rocket attacks from southern Lebanon—they can hit all the way to the Jezreel Valley in south Galilee.

Judaism from the Roman Perspective

✤ ✤ ✤ ✤

For Rome, the Jews represented a frontier province that just wouldn't play the game. For that, they sometimes paid a price.

Cultural Differences

Roman culture and Jewish culture differed in so many ways it's harder to say how they were similar. True, both had farming roots. The Romans had a militaristic streak, whereas by Roman times, the Jews didn't take up arms unless they felt threatened.

When the Romans conquered a people, they allowed limited self-government if the population made its peace with Roman dominance. Jews tended to stick resolutely to their own customs, which made them a stubborn and troublesome group in Roman eyes.

Spiritual Differences

This perplexed the Romans, whose faith was polytheistic; they adopted conquered peoples' gods. The Jews had worshipped only Elohim (God) since before Rome had even been a pleasant Italian cow pasture. To the Romans, the God of Judaism was another deity they would have honored. For Jews to call all other gods but Elohim false, therefore, came as something of a slap in the Roman face. It also symbolized the Jews' unwillingness to accept a gradual transformation into good Romans. Even when Jews settled outside Israel, they tended to cluster in their own communities.

Destruction of the Temple

The center of Judaism was the temple in Jerusalem. The Great Revolt began in A.D. 66 with Greek/Jewish tensions in Judea boiling over into violence. In A.D. 70, the Romans stormed Jerusalem and destroyed the temple (of which the Western or "Wailing" Wall remains today). Many Jews were enslaved; many more scattered about the Mediterranean, the beginning of what modern Jews call the *Diaspora* (which means "scattering"). Judaism had fought the Empire and lost, but the rising Jewish sect called Christianity would eventually conquer the Empire.

Taxation and Vexation

✤ ✤ ✤ ✤

*Some things never change, and taxes—and the men
who collect them—have always been held in contempt.*

Yep, tax collectors were right up there with prostitutes as far as
respectability in ancient Israel. They were insulted, reviled, mocked,
scorned, and snubbed. They were rejected at the temple, avoided
at the marketplace, and unwelcome in the homes of others. Their
wives and children suffered because of the shame of their profession. Yet the job was so rewarding financially that many men were
willing to destroy their reputations and dismiss their ethical, religious, and familial obligations. The Jews who lived under the tax
collectors and their oppressive overlords, the Romans, seethed with
anger and bitterness.

Double Trouble

By the time of the New Testament, Jews living in ancient Israel
were taxed not once but twice—by both their local temple and the
Roman government. Most Jews were happy to tithe to their place
of worship, taking seriously their responsibility to their religion and
to those in need in the Jewish community. The taxes levied by the
Romans, however, were an entirely different matter. The Jews
hated living under Roman occupation and longed for the day
their country would be free. They knew where their tax money
was going—funding Rome's enormous army, bankrolling its never-
ending building projects, and subsidizing the lavish lifestyle of its
aristocracy. Romans and Jews lived side by side in Israel, especially
in the urban areas, and Jews could see that the Romans were "living
large." Very few Jews enjoyed such a lifestyle, but the rare excep-
tions were the tax collectors.

And boy, did Rome need a lot of tax collectors! After all, there
was a poll tax, a city tax, a road tax, a water tax…heck, a Jew
couldn't even *die* without being taxed. There were sales taxes in the
marketplace, but even before goods got there, they were subject to

import and export taxes. With taxes at every turn, it was very, very hard for the Jews to get ahead, and the longer the Romans were in power, the more resentment they felt. By the time of Christ, emotions had reached a boiling point, and many Jews were looking for someone to lead them in a revolution.

A Different Kind of Radical

In ancient Israel, tax collectors were considered traitors by their fellow Jews. They were demonized by the vast majority of Jewish leaders who called for change, whether those leaders were part of the establishment or on the radical fringe. That is why Jews were so shocked and appalled at Jesus' attitude towards both taxes and tax collectors. In Mark 12:13–17, some Pharisees and Herodians try to trap Jesus by asking him whether Jews should pay taxes to Rome. But Jesus knows they are trying to trick him. He calls for a Roman coin, holds it up to them, and asks them, "Whose head is this, and whose title?" When they answer that it is the emperor, Jesus says, "Give to the emperor the things that are the emperor's, and to God the things that are God's."

Jesus did more than just shrug off taxes, however; he actually socialized with tax collectors. One of them, a remarkably short man named Zacchaeus who had been skimming from the taxes he collected, repented of his ways after Jesus dined in his home. Of course, the most famous tax collector in the Bible is Matthew of Galilee. When the Pharisees criticized Jesus for hanging out with Matthew, Jesus told them, "Those who are well have no need of a physician, but those who are sick. Go and learn what this means, 'I desire mercy, not sacrifice.' For I have come to call not the righteous but sinners" (Matthew 9:9–13). This was a statement that was not just shocking in those times, but downright dangerous.

Blood Money

When Judas Iscariot betrayed Jesus to the Jewish authorities, Judas was given 30 pieces of silver in payment. This has led to the phrase "blood money," which is money received in exchange for the life of a human being.

Biblical Women's Daily Lives

❖ ❖ ❖ ❖

There was no gender equality in those days. This in no way means women were unimportant or disposable parts of Israelite society.

Hearth and Home

For most ancient Israelite women, life was homemaking and home-making was life. Most people lived in small houses, perhaps better described as huts. Most women worked lengthy hours caring for children, going to market, gardening, crafting, cooking, and more. Many also worked outside the home, at farming or other jobs.

Childbearing was the center of most adult Israelite women's worlds, and a woman who bore many babies was envied. Equal? Hardly. Essential? Surely. Women gave Israelite society life.

The Law

It isn't accidental that the Hebrew for "wife" (*ishah*) also means "woman," and that for "husband" (*ba'al*) also means "owner" or "proprietor." Adultery was a capital offense, but judges enforced the law more harshly on women. A man could have multiple wives, but no woman could have multiple husbands. A man could divorce his wife for failing to produce children, but she couldn't divorce him.

Deuteronomy states that if a man raped a virgin, they had to marry. A girl often married in her mid-teens or earlier—and she had better be a virgin or she could be stoned. However, if the elders found that the groom had falsely accused the bride of not being a virgin, he received a heavy fine and a whipping.

Power?

A woman who became a judge (Deborah) or a queen (Esther) was powerful indeed. For most Israelite women, however, power came from their wisdom and ability to influence husbands, finances, children's upbringing, and social life. It beggars credibility to picture Israelite women as meek housemaids and baby factories. In every society known, when mama isn't happy, no one is happy.

Quiz

Miracles II

The Bible is full of bizarre happenings.
How much do you know about them?

1. Malchus was with the group of soldiers who came to arrest Jesus. Peter nearly killed Malchus, but Jesus healed him. How?
    a. Jesus closed up the wound in his side
    b. Jesus restored his sight
    c. Jesus put his ear back on
    d. Jesus cast out the demon that possessed him

2. After Jesus healed a man born blind, the Pharisees interrogated the man's parents. Why?
    a. to see if he was really born blind
    b. to see if he was born legitimately
    c. to make sure they had been keeping the law
    d. to investigate their collusion with the Romans

3. Jesus fed 5,000 with five loaves of bread and two fishes. What did he do later with seven loaves?
    a. fed 4,000
    b. cast them upon the water
    c. celebrated Passover with his disciples
    d. made them vanish

4. Moses tried to dazzle the Egyptian pharaoh with miracles the Lord had enabled him to do. How did the pharaoh's own magicians respond?
    a. in awe, they praised the God of the Israelites
    b. they made excuses and left the room
    c. they duplicated the tricks Moses had done
    d. in spite, they turned the Nile River to blood

Answers: 1. c (Luke 22:51; John 18:10); 2. a (John 9:18–19); 3. a (Matthew 15:32–38); 4. c (Exodus 7:11)

Christianity from the Roman Perspective

While the Romans persecuted Christians now and then, clearly the Romans didn't persecute the new faith out of existence. How did Christianity look through Roman eyes?

Beginnings

At first, Christianity looked pretty small and cultish: an offshoot of a strange, stubborn Near Eastern faith called Judaism whose followers worshipped only one god. In this case, of course, Christians were claiming that their deity had risen from death after crucifixion. The Romans had gods for agriculture, war, the hearth, the family, and other aspects of life. Who could get by with only one god? Even the troublesome Jews themselves mostly rejected the new cult that had leapt from their midst. But at the start, naturally, Roman perception of Christians began with Roman perception of Jews, whom they viewed as insular, stubborn, and set in their ways (see page 357).

When a terrible fire torched much of Rome in A.D. 64, Emperor Nero decided to scapegoat Christians in their first major persecution. (Given what most Romans thought of Nero, in some ways that may have been good PR for the Christians.) In any case, there were no more than a few thousand Christians around at that time for Nero to persecute. Against the Empire's millions, it was a tiny movement, and surely they were no meaningful threat so far as the average Roman could discern. Had some prophet told Nero that within three centuries his successor would be a Christian, this effete slob would have laughed very hard before punishing such insolence.

The XX Factor

Christianity went mainstream in the second and third centuries A.D., enjoying a growth rate of about 40 percent per decade. The evidence indicates that Christianity spread faster among women than men, leading to plenty of secondary conversions as pagan men seeking wives ended up marrying Christian women who would certainly seek to raise Christian children. One might say that Christianity snuck up on the Romans through the bedroom door. Christianity condemned abortion and infanticide (neither of which were rare in Roman culture), which helped it outbreed the shrinking Roman pagan family. To Romans, early Christianity looked quite female.

Plague Times

Christianity made its greatest impression on Romans during the era's devastating epidemics. The pagan inclination was to get far away from the diseased. Christians took exactly the opposite tack: They stuck together, nursing one another and often helping sick pagan friends as well. This practice was rooted in scripture, and early Christians took it as a duty of devotion. From the Roman viewpoint, several things were happening, all likely to spread the new faith.

For one thing, Christians were more likely to survive whatever disease was tearing through their city. Common sense says that if you are sick, you are more likely to recover if someone takes care of you, brings you food and water, and cleans up after you. Christians did this, and non-Christian Romans saw it. It was no more strange for a Christian to have pagan friends than it is today for an atheist to have Christian or Jewish friends. It was natural enough for friends to help each other in hardship, but early Christians really worked at it.

Put Yourself in Their Sandals...

Imagine yourself a sick Roman pagan carpenter, saved by the kindness of your Christian friends while many other pagans died. How's that Jesus business looking now? Not only does it look quite nurturing and welcoming, but through pagan eyes it looks like divine favor. Whatever god these people have, you might reason, he has some pull. Evidently more pull than the pagan gods, whose followers' bodies are decaying all over the city because no one will haul them away.

Furthermore, you aren't the only one to see this. Other pagan friends saw it too; could they blame you if you felt you wanted this faith in your life? Would you not seek to embrace them? Many did.

Mystery Author

✤ ✤ ✤ ✤

Who wrote Hebrews? Bible scholars still don't know for sure,
but they have some hunches.

IDing Letters: Most New Testament letter writers identify
themselves. That's how we know Paul authored Romans through
Philemon. Jesus' brother James wrote James. First and Second
Peter are the apostle Peter's works (though there is some debate),
while the apostle John wrote 1–3 John (as well as Revelation and the
Gospel of John). Another brother of Jesus penned Jude.

The Lone Anonymous Letter: Only one New Testament letter—
Hebrews—departs from this norm. Foregoing greetings, it dives
right into teaching that's peppered throughout with Old Testament
passages and written in impeccable Greek. Until recent years, copies
of the King James Bible gave Paul credit for writing Hebrews.
However, earlier manuscripts (found since the KJV's translation)
don't name an author. That's why modern translations and newer
copies of older translations tend to leave the byline blank.

Whodunit?: Paul remains the prime suspect as writer. Tertullian
(A.D. 160–220)—who was alive when the original manuscripts were
around—referred to Hebrews as the Epistle of Barnabas. Martin
Luther guessed that Apollos wrote it. Other nominations are the
apostle Philip or Priscilla. Clement of Alexandria (c. A.D. 150–215)
surmised that Paul wrote it first in Hebrew and then, to account for
the excellent Greek, Luke translated it. This might be the best guess
of all.

Wonderful Irony!: Is it coincidence that the only unidentified
New Testament author wrote the Bible's premier chapter on faith?
Hebrews 11 begins, "Now faith is the assurance of things hoped for,
the conviction of things not seen."

It does make you think!

Israel's Neighbors

PHOENICIANS

They are one of the most influential peoples few today can identify.

Who Were They?
Phoenicia was the coastal land of modern Lebanon and southern Syria, home to a grouping of city-states occupied by the Semitic Canaanite people we call Phoenicians. While they were never an empire, from before 1200 B.C. until the Persian conquest, the Phoenicians operated one of the most famous seafaring and trading cultures in Western history. Sidon, Tyre, Byblos, Acre, and Tripoli were their most important Near Eastern cities, though their African colony of Carthage, founded in 814 B.C. (in modern Tunisia), arguably outshone any of the homeland city-states as a minor empire until the Romans eradicated it. Most importantly, the Phoenicians developed a phonetic alphabet that is the ancestor of all other Western alphabets. Phoenician religion was Canaanite polytheism.

Where Are They Now?
Cyrus of Persia occupied Syrian Phoenicia in 539 B.C. Soon after Alexander the Great conquered the region in 332 B.C., Greek culture swamped Phoenicia. Rome's destruction of Carthage in 143 B.C. dealt the death-stroke to Phoenician identity. Distant Phoenician descendants are found today all along the southern Mediterranean coast from Morocco to Asia Minor and in most major Mediterranean islands, notably Malta.

Biblical Mentions
When one considers the Phoenicians as Canaanites, the biblical interest comes into clear focus. God promised the Israelites a chunk of Canaan—but they were not to marry Canaanites. In general, the Jewish and Christian view of Phoenicia was chilly; they saw it as a land of sin, idolaters, slippery merchants, and hedonists. Isaiah in particular railed about Tyre, characterizing it as a prostitute; Ezekiel prophesied its conquest. Christ visited Phoenicia, and the apostles preached there—as surely they must if they meant to evangelize far and wide; for even as Roman subject cities, Phoenician ports were gateways to the Mediterranean.

The Genealogy of Jesus

❖ ❖ ❖ ❖

If there had been a Social Register in ancient Israel,
Jesus and his family would have been on it.

Jesus was certainly no snob, but one look at his lineage and you'll agree that he had the right to be. Oh, the Romans might have seen the Jews as second-class citizens, but among the Jews themselves, there was a definite pecking order. Jesus could trace his line all the way back through David to Abraham, and that was one big deal.

Poor but Well-Bred

Jesus' family was not wealthy by any means. His father, Joseph, was a humble carpenter. But the family was what we might now call "shabby genteel." A good comparison here in modern America would be someone who had little money but could trace his roots back to the Mayflower. Of course, in Jesus' case, his bloodline meant a lot more than which college society or country club he would be allowed to join. It meant that he was part of a chosen clan within a chosen people. And the one who did the choosing was God.

Matthew 1:17 tells us, "So all the generations from Abraham to David are fourteen generations; and from David to the deportation to Babylon, fourteen generations; and from the deportation to Babylon to the Messiah, fourteen generations." The importance of the number 14 cannot be overstated, for each Hebrew letter has a corresponding number, and when the numbers for the name "David" are added up, they equal 14. This number binds Jesus irrevocably and eternally to the clan of David and the land of Israel, and it makes clear that as David was an earthly king, Jesus is a heavenly king.

Women of the World

Unlike most biblical genealogies, Matthew's genealogy of Jesus includes female descendants. The five women mentioned are Rahab, Ruth, Bathsheba, Tamar, and Jesus' mother, Mary. Of these five, only one, Mary, was a Jewish woman. The other four were gentile women from various foreign countries. By including these gentile women, Matthew may well have been making the statement that Jesus was a Messiah for all people, not just the people of Israel. It is also interesting to note that all five of these women were involved in rather scandalous situations (whether through their own fault or the misinterpretations of those around them), yet Matthew does not hesitate to connect them to Jesus. Is this an implied reference to the salvation of sinners? The inclusion of women in Christ's genealogy also corresponds to Matthew's later use of women as important companions in and witnesseses of Jesus' life.

If anyone gets the short stick in Matthew's genealogy, it's Joseph, Jesus' earthly father. Joseph is not called Jesus' father but "the husband of Mary, of whom Jesus was born." This was no doubt written to stress the importance of the virgin birth and the fact that Joseph was not Jesus' biological father. The apostle Luke is a bit kinder in his genealogy (Luke 3:23), saying that Jesus "was the son (as was thought) of Joseph son of Heli." Unlike Matthew, who only traces Jesus' roots back to Abraham, Luke's lineage of Jesus goes all the way back to Adam. This is probably also a universalist statement by Luke, connecting Jesus not only to the Jewish people, but to all people.

Both Exclusive and Inclusive

What both New Testament genealogies of Christ share is that they are very clearly attempting to show Jesus as the savior of all humankind while still emphasizing his Jewish heritage and his family's religious piety and obedience to the laws of Moses. It is important to Matthew and Luke that we remember that although Jesus was God, he was also human. His familial history affected him as it affects every one of us. Though his teaching and preaching were for all nations, the apostles wanted to remind us that they sprang from a great Jewish tradition and a great Jewish family.

New Testament Greek Words You Should Know

❖ ❖ ❖ ❖

Translations usually get it right,
but sometimes there's a deeper meaning.

1. Agape (uh-GAH-pay)

This is divine love—God's love for humans, our love for God, and the love he puts in our hearts for each other.

John 21 has an interesting exchange between Peter and the risen Christ. Twice Jesus asks, "Do you love me?" He uses a form of *agape,* but Peter responds, "You know that I care about you," using a form of the word *philia,* commonly used for friendship. The third time Jesus asks the question, he seems to come to Peter's level, replacing *agape* with *philia.* There's nothing wrong with friendship, but apparently *agape* is something special, a committed, selfless devotion.

2. Logos (LOG-ahss)

Generally translated "word," *logos* has a much bigger meaning. It could be an idea, a principle, or a reason. Since Plato, Greeks had been looking for a principle of perfect order, connecting all knowledge and all experience in a single, divine idea—a *Logos.*

That's where John starts his Gospel. "In the beginning was the *Logos.*" He describes this *Logos* participating with God in the creation. Greek readers would immediately grasp this concept of an eternal creative principle, and Jewish readers would remember that God used words in his creation. But then John gets to his main point: "The *Logos* became flesh and lived among us." Jesus Christ was the eternal *Logos* in human form.

3. Pneuma (NOO-mah)

This word can mean "breath," "wind," or "spirit." It can refer to the spirit of a person, the Holy Spirit of God, or to other supernatural forces ("evil spirits" or angels). Common to all these meanings is the sense of power and a sense of mystery.

Jesus told Nicodemus, a Pharisee, "The wind [*pneuma*] blows where it chooses, and you hear the sound of it, but you do not know where it comes from or where it goes. So it is with everyone who is born of the Spirit [*pneuma*]" (John 3:8). Same word, two different meanings.

Much could be said about Paul's contrast between *pneuma* and *sarx* (flesh). Our bodies (*sarx*) aren't bad, but apart from the control of the living Spirit, we are the walking dead.

4. *Kenosis* (ke-NO-sis)

The word means "emptying" or "making void." In Greek papyri, it's used for the "unloading" of a supply of corn. A form of the word means "in vain."

Describing how the Son of God came to earth, Paul writes: "though he was in the form of God, [he] did not regard equality with God as something to be exploited, but emptied himself [*kenosis*], taking the form of a slave" (Philippians 2:6–7).

For Jesus, divinity was not some loot to be hoarded. Whatever he had, he gave up, becoming a servant on earth. *Kenosis* is what happens to a jar of water as it is poured out. In the rich language of this servant song, we find Jesus "pouring himself out" on behalf of humanity.

5. *Makarios* (ma-KAR-ee-ahss)

It's hard to find the right English translation for this word. Jesus says, "*Makarios* are the poor in spirit . . . those who mourn . . ." and so on. These are the Beatitudes, and we instantly think of the word "blessed." But that's a little too heavy. The Bible is full of blessings uttered by God and blessings offered to God, and this isn't a "blessing" in that sense.

"Happy are the poor in spirit," say some Bible versions, but that seems a little light. Some go for "fortunate" or even "lucky," but that implies some other force of chance.

The point is that these people are well off. All of these seemingly negative things—mourning, meekness, hunger, and thirst—are actually positives in God's economy.

10 Things

Verses that Changed History

The Bible is the most-read book of all time and the most influential.

1. Isaiah 49:1 (Christopher Columbus): *"Listen, O isles, unto me; and hearken, ye people, from far; The Lord hath called me from the womb"* (KJV).

Christopher Columbus was an avid Bible reader. His journals confirm that he saw himself opening up far-off islands to communication with God.

2. Romans 1:17 (Martin Luther): *"The one who is righteous will live by faith."*

Few movements have been as world-changing as the Protestant Reformation. At the heart of it was Martin Luther, haunted by the scriptural notion that righteousness came by faith and not by religious works.

3. Exodus 1:17 (King James): *"But the midwives feared God, and did not as the king of Egypt commanded them"* (KJV).

King James was annoyed with the Bible commentary on this verse, which suggested it was all right to disobey the king. So when some Puritans proposed a new Bible translation, King James made it happen, gathering a group of scholars to produce the version that bears his name.

4. John 8:32 (Harvard): *"And ye shall know the truth, and the truth shall make you free"* (KJV).

Puritan colonists in Massachusetts founded Harvard College (later University) in 1636 for education in religion, but also "all good literature, arts, and sciences." Jesus' statement here was the basis for its motto.

5. Revelation 19:6 (Handel's *Messiah*): *"Then I heard what seemed to be the voice of a great multitude . . . crying out, 'Hallelujah! For the Lord our God the Almighty reigns.'"*

The best-known classical choral piece comes from George Frideric Handel's *Messiah*. Known as the "Hallelujah Chorus," this song has stirred audiences since its debut in 1742. The "Hallelujah Chorus" comes from the vision in Revelation of God's final victory.

6. Galatians 6:9 (William Wilberforce): *"And let us not be weary in well doing: for in due season we shall reap, if we faint not" (KJV).*

In 1787, William Wilberforce, a member of the British parliament, tried to end the British slave trade. Year after year he made proposals, which always went down in defeat. At one such depressing moment, he received a letter from John Wesley: "Oh, be not weary of well-doing. Go on in the name of God." Wilberforce did, and Britain's slave trade was abolished in 1807.

7. Numbers 23:23 (Telegraph): *"What hath God wrought!" (KJV).*

The telegraph revolutionized communication. Samuel F. B. Morse developed it in the mid-1800s. Morse sent the first message in 1844—"What hath God wrought!" Morse chose the phrase "to ascribe all the honor to whom it truly belongs."

8. Mark 3:25 (Abraham Lincoln): *"And if a house is divided against itself, that house will not be able to stand."*

Abraham Lincoln was a serious student of scripture. He chose this witticism of Jesus as a key text in his efforts to keep the United States united.

9. Exodus 15:1 (Underground Railroad): *"Then sang Moses and the children of Israel this song unto the Lord...I will sing unto the Lord, for he hath triumphed gloriously" (KJV).*

An escaped slave, Harriet Tubman risked her life to free hundreds of other slaves in the mid-1800s, working along the Underground Railroad. This effort was full of biblical imagery, using a system of passwords based on the Exodus account of Moses leading the Israelites out of Egypt.

10. Genesis 1:1–10 (*Apollo 8*): *"In the beginning God created the heaven and the earth..." (KJV).*

In December 1968, the nation was captivated by NASA's moon voyage. On Christmas Eve, the world saw a close-up of the moon and Borman, Lovell, and Anders reading the Bible's opening verses.

The Woman's Bible

❖ ❖ ❖ ❖

In the late 19th century, Elizabeth Cady Stanton and other women's rights activists studied the Bible from a woman's point of view, hoping to prevent men from using scripture to discriminate against women. They published a compendium of biblical excerpts accompanied by feminist commentaries. Later feminists decided to ignore the Bible altogether, dismissing it as male propaganda. In recent times, several fine feminist biblical scholars have emerged.

In the 1890s, when the war between the sexes was at full tilt, some 20 womens' activists got together to study the Bible. They hoped that by subjecting the Bible to the scrutiny of discerning women who would be "quick to see the real purport of the Bible as regards their sex," they could prevent men from using it to discriminate against women. Under the direction of Elizabeth Cady Stanton, the group produced *The Woman's Bible,* which was published in two volumes in 1895 and 1898. The work consists of excerpts from the Bible together with feminist commentaries.

Views on Genesis

The commentaries in *The Woman's Bible* hold that the scriptures contain universal truths but that these truths were recorded by fallible human beings—that is, males—
and were thus subject to human
(male) prejudices. After studying the
two stories of Creation, the women
promoted the version in Genesis 1,
which shows that man and woman were
created together and alludes to "the feminine element in the Godhead, equal in power and glory with that of the masculine." This version, they believed, seems to be "more worthy of an intelligent woman's acceptance" than Genesis 2, which holds that man was created first and then woman was created from one of his ribs. In fact, the commentary says that only one of the

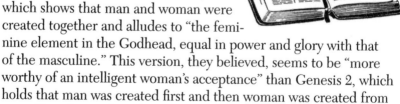

two versions can be true. They surmised that Genesis 1 is true and that some Jewish man had manipulated Genesis 2 to give "heavenly authority" for requiring a woman to obey the man she married.

In discussing Noah's flood, *The Woman's Bible* commented: "The female of each species of animal was preserved; males and females all walked into the ark two by two, and out again in equal and loving companionship." But the commentators go on to perpetuate a female stereotype in discussing the ark itself: "The paucity of light and air in this ancient vessel shows that woman had no part in its architecture, or a series of port holes would have been deemed indispensable."

Current Feminist Biblical Studies

Over the next decades, feminists became more and more critical of what they considered the overbearing patriarchalism of the Bible, and they ended by advising women to abandon the Bible all together. In the 1970s, however, a fresh, clear voice emerged. After closely studying the biblical passages pertaining to gender, Phyllis Trible found that most of the patriarchalism in the Bible was in the eye of earlier interpreters. She held that "the intentionality of biblical faith . . . is neither to create nor perpetuate patriarchy, but rather to function as salvation for both women and men."

Revisiting the creation story, Trible finds the text of Genesis 2 shows that God created male and female as equals. She cites Adam's description of Eve as "bone of my bone and flesh of my flesh" and the statement: "a man leaves his father and his mother and clings to his wife, and they become one flesh" (Genesis 2:23–24). These words, Trible contends, speak unity, solidarity, mutuality, and equality. They describe a perfect union that is shattered only when the couple eat the forbidden fruit and introduce sin into the world. However, Trible holds, even this break was not permanent. The exquisite love poems in the Song of Songs tell of the ideal love between equals, a man and a woman, in a garden much like Eden. The love expressed by this couple, Trible holds, redeems the rupture caused by sin, and men and women are again equals.

Trible was a trailblazer for feminist criticism of the Bible. Under her influence, Cheryl Exum and other feminists have written illuminating, well thought-out commentaries on the Bible.

Granddaddy of Televangelism

Pioneer televangelist Rex Humbard reached millions of people from his state-of-the-art Cathedral of Tomorrow.

Today's televangelists owe a debt to Rex Humbard, a forward-thinking revival preacher who broadcast his first sermon via television in 1949.

Humbard was born on August 13, 1919, in Little Rock, Arkansas. His parents were Pentecostal evangelists who trained Humbard from an early age to go forth and preach. Humbard traveled the country as a revival preacher, often strumming a guitar. In 1952, he became the first evangelist to host a weekly nationwide television program in the United States.

The First Megachurch
In 1958, Humbard built the Cathedral of Tomorrow outside Cuyahoga Falls, Ohio. Famous for its unique, almost space-age design, the $4 million church holds 5,400 parishioners and a large chorus, and it was constructed specifically to accommodate Humbard's televised services.

Music was an integral part of Humbard's ministry, and his broadcasts typically featured the hottest gospel performers, as well as his family. His ministry proved popular, and by the 1970s, Humbard was reaching an estimated 8 million viewers worldwide. At the height of his ministry's popularity, he is believed to have preached to more than 20 million viewers.

A Friend of Elvis
Humbard also hosted large public crusades, drawing huge crowds. In 1977, Humbard spoke at Elvis Presley's funeral because the singer had been a huge fan. Rex Humbard moved to Florida in 1982. He was inducted into the Broadcasters Hall of Fame in 1993, and he passed away of natural causes on September 21, 2007. His legacy lives on in the smiling face of every preacher to grace a television screen.

Quiz

Trees I

Branch out into this test of biblical horticulture.

1. What did God warn would happen if Adam ate from the tree of the knowledge of good and evil (Genesis 2:17)?
    - a. they would become gods themselves
    - b. they would die
    - c. they would be expelled from the Garden of Eden
    - d. they would have children

2. Chased by his pursuers, the rebellious prince Absalom was eventually captured and killed. What did him in?
    - a. he stopped to admire a strange-looking tree
    - b. his picture, posted on a tree, alerted residents to his identity
    - c. a fallen tree blocked his escape route
    - d. his long hair got caught in low-hanging branches

3. Who cursed a fig tree, saying, "May no fruit ever come from you again!"
    - a. Moses
    - b. Jesus
    - c. Elijah
    - d. Eve

4. Why did the tax collector Zacchaeus climb a sycamore tree?
    - a. he was hated, so he was hiding from angry citizens
    - b. he was greedy, so he was reclaiming a treasure he had hidden there
    - c. he was hungry, so he was looking for fruit
    - d. he was short, so he was trying to see over the crowd

Answers: 1. b; 2. d (2 Samuel 18:9–15); 3. b (Matthew 21:19); 4. d (Luke 19:1–3)

Jesus' Mom

✤ ✤ ✤ ✤

No biblical figure is as revered as Mary, the mother of Jesus.

Next to Jesus, Mary is arguably the most influential person in Christianity. Selected by God to bear his only son, she was a follower of Jesus' ministry, and she bore the horrible burden of watching him die on the cross. Considered a saint by most Christians, she is often called upon for solace during difficult times.

Little is written in the New Testament regarding Mary's early life. She is believed to have been born in Galilee around 20 B.C., and she was engaged to a man named Joseph but still a virgin when the angel Gabriel announced to her that she had been chosen by God to bear a holy child. Joseph was understandably surprised by the news, but after being comforted by another angel in a dream, he decided to go forward with the wedding as planned.

Mother and Messiah

After Mary visited her cousin Elizabeth in Judah—during which Elizabeth, who had miraculously become pregnant herself, proclaimed Mary "the mother of my Lord"—Mary and Joseph were told that they had to travel to Bethlehem to participate in a formal census by decree of the Roman emperor Augustus. In Bethlehem, Mary gave birth to Jesus.

Eight days later, the baby was circumcised and given the name Jesus, as Joseph was instructed to do by the angel who had come to him in a dream. Shortly after Jesus' birth, life became difficult for Mary and her family. They learned that King Herod feared the new Messiah and wished him dead, so they fled to Egypt, where they resided until Herod's death. Mary, Joseph, and

Jesus then returned to Nazareth, where Mary lived for most of the rest of her life.

Jesus' Final Moments

Mary and Joseph raised Jesus to adulthood, and Mary was an instrumental part of her son's ministry. In fact, it was at her intercession that Jesus performed his first public miracle, transforming water into wine at a wedding. She followed Jesus as he preached and was present at his crucifixion, standing next to Mary of Clopas, Mary Magdalene, and Jesus' disciples. Many artistic representations of Jesus' death depict Mary cradling his body, a motif known as a pietà, or pity, but such a moment is not found in the Gospels.

According to Acts, Mary was present following the Ascension when Matthias was selected to replace Judas Iscariot, who had fled and ultimately died after helping to deliver Jesus to the authorities. After that, however, Mary pretty much disappears from biblical accounts, though it is believed by many, including the Catholic Church, that she is the heavenly woman mentioned in Revelation.

Ascending Heaven

Mary is believed to have lived with John the Evangelist, referred to in the book of John as "the disciple whom Jesus loved," following Jesus' death. Her own death is not mentioned in scripture, but she is believed by some theologians to have risen to heaven just as her son did. In fact, her corporeal assumption is a basic tenet of the Catholic Church because her tomb was empty when it was opened by the disciples following her death.

Interestingly, the Bible is not the only book in which Mary's story is revealed; she is also mentioned extensively in the Qur'an. In fact, Mary is the only woman to hold such an honor.

Mary, mother of Jesus, has been integral to all aspects of Christianity from the very beginning. The faithful turn to her, as well as to Jesus, for help and guidance during prayer, and her miraculous image has been witnessed at various locations and on an eclectic array of items worldwide for centuries. Holidays are dedicated to her, and songs are sung in her praise.

Such is the remarkable spiritual and historical legacy of a simple young woman from Galilee.

Shavu'ot

*The Feast of Weeks forms an important link to Passover,
and it commemorates God's revelation of the Torah to the Israelites.*

Biblical Basis

Leviticus sets out the holiday's nature in plain words. Fifty days after Passover began, and seven weeks after it ended—thus the name *Shavu'ot* (say it, "shav-oo-OAT"), which means "weeks"—Israel's people were to bring numerous harvested food offerings as sacrifices. However, they were to leave some grain and other crops around the edges of their fields for outsiders and the poor. It was both a first-fruits harvest festival and a time to remember the giving of the Torah, the source of Jewish law and custom that released the people of Moses from idolatry and other sins. As with many Israelite festivals, it was a day of no work.

Biblical Practice

The ancient Israelites practiced the holiday with attentive rigor. Which were the first fruits? The dominant crops of the day were barley and wheat; dominant tree/vine fruits were figs, dates, grapes, pomegranates, and of course, olives. As the first crops began to ripen, the farmer would tie a reed marker to them to ensure that when the harvest came, he could segregate the proper crops and take them to the rabbi.

Modern Practice

Shavu'ot falls on the 6th of Sivan (usually late May). The 49 days after the second day of Passover are called the Omer, so each night observant Jews note how many days left until Shavu'ot. On the night of Shavu'ot, devout Jews stay up as late as possible studying the Torah. If possible, they pull an all-nighter, and in any case, they pray first thing in the morning. Today the first fruits are far more diverse in Israel, such as oranges and bales of hay, for example. At least once during the holiday, Jews eat a meal concentrated on dairy products; this may symbolize arrival in a land of milk and honey (opinions vary). Another modern custom with varying opinions as to its origin involves reading the book of Ruth.

The Evolution of Hell

⚜ ⚜ ⚜ ⚜

We commonly envision hell as a pit of fire ruled by the devil.
People roil and wail in burning pools. It wasn't always like this.

Gloomy Hades

While Zeus became king of the gods, his brother Hades captained a less enviable position: lord of the underworld. The river Styx marked the boundary between the living world and Hades. Hades was dark and dank. Souls wandered through the underworld without purpose or destination. Although some souls received punishment, such as Sisyphus, most were ordinary people. Greece is littered with underground caves carved by ancient waters. It is likely these caves helped give birth to this dreary myth.

Sheol to Hell

Although we often associate the Old Testament with an angry, wrathful God, hell is surprisingly dull by comparison. Sheol, sometimes translated as "grave," is a place not unlike Hades. It is not until the New Testament that we get a better picture of hell as a place of damnation and torment. Intermingling with Zoroastrianism from Persia, we finally see concepts such as Satan, resurrection, and the notion that the damned will rise again upon the return of the Savior.

Inferno

The first part of Dante's *Divine Comedy*, "Inferno," details the poet's guided tour of hell. Hell is fully fleshed out here. It captures all the fears of medieval Europe. There are flames, wailing souls, eternal punishment and the nine circles for nine categories of sin. Trapped in ice and weeping, Satan can only pass the time tormenting other traitors, such as Judas Iscariot. So far from God's love is the deepest part of hell that it is not fiery hot, but rather freezing cold.

In Milton's *Paradise Lost,* Satan regains some of his swagger. He commands the fallen angels, who have lost their war in heaven. As revenge, they attempt to corrupt humanity.

Fast Facts

- Vatican City—home of the pope—is the smallest nation in the world, measuring just 110 acres in size. It also has the smallest population of any nation: around 1,000 residents.

- If you're a museum lover, you definitely need to visit the Vatican. Its many museums and galleries total about nine miles in length. In fact, if you spent just one minute admiring each painting in the Vatican, it would take you nearly four years to complete the tour.

- The Pontifical Swiss Guard were originally employed as the Pope's personal bodyguards. Today, they serve as the military force of the Vatican.

- On May 6, 1527, The Swiss Guard's 189 members managed a heroic last stand on the steps of St. Peter's Basilica against 20,000 mercenary troops under Emperor Charles V, who wanted Pope Clement VII dead. When the fighting ceased, only 42 of the Guard remained alive, and none had escaped injury. However, they were victorious in their goal—Pope Clement managed to escape with his life.

- Not all popes lived under a vow of celibacy. In fact, several popes are known to have fathered children, including Pope Innocent VIII, who had eight offspring. Not so innocent, apparently.

- St. Gelasius I was the first pope to use the title "Vicar of Christ." Though born in Rome, he was also the last pope of African descent.

- Shades of Richard Nixon! St. Pontian, who was pope from A.D. 230 to 235, was the first pope to resign his office.

- Worst. Pope. Ever! Pope John XII—real name: Octavian, Count of Tusculum—is considered by most historians to be the worst pope ever to hold the title. It was alleged that over the course of his reign, he consecrated a 10-year-old boy as bishop of Todi, converted the Lateran Palace into a brothel, raped female pilgrims, stole church offerings, drank toasts to the devil, and tortured anyone who opposed him. He was beaten senseless by the husband of a woman with whom he allegedly had been having an affair. He died a few days later, on May 14, 964.

Where Jesus Walked

Mount Olivet

Also known as the Mount of Olives, it's actually a two-mile-long range of three hills running through east Jerusalem, containing one of the world's richest concentrations of religious history.

In Biblical Times
Jews have greatly desired Mount Olivet as their final resting place since before 2000 B.C., so it was a hill of cemeteries, holiness, and contemplation. Solomon built pagan temples there, surprisingly; Josiah knocked them down, making it also the "Mount of Destruction." It adjoined the Garden of Gethsemane. Ezekiel saw God there; Zechariah prophesied that it would be split to form a valley to allow God's people to flee.

Jesus' Connection
He spent a lot of time on and around Mount Olivet. Matthew 24 has a vivid description of Jesus' prophecies concerning his return, in response to his disciples' questions. He was passing by Mount Olivet on his way to enter Jerusalem when he sent his disciples to fetch him a colt, which he borrowed to make his triumphant entry. Surveying Jerusalem, he wept on its slopes for its fate. According to Acts, Mount Olivet hosted the Ascension. After Christ ascended into heaven, two men in white appeared among the rather stunned disciples to explain what they had just witnessed.

Mount Olivet Today
Its elevation is 2652 feet, giving it a tremendous view of Jerusalem. In Hebrew it is called *Har ha'Zeitim*. Saladin captured Mount Olivet from the Crusaders in A.D. 1187 and converted the Church of the Holy Ascension into a mosque, which it remains to this day. This small structure is said to contain the last footprint of Christ before his Ascension. Mount Olivet hasn't really recovered from the 1948–67 Jordanian occupation, in which vandals damaged many Jewish graves; vandalism remains a problem even today. It remains a traditional place for Jews to lament the destruction of the second temple. Among many shrines and churches on Mount Olivet, a tear-shaped chapel commemorates Jesus' tears for Jerusalem.

The First Christian Emperor

✥ ✥ ✥ ✥

Constantine legalized Christianity in Rome.

Emperor Nero brutally repressed Christians, but Roman toleration was more the norm than the exception. Diocletian led the Great Persecution against Christians in the 4th century. He ruled with the aid of three others, dividing the Roman Empire into fourths. One of the caesars was Constantine's father, Constantius, who was noted for a more lenient hand against Christians.

Religious Tolerance

Constantine's worship was monotheistic. He worshipped Apollo; that, in turn, was often conflated with the God of Christianity during that period. Constantine had a vision the night before his forces captured Rome. As instructed by God, he had his soldiers inscribe a spear with a crossed bar (the Greek Chi-Rho cross) on their shields. His forces carried the day.

Constantine was tolerant toward religion probably due to his upbringing. As a cunning leader and politician, he regarded Christianity pragmatically. It was a fast-growing religion in a cumbersome, far-stretched empire. His use of the Chi-Rho cross was politically savvy; it was a symbol used by both pagans and Christians. By the same token, Constantine openly declared himself a Christian (not just a monotheist) and built many basilicas.

When Constantine traced the boundaries of his new capital, Constantinople (formerly Byzantium), its placement not only signified a shift in power in Rome from the west to the east, but he also claimed God guided the new foundation for the city.

A Religion Legitimized

Constantine gradually transformed Christianity into a part of the political establishment. Pagan tolerance turned to intolerance *against* the pagans, as their temples were banned or torn down. Rome, abandoned as the capital of the empire for Constantinople, became the seat of power for Christendom.

Jesus the Man

⚜ ⚜ ⚜ ⚜

Jesus' corporeal existence is a fact accepted by millions of Christians—but where's the proof?

For nearly 2,000 years, Christians have accepted that Jesus the man actually existed. But where is the hard archaeological proof? Quite simply, there isn't any, experts say. Nothing concrete about or from Jesus has ever been found—not a sandal, not a diary, not the bill from the Last Supper—to prove that he really walked this earth.

Compelling Evidence

There is quite a bit of circumstantial evidence that the story of Jesus' life on earth is fact. The letters of Paul in the New Testament, for example, were written approximately 20 years after Jesus' death—an incident that Paul discusses in detail and thus likely really did occur.

There are also Jewish sources from the period. The historian Josephus, who was born just a few years after Jesus' crucifixion, mentions in his writings a man he refers to as "Jesus, who was called the Messiah or the Christ"—further proof that Jesus almost certainly existed and was remembered by those who had heard about him.

A Historian's Account

Perhaps most compelling, however, are the writings of the Roman historian Tacitus. In his book *Annals,* written around A.D. 117, he discusses the fire that ravaged Rome under the emperor Nero. According to Tacitus, the conflagration was caused by a group known as Christians, who got their name from a spiritual leader who was executed by Pontius Pilate. Tacitus had obviously heard of Jesus, and he discusses him in a way that suggests Jesus was a real person.

Taken together, all of these reports provide irrefutable evidence that Jesus walked the earth as a human being and was not merely the fictional creation of a bunch of religious zealots. Throw in the detailed description of Jesus' life and times as presented in the New Testament, and you have an amazing biography that stands the test of time—and cynicism.

Israel's Neighbors

SELEUCIDS

Alexander the Great (323 B.C.) bequeathed his empire's fragments to his successor generals: the Diadochi, including Seleucus.

Who Were They?
Seleucus was the Greek/Macedonian warlord who inherited Alexander's eastern Persian conquests. (A rival faction, Egypt's Ptolemaic Kingdom, grabbed the Holy Land.) After at first getting kicked out of the area, Seleucus set up shop in Babylon in 312 B.C. almost in rodeo fashion: He tried to hang on while his rival Diadochi tried (and failed) to buck him off. In 198 B.C., the Seleucids seized Palestine from Egypt's Ptolemaic rulers. Both Diadochian dominions brought a steady flow of Greek culture into Palestine. This created a dilemma for the Jews, especially those beginning to disperse around the Mediterranean: How could they preserve their Judaism when swamped in foreign culture? By the time Roman dominion supplanted the last Seleucids in 63 B.C., 250 years of cultural overlay had forever altered the course of biblical faith.

Where Are They Now?
There weren't many actual Seleucids, as it was a political faction. After Rome took over, they submerged partly into the other cultures of the region. Their closest kin would be modern Greeks and Macedonians, though Seleucid genetics form a thin strand throughout the modern Near East.

Biblical Mentions
The Apocrypha's books of Maccabees say much about the Seleucids in the story of the Jewish revolt against the Seleucid Emperor Antiochus IV and his successors (167–160 B.C.). While the Maccabean rebels got bloody noses, they won cultural, fiscal, and religious breathing room. Against such a mighty empire, this must count as a win; it shows just how highly the Maccabees valued their Jewish faith. Perhaps the most important biblical consequence of the Seleucid era was the increasing preeminence of *Koine* Greek. The New Testament was written in Koine, making the Greek cultural imprint on scripture impossible to overstate.

The Power of Three

⚜ ⚜ ⚜ ⚜

This holy mystery is cherished by most Christians,
though none can ever fully comprehend it.

The Trinity—the idea that the three persons of the Father, Son, and Holy Spirit exist in one Godhead—is something that unites most mainstream Christians, whatever other theological differences they might have. Roman Catholics, Orthodox Christians, Anglicans, Presbyterians, Methodists, and Lutherans all believe in the Trinity. This belief is called Trinitarianism, and the *Oxford Dictionary of the Christian Church* describes it as "the central dogma of the Christian Church." But how did a doctrine that is never explicitly stated in the New Testament come to be so widely accepted?

Grasping the Concept

The Trinity is an abstract concept that is not always easy for religious leaders and theologians to explain. One of the reasons the idea is so difficult to convey is because the Trinity is described as "three persons in one being." But the meaning of "persons" back in biblical times was very different from what it is today in modern America. At that time, the Greek word to describe any of the "persons" who made up the Godhead was *hypostasis.* While this word did describe an individual, it always described him in relation to both God and community. This "individualism" is a far cry from the kind envisioned by Thomas Jefferson and other 18th century Enlightenment thinkers, for hypostasis is a religious and mystical idea, not a political theory.

The concept of the Trinity is based upon biblical passages such as Matthew 28:19, which says, "Go therefore and make disciples of all nations, baptizing them in the name of the Father and of the Son and of the Holy Spirit." So while neither Matthew nor any of the Gospel-writing apostles ever flat out say, "The three persons of the Father, the Son, and the Holy Spirit exist in one Godhead," most mainstream Christian theologians argue that the implication is obvious. Why would God's people be baptized in the name of all three if only the Father were God? The logical conclusion, they say, is what is called the Triune God.

A Doctrinal Debut

"Trinity" is derived from the Latin word *trinitas,* which means "three" or "a triad." Translated to Greek, this word is τριασ, and its first known use in Christian history was when Theophilus of Antioch, in A.D. 180, used the phrase "types of the Trinity of God" or "types of threes of God." In the early third century, the Latin theologian Tertullian asserted that the Father, Son, and Holy Spirit are "one in essence, not one in Person." But Trinitarianism was not established as the official belief of the Christian Church until the fourth century, when the First Council of Nicaea adopted the Nicene Creed, which clearly states that Jesus Christ is "God of God, Light of Light, very God of very God, begotten, not made, being of one substance with the Father." From this time on, the Trinity was an orthodox concept accepted by the vast majority of Christians.

The Trinity may be widely accepted now, but in the beginning it was a radical idea that even some followers of Christ found hard to accept. This is because it seemed to many to fly in the face of Old Testament doctrine, perhaps most explicitly stated in Deuteronomy 6:4: "Hear, O Israel: The Lord is our God, the Lord alone." Some early Christians were quite comfortable believing that Jesus was the *son* of God, but they simply could not bring themselves to believe he *was* God. Their Hebrew roots and Old Testament instruction would not allow them to make that theological leap. Some Christian theologians these days, however, claim that the Trinity is foreshadowed in the Old Testament, for example in Genesis 18, when three men accompany God on his appearance to Abraham, and in Genesis 19, when God and two angels visit Lot at Sodom. But are such passages a true presaging of the Trinity, or are these theologians simply seeing what they wish to see? The argument has raged for centuries.

United, but not Universally Accepted

While most Christians profess the Trinity, not all who call themselves Christians do. These Christians are called Nontrinitarians, and though in the minority, they exist all over the world. Not all Nontrinitarians have the same beliefs, however. For example, Bitheists believe that the Godhead is composed of two persons—the Father and Son—rather than three. Ditheists believe that two gods—God and Satan—are constantly working against one another. Some Pentecostals have adopted the "Oneness" belief, which states that God is one spirit who manifests himself in all kinds of different ways, including coming to earth as Jesus Christ. They baptize in the name of Jesus Christ *only*. And then there are Unitarians, some of whom don't believe in any God at all.

Still, these groups are dwarfed by the vast majority of Christians who believe in the Triune God. The believers in the Trinity take to heart the words of John the apostle, who opened his Gospel by saying, "In the beginning was the Word, and the Word was with God, and the Word was God. He was in the beginning with God. All things came into being through him, and without him not one thing came into being."

And since Jesus himself discussed both God and the Holy Spirit, though separately, this is the basis of their belief: Father, Son, and Holy Spirit.

Who Was Jedidiah?

Jedidiah was another name given to Solomon. It means "beloved of the Lord." After David sinned by committing adultery with Bathsheba, their child died. A second child (Solomon) was born, and one name David gave him was Jedidiah, since David had been reassured that the Lord had forgiven him and still loved him, despite his sins.

It's Greek to Me— Septuagint and the Apocrypha

✦ ✦ ✦ ✦

After the conquests of Alexander the Great, the language most spoken in the Near East was Greek. Consequently, the Hebrew scriptures were translated into Greek—supposedly by 70 scribes who independently came up with identical translations. Some of the books included in this translation (the Septuagint) were later demoted to secondary status—and labeled the Apocrypha.

By the third century B.C., most Jews—especially those living outside of Israel—had lost touch with their native Hebrew language. Instead, they spoke Greek—the language of the rulers who had been given power by Alexander the Great after his conquest of the Near East. Pious Jews, then, had a problem. Because their sacred scriptures were available only in Hebrew, they couldn't read them. In response to their quandary, a much-needed Greek version of the Jewish scriptures was started in the middle of the third century B.C. First the Pentateuch (Genesis through Deuteronomy) was translated. Over the next 200 years or so, the remaining books of the Hebrew scriptures were rendered into Greek. No one is really sure who made any of these translations, but there's a wonderful story attached to the translation of the Pentateuch.

A Tale of 72 Scholars

According to an ancient document known as the *Letter of Aristeas,* the Hebrew scriptures were translated into Greek at the request of King Ptolemy II, the son of Ptolemy I, the former general who was made king of Egypt by Alexander the Great. In a letter, a man named Aristeas tells his brother that Ptolemy II had wanted to acquire a copy of every book in the world for his library in Alexandria, the capital of Egypt. After collecting 200,000 volumes, Ptolemy's librarian, Demetrius, told the king that he hoped to add another 300,000 books to the library. Among the missing books, Demetrius said, were the law books of the Jews, which were worthy of translation and inclusion in the royal library.

Anxious to possess a translation of the Jewish books, Ptolemy wrote to Eleazar, the Jewish high priest in Jerusalem, asking him to send 72 scholars to Alexandria to make an accurate Greek translation of the Jewish Law (the Pentateuch). When the 72 scholars arrived in Alexandria (there were 6 scriptural scholars from each of the 12 tribes of Israel), they were served sumptuous feasts and given a quiet place to work on a small island a mile out in the Mediterranean Sea. This would have been the Island of Pharos, where Ptolemy built the lighthouse that was considered one of the Seven Wonders of the Ancient World.

The 72 scholars divided the work among themselves, consulting one another as they progressed. They completed their translation in 72 days. Ptolemy was pleased with the translation, marveling at the genius of the lawgiver. He sent the scholars home with rich gifts.

Or Was It Only 70 Scholars?

The authenticity of the *Letter of Aristeas* is debatable. Some scholars consider the letter to be a fictitious account written well after the time of Ptolemy. Whatever its authenticity, the story captured the imaginations of the people and soon more fanciful versions of the story emerged. In some early Christian versions, the translation was made by only 70 scholars—paralleling the 70 elders who were with Moses at Mount Sinai (Exodus 24:1–14) and the 70 disciples Jesus sent out (Luke 10:1–20). Furthermore, these 70 men worked independently and produced identical translations of the text—word for word. It is probably from the Christian versions of the tale that the translation receives its name, the *Septuagint* (Latin for "seventy").

In any event, the early Christians made the Septuagint their own, using it whenever they referred to the Hebrew Bible. In the New Testament, which is written in Greek, nearly all quotations from the older Scriptures are taken from the Septuagint.

The Official Jewish Bible

In the late first century A.D., Jewish leaders met at Jamnia, Palestine, where for the first time they officially set the canon of the Hebrew Bible. From that time on, the Hebrew Bible could not be changed in any way. In selecting the books to be included, however, the Jewish leaders left out some of the books that had been included in the Septuagint. Although these are worthy books that Jews continue to read and cherish, they are not considered part of the divinely inspired Jewish scriptures. The omitted texts include the books of the Maccabees, Judith, Tobit, the Wisdom of Solomon, Ecclesiasticus (or Sirach), Baruch, the Letter of Jeremiah, and some additional materials included in Esther and Daniel—notably the colorful stories of Susanna and the Elders and Bel and the Dragon.

Christian Old Testament

For some 300 years, Christians continued to follow the Septuagint when dealing with the Old Testament. However, in the late fourth century, while working on the Latin translation of the Bible that would become the Vulgate, Jerome traveled to the Holy Land and, after coming under the influence of Jewish teachers there, decided to distinguish between the strictly canonical books of the Old Testament and what he called ecclesiastical (or church) books—texts included in the Septuagint but not in the Jewish Bible. Augustine disagreed with Jerome, insisting on the ancient church tradition that all books in the Septuagint are equally authoritative. And so the matter stood for more than a millennium.

In the 16th century, Martin Luther broke with tradition by accepting Jerome's position that the so-called Palestinian canon (the one set at Jamnia) was the rightful one, for it was assumed to be the version used by Jesus and the early Christians. (Recent studies have shown that the Septuagint was used in Palestine just as often as any other early version.)

In his 1534 German translation of the Bible, Luther was the first to remove the ecclesiastical books from their traditional places in the Bible and group them in a separate section between the Old and New Testaments, giving them the inaccurate label "Apocrypha" (hidden away). Most Protestant editions of the Bible, if they include these books at all, follow Luther's lead in segregating them, though sometimes they position them to follow the New Testament. Today, the Catholic church labels these books deuterocanonical, meaning that they are divinely inspired and part of the biblical canon but of somewhat secondary importance.

Women Who Wreaked Havoc

✤ ✤ ✤ ✤

When the women in the Bible are good, they're very, very good, but when they're bad, they're rotten. Their degree of rottenness, however, varies—ranging from turning against a brother to initiating a massacre. A few of the more interesting bad women follow.

Athaliah Wipes Out a Family—Almost: A daughter of King Ahab of Israel, Athaliah was an ardent follower of the Canaanite god Baal. As part of a peace treaty between the warring northern and southern kingdoms, Athaliah was married to Jehoram, the king of Judah's son and later king himself. When Jehoram died, Athaliah's son Ahaziah became king of Judah, and Athaliah tried to spread the worship of Baal throughout Judah despite heavy resistance. A year later, Ahaziah and many in his family were assassinated by zealots who were trying to end Baal worship. Athaliah then seized the throne and ruled with a vengeance. To solidify her power, she ordered all males of royal blood murdered, including her own sons and grandsons. As often happens in attempted annihilations, one child, Athaliah's grandson Joash, was saved from the massacre and kept hidden. Six years later, Joash's supporters made him king, executed his hated grandmother, Athaliah, and savagely put down Baal worship.

Delilah Dallies with a Strong Man: Samson, a strongman and judge (ruler) of Israel, had a weakness for foreign women, and Israel's enemies, the Philistines, knew it. Consequently, they paid Delilah, a sly Philistine beauty, to ensnare Samson and ferret out the source of his strength. So Delilah seduced Samson and used her feminine wiles to draw out his secret. Three times Samson gave a wrong answer, and when Delilah pretended to teasingly do what he said would weaken him, he remained strong. Delilah then resorted to a standard trick, saying that if Samson really loved her, he'd trust her. After enduring days of nagging and pestering, Samson caved in and foolishly admitted that he would lose his strength if he broke his vow never to let his head be shaved. So Delilah lulled him to sleep with his head on her lap and shaved him bald. When the weakened

Samson woke, Philistine soldiers bound, blinded, and imprisoned him. Sometime after his hair had begun to grow back, Samson got even, though at a price! When the Philistines brought him into their temple to mock him, Samson grabbed the pillars that supported the structure and brought the building down, killing himself and all the Philistine revelers.

Jezebel Makes a (Bad) Name for Herself: The foreign wife of Israel's King Ahab, Jezebel was a strong-willed promoter of the Canaanite god Baal. This made her the archenemy of the prophet Elijah, who fought her tooth and nail. So fierce was their enmity that Elijah was forced into hiding to save his life. One of Jezebel's most outrageous acts was the seizure of a poor man's family vine-yard. When Ahab tried to buy a vineyard to make it into a personal vegetable garden, Naboth, the vineyard's owner, refused to sell, not wanting to lose his ancestral land. Ahab backed off, but when Jezebel heard what had happened, she had Naboth arrested on trumped-up charges, paid false witnesses to testify against him, had the poor man stoned to death, and seized the vineyard for Ahab. On hearing of this, Elijah came out of hiding to denounce Ahab and Jezebel, predicting that dogs would eat Jezebel. The prophecy came true. When the military commander Jehu overthrew Ahab, Jezebel was thrown from a window—but only after she painted her eyes and adorned her head. "When they went to bury her, they found no more of her than the skull and the feet, and the palms of her hands" (2 Kings 9:35). The name Jezebel has come to stand for a shame-less seductress, a vice in which the queen probably did not indulge, though she was certainly a pattern for evil.

Miriam Turns on Moses: Moses' sister, Miriam, was loving to her brother and helpful, and as a prophetess she sang in triumph after the Israelites passed through the parted waters of the Red Sea. However, after Moses married a Cushite woman, both Miriam and her other brother, Aaron, become angry with him, though no one knew why. Miriam took the lead in confronting Moses, asking: "Has the Lord spoken only through Moses? Has he not spoken through us also?" (Numbers 12:2). This arrogance angered God, who appeared and berated Miriam and Aaron, telling them that he spoke to them only in dreams, visions, and riddles, but he spoke to Moses face to face. So Moses did indeed have a higher standing. As punishment, Miriam contracted leprosy but Moses pleaded with God for her, and her illness lasted only seven days.

Potiphar's Wife Cries Rape: When his jealous brothers sell him into slavery, Joseph, Jacob's favorite son, was taken to Egypt and sold to Potiphar, a high official. Because he was clever and hard-working, Joseph was made supervisor of Potiphar's estate. His youthful good looks caught the eye of Potiphar's wife, who propositioned him. Joseph refused to dishonor his generous master by sleeping with his wife, but the woman persisted. One day she actually grabbed hold of Joseph's garment, which came off in her hand as he ran away. Infuriated, Potiphar's wife cried "rape" and Joseph was put in jail. Fortunately, in prison Joseph became known for interpreting dreams, and when the pharaoh had mystifying dreams, he sent for Joseph. The dreams, Joseph said, predicted a coming famine, so the pharaoh put him in charge of storing up grain and then dispensing it when the famine hit. Joseph ended up saving Egypt as well as his own traitorous brothers, who came to him for grain during the famine. Potiphar's wife had served a purpose, but she was unimportant. We don't even know her name.

Salome Dances While Mom Cheers Her On: When Herod Antipas, the ruler of Galilee, married Herodias, his brother's wife, John the Baptist condemned the union as incestuous, infuriating Herodias. At a birthday bash for Herod, Herodias's sexy young daughter danced for the birthday boy, and he enjoyed it so much that he promised the girl anything she wanted. After consulting with her mother, she demanded John's head—on a platter. When the gory gift was brought to her, she triumphantly presented it to her gloating mother. The story as told in Mark 6:21–28 doesn't give the daughter's name, but historical records show that it was Salome. The dance she performed for Herod was later dubbed the Dance of the Seven Veils.

Sapphira and Her Husband Turn Cheat: In the earliest days of the Church, Christian landowners sold their property and laid the proceeds of the sale at the feet of the apostle Peter to be used for the community. However, as related in Acts of the Apostles 5:1–11, Sapphira conspired with her husband, Ananias, to cheat. Ananias did sell property, but he placed part of the sale money at Peter's feet—keeping the balance. When Peter accused Ananias of deception, the man fell dead at his feet. Three hours later Peter questioned Sapphira, and she lied about the sale. When Peter confronted her with her deception and told her that her husband had died, she too fell dead. Let's be grateful that all sins are not punished so quickly.

The Witch of Endor Raises a Ghost: The least villainous of the lot is the Witch of Endor, who was forced to act because of her illegal status. King Saul had outlawed mediums, but violating his own law, he disguised himself and forced a former medium to raise the ghost of Samuel. The unnamed woman, who was popularly known as the Witch of Endor, resisted, fearing that she would be put to death for violating the king's ban. Only when she discovered that she was dealing with the king himself did she comply—and was herself shocked when Samuel did in fact show up. But Saul paid a bitter price for his action, as Samuel's ghost told him the king would die in battle the next day. The medium then maternally prepared a meal for the distraught Saul. Her story is told in 1 Samuel 28:7–25.

Gomer Cheats on Hosea: Gomer was a prostitute whom the prophet Hosea married on God's orders. God's reason for ordering the marriage was to let Hosea know what it felt like to love someone only to have her run off after other men. God had nurtured the people of Israel, who had deserted him for stone and wooden idols. Hosea loved Gomer, and when she deserted him for other lovers, he brought her back to him, just as God had so often forgiven Israel.

Michal Turns Nag: King Saul's daughter Michal loved David and married him, and when Saul turned against David, she helped David escape. Saul had the marriage annulled and forced Michal to marry someone else. When David became king, he forced Michal to leave her husband and return. This turned Michal against him. When she derided David for dancing in a procession, he swore to never again come to her as a husband, and she died childless.

Quiz

Who Played Whom?

Test your Bible movie casting knowledge!

Following is a list of actors and the roles they portrayed in one of six classic biblical movies: 1. *Samson and Delilah* (1949), 2. *The Ten Commandments* (1956), 3. *Ben-Hur* (1959), 4. *Barabbas* (1961), 5. *The Greatest Story Ever Told* (1965), and 6. *The Bible... In the Beginning* (1966). Can you match the role to the performer?

1. Hedy Lamarr	A. Nefretiri
2. Frank Thring	B. Dathan
3. Michael Parks	C. Barabbas
4. John Huston	D. Pontius Pilate
5. Max von Sydow	E. Joseph of Arimathea
6. Anthony Quinn	F. Lazarus
7. Joanna Dunham	G. Delilah
8. Charlton Heston	H. Jesus
9. Pat Boone	I. Mary Magdalene
10. David McCallum	J. Sephora
11. Richard Harris	K. Peter
12. Yul Brynner	L. Cain
13. Anne Baxter	M. Angel at the Tomb
14. Edward G. Robinson	N. Samson
15. John Derek	O. Judas Iscariot
16. Yvonne De Carlo	P. Adam
17. Franco Nero	Q. Rameses
18. Harry Andrews	R. Moses
19. Arnoldo Foa	S. Abraham
20. Michael Gwynn	T. Noah
21. Victor Mature	U. Abel
22. George C. Scott	V. Joshua

Answers (number in parenthesis refers to movie number in first paragraph): 1. G (1); 2. D (3); 3. P (6); 4. T (6); 5. H (5); 6. C (4); 7. I (5); 8. R (2); 9. M (5); 10. O (5); 11. L (6); 12. Q (2); 13. A (2); 14. B (2); 15. V (2); 16. J (2); 17. U (6); 18. K (4); 19. E (4); 20. F (4); 21. N (1); 22. S (6)

Miraculous

❖ ❖ ❖ ❖

Jesus performed a variety of miracles throughout his life—
everything from raising the dead to turning water into wine.

Jesus proved he was the son of God in many ways over the course
of his life, not the least of which was performing numerous feats
that can only be described as miracles. He refused to perform on
command before skeptics as proof of his divinity, but throughout his
ministry, Jesus' disciples and others were witness to multiple events
that proved beyond doubt that he was
more than a man.

Theologians tend to divide Jesus'
miracles into two groups: those that
affected people, commonly known as
healings, and the control of nature. His
healing miracles are further divided into
three subgroups: curing ailments, exorcisms, and resurrection of the dead—the
latter of which Jesus himself experienced
following his crucifixion.

Healing the Sick

Throughout the New Testament, Jesus is credited with a wide
variety of healing miracles. The three synoptic Gospels tell of Jesus
curing the blind near Jericho as he passed through town. Mark specifically makes mention of a man named Bartimaeus, who was cured
of his blindness by Jesus' healing touch. Matthew also offers an account of two blind men near Jericho who were made to see, but he
provides no names. The healing of two blind men in Galilee is also
mentioned in Matthew.

Restoring sight to the blind was just one kind of healing miracle
performed by Jesus. Matthew, Mark, and Luke all tell of a leper who
was cured early in Jesus' ministry. Jesus asked the man not to reveal
who had cured him, but the man blabbed anyway, an act that dra-
matically increased Jesus' visibility in the region. Later, Jesus is said

to have cured ten lepers he met while on his way to Jerusalem. Only one thanked him, however—a Samaritan.

Helping the Lame to Walk

Jesus also frequently cured the paralyzed and infirm. Several books in the New Testament tell the story of a paralyzed man who was brought to Jesus on a mat. Jesus told the man to stand and walk, and to the awe of everyone in attendance, he did so—miraculously cured of his affliction.

Other healing miracles attributed to Jesus include a woman who had been plagued by bleeding for 12 years, the healing of Simon Peter's mother-in-law, the healing of a man with edema, and the healing of a man with a withered hand, among others.

Jesus was also noted for performing a number of exorcisms over the course of his ministry, including one in the synagogue in Capernaum in which Jesus drives out an evil spirit who says, "What do you want with us, Jesus of Nazareth? Have you come to destroy us? I know who you are—the Holy One of God!"

Raising the Dead

The resurrection of the dead is perhaps Jesus' most astounding healing miracle. He did this three times, according to the Gospels: the daughter of Jairus, a young man from Nain, and Lazarus, who was a close friend of Jesus who had been dead for four days before Jesus commanded him to get up.

Many of Jesus' other miracles involve his supernatural control over nature. Among them:

- turning water into wine at a wedding
- feeding thousands of people with only a few loaves of bread and a handful of fish
- walking on water to meet a boat
- calming a storm while sailing on a lake
- finding a coin in a fish's mouth
- cursing a fig tree and causing it to wither

Jesus' very existence, of course, may be the greatest miracle of all. He was born of a virgin, died and was resurrected, and ascended into heaven. All in all, a pretty tough act to follow.

Moral Majority Maker

The Rev. Jerry Falwell has probably done more than any other evangelist to galvanize the nation's religious conservatives.

Religious and political conservatism has become a social touchstone of sorts in recent years, an ideology that owes much of its current popularity to one man: the Rev. Jerry Falwell.

Falwell was born in Lynchburg, Virginia, on August 11, 1933. His father was a bootlegger during Prohibition, but Falwell followed a different path. In 1956, Falwell founded the Thomas Road Baptist Church in Lynchburg with just 35 members. Today, the church's membership exceeds 24,000.

Family Values

Falwell started *The Old-Time Gospel Hour,* which aired on the radio daily and on local television weekly. The show, which became a global phenomenon, gave Falwell exposure and name recognition, and as his ministry grew, so did his influence. In 1971, Falwell founded Lynchburg Baptist College (now known as Liberty University), and in 1979 he formed the Moral Majority, a right-leaning organization that promoted what Falwell called "pro-traditional family" policies.

Falwell's unrestrained conservatism sometimes made him a social lightning rod. In the 1980s, he fought a bitter legal battle with *Hustler* magazine publisher Larry Flynt over an ad parody. The landmark case became the focus of the 1996 movie *The People vs. Larry Flynt.*

Controversial Comments

Falwell became a vocal social critic whose comments sometimes got him into trouble. In 2001, he was forced to apologize after calling the September 11 terrorist attacks a judgment against America for "throwing God out of the public square." Nonetheless, Falwell remained an influential figure in American religion and politics until the end of his life. He died from heart failure on May 15, 2007.

Biblical Urban Legends

❧ ❧ ❧ ❧

Many wild stories involving the Bible have popped up in recent years. Though fascinating, few of them are true.

Urban legends are as American as apple pie. Traditionally passed along from person to person and usually involving "a friend of a friend," this fascinating aspect of American folklore really picked up steam with the growth of the Internet, which made it possible to transmit urban legends around the world with the click of a mouse.

Urban legends cover a broad array of topics, so it should come as no surprise that many have a biblical angle. Though fun to read, most fall apart under scrutiny and very few are actually true. Here's a sampling of some of the more popular biblical urban legends:

Myth: An unburned Bible was found in the charred rubble of the Pentagon after the terrorist attack on 9/11.

Fact: A total of 189 people perished when American Airlines Flight 77, which had been commandeered by terrorists, crashed into the southwest section of the Pentagon. According to a popular urban legend, a Bible miraculously survived the fiery carnage, a fact many attributed to divine intervention. In truth, a book was found undisturbed by rescue workers, but it was a "bible" of a different kind: a dictionary.

A Gift from the Gideons

Myth: Christians often leave money in Gideon Bibles to reward the next person who turns to the book for solace.

Fact: This legend has been making the rounds for decades, and many people eagerly rifle through the Bibles in their hotel rooms immediately upon check-in hoping to find financial treasure. However, there are few if any verifiable accounts of money being found in a Bible. In truth, it's the Bibles themselves that altruistic evangelists leave—not money within them.

Myth: A father left his only son a spectacular gift within a Bible, but the son, angry at his father's miserly ways, didn't find it until his father's death.

Fact: According to this supposedly true legend, which has circulated for years, the son of a wealthy man wanted only a fancy sports car for his college graduation gift and was angry and upset when he received a gorgeous leather-bound Bible instead. He cast the book aside without looking at it and didn't see it again until he was called home upon his father's passing. While going through his father's possessions, the young man found the Bible still in its gift box. Paging through the book, he found that his father had underlined Matthew 7:11: "And if ye, being evil, know how to give good gifts to your children, how much more shall your Heavenly Father which is in Heaven, give to those who ask Him?" As the son read the words, a car key fell from the back of the Bible. On the tag was the date of his graduation and the words "Paid in Full."

Avoiding the Beast, End Times, and Missing Sun

Myth: Because the book of Revelation states that 666 is the Mark of the Beast, or Antichrist, Christian shoppers often add a small item to their purchases so the total is never $6.66.

Fact: According to store clerks, this one is true—superstitious people often do add a package of gum or other item to change their total if it comes out to $6.66. In fact, it apparently happens quite often.

Myth: Airlines will not pair Christian pilots and copilots out of fear that the Rapture will take them away, leaving the plane without someone to land it.

Fact: Many Christians believe in the Rapture—a time when Jesus will return and call all believers up to heaven, leaving nonbelievers on earth. This belief is based on a passage in 1 Thessalonians, which concludes, "Then we which are alive and remain shall be caught up together with them in the clouds, to meet the Lord in the air: and so we shall be with the Lord."

Are airlines comparing pilots' religious beliefs when making assignments, just to be on the safe side? Not according to FAA officials, who told a reporter, "The FAA does not have any regulations referencing religious beliefs." The nonexistence of such a regulation was also confirmed by a representative of American Airlines.

Myth: NASA scientists have discovered a "missing" day in time that corresponds with biblical accounts of the sun standing still in the sky.

Fact: According to this urban legend, NASA researchers were checking where the sun, moon, and planets would be positioned 100 years and 1,000 years in the future. While running the measurements through a computer, the machine screeched to a halt. While servicing the computer, technicians found a day missing in space in elapsed time, which coincided with a biblical account of the sun standing still. This is a great story, especially if you are a Christian looking for scientific proof of scripture. But according to NASA Public Affairs, it never happened.

Determining a Biblical Center

Myth: The true center of the Bible is Psalm 118.

Fact: Located between the shortest chapter of the Bible and the longest, Psalm 118 is often noted as being the absolute center of the Bible because there are 594 chapters before it, and 594 chapters after it. Add those up, believers say, and you get 1188, or Psalm 118:8, which states what many believe to be the Bible's most important concept: "It is better to take refuge in the Lord than to put confidence in man." The problem is that the math doesn't work for all Bibles, only the one used by most Protestant denominations. So if you're Jewish or Catholic, no such luck.

Female Prophets

Prophetess is used five times in the Old Testament: Miriam (Exodus 15:20); Deborah (Judges 4:4); Huldah (2 Kings 22:14); Isaiah's wife, "the prophetess" (Isaiah 8:3); and Noadiah, a prophetess who opposed Nehemiah (Nehemiah 6:14). Deborah and Huldah exercised significant responsibilities.

God as Potter

✤ ✤ ✤ ✤

The prophet Isaiah describes God as the potter who formed us all,
saying: "O Lord...we are the clay and you are our potter; we are
the work of your hand" (Isaiah 64:8). Jeremiah goes further,
explaining how God created us and shapes us to his satisfaction.

Potters were very important in the daily life of ancient Israel. People
cooked in clay vessels, ate from clay dishes, and stored just about everything in clay jars. The potters who produced these artifacts were
skilled craftsmen who maintained control of every part of a process
that involved several steps.

Before beginning to shape
a vessel, the potter had to
sift dry clay to remove bits of
debris from it and soak the
resulting fine powder in water
until it was the consistency of
dense bread dough. He mixed
the prepared clay thoroughly
by walking on it or kneading it
vigorously by hand. He then
stuck a lump of clay on a potter's wheel and shaped it—an
exacting process that required great skill. Once the pot was shaped
to his satisfaction, the potter put it aside to dry until it was the tex-
ture of leather. Then he carved designs into it or painted it, let it
dry again, and finally, placed the decorated pot inside a kiln, an
extremely hot oven, to harden. After cooling, it was then ready
for use.

The Potter's Wheel

The most difficult part of the process was shaping the vessel on the
potter's wheel, or kick wheel. A kick wheel consisted of two wheels
that were connected by a central spoke or shaft and set on end. The

potter sat in front of this device and turned the lower wheel with his feet in order to make the upper wheel spin. By "kicking" the lower wheel into motion with his feet, the potter left his hands free to shape the clay on the upper wheel. He began the shaping by sticking a lump of prepared clay onto the center of the top wheel and setting the wheel spinning by kicking the lower wheel. He then pressed the lump of clay down firmly onto the center of the top wheel. As the clay began to take shape, the potter pressed his hands gently against the spinning wet clay, both inside and out, applying pressure in the right places to give the clay the desired shape—a long narrow jar, a wide bowl, or some other shape.

Sometimes the clay became too wet or full of air bubbles, causing the potential vessel to collapse, and at other times the vessel got off center and flew off the wheel. When this happened, the potter collapsed the misshaped vessel, pounded the clay back into a solid mound, and started shaping it again. He repeated the process until he succeeded in fashioning a pleasing piece of pottery.

Jeremiah's Prophecy

Jeremiah reports that God sent him to a potter's shop to receive a message for his people. At the shop, Jeremiah watches as the potter tries to shape a pot. "The vessel he was making of clay was spoiled in the potter's hand, and he reworked it into another vessel" (Jeremiah 18:4).

God then tells Jeremiah that he deals with the people of Israel as the potter deals with his clay. "Can I not do with you, O house of Israel, just as this potter has done? says the Lord. Just like the clay in the potter's hand, so are you in my hand, O house of Israel" (Jeremiah 18:6–7). So just as the potter is free to reshape his clay, so too is Yahweh at liberty to do whatever he wishes with the people of Israel—and with us.

Jeremiah's original message was a warning to the people of Israel to conform to God's laws or suffer conquest. If the people did not repent, the Lord would break them (he eventually let them be taken into exile). But God would also reshape the people (on their return from exile). God can also break us if we defy him, but he will never give up on us. He will keep trying to re-form us until we comply with his plan.

Where Jesus Walked

Ephraim

This brief waypoint's location is a mystery.
Can we do anything but speculate about Ephraim?

In Biblical Times
It was near a wilderness, according to John. The most common biblical context for Ephraim involves the Old Testament founder of the Ephraim tribe—the same ones whose hard luck at being able to say "shibboleth" correctly got 42,000 of them slaughtered. Its single mention in scripture suggests it was fairly small. Placing it near a wilderness isn't much help; that would be like us saying a small Nebraska town was near a cornfield.

Jesus' Connection
Christ was at Bethania, where he raised Lazarus from the dead. We know that was along Mount Olivet, very close to Jerusalem. Some Jews believed in him after this event. This got the Jewish priests and Pharisees worried about a Roman crackdown, which might include them as well, and they began plotting his death. Thus, with the arm out for his arrest, Jesus ducked out to Ephraim. From there, he returned to Bethania. He is not mentioned returning to Ephraim.

Ephraim Today
Finding Ephraim is a challenge. It helps if we presume that John's Ephraim has something to do with the Old Testament tribe, which lived roughly north of Jerusalem, west of the Jordan. John's location probably wasn't far from Bethania. After all, while Christ could appear anywhere, he had the disciples along, and there's nothing in the Bible about him teleporting them or himself to Ephraim. Thus, they probably walked. We might begin our search north of Jerusalem, west of the Jordan in the hills of Samaria. How far? Speculating madly (for we must, or give up), suppose ten miles as a long day's walk in hilly terrain; suppose at least half a day for safety and less than two days for convenience. That would put Ephraim some 5 to 20 miles north of Jerusalem. Perhaps someday archaeology will be able to tell us more.

The Book of Job: Why We Suffer

�֍ ✤ ✤ ✤

We've all had bad days, but usually not as bad as Job's.
Out of his story comes an important—if depressing—moral.

A Bad Day

Job is a wealthy and pious man. Satan teases God that the only reason Job is so pious is because he has so much. God tells Satan he can take everything away from Job and he will still be pious.

The next day is a spectacularly bad day for Job. Sabeans take his oxen and asses. A meteor kills his sheep. Brigands carry away his camels. All his servants are slaughtered in the process. A house collapses, killing all his sons and daughters. But Job continues to worship God, saying, "the Lord gave, and the Lord has taken away."

Satan says Job will relent once his health suffers. Again, God grants permission. Job develops sores all over his body but says nothing against God despite his wife's urging. Three friends visit and insist Job must have done something sinful. Job still refuses to curse God, but he asks to state his case before God.

God appears as a whirlwind and chastises Job for demanding that God justify himself. Job repents, and God rewards him.

Satan=Devil?

Strictly translated, it is not the devil who is in the role of Satan here. The satan (there is a definite article) is merely "an adversary." The satan is a member of God's heavenly court and is playing devil's advocate to God's esteem of Job. The satan only acts when given *permission* by God to act. *God* takes responsibility for the suffering inflicted upon Job. He also admits that Job is innocent. While anyone who stole another's herd, murdered their children, and infected them with a skin disease would be singularly punished, God is above justice when it comes to proving a point.

When God appears to Job, he speaks at length about his duties. He doesn't directly answer why Job suffers—why the innocent suffer. His lack of an answer *is* the answer.

What Do the Seraphim Look Like?

✤ ✤ ✤ ✤

When Isaiah was called to be a prophet, he had a vision of the Heavenly Court in which fiery seraphs, or seraphim, flanked the throne of God. Although Isaiah describes the seraphim's wings, he says nothing of the rest of their appearance. The seraphim could have been griffinlike animals, flying serpents, or beings who looked like winged humans. They may also have been related to the cherubim, who also served God in his Heavenly Court.

In the vision Isaiah experienced when he was called to be a prophet, he stood before God, who was seated on a lofty throne with the hem of his garment filling the temple. According to Isaiah: "Seraphs were in attendance above him; each had six wings: with two they covered their faces, and with two they covered their feet, and with two they flew" (Isaiah 6:2).

The fact that the seraphim's wings cover their eyes suggests that the sight of the Almighty is too much for the seraphim to look on. "Feet" in this passage is probably a euphemism for groin—the seraphim use their lower wings to cover their private parts out of modesty. During Isaiah's vision, one of the seraphim takes

a coal from the altar that is below God's throne and touches it to the prophet's lips to purify them and prepare the prophet for his work.

Opinions on what these seraphim may have looked like vary. They may simply have resembled humans with wings. Or they may have been some sort of four-legged winged beasts like the ones the Jews undoubtedly saw in the artworks of Mesopotamian and Egyptian temples. There is also good reason to believe that the seraphim were reptilian in appearance.

Not Quite Dragons

The word *seraphim* is a transliteration of the Hebrew word that roughly means "burning one." In Deuteronomy 8:15, the seraph was a poisonous snake whose venom burned as it killed. In Numbers 21:6–8, Moses uses a bronze seraph, or serpent, to heal some of his people after they are afflicted by poisonous snakes due to their lack of faith. A bronze serpent, said to be the one Moses used, is later kept in the temple, where it is used in healing services. As reported in 2 Kings 18:4, a few years after Isaiah's vision, King Hezekiah smashed the bronze seraph because people were burning incense to it, using it as an idol. But since Isaiah's vision came to him in the same temple before King Hezekiah had destroyed the bronze seraph, the seraphs that were attending God in his vision may have been thought of as the living models for this bronze seraph. In other words, they may have been serpentine in appearance.

The Extended Family

Although the mysterious six-winged seraphim that appear in Isaiah's vision do not show up anywhere else in the Bible, similar entities, called cherubim, or cherubs, do. When Ezekiel is called to be a prophet while exiled in Babylon, he sees opulent and exotic "visions of God," befitting his surroundings in the land of the Babylonians. The visions are full of fire, bright color, and precious jewels and include cherubim, fabulous winged sphinxlike creatures that resemble the Babylonian gods that surround Ezekiel. Unlike seraphim, cherubim appear frequently in the Bible, but their physical descriptions vary widely. Certainly, however, they looked nothing like the fat-faced winged infant cherubs of Renaissance art. Possibly the most notable cherubim in the Bible are the sphinxlike beings who guard Eden's Tree of Life with fiery revolving swords (Genesis 3:24).

In Jewish writings outside the Bible, seraphim are connected with cherubim and ophanim to form the three highest orders of God's attendants. These beings are superior to the angels, who are messengers sent by God on various errands. In popular Jewish culture, the seraphim were represented by serpentine flashes of lightning, while the cherubim were represented by the storm clouds. But none of this is in the Bible. We can only use our own imaginations to guess exactly what the seraphim looked like.

Little Guys Finish First

✤ ✤ ✤ ✤

Zacchaeus was not only of a shrimpy height, he was also a hated tax collector who probably slipped some of the money he collected into his own already bulging pockets. But his faith raised him in stature and brought Jesus to his home as a guest.

Jesus always drew crowds when he came into a town, and Jericho was no exception. A huge mob greeted Jesus as he passed through the city on his way to Jerusalem. And this presented a big problem for Zacchaeus, who was a short man. Zacchaeus appears only in Luke's Gospel, and Luke starts right out by telling us that Zacchaeus was both a tax collector and rich—delivering two strikes against the man before telling us any more about him.

Hated Tax Collectors

The Jews were highly overtaxed, having to pay both their own religious officials and the foreign Roman overlords. The men who collected taxes for the Romans were generally hated because they were Jews who worked for the Romans and because they usually overcharged them and pocketed the difference. John the Baptist urged them to stop overcharging, but few heeded him.

Generally, the Jews placed tax collectors in the category of lowlifes. In one of Jesus' parables, a Pharisee and a tax collector go to the temple to pray. The Pharisee prays haughtily, saying, "God, I thank you that I am not like other people: thieves, rogues, adulterers, or even like this tax collector" (Luke 18:11). His placement of the tax collector among riffraff and sinners is typical of most Jews of his time.

And Zacchaeus was not only a tax collector, but a "chief" tax collector. This means that he supervised a number of lesser tax collectors, probably men who collected money for the Romans at tax offices or tollbooths in places of commerce or transport, such as Jericho, which was an imperial customs station for major routes between Judea and the lands east of the Jordan. So even though

Zacchaeus's position was a lucrative one, it earned the contempt of his own people. However, Jesus remains open to everyone. In the parable of the Pharisee and the tax collector, he much prefers the tax collector, who, albeit uncharacteristically, humbly beats his chest and asks God's forgiveness, while the Pharisee looks down his nose at the world.

Getting Up in the World

As Jesus approaches, Zacchaeus is totally frustrated because he is too short to see him over the crowds. Then an idea comes to him. He quickly climbs a sycamore tree that grows beside the road, and from there he manages to get a good look at Jesus. But Jesus can also see Zacchaeus and, knowing what is in the tax collector's heart, he says: "Zacchaeus, hurry and come down; for I must stay at your house today" (Luke 19:5). So Zacchaeus, overwhelmed, scurries down the tree immediately and offers Jesus the hospitality of his home. The people, of course, grumble against Jesus becoming the guest of a sinner, but both Jesus and Zacchaeus ignore them. Instead, the tax collector, almost babbling with joy, tells Jesus that he will give half of all his wealth to the poor and promises that if he has defrauded anyone he will make restitution four times over. Jesus approves, stating: "Today salvation has come to this house" (Luke 19:9).

Conclusions

Like the tax collector in the parable, Zacchaeus remains open to Jesus and so receives salvation. He stands in sharp contrast to the parable's pompous Pharisee, who boasts of all the good he does but fails to win God's approval. It is not surprising that the story of Zacchaeus appears only in Luke's Gospel, as this is the Gospel that most strongly emphasizes the fact that Jesus came to save all people—Jew and gentile, rich and poor, man and woman, saint and sinner. And Jesus himself underlines this important message by advising his followers that he has come "to seek out and to save the lost" (Luke 19:10).

According to a later tradition, Peter appointed Zacchaeus bishop of Caesarea, a city on Judea's Mediterranean coast, even though Zaccheus was reluctant to accept the office.

Don't Raise the Roof, Lower the Patient

✧ ✧ ✧ ✧

When the house where Jesus is teaching is totally blocked by eager crowds, four ingenious men lower a paralytic through the roof to Jesus, hoping the Lord will heal him.

In Capernaum, so many people mobbed the house where Jesus was teaching that the door was blocked. When four men arrived with a paralyzed man on a stretcher, they couldn't get in. Not about to give up, the men carried the stretcher and its occupant onto the roof.

Getting a man on a stretcher to the roof was not as difficult as it may seem. Because the roof of a house was often used to dry grain, perform household chores, or even sleep on warm nights, there was usually an outside staircase that led up to it. The hard part was manipulating the stairs with the stretcher while keeping the poor man from sliding off and landing on his head—which would produce the very opposite of a cure. But once on the roof, the men had to get their patient down into the room where Jesus was teaching. This was also easier than it may sound.

The typical house in Capernaum was a one-story building with a flat roof. To construct such a roof, wooden beams were placed on the tops of the walls and covered with small branches that were woven together to create a firm surface. A layer of clay-based plaster was then spread across the branches to cover them and fill in the gaps between them. Finally, the plaster was packed down with heavy stonerollers to create a smooth surface.

The men created a hole in the roof by digging away the plaster and cutting away a few of the underlying branches, then they lowered the stretcher down on ropes to land at Jesus' feet. Jesus was so moved by the faith of the men who had brought this paralytic to him that he immediately healed the man, both spiritually and physically, and sent him away carrying his own stretcher. We know nothing of the owner of the house, who was left with a hole in his roof.

10 Things

Bible Translations You've Probably Never Heard Of

From historical to hip, they don't get read much today.

1. The Great Bible (1539) This was the first authorized edition of the Bible in English. Though William Tyndale and John Wycliffe had already been flouting church law by translating scripture for the common folk, it was King Henry VIII who approved this version for his new Anglican church. It was prepared by a Tyndale crony, Miles Coverdale, commissioned by Thomas Cromwell. This was sometimes called the "Chained Bible," because churches would make it available to parishioners (as ordered by Cromwell), but chain it down for safekeeping.

2. The Geneva Bible (1560) For a half-century before the King James Version, this was the standard; it was mass-produced and widely used. When Milton or Shakespeare quoted scripture, it was from this version. The language was vigorous, edgy for its day, a clear improvement over previous translations. Amazingly, this was what modern publishers would call a "study Bible," with an assortment of study guides, introductions, maps, and woodcut illustrations.

3. The Primitive New Testament (1745) Bible translators have always tried to work from the best Hebrew and Greek originals, but archaeologists keep finding new manuscripts, which continually shed new light on the text. Eighteenth-century scholar William Whiston sought to improve on the King James Version by working from some very early ("primitive") Greek manuscripts. A mathematician and scientist, Whiston suggested that Noah's flood had been caused by a comet.

4. A Liberal Translation of the New Testament (1768) A prolific writer and creative thinker, Edward Harwood brought the flowery language of 18th-century English prose to his free (liberal) paraphrase of the New Testament—as we can see in his 77-word subtitle (something about "the True Signification and Force of the Original... transfused into our Language"). His rendering of "Thy kingdom come"? "May the glory of thy moral government be advanced, and the great laws of it be more generally obeyed."

5. The Twentieth Century New Testament (1898–1901) A flood of new Bible translations came along in the 20th century, and this was the first, published in three parts, with a final collection offered in 1904.

 A team of about 20 Britons composed this version, but they weren't professional scholars—they were teachers, homemakers, ministers, and even railroad workers who had studied ancient Greek and wanted to bring the Bible to life in the modern age.

6. Fenton's Bible (1903) In 1853, a young London businessman began work on a personal project, translating the Bible into modern English. Fifty years later he published the complete work: *The Holy Bible in Modern English.* Farrar Fenton wanted to capture the essence of the original, so he treated the psalms as the songs they were. Painstakingly, he fit other poetic books (including Job) into poetic meter. He also tried to put the books of the Bible into chronological order.

7. The Bible in Basic English (1941, 1949) For people just learning to read English, how can they understand the Bible, with its big concepts and massive vocabulary? That was the challenge taken by Samuel Henry Hooke, a British scholar. Using only 850 basic English words (defined by literacy experts), adding 100 words necessary for poetry and 50 distinctly Bible words, Hooke composed this easy-to-read version.

8. The Amplified Bible (1958, 1962) Where the BBE (see above) used fewer words, the Amplified Bible used more. Hebrew and Greek words seldom have direct parallels with English words. Instead, there might be multiple possible translations, nuances, or cultural associations. The Amplified Bible provides alternate readings and explanatory phrases in parentheses and brackets, just to make sure the full sense of the original is honored. It's hard to read out loud, but great for study. This was the first Bible project of the Lockman Foundation, which later sponsored the *New American Standard Bible.*

9. The Berkeley Bible (1945, 1959, 1969) English wasn't the native language of Dutch-born Gerrit Verkuyl, but as an undergrad in the United States, he began to see the need for a modern translation to supersede the KJV. He didn't have much time to work on it for the 40 years after he made the decision, though. As a retiree, he tackled the project, naming it after his new hometown, Berkeley, California. His New Testament, published in 1945, met such critical acclaim that many wanted a complete Bible. Since Old Testament Hebrew was not Verkuyl's specialty, his publisher assembled an all-star team of scholars to finish *The Berkeley Version of the Bible in Modern English* in 1959. (This was revised in 1969 as *The Modern Language Bible.*)

10. The New Testament in the Language of Today (1963) As a pastor in Iowa during the 1930s and '40s, William F. Beck found that even his Sunday school teachers were having trouble understanding the stately KJV language. He began translating New Testament passages from the original Greek into language that made sense to them. After getting a doctorate in New Testament studies, he completed his translation of the NT, stating in his introduction that he wanted to "let God speak the language of today," the kind of language people use over "coffee and doughnuts."

Word Links

Sometimes word links between adjacent books of the Bible can be seen, which probably accounts for their being placed together. The following phrase occurs near the end of the book of Joel (Joel 3:16): "The Lord roars from Zion, and utters his voice from Jerusalem." The next book, Amos, begins with exactly the same phrase (Amos 1:2).

Zealots

✢ ✢ ✢ ✢

*Here's another word that pops up constantly in the Bible.
But what does it mean? Who were these people?*

The zealots were a radical group of Jews in ancient Israel who hated the Roman occupiers with a passion. Well, big deal, you might say: When Judea was occupied by Rome, almost all of the Jews who lived there hated the Romans with a passion. What made the zealots so different? The difference is the lengths the zealots were willing to go in order to free their country from an invader they saw as completely and utterly evil.

United in Hatred...

The term "zealots" does not really refer to one organized group. Rather it is an umbrella term to describe the members of many different anti-Roman bands who were committed to the overthrow of the Roman regime in Israel. The Hebrew word for "zealot," *kanai*, means "one who is jealous on behalf of the Lord" or "one who is passionate for the Lord." The zealots were very active in the first century, and they were looking for a leader, a messiah who would lead them against their oppressive foe. But would that leader be Jesus Christ?

Jesus was either a very small child or a few years away from being born when the Quirinius Census was conducted. The Gospel of Luke and the Gospel of Matthew differ on the year the census occurred, but it was this tax-related census that gave the zealots the issue they needed to really rile the Jewish public. The first century Jewish historian Josephus identifies a Judas of Galilee (not to be confused with the apostle Judas Iscariot who traded Jesus for 30 pieces of silver) as the leader of this rebellion. Judas of Galilee trained his sons James and Simon (also not to be confused with apostles of the same name) to follow in his radical footsteps, and it cost them both their lives: They were executed by procurator Tiberius Julius Alexander in about A.D. 46.

. . . But Divided Over Tactics

Though the vast majority of Jews in ancient Israel did hate the Romans and wanted them gone, many did not support the zealots. A very small minority of Jews were making good money by being the Romans' boot-lickers, and they didn't want to give up their opulent lifestyle. But even many Jews who suffered oppression and poverty could not bring themselves to support the violent ways of some zealot subsets. The Sicarii, for example, were named after the short daggers they used to assassinate Roman officials and their Hebrew collaborators. These fanatics not only terrorized the Romans, but they were willing to kill any Jews who got in the way of their plans for a post-Roman Israel.

What kind of Israel did the zealots want? One that was ruled by the laws of God only. In other words, they wanted a theocracy. But as the zealots became more and more political, many religious Jews backed away from them, feeling that a lust for power was becoming more important to the zealots than serving their common God. Though they hated the Romans for trying to impose paganism on them and destroy their religious heritage, they believed the zealots were doing more harm than good. These moderate Jews wanted to coexist as peacefully and comfortably with the Romans as possible while they hoped for better days in the future. They mocked the zealots as crazy, wild-eyed fanatics, and the zealots mocked them as weak-willed, backstabbing traitors.

Not the Leader They Were Looking For

But what did Jesus of Nazareth think of the zealots? Not a whole lot. In fact, in Luke 21:20–24, Jesus predicts that the rebellion of the zealots will eventually lead to war and the destruction of the temple at Jerusalem: "When you see Jerusalem surrounded by armies, then know that its desolation has come near. . . . Jerusalem will be trampled on by the Gentiles, until the times of the Gentiles are fulfilled." Jesus strongly believed that the zealots were misguided and that a violent uprising against the Romans would only lead to more suffering for the Hebrew people. But he knew that the zealots would not heed his warnings. Indeed, as soon as the zealots realized that Jesus would never agree to supervise their illegal activities, they dropped him and continued their search for a leader elsewhere.

King of Christian Conservatives

Pat Robertson is one of the most recognized Christian broadcasters in the world, thanks to his personal media empire.

For decades, M. G. "Pat" Robertson has been the most prominent face of America's Christian right. In fact, he's so popular that, though he currently holds no official role with any church, millions tune in daily to his television show, *The 700 Club,* to watch Robertson expound on the religious, political, and social issues of the day.

Robertson was born in Lexington, Virginia, on March 22, 1930. His father was U.S. Senator A. Willis Robertson, so politics have been an integral part of Robertson's life since childhood. After college, a stint in the military serving in Korea, and graduation from Yale Law school, Robertson experienced a religious conversion and enrolled in the New York Theological Seminary, where he received a Master of Divinity degree in 1959.

Media Mogul

A year later, Robertson established the Christian Broadcasting Network (CBN) in Virginia Beach, Virginia. He began with a small UHF station in Portsmouth, Virginia, then acquired a local-access cable channel near Hampton Roads. Robertson worked to bring viewers to his start-up network, which is now seen in 180 countries and broadcast in more than 70 languages. (*The 700 Club* remains its most popular program.) He followed CBN with a few other cable channels, which boasted family-friendly entertainment.

In 1977, Robertson founded CBN University (later renamed Regent University) on CBN's Virginia Beach campus; he still holds the position of chancellor. He is also the founder of Operation Blessing International Relief and Development Corporation, American Center for Law and Justice, and The Flying Hospital Inc., among other endeavors.

In 1986, Robertson said he would seek the Republican nomination for president in 1988 if at least three million people promised to campaign on his behalf. When he easily reached that goal, he relinquished his ministerial credentials and turned leadership of CBN over to his son, Tim.

Presidential Platform

Robertson ran on a conservative platform, promoting a ban on pornography, an overhaul of the nation's education system, and the elimination of the Departments of Education and Energy. He was attacked early in his campaign for fudging his military service (he stated in campaign literature that he was a combat Marine who had served in the Korean War; others in his unit disputed his claim of combat service). He placed second in the Iowa caucus. However, he did poorly in subsequent races and lost the nomination to George H. W. Bush.

Shortly after the election, Robertson formed the Christian Coalition, a right-wing organization that supported conservative political candidates. The group was frequently attacked for various improprieties, and Robertson left the Coalition in 2001.

Like many religious leaders, Robertson has held strong, sometimes controversial opinions on numerous issues. Unfortunately, some of his comments have gotten him into hot water. In 1991, for example, he was chastised for promoting a worldwide Jewish conspiracy in his book *The New World Order.*

Robertson has also caught flack for predicting the end of the world (on several occasions, none of which, obviously, came true); claiming to be able to deflect hurricanes through prayer; and for condemning, among other things, the religion of Islam, feminism, homosexuality, and liberal college professors.

Shocking Comment

In early 2010, Robertson made one of his most audacious comments yet—that a devastating earthquake in Haiti was brought on by a "pact with the devil" made by the impoverished nation in the 1800s as it struggled to overthrow French colonialism. Robertson was widely condemned for the comment. His foundation, Operation Blessing International, did send millions in aid to Haiti.

However, Pat Robertson has never let a little criticism keep him from doing God's work, which he continues today as the host of *The 700 Club.* Though he may have angered many over the years, it cannot be denied that Robertson has been an effective leader among America's religious conservatives.

The Miracle at Fatima

❖ ❖ ❖ ❖

When three young children reported seeing the Virgin Mary in 1917,
their story rocked the world—and continues to do so today.

On May 13, 1917, 10-year-old Lucia Santos and her younger cousins
Jacinta and Francisco Marto were tending sheep near their home in
Fatima, Portugal, when they witnessed an apparition of the Virgin
Mary. Their story in itself is not unusual—such accounts have been
reported for thousands of years—but the young girls' tale didn't stop
there. For the next five months, Mary returned, always on the 13th
day (with the exception of August), imploring the children to do
penance and pray for world peace. She also revealed to them three
important secrets, or prophecies.

The girls' incredible story became world news, and thousands
flocked to the small Portuguese village in the hope of witnessing a
miracle. In August, the provincial administrator had the girls locked
up and demanded that they tell him the secrets as revealed by the
Blessed Virgin. The girls refused and were soon released. A few days
later, on the 19th, they reported another apparition.

In October, the "Miracle of the Sun" occurred at the Cova da
Iria, as promised by Mary during one of her earlier visits. Before an
estimated crowd of 70,000, including members of the press, the sun
appeared to change colors, zigzag, or rotate like a fiery wheel. Many
witnesses wept or fell to their knees in prayer.

Three Secrets of Fatima

The secrets revealed by the Blessed Virgin have become one of the
most oft-reported aspects of the Fatima story. The first, according to
Lucia in her *Third Memoir,* was a vision of hell, which appeared as a
great lake of fire. The second secret was instructions on how to save
souls from hell and convert the world to Roman Catholicism. According to Lucia, Mary promised an end to the World War that was
raging at the time, but she warned that if people didn't stop offending God, another world war would soon follow. The consecration

and religious conversion of Russia, then a communist country, was also emphasized.

The third prophecy, which detailed the death of the pope (specifically, "a bishop in white") and other religious persons, wasn't made public by the Vatican until June 26, 2000, even though Lucia had indicated that it could be revealed as early as 1960. Because of the Vatican's unusual secrecy, a variety of rumors quickly spread regarding the contents of the secret, and some believe even today that the report released in 2000 was not the real prophecy, or only part of it.

Followed by Fame

Lucia Santos and her cousins became famous worldwide, and the so-called Miracle at Fatima followed them throughout their lives. Lucia became a Carmelite nun, and she reported several more visits from the Virgin Mary in the years that followed. She died on February 13, 2005—the anniversary day of the first six sightings—at the age of 97, and her room at the convent where she had lived was ordered sealed off by the Vatican.

Francisco and Jacinta Marto, Lucia's cousins, both died young, victims of the Great Spanish Flu Epidemic of 1918–20. Francisco passed away in 1919 and Jacinta in 1920.

The Miracle at Fatima has intrigued religious scholars and the faithful for more than 90 years. The story was turned into a movie, *The Miracle of Our Lady of Fatima* (1952), and has been the topic of several books and magazine articles. The Vatican has gone on record as saying that the reported apparitions are "worthy of belief," and a movement is underway to canonize Lucia Santos, who spent her life devoted to the church.

However, with the passing years, doubt has been cast on the childrens' stories. Some investigators have called the whole thing a hoax or attempted to offer a scientific explanation for events such as the Miracle of the Sun. Nonetheless, the Miracle at Fatima remains firmly etched in the minds of many devout Catholics. To them, the Virgin Mary really did appear to Lucia Santos and her cousins. All we have to do is believe.

Fast Facts

- Until Johannes Gutenberg invented movable type in the 1450s, Bibles were laboriously and meticulously copied by hand, usually by Jewish scribes and Christian monks. However, one scribe apparently wasn't paying attention when he copied 1 Samuel 13:1, which in Hebrew reads: "Saul was one year old when he became king, and he reigned two years over Israel." Since we know that Saul was an adult when he became king and that he reigned for longer than two years, it must be assumed that the sleepy copyist missed at least two numbers.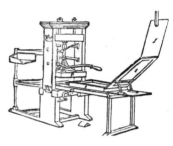

- The third plague on the Egyptians was lice, according to many versions of the Bible. But it didn't take God's hand to make this so—lice were a very common problem during biblical times. In fact, archaeologists have found ancient combs from the region containing dead lice and their eggs.

- Moses—who was called upon more than once to talk of weighty matters—was likely a stutterer. In the Bible, he claims to be "slow of speech," which suggests some kind of impediment.

- Moses was 40 when he fled the courts of Egypt and 80 when he returned. He was 120 when he died.

 - God often used insects as weapons. For example, it is said that he sent swarms of hornets into the land of Canaan ahead of the Israelites to drive out their enemies. Whether this is a literal or symbolic reference remains open to debate.

- It is unknown exactly how many children Adam and Eve had together. Three are mentioned by name—Cain, Abel, and Seth—but Genesis also states that they had many others over the course of their lives.

- Because Adam and Eve were created by God and were not born in the traditional sense, it is unlikely that they had belly buttons.

Forgiveness with a Capital F

✧ ✧ ✧ ✧

*Have you ever blown it so badly that you thought forgiveness
was impossible? Or have you ever chosen to extend forgiveness
rather than take revenge when you've been wronged in a big way?
If so, then you will be able to relate to the emotional
and spiritual power of these passages.*

Story #1: Betrayed by Brothers (Genesis 37, 39—45)

Joseph: Favorite Son

Joseph was one of 12 sons of the Hebrew patriarch Jacob (also
known as Israel). Next to the youngest in birth order, Joseph was a
favorite of his father and enjoyed perks from Dad, such as a spe-
cially made robe unlike anything his older brothers wore. No doubt
the sight of Joseph wearing this obvious token of his father's affections continually provoked the older brothers to jealousy. As if that
wasn't enough to stir the pot of ill-will toward himself, Joseph began
broadcasting the strange dreams he was having, dreams in which
his family members—brothers *and* parents—were bowing down to
honor him.

Brothers Take Their Revenge

You can imagine the deep level of despising that grew over time in
the ten older brothers' hearts. So it was that while they were out
herding sheep some distance from home, they decided to punish the
arrogant little dreamer, Joseph, when they saw him coming. They
knew their father had sent him to bring back a report about how
and what they were doing. Even as Joseph approached, his brothers conspired to kill him and toss him in an empty well. The eldest
brother, Reuben, however, talked them out of murdering Joseph, so
they settled on stripping him of his special robe and lowering him
into one of the empty wells.

Reuben had planned to retrieve Joseph and return him, un-
harmed, to their father, but before he was able to pull off the rescue,

the other brothers saw a band of traveling traders heading down to Egypt. Judah suggested selling Joseph to the caravan, and the others (except Reuben who apparently wasn't there at the moment) agreed. Lifting their little brother from the well, they sold him for 20 pieces of silver, and off he went to Egypt.

Clever Cover-Up

When oldest brother Reuben found out what had happened, he was beside himself. What would he tell his dad? The crime would need a cover-up. They still had Joseph's robe, so they spattered it with goat's blood and told their father that they'd found it, asking him to identify it. Yes, it was Joseph's, and it seemed clear that he'd been attacked and killed by a wild animal. Their grief-stricken father would now live in the belief that he had sent his favorite son to his untimely death.

Best of Times, Worst of Times

Meanwhile, Joseph landed as a servant in the hands of Potiphar, an Egyptian dignitary—captain of the guard—and Joseph did so well as a manager of Potiphar's affairs that Joseph was given charge over all of Potiphar's household. The only problem was that Potiphar's wife liked Joseph a little too much and kept asking him to sleep with her. Joseph resisted, even running out of the house to escape her grasp once. She held onto his robe while he fled, and she used the robe as false evidence that Joseph had tried to rape her. This accusation cost Joseph his job and landed him in prison. However, even in prison he thrived. Soon he was managing the work of the chief jailer.

It was in prison that God gave Joseph the interpretations of two of his fellow prisoners' dreams, both of which came true: One of the men was restored to his position as pharaoh's cupbearer, and the other was executed. Later, the cupbearer remembered Joseph when pharaoh himself had dreams that troubled him. Again, God gave Joseph the ability to understand the dreams, and pharaoh elevated him to second in command over the entire land of Egypt.

Brothers Reunited and Forgiven

The pharaoh's dreams had indicated that there would be seven years of abundant grain followed by seven years of severe famine. Joseph collected and stored grain throughout the land during the seven bountiful years. And then, during the seven years of famine, Joseph saw his own dreams from his youth fulfilled as his brothers came to Egypt seeking grain to feed their families. As they bowed low before him, he recognized them, but they did not recognize him.

Joseph accused them of being spies and sent them back to get their youngest brother (Joseph's only full brother, Benjamin) as evidence that they were telling the truth. Joseph spoke to them through an interpreter, so they didn't know that he could understand them when they talked amongst themselves, lamenting about what they had done to Joseph and how this was surely God's judgment for their evil actions.

After putting his brothers through a nerve-racking ordeal, with which he also mixed in much kindness and generosity, Joseph finally revealed himself to them. And here, the scriptures must speak for themselves:

"Then Joseph could no longer control himself before all those who stood by him, and he cried out, 'Send everyone away from me.' So no one stayed with him when Joseph made himself known to his brothers. And he wept so loudly that the Egyptians heard it, and the household of Pharaoh heard it. Joseph said to his brothers, 'I am Joseph. Is my father still alive?' But his brothers could not answer him, so dismayed were they at his presence.

Then Joseph said to his brothers, 'Come closer to me.' And they came closer. He said, 'I am your brother, Joseph, whom you sold into Egypt. And now do not be distressed, or angry with yourselves, because you sold me here; for God sent me before you to preserve life . . . . So it was not you who sent me here, but God.'"

Story #2: Peter Denies Jesus (Mark 14, John 21)

Daring Declarations

When Jesus made it clear to his disciples that his mission on earth included his death, the disciples, and most notably Peter, boldly announced their intentions to stand with Jesus, even to die with him. "Even though everyone else deserts you," Peter insisted, "I will not."

Jesus knew the truth and told Peter what would happen: "Truly I tell you, this day, this very night, before the cock crows twice, you will deny me three times."

After Jesus was arrested that night, Peter waited in a courtyard while Jesus was being questioned. Those around him began asking whether he was one of Jesus' disciples, and Peter denied it vehemently, saying he didn't even know Jesus, using an oath for emphasis. After the third denial, a rooster crowed, just as Jesus had said it would happen. Realizing his cowardice and unfaithfulness, Peter fled from the courtyard and wept bitterly in shame and remorse.

Moving Restoration

Fast forward to after Jesus' crucifixion and resurrection. Jesus has appeared to his disciples on a number of occasions and this time is feeding them breakfast on the shore of Galilee. Peter is there, and Jesus has already indicated implicitly and explicitly that he hasn't rejected Peter, that Peter is forgiven. In a personal conversation with Peter on the beach, however, Jesus gives Peter a chance to make three declarations of his love for Jesus, forever negating the three denials. Then Jesus calls Peter to the special work he has for him to do, completely forgiving and redeeming Peter's past:

"When they had finished breakfast, Jesus said to Simon Peter, 'Simon son of John, do you love me more than these?' He said to him, 'Yes, Lord; you know that I love you.' Jesus said to him, 'Feed my lambs.' A second time he said to him, 'Simon son of John, do you love me?' He said to him, 'Yes, Lord; you know that I love you.' Jesus said to him, 'Tend my sheep.' He said to him the third time, 'Simon son of John, do you love me?' Peter felt hurt because he said to him the third time, 'Do you love me?' And he said to him, 'Lord, you know everything; you know that I love you.' Jesus said to him, 'Feed my sheep....' After this he said to him, 'Follow me.'"

Quiz

Trees II

Branch out into this test of biblical horticulture.

1. Jesus amazed Nathanael by saying, "I saw you under the fig tree"
   (John 1:45–51). But just before that, what insulting comment did
   Nathanael make?
   - a. "Can anything good come out of Nazareth?"
   - b. "Look, a glutton and a drunkard, a friend of tax collectors and
     sinners!"
   - c. "He saved others; he cannot save himself!"
   - d. "His bodily presence is weak, and his speech contemptible."

2. What angry prophet called himself "a herdsman and a dresser of
   sycamore trees"?
   - a. Joshua
   - b. Elisha
   - c. Amos
   - d. Jonah

3. What couple was visited by three strangers near the "oaks of Mamre"
   and given the laughable news that they would have a child?
   - a. Adam and Eve
   - b. Abraham and Sarah
   - c. David and Bathsheba
   - d. Joseph and Mary

4. According to Jesus, what does a good tree produce (Matthew 7:17)?
   - a. good fruit
   - b. shade and sustenance
   - c. nothing of eternal value
   - d. false prophets

Answers: 1. a; 2. c (Amos 7:14); 3. b (Genesis 18:1–15); 4. a

---

425

The Left Behind Series

✧ ✧ ✧ ✧

*In 1995, conservative minister Tim LaHaye teamed up with
Jerry Jenkins, one-time writer of the popular sports comic-strip
Gil Thorp, to write a novel about the Rapture. Despite featuring
unlikely plot development and dreadful action sequences—not
to mention cries of protest from secular and religious groups
around the world—the novel was a massive hit.*

Thus began the *Left Behind* series, one of the most successful franchises in history. The novel spawned a series of books, several movies, and two video games, garnering billions of dollars in sales. It's no wonder that *Left Behind* has been referred to as the most influential Christian book—other than the Bible—in the past 15 years.

64 million	Number of copies of *Left Behind* books sold since 1995, approximately
75 million	Number of evangelical Christians in United States, conservatively
0.86	Number of copies of *Left Behind* books per evangelical Christian

Good Guys

The good guys make up the Tribulation Force, a small band of born-again Christians devoted to surviving the seven-year period between the Rapture (when believers are taken up in the air to meet Christ) and Christ's Second Coming.

Rayford Steele: Steele, a handsome, tall, airline pilot, lost his wife and son in the Rapture. In the aftermath of the Rapture, Steele sees the error of his godless ways, becomes born again, and is made leader of the "Tribulation Force."

Cameron "Buck" Williams: An award-winning journalist, Williams witnesses all sorts of strange events following the Rapture, which prompt him to become born again and join the Tribulation Force.

Chloe Steele: Rayford's daughter, Chloe, is a junior at Stanford when the Rapture occurs. Chloe eventually meets and marries Buck and creates a co-op for Christians to buy food after the United Nations outlaws it.

Bad Guys

Nicolae Carpathia: The unlikely named Carpathia was the former president of Romania and spends most of his time in the *Left Behind* series as president of the United Nations, riding a white horse, wielding a silly sword, and speaking in ridiculous dialogue. Oh, and he's the Antichrist.

Leon Fortunato: Fortunato is Carpathia's right-hand man and has many of the qualifications to be one of the Antichrist's minions—he's ostentatious, Roman, and Catholic.

The Rapture Will Not Be Televised, but It Might Be Digitized

Left Behind: Eternal Forces was the first big-budget Christian video game—and one of the most controversial. Secular groups laughed at the depiction of Antichrist's minions as electric-guitar-playing secularists, and then got angry when big-box stores such as Wal-Mart stocked the game. Religious groups weren't too happy about it, either: One of the game-play options allowed players to control the devil's forces, with the goal of spreading the Antichrist's message.

A Hebrew Cryptogram

A fascinating literary device found occasionally in the Hebrew Bible is called *atbash*. It created code words by substituting the first letter of the alphabet for the last, the second for the next-to-last, and so on. A famous example is in Jeremiah 51:41, where *Sheshach* is a cryptogram for Babylon.

Israel's Neighbors

NABATEANS

*In south Jordan today, one may visit
beautiful Petra, the Nabatean capital.*

Who Were They?

The Nabateans were an Arabic people, perhaps proto-Arabic, occupying
the land known as Edom. By speaking early Arabic, but writing it in
Aramaic characters, they built the linguistic bridge to the Arabic alphabet.
However, as cosmopolitan traders straddling a crucial route for commodi-
ties, many Nabateans spoke other languages: Aramaic, Greek, and later
Latin. Their independent cultural identity rose on the fringes of Alexander
the Great's conquests in the late 300s B.C. and lasted well past their
annexation to the Roman Empire in A.D. 106. Nabateans were tolerant
polytheists whose architecture, as seen at Petra, was a splendor in red
sandstone. Their water management enabled urban life in the arid region.

Where Are They Now?

A severe earthquake in A.D. 363 badly damaged the water supply systems
in Nabatea (by then, the Roman province of Arabia Petraea). Worse yet,
the caravan routes on which Nabatean urban life so depended had begun
taking other directions, leaving Nabatea high and dry in every sense.
Today their descendants are the region's Arabs, but as the adaptors of
Aramaic writing to Arabic language, any native Arabic speaker (or Muslim,
since the Koran is written in Arabic) partakes of the Nabatean heritage.

Biblical Mentions

Genesis describes a caravan carrying goods, and Josephus believed
the Nabateans were the descendants of Ishmael. The Apocrypha mentions the Nabateans in brief as friends of the Jews during the Maccabean
war. Though not attested to in scripture, while acting as a proxy for the
Romans, Herod the Great made war on the Nabateans in the late first
century B.C. He took some of their land, but Nabatea was hard to hang
onto unless you knew the water secrets. The only scriptural notices of the
Nabateans are vague and brief.

War in Heaven

✦ ✦ ✦ ✦

Angels kill for humanity.

The book of Revelation is one of the most fascinating sections of the Bible because it covers so much material. It reveals the future and how the world will end in a cataclysmic apocalypse, and it delves into the past with a story about the war in heaven between the angels. Perhaps it is because it covers both in so little depth that readers are left wanting more.

Revelation describes a conflict between hosts of angels. Michael leads God's forces against Satan's. Michael's triumph has been depicted by artists showing Michael triumphant over a dragon or serpent (representing Satan). Satan and his army are cast out of heaven forever. It is only during the End Times that Satan and his army leave hell to confront Michael again. It's an amazing story, more amazing perhaps because it is told with brevity. It isn't until Milton's *Paradise Lost* that the war is depicted in full dramatic scope.

Milton's work develops Satan as a tragic figure. Unlike Michael, who bowed down to humankind, Satan believes the angels are superior. Once favored in heaven, he rebels. Michael takes his place and casts him out after a horrible battle. In hell but still undeterred, Satan continues to justify his actions to his fellow fallen angels. He takes the war from heaven to humanity when he appears to Eve.

Other Wars in Heaven

This is not the first time heaven has been the scene of a great war. Many pagan religions describe similar titanic battles. In Greek mythology, Zeus and his brothers and sisters fought their father, Cronus, and his brothers, the Titans. In Norse mythology, Odin and the other two Aesir gods kill the giant Ymir and create the world from his body. The Aesir fight a succession of wars against the giants. Unlike the other "war in heaven" stories that end with good triumphing over evil, the Aesir know that when Ragnarok (the end of the cosmos) comes, all will be lost and the age of the gods over.

Was the Early Christian Movement Poor?

❖ ❖ ❖ ❖

The common presumption is that Christianity built its early base through appeal to the vast Roman lower classes. As neatly as that seems to fit, it isn't true.

The Perception

It makes such an emotionally gratifying story today: The new faith rejected worldly rewards to the promise of a better afterlife; it spoke to the suffering souls who toiled long, menial hours for paltry rewards. The good news spread to slaves, to widows, to all who went about in tattered rags. The snobs snarked at them while munching candied flamingo tongues between orgies in their beautiful villas, but the new converts did not care. With nothing to lose and a bountiful afterlife approaching, they went willingly to the lions, the dungeons, their martyrs' crosses.

It sounds so democratic, so grassroots, so affirming of the basic goodness of the salt-of-the-earth, poor, honest, hardworking, average Joe or Jane. Unfortunately, it was not the case. While some early Christians were martyred, and many were wonderful human beings, most were not dirt poor.

How Do They Start?

Most faiths begin as schisms (splits) or fringe movements. Christianity was both, so the Romans viewed it as many look at some of the odd religious movements of today. We lack hard numbers on early Christian demographics, but we can draw upon modern experience with fringe religions. To join a fringe religion means going away from the mainstream; who does that today? For the most part, those who are not a member of any church or who are receptive to a new viewpoint. College students tend to be among the most receptive. Those who join a new movement are likely to spread it to others, as early Christians did with gusto.

Better educated people more often question social norms, and it was no different in Roman times. Scriptural descriptions of the early Christian church's membership, though sketchy, refer to a variety of social classes. While not many early Christians were wealthy, that was true of overall Roman demographics. Evidence indicates the poor were slightly underrepresented in the early followers of Christ.

For further evidence of this, consider the absence of any truly devastating Roman reaction to early Christianity. Suppose Christianity mobilized mostly slaves, homeless people, and the rest of society's castoffs. The Romans had plenty of bitter experience with slave revolts and mob violence; imagine their reaction to a group that united poor Romans in opposition to the state faith. Roman leaders may have been hidebound, but they were not stupid. If this had been the case, they would have stomped on Christianity far harder than they did. They didn't see the early Christian church as a mass movement of the poor, because it wasn't.

What Did Early Christians Have in Common?

For the most part, early Christians lived in Roman society, a society whose Greco-Roman pagan state faith was past its sell-by date. When a religion becomes a habit rather than a sincere belief, people can drift away. Rome's stolid republic had already given way to a bureaucratic empire that barely even paid lip service to its senate and traditions, which was often ruled by paranoid, sadistic, and/or insane tyrants. As Roman religion was bound up with the state itself, cynicism about the state would tend to affect the state faith.

Into this climate of cynicism came the vibrant message of early Christianity. It gained ground as the Roman Empire suffered turmoil, plagues, and mishaps that the Roman gods seemed unable to deflect. No matter their social class, early Christians were drawn to a faith that seemed to practice what it preached, taught love and community, and couldn't possibly (yet) be considered a tool for the Roman state to manipulate. By the first century A.D. and thereafter, Greco-Roman paganism had little to offer that could compare. A quest for the economic status of early Christians tends to overlook the more important point: When you joined Christianity—rich, poor, or in between—you joined a fraternity/sorority of physical help, spiritual fellowship, and financial support.

Jesus' Best Comebacks

❖ ❖ ❖ ❖

Just because Jesus walked in humility doesn't mean others could walk all over him. Check out these savvy answers that effectively silenced his detractors.

Laying Verbal Land Mines

Jesus' ministry was reaching its climax. The cross was just ahead, and Jesus' words and actions were shining a white-hot spotlight on the pretensions and corruptions of some of the religious leaders. Predictably, the folks in power were nervous and irked. Their position was being threatened by Jesus' popularity. If they could just lead this "wannabe messiah" into making some verbal misstep, they could haul him out of the public eye and deal with him in the courts.

Trap #1: Who Gave You the Right?

The "chief priests and elders" were called the Sanhedrin—a 71-member Jewish religious council made up of Pharisees and Sadducees and presided over by the high priest. In an attempt to draw Jesus into a self-condemning statement, such as claiming to have divine authority, the Sanhedrin confronted him about the audacious things he'd been doing.

Jesus, for example, had recently ridden into the city on a donkey amid shouts of adoration by the people. Just after that, he'd plowed through the temple court, overturning the tables of the moneychangers and driving out the sellers of sacrificial animals, telling them to quit turning the place of prayer into an open market for their thieving enterprises. Wow!

The book of Mark records that "when the chief priests and the scribes heard [about Jesus' latest activities], they kept looking for a way to kill him." But Mark also notes that they were afraid to make waves publicly "because the whole crowd was spellbound by his teaching."

A good way to gain a foothold in the situation, then, would be to discredit Jesus in front of his followers. So while Jesus was teaching in the temple, the ruling council sent representatives to him with a pointed query: "By what authority are you doing these things? Who gave you this authority?"

Comeback #1: You First

Perceiving what they were up to, Jesus said to them, "I will ask you one question; answer me, and I will tell you by what authority I do these things. Did the baptism of John come from heaven, or was it of human origin?"

With his simple yet insightful counter-question, Jesus turned the trap back on his pursuers: If the religious leaders said John the Baptist's ministry was from God, they'd have to admit that they acted in rebellion against God, since they rejected John's baptism. But if they said John wasn't from God, the people would be in an uproar, since they considered him a prophet. Uh, time to beat a hasty retreat: "We do not know," they skirted.

"Neither will I tell you by what authority I am doing these things," Jesus countered.

Score: Jesus 1, Sanhedrin 0

Trap #2: Is Paying Tax to Rome Right or Wrong?

The religious leaders soon devised a plan for Round 2. Perhaps using what they learned from Jesus' last response, they chose a question that would force him to choose between two equally damning answers.

If the Sanhedrin could get Jesus to speak out against paying taxes to Caesar, they could get him in trouble with Rome, but if he spoke favorably about paying taxes, his followers would turn against him. You see, Rome imposed relentless taxes on virtually anything and everything in sight. Jewish tax collectors who worked for Rome were a despised lot. They pilfered their own people by overcharging and then lining their own pockets with the excess. They were viewed as traitors by their fellow Israelites.

So the Pharisees sent some of their own disciples along with a politically affiliated group (referred to as the Herodians) to put the question to Jesus. With veiled malice they flattered, "Teacher, we know that you are sincere, and show deference to no one; for you do not regard people with partiality, but teach the way of God in accordance with truth. Is it lawful to pay taxes to the emperor, or not?"

Comeback #2: Give Caesar His Coins

Jesus wasn't fooled by their fake display of honor. In his response, he didn't cut them any slack for it either: "Why are you putting me to the test?" Then Jesus continued, "Bring me a denarius and let me see it." And when they produced one, he asked them, "Whose head is this, and whose title?"

"The emperor's," they acknowledged.

And then with the greatest of ease, Jesus solved the dilemma: "Give to the emperor the things that are the emperor's, and to God the things that are God's."

Jesus' opponents were amazed and made for the exits once again.

Score: Jesus 2, Sanhedrin 0

Trap #3: Riddle Me This, Jesus

After seeing the Pharisees burned, the Sadducees stepped up to take a crack at Jesus. They approached him with what they felt was an airtight argument supporting one of their distinctive beliefs. The Sadducees took pride in the fact that they didn't consult rabbinic tradition and interpretation, but held exclusively to the Law of Moses as the only authoritative scripture on matters of life and faith. Since nowhere in the Law of Moses does it teach of a resurrection from the dead, the Sadducees didn't believe in an afterlife. This set them apart from the Pharisees, who staunchly held to their belief in a resurrection, as well as to a belief in the existence of angels, something the Sadducees also rejected.

So in an effort to stir the doctrinal pot, the Sadducees spun a riddle: "Teacher, Moses wrote for us that if a man's brother dies, leaving a wife but no child, the man shall marry the widow and raise up children for his brother. There were seven brothers; the first married and, when he died, left no children; and the second married her and died, leaving no children; and the third likewise; none of the seven left children. Last of all, the woman herself died. In the resurrection whose wife will she be? For the seven had married her."

Their implied "So what do you say to that, Jesus? If there really is a resurrection, there's going to be a lot of confusion in the afterlife. See how absurd the notion is?" hung in the air.

Comeback #3: You Don't Know Squat

As Jesus set the record straight, the Sadducees got a cold bucket of truth poured over their suppositions: "Is not this the reason you are wrong, that you know neither the scriptures nor the power of God? For when they rise from the dead, they neither marry nor are given in marriage, but are like angels in heaven. And as for the dead being raised, have you not read in the book of Moses, in the story about the bush, how God said to him, 'I am the God of Abraham, the God of Isaac, and the God of Jacob'? He is God not of the dead, but of the living; you are quite wrong."

With that, the Sanhedrin's hopes of discrediting Jesus in front of his followers were quashed.

Score: *Jesus 3, Sanhedrin 0*

Game over.

Am ha'aretz

Every faith has had backsliders and followers in name only. Ever wonder about the agnostic or irreligious Jews of biblical times? The priests and rabbis called them *Am ha'aretz,* which means "people of the land"—but perhaps "dumb hicks" conveys educated Jews' disdain for their ignorant country cousins. The term is in use today, though its meaning has evolved to mean a Jew who is lax in Jewish observance, while still impling ignorance.

The New Testament refers to the Pharisees and Sadducees upbraiding Jesus for hanging out with "sinners," which likely meant nonobservant Jews—what both groups meant by the scornful term *Am ha'aretz.* Some observant Jews also applied it to Hellenized (Greek-influenced) Jews, from whose ranks Christianity attracted many followers.

Yom Kippur

In the Jewish faith, God makes clear that his people are to set aside a specific day to atone: Yom Kippur.

Biblical Basis
Leviticus says what and when: On the tenth day of the seventh month, from sunset to sunset, Jews are to cleanse themselves of the past year's sin. This means no food, no water, no work, no fun. Scripture makes clear that this is no festival but a solemn day enshrined in Jewish law. While we call it *Yom Kippur* (YOME ki-PUR) today, the Torah calls it *Yom Ha'Kippurim.* It just adds "the" and makes it plural.

Biblical Practice
The Israelites didn't achieve atonement merely by spending the day in fasting and prayer. They also had to give burnt offerings to God: a bull, lambs, a ram, a goat, and accompanying grain, above and beyond any other offerings due. Scripture's repeated emphasis on Yom Kippur makes clear that it was expected not only of all Jews but also of resident non-Jews living among them.

Modern Practice
Like Passover and Chanukah, Yom Kippur is so culturally and spiritually important that even many secular Jews observe it in some way. Before Yom Kippur, Jews must seek to reconcile with anyone they have wronged in the past year, since the day is for atoning only for sins against God. In addition to fasting, abstention, and prayer, on Yom Kippur Jews do not bathe, wear leather shoes, or anoint their bodies (no perfume, no deodorant, etc.). Most wear white.

While no Jew is exempt from Yom Kippur, Jewish law prohibits fasting both by children under nine and women from the first labor pain to three days after childbirth. Older children and women between the third and seventh days after bearing a child may choose to fast. Of course, any danger to life or health can lift any stricture of Yom Kippur. The holiday ends with a long blast on the *shofar* (ram's horn) and much-needed food and drink.

Mary Magdalene After the Gospels

Little is said about Mary Magdalene in the New Testament, but Mary had an active life in the early Christian Church and even has her own gospel. Some go so far as to suggest that Mary and Jesus were married! Who was Mary really?

The Gospel of John repeatedly refers to the disciple whom Jesus loved. Most readers believe that disciple was John. However, there was another disciple who was just as close, if not closer, to Jesus, and it was a woman: Mary Magdalene. From the time she first met Jesus, Mary remained close to him, followed him everywhere, listened to his teaching, and even helped support him financially. She stood at the foot of the cross as he died and was the first to see the risen Lord.

Mary Magdalene and Jesus

Mary is introduced into the Gospels as one of three women "who had been cured of evil spirits and infirmities" (Luke 8:2). Jesus had cast seven demons out of Mary, but this did not mean that she was sinful. The demons could just as well have been the causes of physical or mental illness. Although Mary is popularly represented as a prostitute, there is no reason to believe she was. The label was attached to her centuries later—perhaps because her hometown, Magdala, had a reputation for licentiousness. Nor did Mary Magdalene wash Jesus' feet, as sometimes alleged. The foot washing is done by an unnamed woman just before Mary is introduced, and there is no known connection between the two women.

According to the Gospels (free of unfair traditional associations), Mary Magdalene and the other women Jesus had healed were apparently wealthy, for they followed Jesus during his mission and helped support him financially out of their own means. No details are given of Mary's personal relationship with Jesus, but Mary was among the women who stood at the foot of the cross while Jesus breathed his last and she watched as he was buried. Her faith in Jesus never wavered, but even she did not expect his resurrection.

Mary Magdalene at Jesus' Tomb

All four Gospels name Mary as one of the women who went to Jesus' tomb on Easter Sunday. In the Gospels of Matthew, Mark, and Luke, when the women arrive at the site around dawn they find the tomb empty and are informed by an angel that Jesus has risen. They then run off to tell the apostles. The Gospel of John depicts the incident as a personal story about Mary Magdalene. Mary goes to the tomb just before dawn (the other women aren't mentioned) and sees that the stone blocking the tomb's entrance has been rolled back. In a panic, she then runs back to the city and tells Peter and the "disciple whom Jesus loved" (probably John), "They have taken the Lord out of the tomb, and we do not know where they have laid him" (John 20:2). The two disciples race to the tomb and find that Jesus' body is indeed missing but his burial cloths have been left in the tomb.

The disciples return home, and Mary remains near the tomb, weeping. Then two angels appear inside the tomb and ask Mary why she is weeping. Mary tells them, and then she turns and sees Jesus standing nearby, but she doesn't recognize him, mistaking him for the gardener. It is only when Jesus softly and affectionately speaks her name that Mary realizes she is seeing the risen Christ. Jesus instructs Mary to go tell the disciples all she has seen, and she faithfully does so.

Gospel of Mary

During the early years of Christianity, Mary Magdalene emerged as a major figure and the center of a controversy over the role of women in the church. Much of what we know of her comes from a book entitled the Gospel of Mary, which was probably written in the late first or early second century. Long lost, the Gospel of Mary now survives only in fragments. The surviving text (about half the gospel) begins as Jesus is teaching his disciples, including Mary, that salvation comes from seeking the true spiritual nature of humanity within oneself. Jesus then instructs the disciples to go forth and preach the Gospel and leaves.

The disciples are left puzzled. They have not understood what Jesus was teaching them—except for Mary and Levi (Matthew). Rather than seek peace within, most worry about Jesus' departure and their own deaths. Mary quietly takes over and begins to comfort them and give them further instructions—acting as Jesus had done in the past. She tells them about a vision she has had in which Jesus had told her how to win the battle over the powers of the world that keep the soul ignorant of its own spiritual nature. But Andrew and Peter cannot accept Mary's teaching because they are so offended that Jesus preferred a woman over them. As in the canonical Gospels, the disciples are slow to learn and misunderstand Jesus' teachings at first hearing. (After all, Jesus had predicted his death to them three times and they still did not believe it until it happened.) Levi then reminds Peter that he has an inclination to anger and should keep it in check, adding: "If the Savior considered her to be worthy, who are you to disregard her? For he knew her completely and loved her devotedly." He then advises all the disciples to go out and preach the Gospel as Jesus had instructed.

Mary in Other Writings

Whereas the Gospel of Mary is the most important of the books about Mary Magdalene, many of the other extra-biblical works refer to her, and all speak of her closeness to Jesus. She is often referred to as the favorite of three female companions of Jesus, all called Mary.

The most provocative statement about Mary Magdalene is found in the Gospel of Philip. Although the only surviving copy of that book is dated A.D. 350, it is obviously a copy of an older book, which, in turn, is a collection of sayings that go as far back as the time of Christ. One of the brief entries in this so-called gospel states that the Lord loved Mary Magdalene more than all the disciples, and he used to kiss her on her mouth more than the other disciples. At least, we think the kisses were on the mouth, for the word "mouth" has been torn away. The missing word could conceivably be "cheek" or "hand," though this seems unlikely as these kisses anger the male disciples, who accuse Jesus of loving Mary more than them. The male disciples seem to be suffering from a sort of sibling rivalry, and the situation reflects that of the earlier Gospel of Mary in which the men resent that a woman is taking on the role of spiritual leader.

Much Ado About Kissing

In his super-popular novel *The Da Vinci Code,* Dan Brown made a big thing about the passage in which Jesus kisses Mary, alleging that it proves that Jesus and Mary Magdalene were married. This is not only wildly imaginative, but counterintuitive. If the incident had anything to say about marriage at all, it wouldn't be that the two were man and wife, but just the opposite! A man kissing his wife would not be objectionable, while a man kissing a woman he was not married to (and a disciple at that) might indeed cause a stir. But of course, *The Da Vinci Code* is fiction, so it needn't be true—or even reasonable. Brown could depict Mary as flying around on a broomstick if he wished. A more spiritual take on the kiss, though, is that it symbolized a transmission of knowledge, which the male disciples believed they were more entitled to receive than a woman.

Although some of the teachings in these extra-biblical books were later deemed heretical by a number of Christian thinkers, the writings seem to emphasize that Mary Magdalene was a major figure in the early Church, though her authority was resented by some of the men. In time, men completely took over the leadership of the Church and, deliberately or not, pushed the women into more subservient roles.

The Salt Covenant

Salt was a seasoning to be offered with Israelite sacrifices, and covenants were sealed with sacrificial meals where salt was present. Since salt was also a preservative, a "salt covenant" symbolized eternity. This first referred to the holy offerings due the priests and Levites in perpetuity (Numbers 18:19), and later the eternal kingship that God had given David and his sons (2 Chronicles 13:5).

Great Bible Orators

Have Faith

Kathryn Kuhlman believed the purpose of her ministry was to salvage souls. Divine healing was an added bonus.

Many evangelists offer faith healing as part of their ministry, but only a handful have achieved the level of fame experienced by Kathryn Kuhlman, one of the best-known faith healers of the mid-20th century.

Kuhlman was born on May 9, 1907, in Concordia, Missouri. She claimed to be born again during a revival meeting at age 14, and she began preaching two years later. She became a popular fixture on the national revival circuit and hosted healing crusades starting in the 1940s. Kuhlman had a national weekly TV show, *I Believe in Miracles*, in the 1960s and '70s.

Legacy Preserved

In 1954, Kuhlman established the Kathryn Kuhlman Foundation and followed it with a Canadian branch in 1970. The organization continues today, preserving and promoting Kuhlman's ministerial legacy. She moved to Los Angeles in 1970 and began offering faith-healing services. She saw herself as an heir to Aimee Semple McPherson (see page 294), and she attracted huge crowds.

Many claimed to have been cured as a result of Kuhlman's healing touch—which she always attributed to God—but not everyone was a believer. In 1967, a doctor named William Nolen followed 23 people who claimed to have been cured by Kuhlman. Follow-ups showed no evidence that their conditions were gone or even in remission. In a separate case, a woman with spinal cancer was instructed by Kuhlman to run across the stage to prove that she had been cured. The woman did so, only to have her spine collapse the following day. She died four months later.

Fondly Remembered

Despite such stories, thousands of people remain convinced that Kuhlman possessed healing powers. Kuhlman died following open heart surgery on February 20, 1976.

Where Jesus Walked

Jericho

"And the walls came tumbling down." Its Old Testament significance would be enough to bring Jericho lasting fame—but it also played a part in the walk of Jesus.

In Biblical Times
Jericho is one of earth's most ancient cities, extending well back into the Stone Age—at least 11,000 years (see page 334). It was at one time a Canaanite city, though not after Joshua finished blowing rams' horns outside it for a week. Jericho fell while under Babylonian rule, but the Persian emperor Cyrus returned Jews there from exile to resettle it after he captured the site. It was an outstanding place for a city: Natural irrigation sources nearby made it a true oasis, well situated from a practical defensive standpoint. By Christ's time, it was something of a resort town.

Jesus' Connection
Jericho was an important stop for Christ. Late in his earthly ministry, he restored sight to two blind beggars at Jericho, despite the loud complaints of a large crowd. (Mark and Luke cite just one blind man, Bartimaeus.) Jesus stayed there with a tax collector named Zacchaeus. The crowd groused about Jesus calling Zacchaeus down to meet him, but it paid a dividend of repentance as the taxman promised to give the poor half of his considerable wealth—and to compensate anyone he had ripped off. (Given the dishonesty of tax officials in that day, one supposes Zacchaeus had a busy time keeping his word.) Christ also mentioned Jericho in the parable of the Good Samaritan, who assisted a crime victim on the way to Jericho from Jerusalem.

Jericho Today
Interestingly, Jericho is 800 feet below sea level, roughly ten miles north of the Dead Sea's northernmost extreme. Its population is about 20,000, mostly Arab, and it has some of the most extensive ruins in the Holy Land; its cross-section is a trove of historical knowledge. One major attraction relating to Christ's time is the palace of Herod.

Quiz

Figures of Speech

The Bible has greatly influenced Western culture, language, and literature. How much do you know about words from the Word? Take this quiz and find out!

1. Who asked, "Am I my brother's keeper?"
   a. Jesus' disciple John, speaking of his brother James
   b. Reuben, speaking of his younger brother Joseph
   c. Cain, speaking of his brother Abel
   d. Esau, speaking of his twin, Jacob

2. Who promised that "God helps those who help themselves"?
   a. Moses
   b. writer of Proverbs
   c. Peter's mother-in-law
   d. none of the above

3. The phrase "the apple of his eye" is taken from which of the following?
   a. Garden of Eden story in Genesis
   b. Deuteronomy
   c. Jesus' feeding of the 5,000
   d. none of the above

4. Who was the original "good Samaritan"?
   a. poor widow who helped Elijah
   b. Simon of Cyrene, who carried Jesus' cross
   c. traveler in one of Jesus' parables
   d. Mary Magdalene

Answers: 1. c (Genesis 4:8–9); 2. d (actually, Benjamin Franklin); 3. b (Deuteronomy 32:10; related passages include Psalm 17:8; Proverbs 7:2; Zechariah 2:8); 4. c (Luke 10:25–37)

Was Paul an Anti-Feminist?

❖ ❖ ❖ ❖

*The apostle Paul's instructions to women have raised the ire
of feminists since the Women's Liberation movement began—
and long before that as well. But was Paul the misogynist his
most severe critics claim he was, or was he maybe
even a bit liberal on women's issues for his time?*

If we read selectively, Paul can sound like a full-blooded male chauvinist pig as he orders women to submit to their husbands, dress modestly, keep silent in church, and stop exercising authority over men. To seal the verdict, we can cite 1 Corinthians 7:4: "The wife does not have authority over her own body, but the husband does." Can Paul worm out of that one? Yes, because we're looking at only part of what Paul wrote.

Emphasis on Family

Having stated that women have no authority over their bodies, Paul adds that neither do men have authority over their own bodies—the wife does. When a man and a woman marry they become one flesh, as stated in Genesis. What Paul is really saying here is that both spouses should grant conjugal rights to each other—a liberal stance in a society that gave husbands almost total control over their wives.

On the other hand, for practical reasons, Paul was a staunch believer in structure. All Christian men and women are parts of the body of Christ (the Church), and in order to keep that body functioning at peak level, some sort of organization is needed. Paul favors a Christian version of the traditional patriarchal model of the family, with a hierarchy of submission that runs from God, to Christ, to man, to woman, to child.

Based on this model, Paul instructs wives to obey their husbands for the sake of Christ, but he balances this by telling husbands to treat their wives lovingly—also for Christ's sake. At the same time, any Christian's primary role is as a member of the Christian community, and Paul is quick to acknowledge women in important roles including those of deacon and prophet. He even calls Junia, a Christian woman, an apostle—a high title indeed (Romans 16:7).

Dealing with Local Problems

Many of the seemingly outrageous demands Paul makes on women are not intended for all women. Paul never wrote a book in which he outlined his views, he only wrote letters to particular Christian communities—often to offer solutions to local problems. Consequently, in 1 Corinthians and 1 Timothy, Paul is giving advice on how to deal with certain women who are disrupting worship services or usurping authority over others. He advises the community leaders to tell these women to be silent in church, to not speak or teach, and to comport themselves in an appropriate manner.

There is no reason to believe that Paul means to apply these strictures to all Christian women. He probably meant them to do no more than rule out the abuses he was addressing. Other disciplinarian words are aimed at men throughout Paul's letters, so these few passages should not be seen as attacks on women. On the contrary, Paul seems to have encouraged women to work and speak in the churches. He personally worked closely with women and often praised and thanked them.

Paul's Female Coworkers

Paul acknowledges women associates. First is Phoebe, a deacon and benefactor. Prisca, who worked with Paul, hosted a church in her house, and even risked her neck for Paul. Others include the "apostle" Junia, who spent time with Paul in prison; "those workers in the Lord" Tryphaena and Tryphosa; and a hard-working woman named Mary (Romans 16:1–12). Paul acknowledges that Euodia and Syntyche struggled beside him (Philippians 4:2–3). Finally, in Philippi (Macedonia), Paul made his local headquarters in the home of Lydia, a prosperous woman he had baptized.

In short, Paul advocated new roles for women, which made him radical in his day, but his insistence on a patriarchal family structure may seem confining in today's society. Yet, for Paul, the most important thing about a person is not gender but Christian baptism, for after baptism "There is no longer... male or female; for all of you are one in Christ Jesus" (Galatians 3:28).

A Case for Labor Unions: Was Jesus Unfair?

✧ ✧ ✧ ✧

Jesus told parables in order to shock his audiences into understanding and belief. His parable about workers who receive the same pay whether they worked a few hours or a full day still shakes people up because it seems to violate their fundamental idea of fairness. But we should be careful how we judge this parable, as it might affect us.

The parable of the workers in the vineyard, found in Matthew 20:1–16, begins with Jesus saying: "The kingdom of heaven is like a landowner who went out early in the morning to hire laborers for his vineyard." The landowner hires a group of grape pickers, who agree to work for "the usual daily wage." He then hires a second group of workers at noon and a third group at three o'clock, agreeing to pay them "whatever is right."

When the landowner calls quitting time, he pays all the workers for the day. But—surprise, surprise!—instead of basing their pay on the number of hours they worked he gives everyone the amount he'd promised the first group. The workers in the first group practically go ballistic! Why should someone who worked only a couple of hours get the same pay as they got for slaving in the scorching sun all day? The landowner politely asks the irate workers three questions. First he asks them if they hadn't agreed to work for the wage he'd just paid them. Then he asks them if he isn't allowed to do what he chooses with what belongs to him. Then he gives the zinger: Are you maybe just jealous because I'm generous? Jesus concludes by saying: "So the last will be first, and the first will be last" (Matthew 20:16).

So Do We Call in a Labor Rep?

If we were talking about a real labor case, we'd have a good case against the landowner—especially today, with our concerns for getting equal pay for equal work. But the parable isn't about the fairness of the pay scale. Rather, it's about the surprising upside-down effects of God's generosity.

The key to interpreting this parable comes in the opening words: "The kingdom of heaven is like ..." This is not an earthly vineyard. The workers represent people who come to accept God—and his kingdom—at different stages in their lives. Some people, though far from perfect, live consistently good lives from childhood, while others don't see the light until late in life. But God so loves the world that he brings into heaven all who turn to him, no matter when they do so. And once in (the kingdom of) heaven, everyone will be equal. "The last will be first, and the first will be last." Heaven has no first, last, or middle; it is not like earth.

Should We Complain?

If Jesus came to save sinners, why should we be angry when he does so? Jesus himself said that he came like a physician to heal the (spiritually) sick, not the (spiritually) healthy. Jesus' mission was to forgive sinners, even if they waited until the last minute to turn to him. So, if a particularly bad person repents just before dying, Jesus brings him or her into heaven with the rest of the souls who are saved. And when he does so, does anyone have the right to say: "I've been a good Christian all my life and I deserve to be rewarded, while this person doesn't deserve squat?" If we ever do argue that, we won't be expressing concern for justice; we'll just be spouting jealous drivel.

> ### Archaic Word: Neesing
>
> The King James Version of Job 41:18 says, "By his neesings a light doth shine." What's neesing? It was the 17th-century word for "sneezing."

Instead of being a sourpuss, we should rejoice, saying: "Thank God the poor person found Christ in time to be saved, and thank God I've been fortunate enough to enjoy God's grace my whole life." On the other hand, if we do fall by the wayside in life, won't we want God to forgive us and bring us into heaven if we wake up and smell the coffee only at the last minute? Don't be jealous; celebrate God's great love.

If all employers on earth were like God, we wouldn't need labor unions at all. That's what the parable says.

Possible Authors of the Gospels

✧ ✧ ✧ ✧

Seems pretty simple; each Gospel was written by the book's name-sake, as direct testament of that writer's experiences with Jesus Christ. Indeed, for most of the history of Christianity, this was the unquestioned interpretation. But in the past two centuries, biblical scholars have begun to question these assumptions.

Part of the problem in finding the authors is the phenomenon of "pseudoepigraphy"—falsely attributing a book to an author, often as a means to validate the work. Pseudoepigraphy is common throughout the world and throughout history, but it was especially common in ancient times. Another problem is that most biblical scholars agree that the original Gospels were written in Greek—unlikely if the authors were poor disciples of Jesus who spoke Hebrew or Aramaic. So who were the authors of these important works?

Gospel of Matthew

Until the 18th century, the unquestioned author of the Gospel of Matthew was the apostle Matthew. Matthew was also considered the first Gospel written. By the 19th century, biblical scholars began to question this authorship. Today, the majority of scholars believe the Gospel of Matthew was written by an anonymous Jewish Christian toward the end of the first century. The case for Matthew:

• **Early Christian scholars say it is so.** Papias of Hierapolis, an early Christian writer, states that Matthew wrote a Gospel in Hebrew. Though the Gospel of Matthew was written in Greek, some modern scholars believe the Hebrew book may have been a prototype. Unfortunately, Papias, who is one of the primary sources for much of what we know about early Christian writing, was considered "a man of meager intelligence" by his contemporaries.

• **The writer was probably Jewish.** Textual clues in the narrative, such as a familiarity with Jewish customs and local geography, as well as a familiarity with the Old Testament, indicate the writer was Jewish.

• **The writer didn't like Pharisees.** The Pharisees are depicted in a dim light in Matthew. The Pharisees were hard on tax collectors, and Matthew was a tax collector.

The case against Matthew:
• **Matthew copied Mark.** Though presented first in the New Testament, biblical scholars agree that Matthew was actually written after Mark, using Mark as a source. Evidence for this includes the fact that Matthew incorporates passages from Mark wholesale. Why would an apostle, who was an eyewitness, need to copy from Mark, who was writing everything down secondhand?

• **The book was written in Greek.** Not only was the Gospel written in Greek, but it was an eloquent Greek. Very few people could write at this time, much less in a nonnative language.

Gospel of Mark

Traditionally, the Gospel of Mark was associated with John Mark the Evangelist. The Gospel was written not as an eyewitness account, but as a summary of what Mark had heard from Peter's preaching in Rome. Of all the Gospels, Mark's authorship of the Gospel bearing his name is the one that is most widely accepted. The case for Mark:

• **Church fathers didn't ascribe the Gospel to an apostle.** It would make sense for the early church fathers to ascribe the most important accounts of Jesus' life to apostolic sources—as they did with Matthew and John—to provide added credibility to the text. There is no reason to give credit to Mark, who is a minor character in the New Testament.

• **The book displays an ignorance of Palestine.** An apostle of Jesus would be intimately familiar with Palestine, including its geography. Time and again the author of Mark bungles basic details, which shows that the author probably was not a Jew and was hearing it second-hand.

• **The Gospel seems to be written for gentiles.** The book is written for a gentile audience and seems to be designed to bolster the faith of those under threat of persecution—as Christians were in Rome during the time Mark was there.

The case against Mark:
• **Persecution was widespread.** Just because the Gospel seemed concerned about persecution doesn't mean it was written in

Rome, a main contention of pro-Mark scholars. Skeptics suggest this indicates the writer *could* have been someone other than Mark.

Gospel of Luke

The author of the Gospel of Luke has been assumed to be Luke the Evangelist, during the first century. Luke was a companion of Paul, and so the Gospel is not an eyewitness account. The case for Luke:

• **All early writings attribute the Gospel to Luke.** The oldest surviving manuscript referencing the Gospel, dating back to A.D. 200, attributes the book to Luke.

• **Luke spoke fluent Greek.** The Gospel of Luke was originally written in an eloquent Greek of the sort a highly educated physician might use.

• **The Gospel of Luke and Acts of the Apostles is written by the same person.** Both books exhibit the same writing style and are dedicated to the same patron, Theophilus.

• **Textual clues indicate Luke wrote Acts, and therefore Luke.** At several places in Acts the writer refers to Paul and his companions as "we." Scholars determined that the "we" passages correspond to times when Luke was in Paul's company.

The case against Luke:

• **Contradictions between Acts and Paul's letters.** Multiple contradictions occur in Acts. These contradictions cause skeptics to suggest Luke the physician did not write Acts, since the real Luke, a companion of Paul, would not have made such errors. And since he didn't write Acts, he could not have written the Gospel of Luke.

Gospel of John

The authorship of John is the most hotly debated. Traditionally, the Gospel was ascribed to John the Apostle. The book was said to have been written to refute the heretical writings of the gnostic scholar Cerinthus, who taught that Jesus was separate from Christ. Today most scholars agree that John the Apostle was most likely not the author of the Gospel. The case for John:

• **Every existing manuscript attributes it to him.** While this is not evidence that John wrote the Gospel, it is worth noting that none of the manuscripts we have containing early versions of the Gospel suggest otherwise.

• **The author claims to be an eyewitness.** The manuscript indicates intimate familiarity with Jesus and the other disciples.

The case against John:

• **The book was written well after John's death.** Scholars' best estimates peg the writing of John as A.D. 70. This would be difficult for the apostle John, considering that some scholars believe he was martyred with his brother James decades before.

• **Contradictions with the other Gospels.** John's Gospel is littered with details that are at odds with the synoptic (Matthew, Mark, and Luke) Gospels.

• **John was probably illiterate.** Most scholars now agree that John was illiterate.

So who *did* write the Gospel of John? Over the years, various scholars have put forth theories:

• **Cerinthus:** Cerinthus was a 1st-century gnostic writer who is the author of several important pieces of early Christian writing. The Alogi, a 2nd century Christian sect, attributed the Gospel to him.

• **Mary Magdalene:** Mary Magdalene was not one of the 12 apostles, but she could be interpreted as the "beloved disciple" referred to in John. Additionally, Ephesus, where Mary Magdalene was from, is considered the likely place of origin for the Gospel.

• **John the Elder:** Papias of Hierapolis claims that the Gospel of John is written by "the elder John," leading some to believe that John the Elder is the actual author of the Gospel.

• **Multiple authors:** One of the most popular interpretations is that the Gospel of John was a composite work. The theory holds that the work originated with John's recollections, which were then expanded and formed by multiple authors over several years into the Gospel we have today.

...and Q

Most might associate Q with James Bond, but the Q of the Gospels is more intriguing—a hypothetical, lost source book from which the authors of Matthew and Luke drew inspiration. The possibility of this book was first proffered in the early 19th century. The term Q, which stands for the German word *Quelle* ("source"), was first proffered by German theologian Johannes Weisse in the late 1800s and is theorized to have been a collection of Jesus' sayings.

Where Jesus Walked

Gethsemane

For 150 years, it has been a fixture of Christian hymnals:
"Go to Dark Gethsemane." But where is it?

In Biblical Times

We know relatively little about Gethsemane of old. It rested at the base of Mount Olivet, a peaceful place of beauty, perhaps a biblical equivalent of a city or rural park. Its name means "oil press," which indicates that at one point in time it processed olives from the lush groves giving the mountain its name.

Jesus' Connection

Gethsemane looms gigantic in Jesus' life. Expecting to be arrested and martyred soon, Jesus went there with Peter, James, and John to pray about his despair and sorrow. He asked that this tragic cup be taken from his lips, provided it was God's will. The disciples kept falling asleep on him, and the last time he woke them up was to let them know the arresting party had arrived. Judas, of course, had brought them. The fact that Judas knew he would find Christ at Gethsemane suggests that the garden was familiar to him and his disciples from previous times in Jerusalem. In any case, Christ left Gethsemane for the last time when the priests, elders, and scribes hauled him off to face Pontius Pilate.

Gethsemane Today

Just as we do not know most of the history of Gethsemane (in Hebrew, *Gat Shmanim*), we don't know its actual site beyond the reasonable presumption that it was along the western base of Mount Olivet. Several modern sites compete for the honor, and none can prove their claims. One traditional site is that centering on the Church of All Nations, a beautiful basilica built in the 1920s. The nearby Orthodox Church of St. Mary Magdalene also lays a claim. The Franciscan brethren maintain a garden near both, including some greatly ancient olive trees. Perhaps the precise site is less important than the spiritual significance of what they all represent.

Fast Facts

- The phrase "ashes to ashes, dust to dust" is often recited at funerals. But what you may not have known is that it's a paraphrase of something God said to Adam in the Bible—"You are dust, and to dust you shall return"—a not-so-subtle reminder of how Adam was created.

- Judas Iscariot was paid 30 pieces of silver for turning Jesus over to the Jewish leaders. But it hardly made Judas rich. In fact, it was an almost insultingly small sum, equal to what, back then, you would have had to pay if your ox gored a slave.

- Did you know that Hell exists right here on earth? In the northwest Grand Cayman town of West Bay, to be precise. But don't worry— there are no tormented souls there. This Hell is actually just a group of short, black, limestone formations covering a spit of land about half the size of a football field. It's a popular tourist spot and even has a small post office so you can torment friends and family with postcards from Hell. (There is also a Hell in Norway, which freezes over in winter!)

- The English word "hell" derives from an old Germanic word meaning "hidden place." Other words for hell found in various versions of the Bible include sheol, hades, and gehenna.

- Some scholars believe Jesus gave his famous Sermon on the Mount atop a hill on the north end of the Sea of Galilee that acts as a natural amphitheater. Voices are naturally amplified there, so Jesus, speaking in a normal voice, could easily have been heard as far as 200 yards away.

- Unicorns are mentioned several times throughout the King James Version of the Bible. But rather than magical, single-horned horses, the animals in question were actually oryx, a horselike creature with two long, straight horns. These exotic animals were nearly hunted to extinction in the 19th century, but they are slowly making a comeback.

- The falcon is a bird of prey. About ten species are known from Palestine. In Leviticus 11:14, falcons are mentioned as an abomination, not to be eaten. Job 28:7 speaks of their keen vision. One of the highest Egyptian gods was Horus, a falcon-god.

Was Paul Pro-Slavery?

❧ ❧ ❧ ❧

For two millennia, Paul's writings have been used to justify slavery and to condemn it. It's hard to believe that both sides can find support for their cause in Paul's work, but they can and do. Actually, it's hard to tell exactly where Paul stood on the issue of slavery.

Slavery was an accepted part of the social fabric of the Roman Empire in the first century. There were many kinds of slaves, including heavily abused galley slaves and mine workers, but the slaves Paul knew were mostly household slaves. These slaves were generally treated well, as members of the family, although they could also be abused—just as spouses and children in dysfunctional families are abused today.

Some household slaves were well educated and entrusted with training their master's children or administrating his estate. A hardworking slave could be rewarded with freedom. In this process, called *manumission,* the slave was virtually freed but stayed under the protection of the former owner, who acted as a patron. Eventually the bond of patronage was also dissolved, and the former slave and his descendants were considered free.

Paul's Instructions

When a family converted to Christianity, the slaves often did so too—as seen in the Acts of the Apostles, where the apostle Peter converts the entire household of the Roman soldier Cornelius— slaves included. Paul included slaves in his discussions of how family members should act toward each other. In Ephesians 5:22–6:9 and Colossians 3:18–4:1, he advises wives and children to obey their husbands and fathers but also insists that the husbands and fathers treat their wives and children compassionately. Similarly, Paul continues, slaves should obey their masters even when they aren't looking. Furthermore, they should perform their duties wholeheartedly as though they were doing them for the Lord, rather than for their worldly masters. Conversely, a master should be kind to his slaves, remembering that master and slave both answer to God, who shows no partiality.

Paul holds that it doesn't matter whether a Christian is a slave or free citizen. When someone is called to be a Christian, he should not change who or what he is in the material world. If a slave has the chance to be freed he should grab it, but otherwise he should not be concerned about it. All Christians, slave and free, are the same in the eyes of God, and all Christians, like slaves, were "bought with a price" (1 Corinthians 7:23). This price is the one referred to in Philippians 2:6–11: Jesus, "though he was in the form of God . . . emptied himself, taking the form of a slave" (a human being), and accepted death on a cross to free us from the consequences of sin.

Paul as Con Artist

Only once does Paul write about freeing a slave. The slave in question, Onesimus, had run away from his master, Philemon, and Paul had baptized the runaway and used him as a valued aid. In a letter, Paul hints that Philemon might free Onesimus. But "hints" is an understatement. The letter is a masterful con job.

Paul begins his letter by praising Philemon for being a loving Christian, then he tells him how useful Onesimus has been to him and how he regards the slave as "my own heart" (Philemon 1:12). Paul wants to keep Onesimus with him but won't do so without Philemon's consent. Hoping that Philemon will act voluntarily, Paul is sending Onesimus back, and he offers to pay any expenses incurred by the slave's absence. He hopes Philemon will forgive the runaway.

Paul then hits below the belt by telling Philemon: "I say nothing about your owing me even your own self" (Philemon 1:19)—though in saying he'll say nothing, he says plenty. Paul concludes, "I am writing to you, knowing that you will do even more than I say" (Philemon 1:21).

In short, Philemon would be a jerk to refuse to free Onesimus and return him to Paul. We don't know how Philemon responded, but the fact that the letter was not burned in anger but ended up in the Bible indicates that he probably did free Onesimus.

10 Things

Great Prayers of the Bible

*Scripture is full of brash, heartfelt, angry,
and accidental conversations with God.*

1. Midnight Madness (1 Samuel 3:1–8) As a boy, Samuel lived at the Tabernacle, helping the old priest Eli. He was awakened one night by a voice calling his name. Assuming that Eli was summoning him, he woke up the priest—and was told to go back to bed. This happened a second time, and a third, until Eli realized that it must be the Lord calling the boy. So he gave young Samuel his first lesson in prayer: "If he calls you, you shall say, 'Speak, Lord, for your servant is listening.'" And that's just what the boy did.

2. You Are the Man (Psalm 51) King David had sinned grievously, committing adultery with Bathsheba and then arranging her husband's death. He thought he got away with it, until his trusty prophet, Nathan, told a story about a rich man who robbed and killed a pauper. Furious, David demanded the identity of that rich scoundrel. "You are the man," he was told, and that unleashed an outpouring of repentance in the king's heart, including the personal confession that became Psalm 51: "Create in me a clean heart, O God" (verse 10).

3. Cave Man (1 Kings 19:10, 14) The prophet Elijah had won a great victory, calling fire from heaven and embarrassing an army of false prophets. But the wicked queen was still threatening his life, so he had to flee the country. He landed in a desert cave, where the Lord confronted him: "What are you doing here, Elijah?" The moping prophet answered with a torrent of self-pity—he had worked hard for the Lord, to no avail. This depressed-but-honest prayer serves as a model for those of us who aren't always in a praying mood.

4. Surrounded (2 Kings 6:11–17) An enemy king was convinced that the prophet Elisha was supernaturally snooping on his battle plans, so he sent an army to capture him. Elisha's servant looked out one morning and saw that army surrounding the town. *Uh-oh.* But the prophet seemed unconcerned. "There are more with us than there are with them," Elisha explained, and then he prayed: "O Lord, please open his eyes that he may see." Suddenly the servant saw that "the mountain was full of horses and chariots of fire all around Elisha." It seems the prophet had protection from a greater force.

5. Extension Course (Isaiah 38:3) Good king Hezekiah had taken ill, and the prophet Isaiah offered a bleak prognosis: *Set your house in order, for you shall die.* In tears, Hezekiah implored the Lord for more time, asking him to remember his faithful service. Amazingly, God granted this request. "I have heard your prayer, I have seen your tears; I will add fifteen years to your life."

6. Some Explaining to Do (Habakkuk) "O Lord, how long shall I cry for help, and you will not listen?" That's how the prayer of the prophet Habakkuk begins. He was sick and tired of wicked people winning out, abusing the righteous, while the Lord seemed to sit idly by. The prophet decided to stand in his watchtower until he got a proper explanation. And he got it. The righteous, God said, would live, but through faith. They might have to wait for things to be set right, but it would happen.

7. News from Home (Nehemiah 1—2) Nehemiah had a good gig, serving the king of Persia. But when he learned that his hometown of Jerusalem was in ruins, he felt he had to do something. His plan started with a prayer: a thorough confession of sin; reminding God of his own promises; good wishes for the future of the Jews; and a plea for success as he approached the king with an audacious plan to return to Jerusalem and rebuild the wall. The plea was granted, by God and the king.

8. A Whole Lot of Shakin' (Acts 4:23–31) Peter and John had been arrested for a public disturbance after they healed a lame man. They were released with a slap on the wrist and a stern warning not to preach anymore about Jesus. A lot of good that did! They returned to their congregation, which immediately launched into prayer, praising God and asking for power. "When they had prayed, the place in which they were gathered together was shaken." If your prayer starts an earthquake, you know you're doing something right.

9. The Answer Is No (2 Corinthians 12:1–9) The apostle Paul had a problem. He called it a "thorn in the flesh," but we're not sure what it was: encroaching blindness? epilepsy? migraines? He asked God three times to remove this problem, but that didn't happen. Finally, God responded, "My grace is sufficient for you, for power is made perfect in weakness." It's a great lesson for all of us: God does answer prayer, but sometimes the answer is no.

10. No Limit (Ephesians 3:14–21) The apostle Paul had a special love for the church in Ephesus, where he spent over two years. We see his affection in the poetic prayer included in a letter to them. He wanted them to be "rooted and grounded in love," to know "the breadth and length and height and depth" of Christ's love, which "surpasses knowledge." He asked that they would be "filled with all the fullness of God."

Sadducees

Opponents of the Pharisees, the Sadducees formed the traditional aristocratic Jerusalem temple priesthood. They rejected the oral tradition that would later become the Talmud, basing their faith on strict and literal interpretation of the Torah. The Sadducees gained identity under the Hasmonean Jewish Kingdom of the 2nd century B.C. and seem to have dissipated after the destruction of the temple in A.D. 70. For the most part, Roman authorities found them cooperative, the Romans being rather tolerant on religious matters provided minority religions didn't stir up rebellion.

Sadducees represented one major side of their day's Jewish religious debate, and it was the losing side—especially when it lost its key bastion, the temple. The Pharisee/Sadducee conflict had an economic tinge, because Sadducene Judaism tended to look down on the poor and uneducated. Jesus was no more enamored of the Sadducees than he was of the Pharisees.

The Noahide Covenant

✤ ✤ ✤ ✤

They're simple laws with deep meaning to Judaism.
What does the Noahide Code (or Covenant) mean for humanity?

What They Are—Where Did They Come From?

According to the Talmud, the seven commandments of the Noahide Covenant obligate all humankind. They ordain that:

- One must not murder; human life is a creation in the image of God, therefore holy.
- One must not steal; humankind was supposed to eat only from what God gave, never take what he did not give.
- One must not commit incest or adultery; the handing down of God's commands requires moral, orderly family life.
- One must not eat flesh taken from an animal while alive; the animal soul can't assimilate to the human soul—the animal's soul must have departed before its flesh can be used for meat.
- One must not worship idols or gods other than God; as the ultimate giver of creation and law, humanity owes God its sole spiritual loyalty, thus to worship any other is idolatrous.
- One must not blaspheme against God; he gave the law to humankind, and his name must therefore be kept holy— never blasphemed or cursed.
- People must establish laws and courts of justice; as God made laws to hold humankind accountable, humankind must enforce and administer laws to keep itself in line.

The Talmud derives the Noahide Covenant from Genesis 2:16–17, in which God commands Adam and Eve not to eat from the Tree of Knowledge of Good and Evil.

Implications for Non-Jews

The Noahide Covenant offers gentiles a share in the world to come, provided the gentile obeys the commands because they are God's commands. A gentile who does so will have "righteous gentile" status equal to a Jew, sort of a naturalized spiritual immigrant.

Jesus' Parables: Just Good Stories?

⚜ ⚜ ⚜ ⚜

*Why did Jesus tell parables? One might offer the simplest
answer: "To give comfort and hope to those in need." While this
is generally accurate, his teaching also challenged some and
confronted others. We can learn much about the message
of Jesus from his teaching techniques.*

That Seems Familiar!

The Gospels, especially Matthew and Luke, relate dozens of Christ's
parables. Parables can be engaging, even entertaining. Most speak of
ordinary life events, without naming people. Let's remember Christ's
audience: ordinary people, who could best understand a message
in terms familiar to their daily lives. His listeners understood things
like seeds, salt, light, bread, sheep, taxmen, and shepherds. If Jesus
were physically here on earth today, he might well tell stories about
television, the Internet, and telemarketers. (Imagine his reaction to
someone texting during his parables.) Christ's method could light up
spiritual truths for even the humblest listener.

Not only does analysis tell us this, but Jesus told us straight up
what he was doing (see the parable of sowing seeds on rocks, along
a path, among thorns, and in good soil). He explained parables as a
means to reach those who did not yet know the kingdom of God.

A Life Coach's Teachings

Some people have called a parable "an earthly story with a heavenly
meaning." One might characterize Jesus as an ancient life coach.
He used the analogy of a mustard seed to explain how all would live
within the kingdom of God. In the parable of the great banquet,
Jesus showed that many people would make excuses and decline his
invitation to God's kingdom but many who hadn't gotten an invitation would join—especially the less fortunate. His parable of debts in
Luke 7 explains that the greater the debt forgiven (i.e., our sins), the
greater the relief and appreciation of the debtor (that would be us).

Sometimes he strung parables together or repeated a theme. In the parable of asking a friend for bread at midnight, Christ explains the power of persistent prayer. He reinforced the lesson with the story of the widow who badgered the judge into giving her justice. He immediately followed this with the parable of the Pharisee and the tax collector, teaching his audience to take a humble approach to God rather than handing him a cosmic bill for righteous deeds done. The parable of the rich fool is quite relevant today, as people of wealth often cannot stop seeking more. The one about the cheating manager explains how a person who will be dishonest in small ways will also be dishonest in larger ones, just as a person who shows small acts of faith can aspire to greater ones. Jesus uses this story to teach that one can't serve both wealth and God, and his repetition of this lesson emphasizes the importance he attached to it.

Seeking Meaning

Parables are a classic forest-and-trees dilemma. It's easy to get hung up looking for significance in every little detail, and since the Bible is God's word, one can hardly fault a believer for a zealous search for meaning—yet that can miss the overall point of a given parable. If a parable teaches us one resonant, wholesome lesson, we have learned.

Consider the familiar Good Samaritan parable. Some interpret the story with the wounded man representing Adam, Jerusalem standing for the garden of Eden, Jericho as the world, the priest representing the Old Testament law, the Levite symbolizing the prophets' message, the Samaritan as Christ, the donkey as Christ's crucified body, and the inn as the church! All well and good, but the basic lesson of unselfish caring for the less fortunate mustn't be misplaced in the process. It's certainly more relevant (and reverent) than trying to compare Jesus' body to a donkey!

Revolutionary

Jesus' parables may seem familiar today, but in his day, they presented revolutionary ideas using a familiar mechanism. His teachings turned the status quo on its ear. Thus the genius of the method: It imparted radical ideas in ways so simple and accessible we still learn from them today.

Julian "the Apostate": Scourge of the Faithful

⚜ ⚜ ⚜ ⚜

*Christians hated Julian so much they gave him
the nastiest nickname they could think of. Did he deserve it?*

Who He Was

Flavius Claudius Julianus, also known as Julian Augustus ("Emperor"), had a short but very eventful life. He was born in about A.D. 331 under Constantine I, Rome's first Christian emperor. Julian's father was Constantine's half-brother, making Julian a potential emperor from birth. While he spent most of his youth keeping his head down and his mouth shut, Julian grew up in a Christian home but seems to have gone through the motions; at heart, he was pagan. Since an apostate is one who rejects a faith after having joined it, there's valid question whether Julian deserved the insult.

In 355, Julian's uncle Constantius II Augustus sent his nephew to Gaul as Caesar ("Deputy Emperor"). Some historians say that the idea was for Julian to be out of the way, perhaps even conveniently die in some barbarian revolt. Instead, Julian enjoyed rapid military successes, and his troops pressured him to proclaim himself Augustus. Knowing this would mean civil war, Julian resisted until the troops insisted. Constantine died on the way to confront Julian, leaving the latter as sole Augustus (A.D. 361).

Now Julian tried to turn the clock back by restoring Greco-Roman paganism as the Empire's state faith; he grew a beard suitable for a pagan philosopher (and unfashionable for an Augustus). He could retract all the advantages the Empire had been giving to Christianity, but he could no more make people embrace paganism than his parents had been able to make him believe in Christ as he grew up.

Less than two years into his reign, Julian died on a botched military campaign in Persia. His successors renounced his pro-pagan actions and solidified the Empire's Christianization.

Persecutions

Julian was no Nero, Marcus Aurelius, or Diocletian, martyring hundreds of Christians. (Not to say he martyred *none*.) He was a heavy writer, and with his pen he delighted in goading Christ's followers. His term for Christians was "Galileans." He called Christian churches "charnel houses" because they savaged saints' physical remains. His lack of respect for most of Christianity was quite clear.

Most of Julian's legal actions stripped away special privileges earlier emperors had granted to Christians. Many Christian churches had been built atop unused or dismantled pagan temples, and Julian required those responsible to pay compensation. Hoping to create a schism, he invited argumentative Christian religious leaders back from exile. He sought to weaken Christian religious education and strengthen that of pagans. He tried to rebuild the Jews' temple.

If Julian disliked Christianity and Christians so much, why didn't he play rougher? For that matter, why did he put forth an edict of freedom of religion (A.D. 362)? Because not only was Julian not a brute, he was not an idiot. By his day, Christianity was the majority faith in the Empire. Let's imagine for a moment that he sought to slaughter all Christians. With what army would he attempt this? His own, many of whom were Christians? Would one propose that it begin with a large portion of the troops committing suicide? Even had he been the type, which he was not, mass martyrdoms were simply unrealistic for Julian. He did control the administrative apparatus of the Roman state, and he used it creatively to divide Christianity and foster paganism. One of his pet projects was to emulate (thus undermine) Christianity by developing pagan philanthropy and charity.

Christian Reactions

During Julian's brief reign, he made enemies. Gregory of Nazianzus ranted against Julian while he was alive, perhaps being the first to call him "Apostate." After Julian's death, John Chrysostom laid into Julian as a bigot and enemy of Christianity. Numerous medieval writers demonized Julian for not only being non-Christian and anti-Christian, but for treating Christianity as just another faith.

From Julian's perspective, he was right; from a Christian perspective, they were right. Jews, whom Julian favored, might today reasonably admire Julian. Surely few Christians would.

What Evidence for Jesus Christ Is There Outside the Bible?

⚜ ⚜ ⚜ ⚜

The Bible isn't the only source of information about Jesus.
Various sources attest to his place in history.

Josephus

The Jewish historian T. Flavius Josephus lived from A.D. 37–c.100. His *The Antiquities of the Jews* is quite informative about life in Palestine during Jesus' time, and it describes Jesus this way:

"Now, there was about this time Jesus, a wise man, if it be lawful to call him a man, for he was a doer of wonderful works—a teacher of such men as receive the truth with pleasure. He drew over to him both many of the Jews, and many of the gentiles. He was [the] Christ; and when Pilate, at the suggestion of the principal men among us, had condemned him to the cross, those that loved him at the first did not forsake him, for he appeared to them alive again the third day, as the divine prophets had foretold these and ten thousand other wonderful things concerning him; and the tribe of Christians, so named from him, are not extinct at this day" (18.3.3).

Josephus completed this work around A.D. 93–94. Quite possibly he knew some eyewitnesses to Christ's life. Of course, during his lifetime, the Christian movement was still rather small. Josephus didn't live to see it take over the Western world, so he saw it as a small movement meriting a relatively brief mention. At the time of writing, Josephus enjoyed Roman patronage, suggesting that Roman officials didn't object much to his very flattering portrait of Jesus despite periodic Roman persecution of Christians.

Roman Historians

During the time of Jesus, the Roman Empire controlled Palestine. Suetonius (c. 69–c.130), Pliny the Younger (61–c.112), and Tacitus (c. 55–c.117) are the nearest Roman sources to the period. Writing in the early 2nd century A.D., Suetonius didn't mention Christ, but he did call this new faith "a new and mischievous religious belief" when he described Nero blaming Christians for the burning of Rome. Tacitus had more to say, mentioning Jesus directly while describing the same event:

"To suppress this rumour [blaming him for the fire], Nero fabricated scapegoats—and punished with every refinement the notoriously depraved Christians (as they were popularly called). Their originator, Christ, had been executed in Tiberius' reign by the governor of Judaea, Pontius Pilatus. But in spite of this temporary setback the deadly superstition had broken out afresh, not only in Judaea (where the mischief had started) but even in Rome. All degraded and shameful practices collect and flourish in the capital" (Annals, XV.44.).

Also writing in the early 2nd century A.D., Tacitus didn't conceal his hostility to the Christian movement. He adds that Nero's crude scapegoating didn't fool anyone, and that many pitied the Christians (even if Tacitus himself didn't). What is relevant here: Even though Tacitus held Christianity in scathing contempt, he didn't doubt Christ's existence. Of course, we can't know if either Roman author, in their youth or middle ages, ever met a living eyewitness to Jesus' life. All their information about him was likely second-hand at best.

Pliny exchanged letters with Emperor Trajan (A.D. 98–117) in A.D. 111–113, while governing Roman provinces in modern Turkey. He found the Christians perplexing and stubborn, yet one senses a hint of grudging respect on Pliny's part as he writes:

"Those who denied that they were or had been Christians, when they invoked the gods in words dictated by me, offered prayer with incense and wine to your image, which I had ordered to be brought for this purpose together with statues of the gods, and moreover cursed Christ—none of which those who are really Christians, it is said, can be forced to do—these I thought should be discharged" (*Letters* 10.96–97).

While this doesn't speak directly about Jesus' life, Pliny certainly documents that Christ's sincere believers remained true to him, and that they swore "not to commit fraud, theft or adultery, nor falsify their trust . . . " It seems that Pliny's local Christian community emphasized the Ten Commandments—rightfully so!

Saul of Tarsus: Before He Was Paul

❖ ❖ ❖ ❖

Paul, author of 13 epistles of the New Testament, was previously Saul—a persecutor of Christians. What was Saul like?

Early Life

Saul—in Hebrew, *Sha'ul*—came from a respectable Pharisee family in Tarsus, in modern southern Turkey. He was a citizen of the Roman Empire. Our best guess at his birth year is A.D. 5, so he was a few years younger than Jesus. On his eighth day of life, he was circumcised, as *Halakhah* (Jewish law) mandated.

Saul was raised in Jerusalem. He grew up bookish (scrollish?) as an observant Jew following Pharisaic (rabbinic) Jewish law. If he had anything like a modern bar mitzvah, his parents were likely proud of him. It is unlikely he worked on the Sabbath, ate clams, or failed to fast on Yom Kippur, for example. He described his young self as zealous for Jewish tradition, which is consistent with the later passionate evangelist: Neither Saul nor Paul ever did anything halfway.

Maturity

As a highly literate member of his day's establishment, Saul was a rising star in the Jerusalem priesthood. Paul admits that Saul persecuted Christians violently. Saul approved of Stephen's stoning martyrdom. He operated in Gestapo fashion, going from house to house in Jerusalem, hauling Christians off to jail. Nor was that the last of their troubles with Saul; when the Christians' friends wrote them letters in jail, Saul used the letters to hunt down said friends so they too could enjoy the hospitality of prison.

All that changed, of course, when Jesus appeared to Saul on the road to Damascus to ask why Saul was picking on him. Like any sane man suddenly blinded by a bright light and a heavenly voice, Saul panicked and asked (yes, we're paraphrasing), "Who wants to know?" "Jesus," said Jesus. "I would be the guy you've been persecuting." "My bad," said Saul. "What now?" In that moment, Saul's life—and history—altered forever.

Lots for Broadcloth

✣ ✣ ✣ ✣

At the crucifixion, the Roman soldiers on guard divided Jesus' clothes evenly among themselves, but they threw dice to see who'd get his tunic. Obviously there was something special about the garment.

When Roman soldiers assisted at an execution, they generally took the condemned man's clothes as booty. All four Gospels report that soldiers divided Jesus' garments among themselves, but only John's Gospel gives the full details. After dividing most of Jesus' clothing evenly among them, four soldiers cast lots (played dice) for the remaining tunic. Why?

A tunic consisted of a length of fabric with an opening cut at its center. Jesus would have slipped his head through the opening, gathered in the material at his waist, and tied it with a cloth or leather belt. He would have also worn another garment over the tunic and put sandals on his feet. According to John 19:23, Jesus' tunic "was seamless, woven in one piece, top to bottom." Most looms of Jesus' time produced cloth that was about three feet wide, and two panels had to be sewn together to make a tunic, but the looms in Galilee, where Jesus grew up, were wide enough to weave a tunic in one piece. A tunic with no seam was more valuable than a seamed one. Because the soldiers knew this, they played dice to win this prize garment.

What It All Means

By dividing Jesus' clothes, the soldiers enacted what is described in Psalm 22:18: "They divide my clothes among themselves, and for my clothing they cast lots." Although this psalm was probably composed to express the anguish of a dying man, many saw it as a prophecy describing the Messiah's passion. The scene may have had deeper significance as well. Some early commentators believe that John was comparing Jesus to the patriarch Joseph, whose brothers stripped off the special long coat his father had given him and sold him into slavery. Others believe the seamless tunic brought to mind a priest's tunic, signifying that Jesus died as a priest.

Rights for All

*Martin Luther King Jr. picked up the mantle
of civil rights early in his career as a minister.*

Martin Luther King Jr. is revered as a civil rights leader, but it's easy to forget that he was a minister before assuming the national stage as an activist on behalf of the poor and disenfranchised. The former understandably led him to the latter.

King was born on January 15, 1929, in Atlanta, Georgia, the son of the Rev. Martin Luther King Sr. A gifted student, he entered Morehouse College when he was just 15, and he graduated in 1948 with a bachelor's degree in sociology. He then enrolled in Crozer Theological Seminary in Chester, Pennsylvania, graduating in 1951 with a bachelor of divinity degree. In addition, King earned a doctorate of philosophy degree from Boston University.

The Fight for Civil Rights

King became pastor of the Dexter Avenue Baptist Church in Montgomery, Alabama, in 1954. By then, he had become deeply involved in the cause of civil rights for African Americans, and in 1955 he led the Montgomery Bus Boycott, which lasted 382 days. During that time, King was arrested, his home was bombed, and he was subjected to tremendous personal abuse. But as a result of that protest, the United States Supreme Court declared unconstitutional all laws requiring segregation on buses. For the first time in history, blacks and whites could ride municipal buses as equals.

The Montgomery Bus Boycott placed King in the national spotlight and established him as a leading spokesman in the fight for civil rights. In 1957, he was elected president of the Southern Christian Leadership Conference, which was organized to provide leadership for the burgeoning movement. King traveled the nation and the world on behalf of injustice, advocating nonviolent protest to enact social change.

In the years that followed, King worked tirelessly to ensure equal rights for all. He promoted voter registration drives for African Americans in

Alabama and directed a peace march on Washington, D.C., that drew a quarter of a million people. It was during that event, on the steps of the Lincoln Memorial, that King delivered his famous "I Have a Dream" speech, in which he passionately advocated for racial equality and the end of discrimination.

A Personal Toll

King suffered greatly in his fight for civil rights, especially in the South. He was arrested more than 20 times, assaulted at least four times, and the subject of several bomb threats. Those who followed him in the protests that he organized were often assaulted with fire hoses or set upon by police dogs. But King refused to give up, and as a result of his efforts was named Man of the Year by *Time* magazine in 1963. A year later, he was awarded the Nobel Prize in Peace, the youngest man ever to receive the prize. Upon learning of the honor, King announced that he would donate the $54,123 prize money to help advance the civil rights movement.

On the evening of April 4, 1968, King was standing on a second-floor balcony at the Lorraine Motel in Memphis, Tennessee, where he was to lead a protest march on behalf of striking garbage workers, when he was felled by an assassin's bullet. James Earl Ray pleaded guilty to King's murder and was sentenced to 99 years in prison, though he later recanted his confession and spent the rest of his life claiming King's death was part of a conspiracy.

Since his death, Martin Luther King has become a cultural and socio-logical icon, and memorials to him are numerous throughout the United States. A law making King's birthday a federal holiday was signed by President Ronald Reagan in 1983, and the holiday—observed on the third Monday in January—was first observed by a majority of states in 1986.

Bono Honors Jesus and King

"Pride (In the Name of Love)," was recorded in 1984 and released on *The Unforgettable Fire* album. The song is about both Jesus ("one man betrayed with a kiss") and Martin Luther King Jr. Bono gave his all, shouting the lyrics from the depths of his soul. But don't rely on him for a history lesson; the lyric referring to Dr. King ("Early morning, April four/Shot rings out in the Memphis sky...") is incorrect—King was killed around 6:00 P.M. Bono now sings "Early evening, April four" in live shows.

James's Letter Gets a Bad Rap

✤ ✤ ✤ ✤

*Did you know that Martin Luther once called
James an "epistle of straw"? Here's why.*

Luther's Objection to James

Imagine believing that God would never want a relationship with
you unless you did all the right things. Imagine, too, always feeling estranged from God or afraid of him because you knew you
just weren't living up to his standards. This is a basic description of
Martin Luther's religious reality before he began studying the New
Testament scriptures for himself.

Once Luther began reading, what he discovered rocked his world. A light went on when he
read about spiritual justification—that is, restoration of relationship with God—by grace
through faith in Christ's atoning work. As
Luther read through Paul's writings, his
old ideas about salvation by good works
were blown out of the water. He joyfully embraced this biblical explanation
of salvation. No longer miserable in his
relationship with God, Luther preached
this gospel of grace to others who languished under the load of trying to be good enough.

That's why when Luther read the book of James, it was like an
LP record being scratched mid-song. Paul's message seemed under-
mined by James's words: "But someone will say, 'You have faith and I
have works.' Show me your faith apart from your works, and I by my
works will show you my faith. . . . You see that a person is justified by
works and not by faith alone."

It's easy to see how a man just escaping a works-based concept
of salvation might react the way Luther did to James's treatise on
practical Christian living. Feeling it lacked the life-giving spiritual

substance and nourishment of Paul's teachings about Christ—even concluding that it contradicted the idea of salvation by faith alone— Luther dubbed James a "gospel of straw."

Who's Right, James or Paul?

Well... they both are! Have you ever told your more "adventurous" child that the curfew is 11:00 P.M., while you've had to urge your homebody to go out and spend more time with friends? You don't have a double standard. You have kids with different needs. One needs to be reined in. The other needs to be encouraged forward.

That's how the differences between Paul's message and James's can be cleared up. The audiences needed different kinds of direction because they were mistaken in different ways about the role of faith and works.

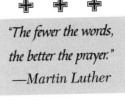

"The fewer the words, the better the prayer."
—Martin Luther

Paul's audience, in the book of Romans, had some serious legalists who were struggling to venture out into the life of faith. They were trusting in a false "safety net" of good works to save them, rather than recognizing that no matter how many good works they did, there would still be a deficit between that and perfection. Their piety wasn't going to get them into heaven; only faith in Jesus could do that.

On the contrary, some of the people in James's audience apparently had the idea they could coast into heaven on a free grace ticket while living like the devil here on earth. James needed to explain that a true saving faith in Christ has a transforming effect on one's heart and mind, on both words and actions. Good works flow out of real faith.

Of Carts and Horses

The relationship between faith and works is as simple as the old horse-and-cart metaphor. The "horse" of saving faith pulls the "cart" of good works. You can't get the cart of works ahead of the horse of faith, but a life of true faith will *always* have good works following behind—works that bring glory to God, bless others, and bring personal joy. No straws attached.

Where Jesus Walked

Golgotha

Also known as Calvary, the site of the crucifixion would arguably be the holiest site in Christendom—if we knew where it was.

In Biblical Times
Gulgalta, as it was called in Aramaic, was Jerusalem's traditional site for executions, of which crucifixion was by no means the only form—just one of the most agonizing. It remains unclear whether its translation "Place of the Skull" refers to the shape of the hill or to the skull as an emblem of what it meant to end up there. Since there aren't any other known references to executions there outside scripture, and none at all after Christ's crucifixion, perhaps the tradition died out in the first centuries A.D.

Jesus' Connection
Christ, of course, was abused all the way to Golgotha. According to John, he had to carry the cross himself; the other three Gospels say that the lynch mob grabbed a poor wayfarer named Simon of Cyrene and made him lug the cross.

However the cross arrived, the Gospels are in no conflict as to its use. Jesus endured the kind of death few today can imagine; after his death, Pilate granted possession of his body to Joseph of Arimathea. With help from Nicodemus, Jesus' mother Mary, and Mary Magdalene, Joseph helped prepare Christ's body for burial according to Jewish tradition.

Golgotha Today
As with numerous sites, the disuse of centuries caused future generations to forget the location of Golgotha. In A.D. 325, however, Roman Emperor Constantine I's mother, Helena, went to Palestine and decided she had discovered Golgotha, Jesus' tomb, and indeed the True Cross. Constantine then built the Church of the Holy Sepulchre on the supposed spot of the crucifixion. Should we believe Helena? There's no objective evidence for her findings, but they meet one essential requirement. Her site is outside the New Testament era walls of the city—as Golgotha had to be, for executions weren't done within Jerusalem's walls.

End of Days

§ § § §

*Is the book of Revelation a true warning of the
coming apocalypse, or merely a vivid historical allegory?*

Of the 66 books contained within the Old and New Testaments, few
have engendered as much discussion and controversy as the last—
the book of Revelation. Biblical scholars have studied and debated
its history, context, and meaning for centuries, and still the discussion continues. The biggest question remains: Is Revelation supposed to be taken as a factual prophecy of the end times, or was it
written as a clever way to
encourage early Chris-
tians to maintain their
faith?

Which John?

The prophetic author
of Revelation calls him-
self "John to the seven
churches that are in Asia,"
and is assumed by most scholars to be the apostle John. (Some theologians disagree with that assumption, suggesting instead that the
author may actually have been a disciple of John.) Revelation is the
only book within the Bible that discusses the apocalypse at length,
though short passages about the event can be found in a handful of
other gospels and epistles.

Indeed, it is the book's vivid description of the apocalypse—the
final conflict between good and evil—that so effectively holds the
imagination. It begins with a time of great tribulation on earth that
includes both natural disasters and war on an almost unimaginable
scale. Jesus, referred to in Revelation as the "Lamb," eventually
saves the faithful, destroys the wicked, and ushers in an era of peace.
A second, brief period of conflict follows, after which Jesus permanently banishes the wicked and the devout are brought to a heavenly
city to live forever in the presence of God and Christ.

Cast of Characters

Like any good story, Revelation features several compelling characters, including a heroic Jesus; his adversary, Satan (who is referred to by many names in Revelation, including "the dragon," "the Beast" and the "False Prophet"); the archangel Michael, who helps defeat Satan; the so-called Whore of Babylon (who isn't what you think); and the Four Horsemen of the Apocalypse.

One reason Revelation is so difficult to read and understand today is the archaic language and style in which it was written. The book is filled with bizarre symbolism and strange allegorical language that was common at the time it was created, around A.D. 96, but which modern readers understandably find hard to decipher.

When one considers the period in which Revelation was written, however, its complex use of metaphor, allegory, and symbolism becomes clear. Christianity was still in its infancy and facing attacks on a variety of fronts. Christians were persecuted by the Romans, and theologians now believe Revelation was actually a coded call to arms to stand firm against adversity. Those who follow the word of Christ even at the risk of death, the story suggests, will find themselves justly rewarded by God.

Symbolism Aplenty

Particularly intriguing is Revelation's extensive use of symbolism. For example, Jesus is said to have seven horns and seven eyes. This shouldn't be taken as a literal description, scholars say, but refers to Jesus' universal power and knowledge, based on the unique symbolism of the number seven. (Colors, metals, and clothing also have special symbolic significance.) Similarly, the so-called Whore of Babylon is not a woman but a reference to Rome, which at the time was a pagan state in which the practice of Christianity was often punished. Such an obscure reference meant nothing to the Romans but was easily understood by those with knowledge of the Old Testament.

Ultimately, when reading Revelation, it's important to focus on its underlying message rather than obsessing about its over-the-top literary devices. At its essence, Revelation, while perhaps frightening in its details regarding the end of the world, promotes a very basic Christian tenet: That genuine, heartfelt belief will ultimately be rewarded by eternal life in the heavenly kingdom of God.

Quiz

Famous Last Words

A person's final words are the ones we remember. The conclusion of a talk may be the part that rings in our ears for a long time afterward. So what about the books of the Bible—do they go out with a bang or a whimper? Test yourself and see.

Which Bible Book Ends...?

1. "In those days there was no king in Israel; all the people did what was right in their own eyes."

2. "But grow in the grace and knowledge of our Lord and Savior Jesus Christ. To him be the glory both now and to the day of eternity. Amen."

3. "Obed of Jesse, and Jesse of David."

4. "He will turn the hearts of parents to their children and the hearts of children to their parents, so that I will not come and strike the land with a curse."

5. "But you, go your way, and rest; you shall rise for your reward at the end of the days."

6. "But there are also many other things that Jesus did; if every one of them were written down, I suppose that the world itself could not contain the books that would be written."

7. "Give her a share in the fruit of her hands, and let her works praise her in the city gates."

8. "And for all the mighty deeds and all the terrifying displays of power that Moses performed in the sight of all Israel."

9. "And they shall go out and look at the dead bodies of the people who have rebelled against me; for their worm shall not die, their fire shall not be quenched, and they shall be an abhorrence to all flesh."

Answers: 1. Judges, 2. 2 Peter, 3. Ruth, 4. Malachi, 5. Daniel, 6. John, 7. Proverbs; 8. Deuteronomy, 9. Isaiah

Index

(continued on page 484)

(continued on page 490)

Contributing Writers

✂ ✂ ✂ ✂

Jeanette Dall tried to be a Bible hero to the young children in her classes that she taught for 20+ years. She found that kids in the 21st century are not very different from Bible-time kids. They are full of energy, like to play, get in trouble, and are mischievous—often testing the patience of the teacher. The best solutions to the problems were lots of prayer and love. In addition to working with children, Jeanette enjoys gardening, reading, and traveling.

Christine Dallman grew up in a Bible-believing church, graduated from Bible college, and writes Bible curriculum for adults on a quarterly basis. She's even been known to name her cats for biblical characters: Simon, the Siamese-tabby mix, being her latest misnomer.

Dave Gerardi is a New York–based writer whose work has appeared in *Newsweek, ESPN,* and dozens of other publications. He is currently ignoring his humor site, MaximumAwesome.com. Dave really, really, really wants to pitch a Bible movie script for George Lucas to direct.

Jack Greer gleaned everything he knows about the Bible from watching Monty Python's *Life of Brian.* He lives and writes on a houseboat in Lake Michigan with two dogs, two cats, and two of every other species on earth. (OK, it just seems like that sometimes.)

Robert V. Huber is an editor and writer who has contributed to and created books on a wide variety of topics, ranging from do-it-yourself manuals to law books for laypeople and more than a dozen books on the Bible. Not satisfied with having heard God's voice from the burning bush, he is still searching for the punch line to the human comedy, so he teaches graduate courses in scripture, which he takes seriously, though he always enjoys finding humor in the sacred texts. For a reality check he attends opera performances regularly—make that fanatically.

J. K. Kelley has a B.A. in history from the University of Washington in Seattle. He has contributed to numerous *Armchair Reader*™ books and gives thanks that he doesn't have to pass the Lutheran Church-Missouri

Synod's confirmation exam again today. He resides in the desiccated sage-brush of eastern Washington with his wife, Deb; his parrot, Alex; Fabius the Labrador Retriever; and Leonidas the Miniature Schnauzer.

Martin H. Manser (B.A., master of philosophy) is a professional reference-book editor based in England. He has compiled or edited more than 200 English-language and Bible-reference titles designed to help readers get into the Bible. After editing all these, he still enjoys reading the Bible for himself.

Randy Petersen, author of *Bible Fun Stuff* and *The Family Book of Bible Fun,* is really rather depressed. But that's okay; surely there are other books to write with "fun" and "Bible" in the title. When not writing books, Randy directs plays in local theaters, plans things at his church, teaches at a community college, plays softball, and does other things that require lots of work for little money. Not that he's complaining.

Betsy Rossen Elliot is a lifelong resident of Chicagoland who lives with her husband and petite cat, Hoppy. She takes pride in having helped write features and sidebars for study and reference Bibles. Her most recent book is *1,000s of Amazing Uses for Everyday Products.* Other interests include music, photography, and variations on the theme of chocolate.

Donald Vaughan is a Raleigh, North Carolina–based freelance writer whose work has appeared in an eclectic array of publications, including *Military Officer* magazine, *Cat Fancy,* and *MAD* magazine. He spends his free time wondering why there has never been a Pope Clyde.

Kelly Wittmann may look like a female serial killer in her driver's license photo, but she's actually a mild-mannered freelance writer who has contributed to six *Armchair Reader*™ books. When not having bizarre, surrealistic Synthroid dreams, she guiltily and surreptitiously watches her *Little House on the Prairie* and *The Waltons* DVDs. Don't tell!